FOURTH EDITION

Reinforced Concrete Design

Leonard Spiegel, P.E.
Consulting Engineer

George F. Limbrunner, P.E.
Hudson Valley Community College

PRENTICE HALL
Upper Saddle River, New Jersey   Columbus, Ohio

Library of Congress Cataloging-in-Publication Data

SPIEGEL, LEONARD.
    Reinforced concrete design/Leonard Spiegel, George Limbrunner.—
4th ed.
        p.   cm.
    Includes bibliographical references and index.
    ISBN 0–13–490202–5
    1. Reinforced concrete construction.   I. Limbrunner, George F.
II. Title.
TA683.2.S58   1998
624.1'8341—dc21

97–19010
CIP

Cover art/photo: Ewing Galloway
Editor: Ed Francis
Production Editor: Christine M. Harrington
Production Coordinator: Kathleen M. Lafferty/Roaring Mountain Editorial Services
Design Coordinator: Karrie Converse
Cover Designer: Rod Harris
Production Manager: Laura Messerly
Marketing Manager: Danny Hoyt

This book was set in Times Roman by The Clarinda Company
and was printed and bound by R. R. Donnelley & Sons Company.
The cover was printed by Phoenix Color Corp.

 © 1998, 1992, 1986, 1980 by Prentice-Hall, Inc.
Simon & Schuster/A Viacom Company
Upper Saddle River, New Jersey 07458

Printed in the United States of America

10   9   8   7   6   5   4   3   2   1

ISBN: 0-13-490202-5

Prentice-Hall International (UK) Limited, *London*
Prentice-Hall of Australia Pty. Limited, *Sydney*
Prentice-Hall of Canada, Inc., *Toronto*
Prentice-Hall Hispanoamericana, S. A., *Mexico*
Prentice-Hall of India Private Limited, *New Delhi*
Prentice-Hall of Japan, Inc., *Tokyo*
Simon & Schuster Asia Pte. Ltd., *Singapore*
Editora Prentice-Hall do Brasil, Ltda., *Rio de Janeiro*

DEDICATION

Leonard Spiegel
1922–1996

This edition of *Reinforced Concrete Design* is dedicated to the memory of Dr. Leonard Spiegel, who passed away suddenly during the final stages of its preparation. Len was an accomplished engineer, a dedicated educator, and a leader in the community. He was a colleague and a professional associate as well as a personal friend and mentor. Our more than 20 years of writing began with his suggestion and flourished because of his vigorous enthusiasm. Len enriched many lives. We will miss him and we will cherish his memory.

NOTICE TO THE READER

The information contained in this book has been prepared in accordance with recognized engineering principles and is for general information only. Although it is believed to be accurate, this information should not be used for any specific application without competent professional examination and verification of its accuracy, suitability, and applicability by a licensed professional engineer, architect, or designer. The authors and publisher of this book make no warranty of any kind, expressed or implied, with regard to the material contained in this book nor shall they be liable for any special, consequential, or exemplary damages resulting, in whole or in part, from the reader's use of or reliance on this material.

Contents

CHAPTER 3   REINFORCED CONCRETE BEAMS: T-BEAMS AND DOUBLY REINFORCED BEAMS   72

Preface

The primary objective of *Reinforced Concrete Design,* 4th edition, is to furnish the reader with a basic understanding of the strength and behavior of reinforced concrete members and simple concrete structural systems.

With relevant reinforced concrete research and literature increasing at an exponential rate, it is the intent of this book to translate this vast amount of information and data into an integrated source that reflects the latest information available. It is not intended to be a comprehensive theoretical treatise of the subject, because it is our belief that such a document could easily obscure the fundamentals that we strive to emphasize in the engineering technology programs. In addition, we are of the opinion that adequate comprehensive books on reinforced concrete design do exist for those who seek the theoretical background, the research studies, and more rigorous applications.

This fourth edition has been prepared with the primary objective of updating its contents to conform to the latest *Building Code Requirements for Structural Concrete (ACI 318-95)* of the American Concrete Institute. Since the ACI Code serves as a design standard in the United States, we strongly recommend that the code be used as a companion publication to this book.

In addition to the necessary changes to conform to the new code, many sections have been rewritten and new homework problems have been added. Answers to selected problems are furnished at the back of the text.

Throughout the four editions, the text content has remained primarily an elementary, noncalculus, practical approach to the design and analysis of reinforced concrete structural members using numerous examples and a step-by-step solution format. In addition, chapters use a conceptual approach on such topics as prestressed concrete and detailing of reinforced concrete structures. The metric system (SI), the use of which is gradually gaining momentum in the reinforced concrete design and construction field in the United States, is introduced in a separate appendix with several example problems.

Since form design is an important consideration in most structural design problems involving concrete members, the chapter on the design of job-built forms (which was introduced in the second edition) has been updated to conform to the latest applicable codes, standards, and guides.

This book has been thoroughly tested over the years in our engineering technology programs and should serve as a valuable design guide and source for technologists, technicians, and engineering and architectural students. In addition, it will aid engineers and architects preparing for state licensing examinations for professional registration.

We extend our thanks to the reviewers of this edition for their help and constructive suggestions: Dr. Mark H. Hasso, Wentworth Institute of Technology; Joseph Murphy, Penn College; and Paresh S. Shettigar, Hawkeye Community College.

As in the past, we are indebted to our students and colleagues who have provided constructive comments and input for this edition.

Leonard Spiegel
George F. Limbrunner

CHAPTER 1

Materials and Mechanics of Bending

1-1

CONCRETE

Concrete consists primarily of a mixture of cement and fine and coarse aggregates (sand, gravel, crushed rock, and/or other materials) to which water has been added as a necessary ingredient for the chemical reaction of curing. The bulk of the mixture consists of the fine and coarse aggregates. The resulting concrete strength and durability are a function of the proportions of the mix as well as other factors, such as the concrete placing, finishing, and curing history.

The compressive strength of concrete is relatively high. Yet it is a relatively brittle material, the tensile strength of which is small compared with its compressive strength. Hence steel reinforcing rods (which have high tensile and compressive strength) are used in combination with the concrete; the steel will resist the tension and the concrete the compression. *Reinforced concrete* is the result of this combination of steel and concrete. In many instances, steel and concrete are positioned in members so that they both resist compression.

1-2

THE ACI BUILDING CODE

The design and construction of reinforced concrete buildings is controlled by the "Building Code Requirements for Structural Concrete" (ACI 318-95) of the American Concrete Institute (ACI) [1]. The use of the term *code* in this text refers to the ACI Code unless otherwise stipulated. The code is revised, updated, and reissued on an approximate 6-year cycle. (The previous edition, ACI 318-89, was published in 1989.) The code itself has no legal status. It has been incorporated into the building codes of almost all states and municipalities throughout the United States, however. When so incorporated, it has official sanction, becomes a legal document, and is part of the law controlling reinforced concrete design and construction in a particular area.

1-3

CEMENT AND WATER

Structural concrete uses, almost exclusively, hydraulic cement. With this cement, water is necessary for the chemical reaction of *hydration*. In the process of hydration, the cement sets and bonds the fresh concrete into one mass. *Portland cement,* which originated in England, is undoubtedly the most common form of cement.

Portland cement consists chiefly of calcium and aluminum silicates. The raw materials are limestones, which provide calcium oxide (CaO), and clays or shales, which furnish silicon dioxide (SiO_2) and aluminum oxide (Al_2O_3). Following processing, cement is marketed in bulk or in 94 lb (1 ft³) bags.

In fresh concrete, the ratio of the amount of water to the amount of cement, by weight, is termed the *water/cement ratio*. This ratio can also be expressed in terms of gallons of water per bag of cement. For complete hydration of the cement in a mix, a water/cement ratio of 0.35 to 0.40 (4 to 4½ gal/bag) is required. To increase the *workability* of the concrete (the ease with which it can be mixed, handled, and placed), higher water/cement ratios are normally used.

1-4

AGGREGATES

In ordinary structural concretes the aggregates occupy approximately 70% to 75% of the volume of the hardened mass. Gradation of aggregate size to produce close packing is desirable because, in general, the more densely the aggregate can be packed, the better are the strength and durability.

Aggregates are classified as fine or coarse. *Fine aggregate* is generally sand and may be categorized as consisting of particles that will pass a No. 4 sieve (four openings per linear inch). *Coarse aggregate* consists of particles that would be retained on a No. 4 sieve. The maximum size of course aggregate in reinforced concrete is governed by various ACI Code requirements. These requirements are established primarily to ensure that the concrete can be placed with ease into the forms without any danger of jam-up between adjacent bars or between bars and the sides of the forms.

1-5

CONCRETE IN COMPRESSION

The theory and techniques relative to the design and proportioning of concrete mixes, as well as the placing, finishing, and curing of concrete, are outside the scope of this book and are adequately discussed in many other publications [2–5]. Field testing, quality control, and inspection are also adequately covered elsewhere. This is not to imply that these are of less importance in overall concrete construction technology but only to reiterate that the objective of this book is to deal with the design and analysis of reinforced concrete members.

We are concerned primarily with how a reinforced concrete member behaves when subjected to load. It is generally accepted that the behavior of a reinforced concrete member under load depends on the stress-strain relationship of the materials, as well as the type of stress to which it is subjected. With concrete used principally in compression, the compressive stress-strain curve is of primary interest.

The compressive strength of concrete is denoted f_c' and is assigned the units *pounds per square inch* (psi). For calculations, f_c' is frequently used with the units *kips per square inch* (ksi).

A test that has been standardized by the American Society for Testing and Materials (ASTM) [6] is used to determine the compressive strength (f_c') of concrete. The test involves compression loading to failure of a specimen cylinder of concrete. The compressive strength so determined is the highest compressive stress to which the specimen is subjected. Note in Figure 1-1 that f_c' is not the stress that exists in the specimen at failure but that which occurs at a strain of about 0.002. Currently, 28-day concrete strengths (f_c') range from 2500 to 9000 psi, with 3000 to 4000 psi being common for reinforced concrete structures and 5000 to 6000 psi being common for prestressed concrete members. Concretes of much higher strengths have been achieved under laboratory conditions. The curves shown in Figure 1-1 represent the result of compression tests on 28-day standard cylinders for varying design mixes.

A review of the stress-strain curves for different-strength concretes reveals that the maximum compressive strength is generally achieved at a unit strain of approximately 0.002 in./in. Stress then decreases, accompanied by additional strain. Higher-strength concretes are more brittle and will fracture at a lower maximum strain than the lower-strength concretes will. The initial slope of the curve varies, unlike that of steel, and only approximates a straight line. For steel, where stresses are below the yield point and the material behaves elastically, the stress-strain plot will be a straight line. The slope of the straight line is the modulus of elasticity. For concrete, however, we observe that the straight-line portion of the plot is very short, if it exists at all. There-

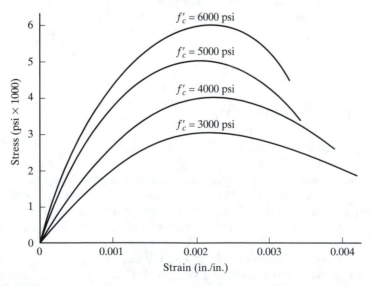

FIGURE 1-1 Typical stress-strain curves for concrete.

fore, there exists no constant value of modulus of elasticity for a given concrete since the stress-strain ratio is not constant. It may also be observed that the slope of the initial portion of the curve (if it approximates a straight line) varies with concretes of different strengths. Even if we assume a straight-line portion, the modulus of elasticity is different for concretes of different strengths. At low and moderate stresses (up to about $0.5f'_c$), concrete is commonly assumed to behave elastically.

The ACI Code, Section 8.5.1, provides the accepted empirical expression for *modulus of elasticity:*

$$E_c = w_c^{1.5}33\sqrt{f'_c}$$

where

E_c = modulus of elasticity of concrete in compression (psi)

w_c = unit weight of concrete (lb/ft^3)

f'_c = compressive strength of concrete (psi)

This expression is valid for concretes having w_c between 90 and 155 lb/ft^3. For normal-weight concrete, w_c may be taken as 145 lb/ft^3, and

$$E_c = 57,000\sqrt{f'_c} \qquad \text{(see Table A-6 for values of } E_c\text{)}$$

It should also be noted that the stress-strain curve for the same-strength concrete may be of different shapes if the condition of loading varies appreciably. With different *rates of strain* (loading), we will have different-shape curves. Generally, the maximum strength of a given concrete is smaller at slower rates of strain.

Concrete strength varies with time, and the specified concrete strength is usually that strength that occurs 28 days after the placing of concrete. A typical strength-time curve for normal stone concrete is shown in Figure 1-2. Generally, concrete

FIGURE 1-2   Strength-time relationship for concrete.

attains approximately 70% of its 28-day strength in 7 days and approximately 85% to 90% in 14 days.

Concrete, under load, exhibits a phenomenon termed *creep*. This is the property by which concrete continues to deform (or strain) over long periods of time while under constant load. Creep occurs at a decreasing rate over a period of time and may cease after several years. Generally, high-strength concretes exhibit less creep than do lower-strength concretes. The magnitude of the creep deformations is proportional to the magnitude of the applied load as well as to the length of time of load application.

1-6

CONCRETE IN TENSION

The tensile and compressive strengths of concrete are not proportional, and an increase in compressive strength is accompanied by an appreciably smaller percentage increase in tensile strength. According to the ACI Code Commentary, the tensile strength of normal-weight concrete in flexure is about 10% to 15% of the compressive strength.

The true tensile strength of concrete is difficult to determine. One common approach has been to use the *modulus of rupture* f_r (which is the maximum tensile bending stress in a plain concrete test beam at failure) as a measure of tensile strength. The ACI Code recommends that the modulus of rupture f_r be taken as 7.5 $\sqrt{f_c'}$ for normal-weight concrete (with f_c' in psi). The moment that produces a tensile stress just equal to the modulus of rupture is termed the *cracking moment* M_{CR} and may be calculated using methods discussed in Section 1-8.

The *split-cylinder test* has also been used to determine the tensile strength of concrete and is generally accepted as a good measure of the true tensile strength. The split-cylinder test uses a standard 6-in.-diameter, 12-in.-long cylinder placed on its side in a testing machine. A compressive line-load is applied uniformly along the length of the cylinder, with support furnished along the full length of the bottom of the cylinder. The compressive load produces a transverse tensile stress, and the cylinder will split in half along a diameter when its tensile strength is reached. The tensile stress at which splitting occurs is referred to as the *splitting tensile strength* f_{ct} and may be calculated by the following expression derived from the theory of elasticity:

$$f_{ct} = \frac{2P}{\pi LD}$$

where

f_{ct} = splitting tensile strength (psi)

P = applied load at splitting (lb)

L = length of cylinder (in.)

D = diameter of cylinder (in.)

According to the ACI Code Commentary, for normal-weight concrete the splitting tensile strength f_{ct} is approximately equal to $6.7\sqrt{f_c'}$.

1-7

REINFORCING STEEL

Concrete cannot withstand very much tensile stress without cracking; therefore, tensile reinforcement must be embedded in the concrete to overcome this deficiency. In the United States this reinforcement is in the form of steel reinforcing bars or welded wire fabric composed of steel wire. In addition, reinforcing in the form of structural steel shapes, steel pipe, steel tubing, and high-strength steel tendons is permitted by the ACI Code. Many other approaches have been taken in the search for an economical reinforcement for concrete. Principal among these are the fiber-reinforced concretes, where the reinforcement is obtained through the use of short fibers of steel or other materials, such as fiberglass. For the purpose of this book, our discussion will primarily include steel reinforcing bars and welded wire fabric. High-strength steel tendons are used mainly in prestressed concrete construction (see Chapter 11).

The specifications for steel reinforcement published by the American Society for Testing and Materials (ASTM) are generally accepted for the steel used in reinforced concrete construction in the United States and are identified in the ACI Code, Section 3.5.

The steel bars used for reinforcing are, almost exclusively, round deformed bars with some form of patterned ribbed projections rolled onto their surfaces. The patterns vary depending on the producer, but all patterns should conform to ASTM specifications. The bars vary in designation from No. 3 through No. 11, with two additional bars, No. 14 and No. 18.

For bars No. 3 through No. 8, the designation represents the bar diameter in eighths of an inch. The No. 9, No. 10, and No. 11 bars have diameters that provide areas equal to 1-in.-square bars, 1⅛-in.-square bars, and 1¼-in.-square bars, respectively. The No. 14 and No. 18 bars correspond to 1½-in.-square bars and 2-in.-square bars, respectively, and are generally available only by special order. Round, plain, reinforcing bars are permitted for spirals (lateral reinforcing) in concrete compression members.

ASTM specifications require that identification marks be rolled onto the bar to provide the following information: a letter or symbol indicating the producer's mill, a number indicating the size of the bar, a symbol or letter indicating the type of steel from which the bar was rolled, and for grade 60 bars, either the number 60 or a single continuous longitudinal line (called a *grade line*) through at least five deformation spaces. The *grade* indicates the minimum specified yield stress in ksi. For instance, a grade 60 steel bar has a minimum specified yield stress of 60 ksi. No symbol indicating grade is rolled onto grade 40 or 50 steel bars. Grade 75 bars can have either two grade lines through at least five deformation spaces or the grade mark 75. Reference 7 is an excellent resource covering the various aspects of bar identification.

Reinforcing bars are usually made from newly manufactured steel (billet steel). Bars rerolled from railroad rails (rail steel) and used axles (axle steel) are relatively uncommon. Steel types and ASTM specification numbers for bars are tabulated in Table A-1. As may be observed in the tabulation, some ASTM designations include more than one grade of steel. For example, ASTM A615, which is new billet steel, is available in grades 40, 60, and 75. (The full range of bar sizes is not available in grades 40 and 75, however.) ASTM A706, low-alloy steel, which is intended primarily for welding, is available in only one grade. Tables A-2 and A-3 contain useful information on cross-sectional areas of bars.

The most useful physical properties of reinforcing steel for reinforced concrete design calculations are yield stress (f_y) and modulus of elasticity. A typical stress-strain diagram for reinforcing steel is shown in Figure 1-3a. The idealized stress-strain diagram of Figure 1-3b is discussed in Chapter 2.

The yield stress (or yield point) of steel is determined through procedures governed by ASTM standards. For practical purposes, the yield stress may be thought of as that stress at which the steel exhibits increasing strain with no increase in stress. The yield stress of the steel will usually be one of the known (or given) quantities in a reinforced concrete design or analysis problem. See Table A-1 for the range of f_y.

The modulus of elasticity of carbon reinforcing steel (the slope of the stress-strain curve in the elastic region) varies over a very small range and has been adopted as 29,000,000 psi (ACI Code, Section 8.5.2).

Unhindered corrosion of reinforcing steel will lead to cracking and spalling of the concrete in which it is embedded. Quality concrete, under normal conditions, pro-

FIGURE 1-3 Stress-strain diagram for reinforcing steel.

vides good protection against corrosion for steel that is embedded in the concrete with adequate cover (minimum requirements are discussed in Chapter 2). This protection is attributed to, among other factors, the high alkalinity of the concrete. Where reinforced concrete structures (or parts of structures) are subjected to corrosive conditions, however, some type of corrosion protection system should be used to prevent deterioration. Examples of such structures are bridge decks, parking garage decks, wastewater treatment plants, and industrial and chemical processing facilities.

One method used to minimize the corrosion of the reinforcing steel is to coat the bars with a suitable protective coating. The protective coating can be a nonmetallic material such as epoxy or a metallic material such as zinc (galvanizing). The ACI Code requires epoxy-coated reinforcing bars to comply with ASTM A775 or ASTM A394 and galvanized bars to comply with ASTM A767. The bars that are to be epoxy coated or zinc coated (galvanized) must meet the code requirements for uncoated bars as tabulated in Table A-1.

Steel reinforcing bars are readily available in straight lengths of 60 ft. Smaller sizes are also available in coil stock for use in automatic bending machines.

Welded wire fabric (commonly called *mesh*) is another type of reinforcement. It consists of cold-drawn wire in orthogonal patterns, square or rectangular, resistance welded at all intersections. It may be supplied in either rolls or sheets, depending on wire size. Fabric with wire diameters larger than about ¼ in. is usually available only in sheets.

Both plain and deformed welded wire fabric are available. Welded plain wire fabric must conform to ASTM A185 and be made of wire conforming to ASTM A82. Welded deformed wire fabric must conform to ASTM A497 and be made of wire conforming to ASTM A496. Both materials have a yield strength of 70,000 psi. For both materials, the code has assigned a yield strength value of 60,000 psi but makes provision for the use of higher-yield strengths provided that the stress corresponds to a strain of 0.35%. The deformed wire is usually more expensive, but it can be expected to have an improved bond with the concrete.

A rational method of designating wire sizes to replace the formerly used gage system has been adopted by the wire industry. Plain wires are described by the letter W followed by a number equal to 100 times the cross-sectional area of the wire in square inches. Deformed wire sizes are similarly described, but the letter D is used. Thus a W9 wire has an area of 0.090 in.^{2}, and a D8 wire has an area of 0.080 in.^{2}. A W8 wire has the same cross-sectional area as the D8 but is plain rather than deformed. Sizes between full numbers are given by decimals, such as W9.5.

Generally, the fabric is indicated by the symbol WWF, followed by spacings first of longitudinal wires, then of transverse wires, and last by the sizes of longitudinal and transverse wires. Thus WWF6 × 12-W16 × W8 indicates a plain welded wire fabric with 6 in. longitudinal spacing, 12 in. transverse spacing, and a cross-sectional area equal to 0.16 in.^{2} for the longitudinal wires and 0.08 in.^{2} for the transverse wires.

Additional information about welded wire fabric, as well as tables relating size number with wire diameter, area, and weight, may be obtained through the Wire Reinforcement Institute [8] or the Concrete Reinforcing Steel Institute [9].

PHOTO 1-1 Concrete construction in progress. Note formwork, reinforcing bars, and pumping of concrete.

Most concrete is reinforced in some way to resist tensile forces. Some structural elements, particularly footings, are sometimes made of *plain concrete,* however. Plain concrete is defined as structural concrete with no reinforcement or with less reinforcement than the minimum amount specified for reinforced concrete. Plain concrete is discussed further in Chapter 10.

1-8

BEAMS: MECHANICS OF BENDING REVIEW

The concept of bending stresses in homogeneous elastic beams is generally discussed at great length in all strength of materials textbooks and courses.

Beams composed of material such as steel or timber are categorized as homogeneous, with each exhibiting elastic behavior up to some limiting point. Within the limits of elastic behavior, the internal bending stress distribution developed at any cross section is linear (straight line), varying from zero at the neutral axis to a maximum at the outer fibers.

The accepted expression for the bending stress is termed the *flexure formula,* where

$$f_b = \frac{Mc}{I}$$

where

f_b = calculated bending stress at the outer fiber of the cross section

M = the applied moment

   c = distance from the neutral axis to the outside tension or compression fiber of
      the beam

   I = moment of inertia of the cross section about the neutral axis.

The flexure formula represents the relationship between bending stress, bending moment, and the geometric porperties of the beam cross section. By rearranging the flexure formula, the maximum moment that may be applied to the beam cross section, called the *resisting moment M_R,* may be found:

$$M_R = \frac{F_b I}{c}$$

where F_b = the allowable bending stress.

   This procedure is straightforward for a beam of known cross section for which the moment of inertia can easily be found. For a reinforced concrete beam, however, the use of the flexure formula presents some complications, since the beam is not homogeneous and concrete does not behave elastically over its full range of strength. As a result, a somewhat different approach that uses the beam's internal bending stress distribution is recommended. This approach is termed the *internal couple method.*

   Recall from strength of materials that a couple is a pure moment composed of two equal, opposite, and parallel forces separated by a distance called the *moment arm,* which is commonly denoted Z. In the internal couple method, the couple represents an internal resisting moment and is composed of a compressive force C above the neutral axis (assuming a single-span simply supported beam that develops compressive stress above the neutral axis) and a parallel internal tensile force T below the neutral axis.

   As with all couples, and since the forces acting on any cross section of the beam must be in equilibrium, C must equal T. The internal couple must be equal and opposite to the bending moment at the same location, which is computed from the external loads. It represents a couple developed by the bending action of the beam.

   The internal couple method of determining beam strength is more general and may be applied to homogeneous or nonhomogeneous beams having linear (straight-line) or nonlinear stress distributions. For reinforced concrete beams, it has the advantage of using the basic resistance pattern that is found in the beam.

   The following three analysis examples dealing with plain (unreinforced) concrete beams provide an introduction to the internal couple method. Note that the unreinforced beams are considered homogeneous and elastic. This is valid if the moment is small and tensile bending stresses in the concrete are low (less than the tensile bending strength of the concrete) with no cracking of the concrete developing. For this conditon, the entire beam cross section carries bending stresses. Therefore, the analysis for bending stresses in the uncracked beam can be based on the properties of the gross cross-sectional area using the elastic-based flexure formula. The use of the flexure formula is valid as long as the maximum tensile stress in the concrete does not exceed the modulus of rupture f_r. If a moment is applied that causes the maximum tensile stress just to reach the modulus of rupture, the cross section will be on the verge of cracking.

These examples use both the internal couple approach and the flexure formula approach so that the results may be compared.

Example 1-1

A normal-weight plain concrete beam is 6 in. × 12 in. in cross section, as shown in Figure 1-4. The beam is simply supported on a span of 4 ft and is subjected to a midspan concentrated load of 4500 lb. Assume $f'_c = 3000$ psi.

(a) Calculate the maximum concrete tensile stress using the internal couple method.

(b) Repeat part (a) using the flexure formula approach.

(c) Compare the maximum concrete tensile stress with the value for modulus of rupture f_r using the ACI recommended value based on f'_c.

Load Diagram
(a)

Section A–A
(b)

FIGURE 1-4　Sketch for Example 1-1.

Solution:

Calculate the weight of the beam (weight per unit length):

$$\text{weight of beam} = \text{volume per unit length} \times \text{unit weight}$$

$$= \frac{6 \text{ in. } (12 \text{ in.})}{144 \text{ in.}^2/\text{ft}^2}(150 \text{ lb/ft}^3)$$

$$= 75 \text{ lb/ft}$$

Calculate the maximum applied moment:

$$M_{max} = \frac{PL}{4} + \frac{wL^2}{8}$$

$$= \frac{4500 \text{ lb (4 ft)}}{4} + \frac{75 \text{ lb/ft (4 ft)}^2}{8}$$

$$= 4650 \text{ ft-lb}$$

(a) Internal couple method:

1.   Since the beam is homogeneous, elastic, and symmetrical with respect to both the X-X and Y-Y axes, the neutral axis (N.A.) is at midheight. Stresses and strains vary linearly from zero at the neutral axis (which is also the centroidal axis) to a maximum at the outer fiber. Since the member is subjected to positive moment, the area above the N.A. is stressed in compression and the area below the N.A. is stressed in tension. These stresses result from the bending behavior of the member and are shown in Figure 1-5.

2. C represents the resultant compressive force above the N.A. T represents the resultant tensile force below the N.A. C and T each act at the centroid of their respective triangles of stress distribution. Therefore, $Z = 8$ in. C and T must be equal (since $\Sigma H_F = 0$). The two forces act together to form the internal couple (or internal resisting moment) of magnitude CZ or TZ.

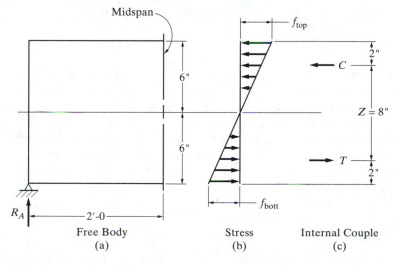

FIGURE 1-5   Sketch for Example 1-1.

3. The internal resisting moment must equal the bending moment due to external loads at any section. Therefore,

$$M = CZ = TZ$$

$$4650 \text{ ft-lb } (12 \text{ in./ft}) = C \ (8 \text{ in.})$$

from which

$$C = 6975 \text{ lb} = T$$

4. $C = $ average stress $\times$ area of beam on which stress acts

$$C = \tfrac{1}{2} f_{top} \ (6 \text{ in.}) \ (6 \text{ in.}) = 6975 \text{ lb}$$

Solving for f_{top} yields

$$f_{top} = 388 \text{ psi} = f_{bott}$$

(b) Flexure formula approach:

$$I = \frac{bh^3}{12} = \frac{6(12^3)}{12} = 864 \text{ in.}^4$$

$$f_{top} = f_{bott} = \frac{Mc}{I} = \frac{4650 \ (12) \ (6)}{864} = 388 \text{ psi}$$

(c) The modulus of rupture is

$$f_r = 7.5 \sqrt{f_c'} = 7.5\sqrt{3000}$$

$$f_r = 411 \text{ psi}$$

The calculated tensile stress (f_{bott}) of 388 psi is about 6% below the modulus of rupture, the stress at which flexural cracking would be expected.

Example 1-1 is based on elastic theory and assumes the following: (1) a plane section before bending remains a plane section after bending (the variation in strain throughout the depth of the member is linear from zero at the neutral axis), and (2) the modulus of elasticity is constant; therefore, stress is proportional to strain and the stress distribution throughout the depth of the beam is also linear from zero at the neutral axis to a maximum at the outer fibers.

The internal couple approach may also be used to find the moment strength (resisting moment) of a beam.

Example 1-2

Calculate the cracking moment M_{CR} (which for an unreinforced concrete beam is the resisting moment) for the plain concrete beam shown in Figure 1-6. Assume normal-weight concrete and $f_c' = 4000$ psi.

FIGURE 1-6   Sketch for Example 1-2.

(a) Use the internal couple method.
(b) Check using the flexure formula.

Solution:

The moment that produces a tensile stress just equal to the modulus of rupture f_r is called the cracking moment M_{CR}. The modulus of rupture is calculated from ACI Equation (9-9):

$$f_r = 7.5\sqrt{f_c'} = 7.5\sqrt{4000} = 474 \text{ psi}$$

For convenience, we will use force units of kips (1 kip = 1000 lb). Therefore, $f_r = 0.474$ ksi.

(a) Using the internal couple method,

$$Z = 14 - 2(2.33) = 9.34 \text{ in.}$$

$$C = T = \tfrac{1}{2}(0.474)\,(8)\,(7) = 13.27 \text{ kips}$$

$$M_{CR} = CZ = TZ = \frac{13.27\,(9.34)}{12} = 10.33 \text{ ft-kips}$$

(b) Check using the flexure formula:

$$f = \frac{Mc}{I}$$

$$M_R = M_{CR} = \frac{f_r I}{c}$$

$$I = \frac{bh^3}{12} = \frac{8(14)^3}{12} = 1829 \text{ in.}^4$$

$$M_{CR} = \frac{f_r I}{c} = \frac{0.474(1829)}{7(12)} = 10.32 \text{ ft-kips}$$

The internal couple method may also be used to analyze irregularly shaped cross sections, although for homogeneous beams it is more cumbersome than the use of the flexure formula.

Example 1-3

Calculate the cracking moment (resisting moment) for the T-shaped unreinforced concrete beam shown in Figure 1-7. Use $f'_c = 4000$ psi. Assume positive moment (compression in the top). Use the internal couple method and check using the flexure formula.

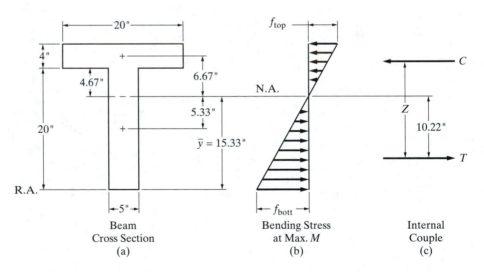

FIGURE 1-7   Sketch for Example 1-3.

Solution:

The neutral axis must be located so that the strain and stress diagrams may be defined. The location of the neutral axis with respect to the noted reference axis is calcualted from

$$\bar{y} = \frac{\Sigma(Ay)}{\Sigma A}$$

$$= \frac{4(20)(22) + 5(20)(10)}{4(20) + 5(20)}$$

$$= 15.33 \text{ in.}$$

The bottom of the cross section is stressed in tension. Note that the stress at the bottom will be numerically larger than at the top because of the relative distances from the N.A. The stress at the bottom of the cross section will be set equal to the modulus of rupture:

$$f_{\text{bott}} = f_r = 7.5\sqrt{f_c'} = 7.5\sqrt{4000} = 474 \text{ psi} = 0.474 \text{ ksi}$$

Using similar triangles in Figure 1-7b, the stress at the top of the flange is

$$f_{\text{top}} = \frac{8.67}{15.33}(0.474) = 0.268 \text{ ksi}$$

Similarly, the stress at the bottom of the flange is

$$f_{\text{bott of flange}} = \frac{4.67}{15.33}(0.474) = 0.1444 \text{ ksi}$$

The total tensile force can be evaluated as follows:

$$T = \text{average stress} \times \text{area}$$

$$= \tfrac{1}{2}(0.474)(15.33)(5) = 18.17 \text{ kips}$$

and its location below the N.A. is calculated from

$$\tfrac{2}{3}(15.33) = 10.22 \text{ in.} \qquad \text{(below the N.A.)}$$

The compressive force will be broken up into components because of the irregular area, as shown in Figure 1-8. Referring to both Figure 1-7 and Figure 1-8, the component internal compressive forces, component internal couples, and M_R may now be evaluated. The component forces are first calculated:

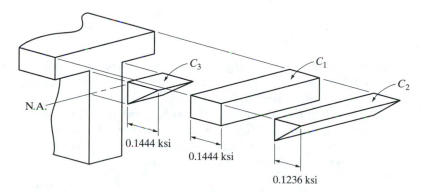

FIGURE 1-8 Component compressive forces for Example 1-3.

$$C_1 = 0.1444\ (20)(4) = 11.55 \text{ kips}$$

$$C_2 = \tfrac{1}{2}(0.1236)(20)(4) = 4.94 \text{ kips}$$

$$C_3 = \tfrac{1}{2}(0.1444)(5)(4.67) = 1.686 \text{ kips}$$

$$\text{total } C = C_1 + C_2 + C_3 = 18.18 \text{ kips}$$

$$C \approx T \qquad\qquad\qquad\qquad \text{(O.K.)}$$

Next we calculate the moment arm distance from each component compressive force to the tensile force T:

$$Z_1 = 10.22 + 4.67 + \tfrac{1}{2}(4.00) = 16.89 \text{ in.}$$

$$Z_2 = 10.22 + 4.67 + \tfrac{2}{3}(4.00) = 17.56 \text{ in.}$$

$$Z_3 = 10.22 + \tfrac{2}{3}(4.67) = 13.33 \text{ in.}$$

The magnitudes of the component internal couples are then calculated from force × moment arm as follows:

$$M_{R_1} = 11.55\ (16.89) = 195.1 \text{ in.-kips}$$

$$M_{R_2} = 4.94\ (17.56) = 86.7 \text{ in.-kips}$$

$$M_{R_3} = 1.686\ (13.33) = 22.5 \text{ in.-kips}$$

$$M_{CR} = M_R = M_{R_1} + M_{R_2} + M_{R_3} = 304 \text{ in.-kips}$$

Check using the flexure formula. The moment of inertia is calculated using the transfer formula from statics:

$$I = \Sigma I_o + \Sigma A d^2$$

$$= \tfrac{1}{12}(20)(4^3) + \tfrac{1}{12}(5)(20^3) + 4(20)(6.67^2) + 5\ (20)(5.33^2)$$

$$= 9840 \text{ in.}^4$$

$$M_{CR} = M_R = \frac{f_r I}{c} = \frac{0.474(9840)}{15.33} = 304 \text{ in.-kips} \qquad \text{(Checks O.K.)}$$

As mentioned previously, the three examples are for plain, unreinforced, and uncracked concrete beams that are considered homogeneous and elastic within the bending stress limit of the modulus of rupture. The internal couple method is also applicable to nonhomogeneous beams with nonlinear stress distributions of any shape, however. Since reinforced concrete beams are nonhomogeneous, the flexure formula is not directly applicable. Therefore, the basic approach used for reinforced concrete beams is the internal couple method.

REFERENCES

[1] "Building Code Requirements for Structural Concrete" (ACI 318-95). American Concrete Institute, P.O. Box 9094, Farmington Hills, MI 48333.

[2] ACI Committee 211. "Standard Practice for Selecting Proportions for Normal, Heavyweight, and Mass Concrete" (ACI 211.1-91). American Concrete Institute.

[3] George E. Troxell, Harmer E. Davis, and Joe W. Kelly. *Composition and Properties of Concrete,* 2nd ed. New York: McGraw-Hill Book Company, 1968.

[4] *Design and Control of Concrete Mixtures,* 13th ed. Engineering Bulletin of the Portland Cement Association, 5420 Old Orchard Road, Skokie, IL 60077-1083, 1994.

[5] Joseph J. Waddell, ed. *Concrete Construction Handbook,* 2nd ed. New York: McGraw-Hill Book Company, 1974.

[6] "ASTM Standards." American Society for Testing and Materials, 1916 Race Street, Philadelphia, PA 19103.

[7] "Manual of Standard Practice," 1990 ed. Concrete Reinforcing Steel Institute, 933 North Plum Grove Road, Schaumburg, IL 60173.

[8] Wire Reinforcement Institute, 7900 West Park Drive, McLean, VA 22101.

[9] Concrete Reinforcing Steel Institute, 933 North Plum Grove Road, Schaumburg, IL 60173.

PROBLEMS

Note: In the following problems, assume plain concrete to have a weight of 150 pcf (conservative) unless otherwise noted.

1-1. The unit weight of normal reinforced concrete is commonly assumed to be 150 lb/ft^3. Find the weight per lineal foot (lb/ft) for a reinforced concrete beam that:

(a) Has a rectangular cross section 16 in. wide and 28 in. deep.

(b) Has a cross section as shown in the accompanying diagram.

1-2. Determine E_c values for the various combinations of concrete having f'_c of 2000 psi, 2500 psi, and 3000 psi and unit weights w_c of 115 pcf, 125 pcf, and 135 pcf. Show your results in a tabular format.

1-3. A normal-weight concrete test beam 6 in. by 6 in. in cross section and supported on a simple span of 24 in. was loaded with a point load at midspan. The beam failed at a load of 2100 lb. Using this information, determine the modulus of rupture f_r of the concrete and compare with the value obtained based on an assumed concrete strength f'_c of 3000 psi.

PROBLEM 1-1

1-4. A plain concrete beam has cross-sectional dimensions of 10 in. by 10 in. The concrete is known to have a modulus of rupture f_r of 350 psi. The beam spans between simple supports. Determine the span length at which this beam will fail due to its own weight. Assume a unit weight of 145 pcf.

1-5. The normal-weight plain concrete beam shown is on a simple span of 10 ft. It carries a dead load (which includes the weight of the beam) of 0.5 kip/ft. There is a concentrated load of 2 kips located at midspan. Use $f_c' = 4000$ psi. Compute the maximum bending stress. Use the internal couple method and check with the flexure formula.

PROBLEM 1-5   **PROBLEM 1-6**

1-6. Calculate the cracking moment (resisting moment) for the unreinforced concrete beam shown. Assume normal-weight concrete with $f_c' = 3000$ psi. Use the internal couple method and check with the flexure formula.

1-7. Rework Example 1-3 but invert the beam so that the flange is on the bottom and the web extends vertically upward. Calculate the cracking moment using the internal couple method and check using the flexure formula.

1-8. Calculate the cracking moment (resisting moment) for the U-shaped unreinforced concrete beam shown. Assume normal-weight concrete with $f_c' = 3500$ psi. Use the internal couple method and check with the flexure formula.

PROBLEM 1-8

1-9. The plain concrete beam shown is used on a 12 ft simple span. The concrete is normal-weight with $f_c' = 3000$ psi.
   (a) Calculate the cracking moment.
   (b) Calculate the value of the concentrated load P at midspan that would cause the concrete beam to crack. (Be sure to include the weight of the beam.)

PROBLEM 1-9

CHAPTER 2

Rectangular Reinforced Concrete Beams and Slabs: Tension Steel Only

2-1

INTRODUCTION

When a beam is subjected to bending moments (also termed *flexure*), bending strains are produced. Under positive moment (as normally defined), compressive strains are produced in the top of the beam and tensile strains are produced in the bottom. These *strains* produce *stresses* in the beam, compression in the top and tension in the bottom. Bending members must therefore be able to resist both tensile and compressive stresses.

For a concrete flexural member (beam, wall, slab, and so on) to have any significant load-carrying capacity, its basic inability to resist tensile stresses must be overcome. By embedding reinforcement (usually steel bars) in the tension zones, we create a *reinforced concrete* member. When properly designed and constructed, members composed of these materials perform very adequately when subjected to flexure.

Initially, we will consider simply supported single-span beams that, since they carry only positive moment (tension in the bottom), will be reinforced with steel placed near the bottom of the beam.

2-2

METHODS OF ANALYSIS AND DESIGN

In the beam examples in Chapter 1, we assumed both a straight-line strain distribution and straight-line stress distribution from the neutral axis to the outer fibers. This, in effect, stated that stress was proportional to strain. This analysis is sometimes called *elastic design.*

As stated in Chapter 1, elastic design is considered valid for the homogeneous plain concrete beam as long as the tensile stress does not exceed the modulus of rupture, that stress at which tensile cracking commences. With homogeneous materials used in construction, such as structural steel and timber, the limit of stress-strain proportionality is generally termed the *proportional limit.* Note that the modulus of rupture for the plain concrete beam may be considered analogous to the proportional limit for structural steel and timber with respect to the limit of stress-strain proportionality.

With structural steel, the proportional limit and yield stress have nearly the same value, and when using the allowable stress design (ASD) method, an allowable bending stress is determined by applying a factor of safety to the yield stress.

With timber, the determination of an allowable bending stress is less straightforward, but it may be thought of as some fraction of the breaking bending stress. Using the allowable bending stress and the assumed linear stress-strain relationship, both the analysis and design of timber members and structural steel members (using the ASD method) are performed by a method that is similar to that used in the Chapter 1 examples.

Even though a reinforced concrete beam was known to be a nonhomogeneous member, for many years the elastic behavior approach was considered to be valid for concrete design, and it was known as the *working stress design* (WSD) method. The basic assumptions for the WSD method were as follows: (1) a plane section before bending remains a plane section after bending; (2) Hooke's law (stress is proportional to strain) applies to both the steel and concrete; (3) the tensile strength of concrete is zero and the reinforcing steel carries all the tension; and (4) the bond between the concrete and the steel is perfect, so no slip occurs.

Based on these assumptions, the flexure formula was still used even though the beam was nonhomogeneous. This was accomplished by theoretically transforming one material into another based on the ratio of the concrete and steel moduli of elasticity.

Currently, a more modern and realistic approach to the analysis and design of reinforced concrete is used. One basis for this approach is that at some point in the loading, the proportional stress-strain relationship for the compressive concrete ceases to exist. When first developed, this method was called the *ultimate strength design* (USD) method. Since then, the name has been changed to the *strength design method*. Although the strength design method is the predominant design and analysis method for reinforced concrete, the use of the WSD method is still acceptable in the 1995 ACI Building Code and is designated the *Alternate Design Method*. This method, which is found in the appendix of ACI 318-95, is similar to the WSD method of previous ACI building codes.

The assumptions for the strength design method are similar to those itemized for the WSD method, with one notable exception. Research has indicated that the compressive concrete stress is approximately proportional to strain only up to moderate loads. With an increase in load, the approximate proportionality ceases to exist, and the compressive stress diagram takes a shape similar to the concrete compressive stress-strain curve of Figure 1-1. Additional assumptions for strength design are discussed in Section 2-4.

The difference in approach of the two methods may be briefly expressed at this point. In the working stress method, actual working loads, now called *service loads*, were used, and a member was designed or analyzed based on an allowable compressive bending stress (generally $0.45f'_c$) and a compressive stress pattern that was assumed to vary linearly from zero at the neutral axis. Additionally, an allowable reinforcing steel tensile stress was used. In the strength design method, service loads are amplified using load factors. Members are then designed so that their practical strength at failure, which is somewhat less than the true strength at failure, is sufficient to resist the amplified loads. The strength at failure is still commonly called the *ultimate strength,* and the load at or near failure is commonly called the *ultimate load.* The stress pattern assumed for strength design is such that predicted strengths are in substantial agreement with test results.

2-3

BEHAVIOR UNDER LOAD

Before discussing the strength design method, let us review the behavior of a long-span rectangular reinforced concrete beam as the load on the beam increases from zero to the magnitude that would cause failure.

At very small loads, assuming that the concrete has not cracked, both concrete and steel will resist the tension, and concrete alone will resist the compression. The stress distribution will be as shown in Figure 2-1. The strain variation will be linear from the neutral axis to the outer fiber. Note that stresses also vary linearly from

FIGURE 2-1   Flexural behavior at very small loads.

zero at the neutral axis and are, for all practical purposes, proportional to strains. This will be the case when stresses are low (below the modulus of rupture).

At moderate loads, the tensile strength of the concrete will be exceeded, and the concrete will crack (hairline cracks) in the manner shown in Figure 2-2. Since the concrete cannot transmit any tension across a crack, the steel bars will then resist the entire tension. The stress distribution at or near a cracked section then becomes as shown in Figure 2-2. This is approximately valid up to a concrete stress f_c of about $f_c'/2$.

FIGURE 2-2   Flexural behavior at moderate loads.

FIGURE 2-3   Flexural behavior near ultimate load.

The concrete compressive stress is still assumed to be proportional to the concrete strain.

With further load increase, the compressive strains and stresses will increase; they will cease to be proportional, however, and some nonlinear stress curve will result on the compression side of the beam. This stress curve above the neutral axis will be essentially the same shape as the concrete stress-strain curve (see Figure 1-1). The stress and strain distribution that exists at or near the ultimate load is shown in Figure 2-3. Eventually, the ultimate capacity of the beam will be reached and the beam will fail. The actual mechanism of the failure is discussed later in this chapter.

At this point, the reader may well recognize that the process of attaining the ultimate capacity of a member is irreversible. The member has cracked and deflected significantly; the steel has yielded and will not return to its original length. If other members in the structure have similarly reached their ultimate capacities, the structure itself is probably crumbling and in a state of distress or partial ruin, even though it may not have completely collapsed. Naturally, although we cannot ensure that this state will never be reached, factors are introduced to create the commonly accepted margins of safety. Nevertheless, the ultimate capacities of members are, at present, the basis for reinforced concrete analysis and design.

In this text, it is in such a context that we will speak of failures of members.

2-4

STRENGTH DESIGN METHOD ASSUMPTIONS

The development of the strength design approach depends on the following basic assumptions:

1.   A plane section before bending remains a plane section after bending. That is, the strain throughout the depth of the member varies linearly from zero at the neutral axis. Tests have shown this assumption to be essentially correct.

2.   Stresses and strains are approximately proportional only up to moderate loads (assuming that the concrete stress does not exceed approximately $f_c'/2$). When the load is increased and approaches an ultimate load, stresses and strains are no longer proportional. Hence the variation in concrete stress is no longer linear.

3.   In calculating the ultimate moment capacity of a beam, the tensile strength of the concrete is neglected.

4.   The maximum usable concrete compressive strain at the extreme fiber is assumed equal to 0.003. This value is based on extensive testing, which indicated that the flexural concrete strain at failure for rectangular beams generally ranges from 0.003 to 0.004 in./in. Hence the assumption that the concrete is about to crush when the maximum strain reaches 0.003 is slightly conservative.

5.   The steel is assumed to be uniformly strained to the strain that exists at the level of the centroid of the steel. Also, if the strain in the steel (ϵ_s) is less than the yield strain of the steel (ϵ_y), the stress in the steel is $E_s\epsilon_s$. This assumes that for stresses less than f_y, the steel stress is proportional to strain. For strains equal to or greater than ϵ_y, the stress in the reinforcement will be considered independent of strain and equal to f_y. See the idealized stress-strain diagram for steel shown in Figure 1-3b.

6.   The bond between the steel and concrete is perfect and no slip occurs.

Assumptions 4 and 5 constitute what may be termed *code criteria* with respect to failure. The true ultimate strength of a member will be somewhat greater than that computed using these assumptions. The strength method of design and analysis of the ACI Code is based on these criteria, however, and consequently so is our basis for bending member design and analysis.

2-5

FLEXURAL STRENGTH OF RECTANGULAR BEAMS

Based on the assumptions previously stated, we can now examine the strains, stresses, and forces that exist in a reinforced concrete beam that is subjected to its *ultimate moment,* that is, the moment that exists just prior to the failure of the beam. (This moment may also be called the beam's *nominal moment strength.*) In Figure 2-4 the assumed beam has a width b and an effective depth d and is reinforced with a steel area of A_s. (A_s is the total *cross-sectional area* of tension steel present.)

Based on the preceding assumptions, it is possible that a beam may be loaded to the point where the maximum tensile steel unit stress equals its yield stress (as a limit) and the concrete compressive strain is less than 0.003 in./in. It is also possible that in another beam, the maximum concrete compressive strain will equal 0.003

Beam Diagram

FIGURE 2-4   Beam subjected to ultimate moment.

in./in. and the tensile steel unit stress will be less than its yield stress f_y. When either condition occurs, it implies a specific mode of failure, which will be discussed later.

As stated previously, the compressive stress distribution above the neutral axis for a flexural member is similar to the concrete compressive stress-strain curve as depicted in Figure 1-1. As may be observed in Figure 2-4, the ultimate compressive stress f_c' does not occur at the outer fiber. Neither is the shape of the curve the same for different-strength concretes. Actually, the magnitudes of the compressive concrete stresses are defined by some irregular curve, which could vary not only from concrete to concrete but also from beam to beam. Present theories accept that, at ultimate moment, compressive stresses and strains in concrete are not proportional. Although strains are assumed linear, with maximum strain of 0.003 in./in. at the extreme outer compressive fiber, the maximum concrete compressive stress f_c' develops at some intermediate level near, but not at, the extreme outer fiber.

The flexural strength or resisting moment of a rectangular beam is created by the development of these internal stresses that in turn may be represented as internal forces. As observed in Figure 2-4, N_C represents a theoretical internal resultant compressive force that in effect constitutes the total internal compression above the neutral axis. N_T represents a theoretical internal resultant tensile force that in effect constitutes the total internal tension below the neutral axis.

These two forces, which are parallel, equal, and opposite and separated by a distance Z, constitute an internal resisting couple whose maximum value may be termed the *nominal moment strength* of the bending member.

As a limit, this nominal moment strength must be capable of resisting the actual design bending moment induced by the applied loads. Consequently, if we wish to design a beam for a prescribed loading condition, we must arrange its concrete dimensions and the steel reinforcements so that it is capable of developing a moment strength at least equal to the maximum bending moment induced by the loads.

The determination of the moment strength is complex because of the shape of the compressive stress diagram above the neutral axis. Not only is N_C difficult to evaluate, but its location relative to the tensile steel is difficult to establish. Since the moment strength is actually a function of the magnitude of N_C and Z, however, it is not really necessary to know the exact shape of the compressive stress distribution above the neutral axis. To determine the moment strength, it is only necessary to know (1) the total resultant compressive force N_C in the concrete and (2) its location from the outer compressive fiber (from which the distance Z may be established).

These two values may easily be established by replacing the unknown complex compressive stress distribution by a fictitious one of simple geometrical shape, provided that the fictitious distribution results in the same total compressive force N_C applied at the same location as in the actual distribution when it is at the point of failure.

2-6

EQUIVALENT STRESS DISTRIBUTION

For purposes of simplification and practical application, a fictitious but equivalent rectangular concrete stress distribution was proposed by Whitney [1] and subsequently adopted by the ACI Code (Sections 10.2.6 and 10.2.7). The ACI Code also stipulates that other compressive stress distribution shapes may be used, provided that the results are in substantial agreement with comprehensive test results. Because of the simplicity of the rectangular shape, however, it has become the more widely used fictitious stress distribution for design purposes.

With respect to this equivalent stress distribution as shown in Figure 2-5, the average stress intensity is taken as $0.85f_c'$ and is assumed to act over the upper area of the beam cross section defined by the width b and a depth of a. The magnitude of a may be determined by

$$a = \beta_1 c$$

where

c = distance from the outer compressive fiber to the neutral axis

β_1 = a constant that is a function of the strength of the concrete; the value of β_1 is taken as 0.85 for $f_c' \leq 4000$ psi and is reduced continuously at a rate of 0.05 for each 1000 psi of strength in excess of 4000 psi; β_1 must not be taken less than 0.65

FIGURE 2-5   Equivalent stress block for strength design and analysis.

It is in no way maintained that the compressive stresses are actually distributed in this most unlikely manner. It is maintained, however, that this equivalent rectangular distribution gives results close to those of the complex actual stress distribution. An isometric view of the accepted internal relationships is shown in Figure 2-6.

Using the equivalent stress distribution in combination with the strength design assumptions, we may now determine the nominal moment strength M_n of rectangular reinforced concrete beams that are reinforced for tension only.

The nominal moment strength determination is based on the assumption that the member will have the exact dimensions and material properties used in the design computations. As discussed in Section 2-9, the nominal moment strength will be further reduced when it is used in practical analysis and design work.

FIGURE 2-6   Equivalent stress block for strength design and analysis.

Example 2-1

Determine M_n for a beam of cross section shown in Figure 2-7, where $f_c' = 4000$ psi. Assume A615 grade 60 steel.

FIGURE 2-7   Sketch for Example 2-1.

Solution:

1.   We will assume that f_y exists in the steel, subject to later check. By $\Sigma H = 0$,

$$N_C = N_T$$

$$(0.85f_c')ab = A_s f_y$$

$$a = \frac{A_s f_y}{0.85f_c' b} = \frac{2.37(60)}{0.85(4)(10)} = 4.18 \text{ in.}$$

This is the depth of the stress block that must exist if there is to be horizontal equilibrium.

2.   Calculate M_n:

$$M_n = N_C \left(d - \frac{a}{2} \right) \quad \text{or} \quad N_T \left(d - \frac{a}{2} \right)$$

Based on the concrete,

$$M_n = (0.85f_c')ab \left(d - \frac{a}{2} \right)$$

$$= 0.85(4.0)(4.18)(10)\left(23 - \frac{4.18}{2} \right)$$

$$= 2970 \text{ in.-kips}$$

$$\frac{2970}{12} = 247 \text{ ft-kips}$$

or, based on the steel,

$$M_n = A_s f_y \left(d - \frac{a}{2} \right)$$

$$= 2.37(60)(20.9)$$

$$= 2970 \text{ in.-kips}$$

3.   In the foregoing computations, the assumption was made that the steel reached its yield strain (and therefore its yield stress) before the concrete reached its "ultimate" (by definition) strain of 0.003. This assumption will now be checked.

Referring to Figure 2-8, we may locate the neutral axis as follows:

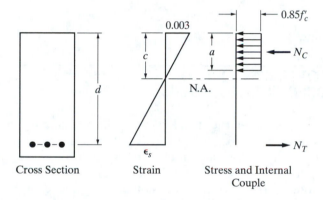

Cross Section   Strain   Stress and Internal
                                             Couple

FIGURE 2-8   Steel strain check.

$$a = \beta_1 c \qquad \text{(ACI Code, Section 10.2.7)}$$

$$\beta_1 = 0.85 \qquad \text{since } f_c' = 4000 \text{ psi}$$

Therefore,

$$c = \frac{a}{0.85} = \frac{4.18}{0.85} = 4.92 \text{ in.}$$

By similar triangles in the strain diagram, we may find the strain in the steel when the concrete strain is 0.003:

$$\frac{0.003}{c} = \frac{\epsilon_s}{d - c}$$

Then

$$\epsilon_s = \frac{d - c}{c}(0.003) = \frac{23 - 4.92}{4.92}(0.003)$$

$$= 0.011 \text{ in./in.}$$

The strain at which the steel yields (ϵ_y) may be determined from the basic definition of the modulus of elasticity, E = stress/strain:

$$\epsilon_y = \frac{f_y}{E_s} = \frac{60,000}{29,000,000} = 0.00207 \text{ in./in.} \qquad \text{(see Table A-1)}$$

This represents the strain in the steel when the stress first reaches 60,000 psi.

Since the actual strain in the steel (0.011) is greater than the yield strain (0.00207), the steel reaches its yield stress before the concrete reaches its strain of 0.003, and the assumption that the stress in the steel is equal to the yield stress was correct. (See assumption 5 in Section 2-4 and the idealized stress-strain diagram for steel shown in Figure 1-3b.)

2-7
BALANCED, OVERREINFORCED, AND UNDERREINFORCED BEAMS

In Figure 2-8 the *ratio* between the steel strain and the maximum concrete strain is fixed once the neutral axis is established. The location of the neutral axis will vary based on the amount of tension steel in the cross section, since the stress block is just deep enough to ensure that the resultant compressive force is equal to the resultant tensile force ($\Sigma H = 0$). If more tension bars are added to the bottom of a reinforced concrete cross section, the depth of the compressive stress block will be greater, and therefore the neutral axis will be lower. Referring again to Figure 2-8, if there were just enough steel to put the neutral axis at a location where the yield strain in the steel and the maximum concrete strain of 0.003 existed at the same time, the cross section would be said to be *balanced* (see the ACI Code, Section 10.3.2). The amount of steel required to create this condition is large, and balanced beams are not generally economical. However, the balanced condition is the dividing line between two distinct types of reinforced concrete beams that are characterized by their failure modes. If a beam has more steel than is required to create the balanced condition, the beam is said to be *overreinforced*. The additional steel will cause the neutral axis to be low (see Figure 2-9). This will in turn cause the concrete to reach a strain of 0.003 *before* the steel yields. Should more moment (and therefore strain) be applied to the beam cross section, failure will be initiated by a sudden crushing of the concrete.

If a beam has less steel than is required to create the balanced condition, it is said to be *underreinforced*. The neutral axis will be higher than the balanced neutral axis, and the steel will reach its yield strain (and therefore its yield stress) before the concrete reaches a strain of 0.003. Figure 2-9 shows these variations in neutral axis location for beams that are on the verge of failure. In each case the

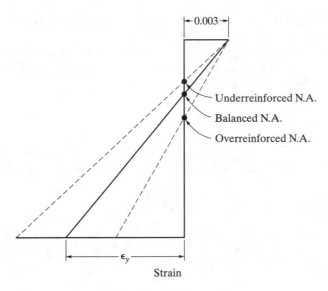

FIGURE 2-9 Variation in neutral-axis locations.

concrete has been strained to 0.003. Following the underreinforced case through to failure, we see that a slight additional load will cause the steel to stretch a considerable amount. The strains in the concrete and the steel continue to increase. The tensile force is not increasing, however, since the steel stress has reached f_y and is not increasing. Since the compressive force cannot increase ($\Sigma H = 0$), and since the concrete strain and therefore its stress are increasing, the area under compression must be decreasing and the neutral axis must rise. This process continues until the reduced area fails in compression as a secondary effect. This failure due to yielding is a gradual one, with the beam showing greatly increased deflection after the steel reaches the yield point; hence there is adequate warning of impending failure. The steel, being ductile, will not actually pull apart even at failure of the beam.

2-8

REINFORCEMENT RATIO LIMITATIONS AND GUIDELINES

Although failure due to yielding of the steel is gradual, with adequate warning of collapse, failure due to crushing of the concrete is sudden and without warning. The first type of failure is preferred, and it is ensured by restrictions of the ACI Code. The code stipulates in Section 10.3.3 that the amount of tensile steel must not exceed 0.75 times the amount of steel that would produce balanced conditions. This is an attempt to ensure a ductile failure that is produced by yielding of the steel, as compared with the brittle type of failure that occurs when the failure is in compression. This may be expressed as $A_s \leq 0.75A_{sb}$.

The code puts this stipulation in terms of a *reinforcement ratio,* sometimes called the *steel ratio.* This is a ratio of A_s to the product of beam width b and effective depth d and is denoted by the Greek lowercase rho (ρ):

$$\rho = \frac{A_s}{bd}$$

According to the ACI Code, the maximum permissible reinforcement ratio is 0.75 times that steel ratio that would produce the balanced condition (ρ_b). This may be expressed as

$$\rho_{max} = 0.75\rho_b$$

The use of the reinforcement ratio concept will be convenient in later calculations, since, if ρ_b (or A_{sb}) is known, the determination of whether a beam is underreinforced may be quickly accomplished.

Example 2-2

Using Example 2-1, determine the amount of steel required to create the balanced condition, where $d = 23$ in. and $b = 10$ in. From Table A-1, $\epsilon_y = 0.00207$ in./in. By definition of the balanced condition, the strain diagram must be as shown in Figure 2-10.

Strain   Stress and Internal Couple

FIGURE 2-10   Sketch for Example 2-2.

Solution:

1.
$$\frac{c_b}{0.003} = \frac{d - c_b}{0.00207}$$

$$0.00207c_b = 0.003(23 - c_b)$$

$$0.00207c_b + 0.003c_b = 0.069$$

$$c_b = \frac{0.069}{0.00507} = 13.6 \text{ in.}$$

2.
$$a_b = \beta_1 c_b = 0.85(13.6) = 11.6 \text{ in.}$$

3.
$$N_{Cb} = (0.85f_c')a_b b = 0.85(4.0)(11.6)(10)$$

$$= 393 \text{ kips}$$

$$N_{Tb} = A_{sb}f_y$$

$$N_{Tb} = N_{Cb}$$

4.   Therefore,

$$\text{required } A_{sb} = \frac{N_{Tb}}{f_y} = \frac{N_{Cb}}{f_y}$$

$$= \frac{393}{60} = 6.56 \text{ in.}^2$$

Comparing the balanced area of steel required with the actual amount of steel present (three No. 8 bars = 2.37 in.^{2}), we see that this is an *underreinforced* beam that is controlled by the steel yielding.

Check the code requirement for a ductile-type beam (ACI Code, Section 10.3.3). The maximum A_s allowed is

$$0.75A_{sb} = 0.75(6.56 \text{ in.}^2) = 4.92 \text{ in.}^2 > 2.37 \text{ in.}^2 \qquad \text{(O.K.)}$$

At this point, it may be noted again that heavily reinforced beams are less efficient than their more lightly reinforced counterparts. One structural reason for this is that, for a given beam size, an increase in A_s is accompanied by a decrease in the lever arm of the internal couple ($Z = d - a/2$). This may be illustrated by doubling the tension steel for the beam of Example 2-1 and recalculating M_n:

$$A_s = 2(2.37) = 4.74 \text{ in.}^2 \qquad \text{(100\% increase)}$$

$$a = \frac{A_s f_y}{0.85f_c'b} = \frac{4.74(60)}{0.85(4)(10)} = 8.36 \text{ in.}$$

$$M_n = 0.85f_c'ab\left(d - \frac{a}{2}\right) = 0.85(4)(8.36)(10)\left(23 - \frac{8.36}{2}\right) = 446 \text{ ft-kips}$$

For the beam of Example 2-1, M_n was 247 ft-kips; therefore,

$$\frac{446 - 247}{247} \times 100 = 80\% \text{ increase}$$

Instead of using the preceding laborious technique for determining the balanced steel, a general expression for the reinforcement ratio that would produce the balanced condition (ρ_b) may be derived with reference to Figure 2-11.

The neutral axis for the *balanced condition* is located by using similar triangles:

$$\frac{c_b}{0.003} = \frac{d}{0.003 + \dfrac{f_y}{E_s}}$$

Reorganizing and substituting, with $E_s = 29,000,000$ psi, yields

$$c_b = \frac{0.003}{0.003 + f_y/29,000,000}(d)$$

$$= \frac{87,000}{87,000 + f_y}(d) \qquad\qquad (2\text{–}1)$$

Since $N_{Cb} = N_{Tb}$ ($\Sigma H = 0$),

$$(0.85f_c')\beta_1 c_b b = A_{sb}f_y$$

$$c_b = \frac{A_{sb}f_y}{(0.85f_c')\beta_1 b}$$

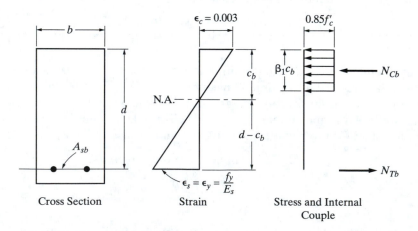

Cross Section   **Strain**   **Stress and Internal Couple**

FIGURE 2-11   The balanced condition.

Since $A_{sb} = \rho_b bd$,

$$c_b = \frac{\rho_b bd f_y}{(0.85 f_c')\beta_1 b} = \frac{\rho_b d f_y}{(0.85 f_c')\beta_1} \tag{2-2}$$

Equations (2-1) and (2-2) may now be equated and solved for ρ_b:

$$\rho_b = \frac{0.85 f_c' \beta_1}{f_y} \left(\frac{87,000}{f_y + 87,000} \right) \tag{2-3}$$

Note that in Equation (2-3) the units are pounds and inches.

The value of ρ_b can be easily calculated for different combinations of f_c' and f_y and subsequently tabulated. The upper limit for the reinforcement ratio set by the ACI Code is $0.75\rho_b$, however. Table A-5 gives values of $0.75\rho_b$ for various combinations of steel yield stress and concrete strength. This table may be used for quick reference to determine if a beam is acceptable with respect to ductility, under the present ACI Code.

Hence the concept of a balanced section serves as a datum or reference as to whether a design or analysis conforms to the specific mode of failure as prescribed by the ACI Code. Where the area of steel is in excess of the area of steel required for the balanced condition, a brittle form of failure will occur. Where the area of steel is less than the area of steel required for the balanced condition, a ductile mode of failure will occur.

Example 2-3 _____

Recheck Example 2-1 for ductility using $0.75\rho_b$ as a limit.

Solution:

$$\rho = \frac{A_s}{bd} = \frac{2.37}{10(23)} = 0.0103$$

From Table A-5 for $f_y = 60,000$ psi and $f_c' = 4000$ psi,

$$\rho_{max} = 0.75\rho_b = 0.0214$$

$$0.0103 < 0.0214$$

The code requirement may also be expressed as $A_{s,max} = 0.75 A_{sb}$. Recall that A_{sb} was calculated in Example 2-2.

$$A_{s,max} = 0.75(6.56) = 4.92 \text{ in.}^2 > 2.37 \text{ in.}^2 \qquad \text{(O.K.)}$$

Section 10.5.1 of the ACI Code also establishes a lower limit on the amount of tension reinforcement for flexural members. The code states that where tensile reinforcement is required by analysis, the steel area A_s shall not be less than that given by

$$A_{s,\mathrm{min}} = \frac{3\sqrt{f_c'}}{f_y} b_w d \geq \frac{200}{f_y} b_w d$$

(Note that for rectangular beams, $b_w = b$.)

$A_{s,\mathrm{min}}$ is conveniently calculated using Table A-5 where the larger of $3\sqrt{f_c'}/f_y$ and $200/f_y$ is tabulated. Note that $A_{s,\mathrm{min}}$ is the product of the tabulated value and $b_w d$.

The lower limit guards against sudden failure essentially by ensuring that a beam with a very small amount of tensile reinforcement has a greater moment strength as a reinforced concrete section than that of the corresponding plain concrete section computed from its modulus of rupture. Alternatively, it is satisfactory to provide an area of tensile reinforcement that is one-third greater than that required by analysis (ACI Code, Section 10.5.3).

Minimum required reinforcement in structural slabs (see Section 2-13) is governed by the required shrinkage and temperature steel as outlined in the ACI Code, Section 7.12.

2-9

STRENGTH REQUIREMENTS

The basic criterion for strength design may be expressed as

strength furnished $\geq$ strength required

All members and all sections of members must be proportioned to meet this criterion.

The required strength may be expressed in terms of design loads or their related moments, shears, and forces. Design loads may be defined as service loads multiplied by the appropriate *load factors*. (When the word *design* is used as an adjective throughout the ACI Code, it indicates that load factors are included.) The subscript u is used to indicate design loads, moments, shears, and forces.

For example, the *design load* $w_u = 1.4w_{\mathrm{DL}} + 1.7w_{\mathrm{LL}}$, and the required or *design moment* strength for dead and live load is $M_u = 1.4M_{\mathrm{DL}} + 1.7M_{\mathrm{LL}}$, where 1.4 and 1.7 are the load factors. This is, in effect, a safety provision. The load factors attempt to assess the possibility that prescribed service loads may be exceeded. Obviously, a specified live load is more apt to be exceeded than a dead load, which is largely fixed by the weight of the structure. With regard to the weight of the structure, recall that the unit weight of reinforced concrete is taken as 150 lb/ft^3. The ultimate strength of the members must take into account the total of all service loads, each multiplied by its respective load factor. Load factors are different in magnitude for dead load, live load, wind, or earthquake loading.

For dead and live loads, the ACI Code, Section 9.2, specifies that design loads, design shears, and design moments be obtained from service loads by using the relation

$$U = 1.4D + 1.7L \qquad\qquad \text{ACI Eq. (9-1)}$$

where U is any of the design strengths, D the service dead load, and L the service live load. Load factors for other types of loading, as well as combinations of loads, may be obtained from Section 9.2 of the ACI Code.

A second safety provision provided in the ACI Code, Section 9.3, is the reduction of the theoretical capacity of a structural element by a *strength reduction factor* ϕ. This provides for the possibility that small adverse variations in material strengths, workmanship, and dimensions, although within acceptable tolerance and limits of good practice, may combine to result in undercapacity. In effect, the ϕ factor, when multiplied by the nominal strength of a member, will furnish us with a practical strength that is obviously less than the nominal strength.

In assigning strength reduction factors, the degree of ductility and the importance of the member as well as the degree of accuracy with which the strength of the member can be established are considered. The ACI Code, Section 9.3, provides for these variables by using the following ϕ factors:

bending	= 0.90
shear and torsion	= 0.85
compression members (spirally reinforced)	= 0.75
compression members (tied)	= 0.70
bearing on concrete	= 0.70

Hence we can state that the practical moment strength will equal the nominal moment strength M_n multiplied by the ϕ factor:

$$\text{practical moment strength} = \phi M_n$$

2-10

RECTANGULAR BEAM ANALYSIS FOR MOMENT (TENSION REINFORCEMENT ONLY)

The *flexural analysis problem* is characterized by knowing precisely what comprises the cross section of a beam. That is, the following things are *known:* tension bar size and number (or A_s), beam width (b), effective depth (d) or total depth (h), f'_c, and f_y. To be found, basically, is the beam strength, although this may be manifested in various ways: Find ϕM_n, check the adequacy of the given beam, or find an allowable load that the beam can carry. The *flexural design problem,* on the other hand, requires the determination of one or more of the dimensions of the cross section or the determination of the main tension steel to use. It will be important to recognize the differences between these two types of problems because the methods of solution are different.

Example 2-4 _____

Determine if the beam shown in Figure 2-12 is adequate as governed by the ACI Code (318-95).

Solution:

For superimposed service loads,

$$\text{uniform dead load} = 0.8 \text{ kip/ft} \qquad \text{(excludes beam weight)}$$

$$\text{uniform live load} = 0.8 \text{ kip/ft}$$

$$\text{concentrated live load} = 12 \text{ kips} \qquad \text{(located at midspan)}$$

Assume $f_c' = 4000$ psi and A615 grade 60 billet steel ($f_y = 60,000$ psi).

A logical approach to this type of problem is to compare the practical moment strength (ϕM_n) with the applied design moment resulting from the *factored* loads. This latter moment will be noted M_u. If the beam is adequate for the moment, $\phi M_n \geq M_u$. The procedure outlined here for ϕM_n is summarized in Section 2-11.

FIGURE 2-12   Sketch for Example 2-4.

Determination of ϕM_n

1.   Given:

$$f_y = 60{,}000 \text{ psi}$$

$$b = 12 \text{ in.}$$

$$d = 17.5 \text{ in.}$$

$$A_s = 4.00 \text{ in.}^2 \qquad \text{(Table A-2)}$$

$$f_c' = 4000 \text{ psi}$$

2.   To be found: ϕM_n.

3.
$$\rho = \frac{A_s}{bd} = \frac{4.00}{12(17.5)} = 0.0190$$

4.   From Table A-5, $0.75\rho_b = 0.0214$. Because $0.0190 < 0.0214$, failure by yielding of steel is assured. Also, from Table A-5:

$$A_{s,\min} = 0.0033 b_w d$$

$$= 0.0033(12)(17.5) = 0.69 \text{ in.}^2$$

$$4.00 \text{ in.}^2 > 0.69 \text{ in.}^2 \qquad\qquad\qquad \text{(O.K.)}$$

5.
$$a = \frac{A_s f_y}{(0.85 f_c')b}$$

$$= \frac{4.00(60)}{0.85(4)(12)} = 5.88 \text{ in.}$$

6.
$$Z = d - \frac{a}{2} = 17.5 - \frac{5.88}{2} = 14.6 \text{ in.}$$

7.   Based on steel:

$$M_n = A_s f_y Z$$

$$= 4.00(60)(14.6) = 3490 \text{ in.-kips}$$

$$\frac{3490}{12} = 291 \text{ ft-kips}$$

8.
$$\phi M_n = 0.9(291) = 262 \text{ ft-kips}$$

Find M_u: Since the given service dead load excluded the beam weight, it will now be calculated:

$$\text{beam weight} = \frac{20(12)}{144}(0.150) = 0.25 \text{ kip/ft}$$

superimposed uniform dead load = 0.80 kip/ft

total service uniform dead load = 1.05 kips/ft = w_{DL}

total service uniform live load = 0.80 kip/ft = w_{LL}

Total factored uniform load:

$$w_u = 1.4w_{DL} + 1.7w_{LL}$$

$$= 1.4(1.05) + 1.7(0.80) = 2.83 \text{ kips/ft}$$

Superimposed concentrated live load = 12 kips = P_{LL}.

Total factored concentrated load:

$$P_u = 1.7P_{LL} = 1.7(12) = 20.4 \text{ kips}$$

$$M_u = \frac{w_u \ell^2}{8} + \frac{P_u \ell}{4}$$

$$= \frac{2.83(20)^2}{8} + \frac{20.4(20)}{4}$$

$$= 243.5 \text{ ft-kips} < 262 \text{ ft-kips}$$

Therefore, the beam is adequate.

The present ACI Code (1995) has placed the upper limit of $0.75\rho_b$ on the reinforcement ratio. The older working stress design codes did not restrict ρ in this manner; therefore, overreinforced beams do exist in structures. Although these are not acceptable within the philosophy of the 1995 code, they have been serviceable and their moment capacity can logically be found by using no more steel than that represented by $0.75\rho_b$. Essentially, this approach ignores the strength of any steel that is in excess of 75% of the amount of steel that would produce the balanced condition.

Example 2-5

Find ϕM_n for the beam of cross section shown in Figure 2-13. This beam was designed using the older working stress design codes. Steel is billet steel, A615 grade 40. Concrete strength is 3000 psi.

Solution:

1.   Given:

$$f_y = 40,000 \text{ psi}$$

$$f'_c = 3000 \text{ psi}, \qquad d = 20 \text{ in.}$$

$$b = 11 \text{ in.}, \qquad A_s = 7.62 \text{ in.}^2$$

FIGURE 2-13   Sketch for Example 2-5.

2.   To be found: ϕM_n.

3.
$$\rho = \frac{A_s}{bd} = \frac{7.62}{11(20)} = 0.0346$$

4. $0.75\rho_b = 0.0278 = \rho_{max}$. Since $\rho > 0.75\rho_b$, we will use $\rho = 0.0278$ as a maximum. Therefore,

$$\text{effective } A_s = \rho bd = 0.0278(11)(20)$$
$$= 6.12 \text{ in.}^2$$

5.
$$a = \frac{A_s f_y}{0.85 f_c' b} = \frac{6.12(40)}{0.85(3)(11)} = 8.73 \text{ in.}$$

6.
$$Z = d - \frac{a}{2} = 20 - \frac{8.73}{2} = 15.6 \text{ in.}$$

7.
$$M_n = A_s f_y Z = 6.12(40(15.6) = 3820 \text{ in.-kips}$$

8.
$$\phi M_n = (0.9)\frac{3820}{12} = 286 \text{ ft-kips}$$

2-11

SUMMARY OF PROCEDURE FOR RECTANGULAR BEAM ANALYSIS FOR ϕM_n (TENSION REINFORCEMENT ONLY)

1.   List the known quantities. Use a sketch.
2.   Determine what is to be found. (An "analysis" may require any of the following to be found: ϕM_n, allowable service live load or dead load, maximum allowable span.)

3.   Calculate the reinforcement ratio:

$$\rho = \frac{A_s}{bd}$$

4.   Compare the actual ρ with $0.75\rho_b$ and A_s with $A_{s,min}$ to determine if the beam cross section is acceptable.

5.   Calculate the depth of the (rectangular) compressive stress block:

$$a = \frac{A_s f_y}{(0.85 f_c')b}$$

6.   Calculate the internal couple lever arm length:

$$Z = d - \frac{a}{2}$$

7.   Calculate the nominal moment strength M_n:

$$M_n = N_T Z = A_s f_y Z$$

or

$$M_n = N_C Z = 0.85 f_c' abZ$$

8.   Calculate the practical moment strength ϕM_n.

A flow diagram of this procedure is presented in Appendix B.

2-12

SLABS: INTRODUCTION

Slabs constitute a specialized category of bending members and are used in both structural steel and reinforced concrete structures. Probably the most basic and common type of slab is termed a *one-way slab*. A one-way slab may be described as a structural reinforced concrete slab supported on two opposite sides so that the bending occurs in one direction only, that is, perpendicular to the supported edges.

If a slab is supported along all four edges, it may be designated as a *two-way slab,* with bending occurring in two directions perpendicular to each other. If the ratio of the lengths of the two perpendicular sides is in excess of 2, however, the slab may be assumed to act as a one-way slab with bending primarily occurring in the short direction.

A specific type of two-way slab is categorized as a *flat slab*. A flat slab may be defined as *a concrete slab reinforced in two or more directions, generally without beams or girders to transfer the loads to supporting members.* The slab, then, could be considered to be supported on a grid of shallow beams, which are themselves integral with and have the same depth as the slab. The columns tend to punch upward through the slab, resulting in a high shearing stress along with inclined slab

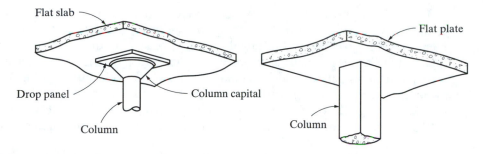

FIGURE 2-14   Reinforced concrete slabs.

cracking. (This "punching shear" is considered later in the discussion on column footings.) Thus it is common to both thicken the slab in the vicinity of the column, utilizing a *drop panel,* and at the same time enlarge the top of the column in the shape of an inverted frustum called a *column capital* (see Figure 2-14). Another type of two-way slab is a *flat plate.* This is similar to the flat slab, without the drop panels and column capitals; hence it is a slab of constant thickness supported directly on columns. Generally, the flat plate is used where spans are smaller and loads lighter than those requiring a flat slab design (see Figure 2-14).

2-13

ONE-WAY SLABS: ANALYSIS FOR MOMENT

In our discussion of slabs, we will be primarily concerned with one-way slabs. Such a slab is assumed to be a rectangular beam with a width $b = 12$ in. When loaded with a uniformly distributed load, the slab deflects so that it has curvature, and therefore bending moment, in only one direction. Hence the slab is analyzed and designed as though it were composed of 12-in.-wide segments placed side by side with a total depth equal to the slab thickness. With a width of 12 in., the uniformly distributed load, generally specified in pounds per square foot (psf) for buildings, automatically becomes the load per linear foot (lb/ft) for the design of the slab (see Figure 2-15).

FIGURE 2-15   One-way slab.

In the one-way slab the main reinforcement for bending is placed perpendicular to the supports. Since analysis and design will be done for a typical 12-in.-wide segment, it will be necessary to specify the amount of steel in that segment. Reinforcing steel in slabs is normally specified by bar size and center-to-center spacing, and the amount of steel considered to exist in the 12-in.-wide typical segment is an *average amount*. Table A-4 is provided to facilitate this determination. For example, if a slab is reinforced with No. 7 bars spaced 15 in. apart (center to center), a typical 12-in.-wide segment of the slab would contain an average steel area of 0.48 in.^{2}. This is sometimes denoted 0.48 in.^{2}/ft.

In addition, the ACI Code stipulates that reinforcement for shrinkage and temperature stresses normal to the principal reinforcement must be provided in structural floor and roof slabs where the principal reinforcement extends in one direction only. The ACI Code further states that for grade 40 or 50 deformed bars, the minimum area of such steel must be $A_s = 0.0020bh$, and for grade 60 deformed bars, the minimum area must be $A_s = 0.0018bh$, where b = width of member (12 in. for slabs) and h = total slab thickness. The ACI Code also stipulates that in structural slabs of uniform thickness, the minimum amount of reinforcement in the direction of the span (principal reinforcement) must not be less than that required for shrinkage and temperature reinforcement (ACI Code, Section 10.5.4).

The principal reinforcement shall not be spaced farther apart than three times the slab thickness nor more than 18 in. Shrinkage and temperature reinforcement shall not be spaced farther apart than five times the slab thickness nor more than 18 in.

The required thickness of a one-way slab may depend on the bending, deflection, or shear strength requirements. The ACI Code imposes span/depth criteria in an effort to prevent excessive deflection, which might adversely affect the strength or performance of the structure at service loads. Table 9.5a of the ACI Code establishes minimum thicknesses for beams and one-way slabs in terms of fractions of the span length. These may be used for members not supporting or attached to construction likely to be damaged by large deflections. If the member supports such construction, deflections must be calculated. For members of lesser thickness than that indicated in the table, deflection should be computed, and if satisfactory, the member may be used. The tabular values are for use with nonprestressed reinforced concrete members made with normal-weight concrete and grade 60 reinforcement. If a different grade of reinforcement is used, the tabular values must be multiplied by a factor equal to

$$0.4 + \frac{f_y}{100,000}$$

As an example, for simply supported solid one-way slabs of normal-weight concrete and grade 60 steel, the minimum thickness required when deflections are not computed equals $\ell/20$, where ℓ is the span length of the slab. Deflections are discussed further in Chapter 7.

According to the ACI Code, Section 7.7.1, the concrete protection for reinforcement in slabs must be not less than ¾ in. for surfaces not exposed directly to the weather or in contact with the ground. This is applicable for No. 11 and smaller bars. For surfaces exposed to the weather or in contact with the ground, the minimum concrete protection for reinforcement is 2 in. for No. 6 through No. 18 bars and 1½ in. for No. 5 and smaller bars. If a slab is cast against and permanently exposed to the ground, the minimum concrete cover for all reinforcement is 3 in.

Example 2-6

A one-way structural interior slab having the cross section shown spans 12 ft. The steel is A615 grade 40. The concrete strength is 3000 psi, and the cover is ¾ in. Determine the service live load (psf) that the slab can support.

Solution:

From Figure 2-16, the bars in this slab are No. 5 bars spaced 7 in. apart. This is sometimes denoted "7 in. o.c." (7 in. on center), meaning 7 in. center-to-center distance. They are perpendicular to the supports.

FIGURE 2-16   Sketch for Example 2-6.

1.   Given:

$$A_s = 0.53 \text{ in.}^2/\text{ft} \qquad (\text{Table A-4})$$

$$f'_c = 3,000 \text{ psi}, \qquad f_y = 40,000 \text{ psi}$$

$$b = 12 \text{ in.}$$

$$d = 6.5 - 0.75 - \frac{0.625}{2} = 5.44 \text{ in.}$$

2.   Find ϕM_n and the permissible service live load.

3.
$$\rho = \frac{A_s}{bd} = \frac{0.53}{12(5.44)} = 0.0081$$

4. From Table A-5, $\rho_{max} = 0.75\rho_b = 0.0278$, and

$$0.0081 < 0.0278 \qquad \text{(O.K.)}$$

The minimum A_s is that required for shrinkage and temperature steel.

$$A_{s,min} = 0.0020bh = 0.0020(12)(6.5) = 0.16 \text{ in.}^2/\text{ft}$$

$$0.53 > 0.16 \qquad \text{(O.K.)}$$

5.
$$a = \frac{A_s f_y}{(0.85f_c')b} = \frac{0.53(40)}{0.85(3)(12)} = 0.69 \text{ in.}$$

6.
$$Z = d - \frac{a}{2} = 5.44 - \frac{0.69}{2} = 5.10 \text{ in.}$$

7.
$$M_n = A_s f_y Z = 0.53(40)(5.10) = 108 \text{ in.-kips (per foot of slab width)}$$

8.
$$\phi M_n = 0.9 M_n = 0.9(108) = \frac{97.2}{12} = 8.1 \text{ ft-kips}$$

The service live load that the slab can support will be found next. (The notation M_u is used to denote moment resulting from *factored* applied loads.) Since

$$M_u = \frac{w_u \ell^2}{8}$$

the total factored design load that can be supported by the slab is

$$w_u = \frac{8M_u}{\ell^2}$$

Since, as a limit, $M_u = \phi M_n$,

$$w_u = \frac{8\phi M_n}{\ell^2} = \frac{8(8.1)}{12^2} = 0.450 \text{ kip/ft}$$

The slab weight is

$$w_{DL} = \frac{6.5(12)}{144}(0.150) = 0.081 \text{ kip/ft}$$

Since the total factored design load is

$$w_u = 1.4w_{DL} + 1.7w_{LL}$$

w_{LL} may be found from

$$w_{LL} = \frac{w_u - 1.4w_{DL}}{1.7} = \frac{0.45 - 1.4(0.081)}{1.7}$$

$$= 0.198 \text{ kip/ft}$$

Since the segment is 12 in. wide, this is equivalent to 198 psf. It will be noted that the procedure for finding ϕM_n for a one-way slab is almost identical to that for a beam. See Section 2-11 for a summary of this procedure.

2-14

RECTANGULAR BEAM DESIGN FOR MOMENT (TENSION REINFORCEMENT ONLY)

In the design of rectangular sections for moment, with f'_c and f_y usually prescribed, *three basic quantities* are to be determined: beam width, beam depth, and steel area. It should be recognized that there is a large multitude of combinations of these three quantities that will satisfy the moment strength required in a particular application. Theoretically, a wide, shallow beam may have the same ϕM_n as a narrow, deep beam. It must also be recognized that practical considerations and code restraints will affect the final choices of these quantities. There is no easy way to determine the *best* cross section, since economy depends on much more than simply the volume of concrete and amount of steel in a beam.

Using the internal relationships previously developed for beam analysis, modifications may be made whereby the design process may be simplified. We have previously developed the analysis expression for the resisting moment of a rectangular beam with tension reinforcement only:

$$\phi M_n = \phi N_C Z = \phi N_T Z$$

and

$$\phi M_n = \phi (0.85 f'_c) ba \left(d - \frac{a}{2} \right)$$

where

$$a = \frac{A_s f_y}{(0.85 f'_c) b}$$

The use of these formulas will now be simplified through the development of design constants, which will subsequently be tabulated:

$$\rho = \frac{A_s}{bd} \qquad \text{therefore, } A_s = \rho bd$$

$$a = \frac{A_s f_y}{(0.85 f'_c) b} = \frac{\rho bd f_y}{(0.85 f'_c) b} = \frac{\rho d f_y}{0.85 f'_c}$$

Arbitrarily define ω (omega):

$$\omega = \rho \frac{f_y}{f'_c}$$

Then

$$a = \frac{\omega d}{0.85}$$

Substitute into the ϕM_n expression:

$$\phi M_n = \phi(0.85f_c')(b)\frac{\omega d}{0.85}\left[d - \frac{\omega d}{2(0.85)}\right]$$

Simplify and rearrange:

$$\phi M_n = \phi bd^2 f_c'\omega(1 - 0.59\omega)$$

Arbitrarily define $\overline{k}$:

$$\overline{k} = f_c'\omega(1 - 0.59\omega)$$

The term $\overline{k}$ is sometimes called the *coefficient of resistance*. It varies with ρ, f_c', and f_y. Tables A-7 through A-11 give the value of $\overline{k}$ in ksi for values of ρ and various combinations of f_c' and f_y. The maximum ρ tabulated in each table is $0.75\rho_b$. The general analysis expression for ϕM_n may now be written as

$$\phi M_n = \phi bd^2\overline{k}$$

In this form, it may readily be used for design purposes. Since $\overline{k}$ is in units of ksi and b and d are in inches, ϕM_n will have units of in.-kips. If the desired ϕM_n is to be in ft-kips, the expression may be written as

$$\phi M_n = \frac{\phi bd^2}{12}\overline{k}$$

These expressions may also be used to simplify rectangular beam *analysis*. As an example, let us recompute the practical moment strength ϕM_n for Example 2-4:

1.
$$\rho = \frac{A_s}{bd} = \frac{4.0}{12(17.5)} = 0.0190$$

2.   From Table A-10, $\overline{k} = 0.9489$ (ksi). Thus

$$\phi M_n = \frac{\phi bd^2\overline{k}}{12} = 0.9(12)\frac{(17.5)^2}{12}(0.9489)$$

$$= 262 \text{ ft-kips}$$

As may be observed, this analysis approach is shorter and simpler than that of Example 2-4, yields the same results, and is equally acceptable.

Using the newly developed expressions and relationships for design problems, the first example will be one where the cross section (b and h) is known by either practical or architectural considerations, leaving the selection of the reinforcing bars as the only unknown.

Material properties, sizes, and availability of reinforcing steel in the form of bars and welded wire fabric were discussed in Section 1-7. In our discussion, we will be concerned with bars only and the ACI Code recommendations as to details governing minimum clearance and cover requirements for steel reinforcing bars. Clearance details are governed by the requirement for concrete to pass through a layer of bars without undue segregation of the aggregates. Cover details are governed by the necessity that the concrete provide protection against corrosion for the bars. Required minimums of both spacing and cover also play a role in preventing the splitting of the concrete in the proximity of highly stressed tension bars.

Spacing requirements in the ACI Code indicate that the clear space between bars in a single layer shall be not less than:

1.   The bar diameter, but not less than 1 in. (ACI Code, Section 7.6.1)
2. $1\frac{1}{3} \times$ maximum aggregate size (ACI Code, Section 3.3.2)

Also, should multiple layers of bars be necessary, a 1 in. minimum clear distance is required between layers (ACI Code, Section 7.6.2) and bars in the upper layers shall be placed directly above bars in the bottom layer.

Cover requirements for cast-in-place concrete are stated in the ACI Code, Section 7.7.1. This listing is extensive. For beams, girders, and columns not exposed to the weather or in contact with the ground, however, the minimum concrete cover on any steel is $1\frac{1}{2}$ in.

Table A-3 combines spacing and cover requirements into a tabulation of minimum beam widths for multiples of various bars. The assumptions are stated. It should be noted that No. 3 stirrups are assumed. Stirrups are a special form of reinforcement that primarily resist shear forces and will be discussed in Chapter 4. Stirrups are common in rectangular beams and will be assumed to exist in all further examples and problems in this text. One type of stirrup, called a *loop stirrup,* can be observed in Figure 2-17, in Example 2-7.

Example 2-7 _____

Design a rectangular reinforced concrete beam to carry a service dead load moment of 50 ft-kips (which includes the moment due to the weight of the beam) and a service live load moment of 100 ft-kips. Architectural considerations require the beam width to be 10 in. and the total depth (h) to be 25 in. Use $f'_c = 3000$ psi and $f_y = 60,000$ psi.

Of the three basic quantities to be found, two are specified in this example, and the solution for the required steel area is direct. The procedure outlined here is summarized in Section 2-15.

Solution:

1.   The total design moment is

$$M_u = 1.4M_{\text{DL}} + 1.7M_{\text{LL}}$$

$$= 1.4(50) + 1.7(100)$$

$$= 240 \text{ ft-kips}$$

2.   Estimate d to be equal to $h - 3$ in.:

$$d = 25 - 3 = 22 \text{ in.}$$

Since $\phi M_n = \phi b d^2 \bar{k}$ and since ϕM_n must equal M_u as a lower limit, the expression may be written as $M_u = \phi b d^2 \bar{k}$ and

$$\text{required } \bar{k} = \frac{M_u}{\phi b d^2} = \frac{240(12)}{0.9(10)(22)^2} = 0.6612 \text{ ksi}$$

3.   From Table A-8, $\bar{k}$ of 0.6649 ksi will be provided if the steel ratio $\rho = 0.0131$. Therefore, required $\rho = 0.0131$. From Table A-5,

$$0.75\rho_b = 0.0161 = \rho_{\max}$$

4. $$\text{required } A_s = \rho b d$$

$$= 0.0131(10)(22) = 2.88 \text{ in.}^2$$

Check $A_{s,\min}$. From Table A-5,

$$A_{s,\min} = 0.0033 b_w d$$

$$= 0.0033(10)(22) = 0.73 \text{ in.}^2 \qquad \text{(O.K.)}$$

5.   Select the bars. Theoretically, any bar or combination of bars that provides at least 2.88 in.^{2} of steel area will satisfy the design requirements. Preferably, no fewer than two bars should be used. The bars should be of the same diameter and placed in one layer whenever possible. We next consider the bar selection based on the foregoing required A_s (2.88 in.^{2}). The following combinations may be considered:

$$2 \text{ No. 11 bars: } A_s = 3.12 \text{ in.}^2$$
$$3 \text{ No. 9 bars: } A_s = 3.00 \text{ in.}^2$$
$$4 \text{ No. 8 bars: } A_s = 3.16 \text{ in.}^2$$
$$5 \text{ No. 7 bars: } A_s = 3.00 \text{ in.}^2$$

A review of Table A-3 indicates that the most acceptable combination is three No. 9 bars. The width of beam required for three No. 9 bars is 9½ in., which is satisfactory.

At this point we should check the actual effective depth d and compare it with the estimated d:

$$\text{actual } d = 25 - 1.5 - 0.38 - \frac{1.128}{2} = 22.6 \text{ in.}$$

This is slightly in excess of the estimated d and is therefore conservative (on the safe side). Because of the small difference, no revision is either suggested or required.

6.   Generally, concrete dimensions should be to the ½ in. The final design sketch should show the following (see Figure 2-17):

FIGURE 2-17   Design sketch for Example 2-7.

a.   Beam width
b.   Total beam depth
c.   Main reinforcement size and number of bars
d.   Cover on reinforcement
e.   Stirrup size

A second type of design problem is presented in Example 2-8. This may be categorized as a *free design* because of the *three* unknown variables: beam width, beam depth, and area of reinforcing steel. There are therefore a large number of combinations of these variables that will theoretically solve the problem. We do have some idea as to the required or desired relationships between these unknowns, however.

We know that the steel area must be greater than $A_{s,\text{min}}$ and that the steel ratio ρ must be less than ρ_{max}, which in effect establishes the range of the acceptable amount of steel. Table A-5 contains recommended values of ρ to use for design purposes. These are recommended maximum values. Try not to use larger ρ values. If larger values are used, a smaller concrete section will result with potential deflection problems.

These ρ values are based on the 1963 ACI Code (Part II), which stipulated that

$$\text{where } \rho > \frac{0.18f_c'}{f_y}, \text{ deflection must be checked}$$

$$\text{where } \rho < \frac{0.18f_c'}{f_y}, \text{ deflection need not be checked}$$

This stipulation was deleted in subsequent ACI Codes. Nevertheless, it remains a valid guide for selecting a preliminary value for the reinforcement ratio. The assumption of a value for reinforcement ratio will reduce from three to two the number of unknown quantities to be determined (yet to be found will be *b* and *d*).

Experience and judgment developed over the years have also established a range of acceptable and economical depth/width ratios for rectangular beams. Although there is no code requirement for the d/b ratio to be within a given range, rectangular beams commonly have d/b ratios between 1 and 3. *Desirable d/b* ratios lie between 1.5 and 2.2. There are situations in which d/b ratios outside this range have applications, however. Therefore, it is the designer's choice.

Example 2-8

Design a simply supported rectangular reinforced concrete beam with tension steel only to carry a service dead load of 0.9 kip/ft and a service live load of 2.0 kips/ft. (The dead load does not include the weight of the beam.) The span is 18 ft. Assume No. 3 stirrups. Use $f_c' = 4000$ psi and $f_y = 60,000$ psi. See Figure 2-18.

FIGURE 2-18   Sketch for Example 2-8.

Solution:

1. Find the applied design moment M_u, temporarily neglecting the beam weight, which will be included at a later step:

$$w_u = 1.4w_{DL} + 1.7w_{LL}$$

$$= 1.4(0.9) + 1.7(2.0) = 4.66 \text{ kips/ft}$$

Note that this is the factored design load,

$$M_u = \frac{w_u \ell^2}{8} = \frac{4.66\,(18)^2}{8} = 189 \text{ ft-kips}$$

2. Assume a value for ρ. Use $\rho = 0.0120$ (see Table A-5).
3. From Table A-10, $\overline{k} = 0.6438$ ksi.
4. At this point we have two unknowns, b and d, which can be established using two different approaches. One approach is to assume b and then solve for d. This is logical since practical and architectural considerations often establish b within relatively narrow limits.

Assuming that $b = 11$ in. and utilizing the relationship $M_u = \phi b d^2 \overline{k}$,

$$\text{required } d = \sqrt{\frac{M_u}{\phi b \overline{k}}} = \sqrt{\frac{189(12)}{0.9(11)(0.6438)}} = 18.9 \text{ in.}$$

A check of the d/b ratio gives $18.9/11 = 1.72$, which is a reasonable value.

5. At this point, the beam weight may be estimated. Realizing that the total design moment will increase, the final beam size may be estimated to be about 11 in. × 23 in. for purposes of calculating its weight. Thus

$$\text{beam dead load} = \frac{11(23)}{144}(0.150) = 0.264 \text{ kip/ft}$$

6. The additional M_u due to beam weight is

$$M_u = 1.4 \frac{0.264(18)^2}{8} = 15 \text{ ft-kips}$$

$$\text{total } M_u = 189 + 15 = 204 \text{ ft-kips}$$

7. Using the same ρ, $\overline{k}$, and b as previously, compute the new required d:

$$\text{required } d = \sqrt{\frac{M_u}{\phi b \overline{k}}} = \sqrt{\frac{204(12)}{0.9(11)(0.6438)}} = 19.6 \text{ in.}$$

A check of the d/b ratio gives $19.6/11 = 1.78$, which is reasonable.

8. $$\text{required } A_s = \rho b d$$
    $$= 0.0120(11)(19.6) = 2.59 \text{ in.}^2$$

Check $A_{s,\min}$. From Table A-5,

$$A_{s\min} = 0.0033 b_w d$$
$$= 0.0033(11)(19.6) = 0.71 \text{ in.}^2 \qquad \text{(O.K.)}$$

9. From Table A-2, select three No. 9 bars. Therefore, $A_s = 3.00$ in.^{2}. From Table A-3,

$$\text{minimum required } b = 9.5 \text{ in.} \qquad \text{(O.K.)}$$

10. Determine the total beam depth h:

$$\text{required } h = 19.6 + \frac{1.13}{2} + 0.38 + 1.5 = 22.04 \text{ in.}$$

Round up to the next ½ in. and use $h = 22.5$ in. The actual effective depth d may now be checked:

$$d = 22.5 - 1.5 - 0.38 - \frac{1.13}{2} = 20.06 \text{ in.} > 19.6 \text{ in.} \qquad \text{(O.K.)}$$

11. A design sketch is shown in Figure 2-19. This design is not necessarily the best. The final ρ is

$$\frac{3.0}{11(20.06)} = 0.0136$$

and the final d/b ratio is

$$\frac{20.06}{11} = 1.82$$

FIGURE 2-19   Design sketch for Example 2-8.

The design moment was based on a section 11 in. × 23 in., where the designed beam turned out to be 11 in. × 22½ in. Small modifications in proportions could very well make more efficient use of the steel and concrete provided.

The percentage of overdesign could be determined (not necessary, however) by analyzing the designed cross section and comparing moment strength with applied moment.

A second approach to this problem would be to establish a desired d/b ratio and then mathematically solve for b and d. For example, if we establish a desirable d/b ratio of 2.0, then $d = 2b$. Again using the relationship $M_u = \phi b d^2 \overline{k}$,

$$\text{required } bd^2 = \frac{M_u}{\phi \overline{k}} = \frac{189(12)}{0.9(0.6438)} = 3914 \text{ in.}^3$$

We can substitute for d as follows:

$$\text{required } bd^2 = 3914 \text{ in.}^3$$

$$b(2b)^2 = 3914 \text{ in.}^3$$

$$b^3 = \frac{3914}{4} = 979 \text{ in.}^3$$

$$\text{required } b = \sqrt[3]{979} = 9.93 \text{ in.}$$

Hence, assuming that $b = 10$ in., the required effective depth d can then be calculated in a manner similar to that previously used.

2-15

SUMMARY OF PROCEDURE FOR RECTANGULAR REINFORCED CONCRETE BEAM DESIGN FOR MOMENT (TENSION REINFORCEMENT ONLY)

A. Cross Section (b and h) Known; Find the Required A_s

1. Convert the service loads or moments to design M_u (include the beam weight).
2. Based on knowing h, estimate d by using the relationship $d - h = 3$ in. (conservative for bars in a single layer). Calculate the required $\overline{k}$:

$$\text{required } \overline{k} = \frac{M_u}{\phi bd^2}$$

3. From Tables A-7 through A-11, find the required steel ratio ρ.
4. Compute the required A_s:

$$\text{required } A_s = \rho bd$$

Check $A_{s,\text{min}}$. Use Table A-5.

5. Select the bars. Check to see if the bars can fit into the beam in one layer (preferable). Check the actual effective depth and compare with the assumed effective depth. If the actual effective depth is slightly in excess of the assumed effective depth, the design will be slightly conservative (on the safe side). If the actual effective depth is less than the assumed effective depth, the design is on the unconservative side and should be revised.
6. Sketch the design. (See Example 2-7, step 6, for a discussion.)

B. Design for Cross Section and Required A_s

1. Convert the service loads or moments to design moment M_u. An estimated beam weight may be included in the dead load if desired. Be sure to apply the load factor to this additional dead load.
2. Select a desired steel ratio ρ. (See Table A-5 for recommended values. Use the ρ values from Table A-5 unless a small cross section or decreased steel is desired.)
3. From Tables A-7 through A-11, find $\overline{k}$.
4. Assume b and compute the d required:

$$\text{required } d = \sqrt{\frac{M_u}{\phi b \overline{k}}}$$

If the *d/b* ratio is reasonable (1.5 to 2.2), use these values for the beam. If the *d/b* ratio is not reasonable, increase or decrease *b* and compute the new required *d*.

5. Estimate *h* and compute the beam weight. Compare this with the estimated beam weight if an estimated beam weight was included.

6. Revise design M_u to include the moment due to the beam's own weight using the latest weight determined. Note that at this point, one could revert to step 2 in design procedure A, where the cross section is known.

7. Using *b* and $\bar{k}$ previously determined along with the new total design M_u, find the new required *d*:

$$\text{required } d = \sqrt{\frac{M_u}{\phi b \bar{k}}}$$

Check to see if the *d/b* ratio is reasonable.

8. Find the required A_s:

$$\text{required } A_s = \rho b d$$

Check $A_{s,\min}$. Use Table A-5.

9. Select the bars and check to see if the bars can fit into a beam of width *b* in one layer (preferable).

10. Establish the final *h,* rounding this upward to the next ½ in. This will make the actual effective depth greater than the design effective depth, and the design will be slightly conservative (on the safe side).

11. Sketch the design. (See Example 2-7, step 6, for a discussion.)

A flow diagram of this procedure is presented in Appendix B.

2-16

DESIGN OF ONE-WAY SLABS FOR MOMENT (TENSION REINFORCEMENT ONLY)

As higher-strength steel and concrete have become available for use in reinforced concrete members, the sizes of the members have decreased. *Deflections* of members are affected very little by material strength but are affected greatly by the size of a cross section and its related moment of inertia. Therefore, deflections will be larger for a member of high-strength materials than would be the deflections for the same member fabricated from lower-strength materials, since the latter member will be essentially larger in cross-sectional area. Deflections are discussed in detail in Chapter 7. As discussed previously, one method that the ACI Code allows to limit adverse deflections is the use of a minimum thickness (see Section 2-13). A slab that meets the minimum thickness requirement must still be designed for flexure. Deflections need not be calculated or checked unless the slab supports or is attached to construction likely to be damaged by large deflections, however.

Example 2-9 illustrates the use of the ACI minimum thickness for one-way slabs. With respect to the span length to be used for design, the ACI Code, Section 8.7.1, recommends for beams and slabs not integral with supports:

$$\text{span length} = \text{clear span} + \text{depth of member}$$

but not to exceed the distance between centers of supports. For design purposes, we will use the distance between centers of supports, since the slab thickness is not yet determined.

Example 2-9

Design a simple span one-way slab to carry a uniformly distributed live load of 400 psf. The span is 10 ft (center to center of supports). Use $f_c' = 4000$ psi and $f_y = 60,000$ psi. Conform to the ACI minimum thickness requirement and make the slab thickness to a ¼-in. increment.

Solution:

Determine the required minimum h and use this to estimate the slab dead weight.

1. From ACI Table 9.5(a),

$$\text{minimum } h = \frac{\ell}{20} = \frac{10(12)}{20} = 6.0 \text{ in.}$$

   Try $h = 6$ in. and design a 12-in.-wide segment.

2. Determine the slab weight dead load:

$$\frac{6(12)}{144}(0.150) = 0.075 \text{ kip/ft}$$

   The total design load is

$$w_u = 1.4\, w_{\text{DL}} + 1.7 w_{\text{LL}}$$

$$= 1.4(0.075) + 1.7(0.400)$$

$$= 0.785 \text{ kip/ft}$$

3. Determine the design moment:

$$M_u = \frac{w_u \ell^2}{8} = \frac{0.785(10)^2}{8} = 9.81 \text{ ft-kips}$$

4. Establish the approximate d. Assuming No. 6 bars and minimum concrete cover on the bars of ¾ in.,

$$\text{assumed } d = 6.0 - 0.75 - 0.375 = 4.88 \text{ in.}$$

5. Determine the required $\bar{k}$:

$$\bar{k} = \frac{M_u}{\phi b d^2}$$

$$= \frac{9.81(12)}{0.9(12)(4.88)^2} = 0.4577 \text{ ksi}$$

6. From Table A-10, for a required $\bar{k} = 0.4577$, the required $\rho = 0.0083$. (Note that the required ρ selected is the next *higher* value from Table A-10.) Thus

$$\rho_{max} = 0.0214 > 0.0083 \qquad \text{(O.K.)}$$

Use $\rho = 0.0083$.

7. $$\text{required } A_s = \rho b d = 0.0083(12)(4.88) = 0.49 \text{ in.}^2/\text{ft}$$

8. Select the main steel (from Table A-4). Select No. 5 bars at 7½ in. o.c. ($A_s = 0.50$ in.^{2}). The assumption on bar size was satisfactory. The code requirements for maximum spacing have been discussed in Section 2-13. Minimum spacing of bars in slabs, practically, should not be less than 4 in., although the ACI Code allows bars to be placed closer together, as discussed in Example 2-7. Check the maximum spacing (ACI Code, Section 7.6.5):

$$\text{maximum spacing} = 3h \quad \text{or} \quad 18 \text{ in.}$$

$$3h = 3(6) = 18 \text{ in.}$$

$$7\tfrac{1}{2} \text{ in.} < 18 \text{ in.} \qquad \text{(O.K.)}$$

Therefore, use No. 5 bars at 7½ in. o.c.

9. Select shrinkage and temperature reinforcement (ACI Code, Section 7.12):

$$\text{required } A_s = 0.0018bh$$

$$= 0.0018(12)(6) = 0.13 \text{ in.}^2/\text{ft}$$

Select No. 3 bars at 10 in. o.c. ($A_s = 0.13$ in.^{2}) or No. 4 bars at 18 in. o.c. ($A_s = 0.13$ in.^{2}):

$$\text{maximum spacing} = 5h \quad \text{or} \quad 18 \text{ in.}$$

Use No. 3 bars at 10 in. o.c.

10. The main steel area must exceed the area required for shrinkage and temperature steel (ACI Code, Section 10.5.3):

$$0.50 \text{ in.}^2 > 0.13 \text{ in.}^2 \qquad \text{(O.K.)}$$

11. A design sketch is shown in Figure 2-20.

FIGURE 2-20   Design sketch for Example 2-9.

2-17

SUMMARY OF PROCEDURE FOR DESIGN OF ONE-WAY SLABS FOR MOMENT (TO SATISFY ACI MINIMUM *h*)

1. Compute the minimum *h* based on the ACI Code, Table 9.5(a). Round off *h* to the next higher ¼ in. and use that dimension.
2. Compute the slab weight and compute w_u (total design load).
3. Compute the design moment M_u.
4. Calculate an assumed effective depth *d* (assuming No. 6 bars and ¾ in. cover) by using the relationship

$$d = h - 1.12 \text{ in.}$$

5. Calculate the required $\bar{k}$:

$$\text{required } \bar{k} = \frac{M_u}{\phi b d^2}$$

6. From Tables A-7 through A-11, find the required steel ratio ρ. (This must be less than ρ_{max}. If the required $\rho > \rho_{max}$, the slab must be made thicker.)
7. Compute the required A_s:

$$\text{required } A_s = \rho b d$$

8. Select the main steel (Table A-4). Check with maximum spacing 3*h* or 18 in. Check the assumption of step 4.
9. Select shrinkage and temperature steel as per the ACI Code:

$$\text{required } A_s = 0.0020bh \qquad \text{(grade 40 and 50 steel)}$$

$$\text{required } A_s = 0.0018bh \qquad \text{(grade 60 steel)}$$

Check with maximum spacing 5*h* or 18 in.

10. The main steel area *cannot* be less than the area of steel required for shrinkage and temperature.
11. Sketch the design.

2-18

SLABS ON GROUND

The previous discussion primarily concerns itself with a structural slab. Another category of slabs, generally used as a floor, may be termed a *slab on grade* or a *slab on ground*. As the name implies, it is a slab that is supported throughout its entire area by some form of subgrade. The design of such a slab is significantly different from the design of a structural slab.

A theoretical approach to determine the required floor slab thickness must consider the following factors:

1. Strength of subgrade and subbase
2. Strength of concrete
3. Magnitude and type of load (including contact area of loads)

The subgrade is the natural ground, graded and compacted, on which the floor is built. The pressure on the subgrade is generally low due to the rigidity of the concrete floor slab. The floors do not necessarily require strong support from the subgrade. It is important that the subgrade support be reasonably uniform without abrupt changes, horizontally, from hard to soft, however. The upper portion of the subgrade should be of uniform material and density.

The subbase is usually a thin layer of material placed on top of the prepared subgrade. It is generally used when a uniform subgrade cannot be developed by grading and compaction. It will serve to equalize minor surface defects as well as provide a capillary break and a working platform for construction activities. A 4 in. minimum thickness, compacted to a high density, is suggested.

The concrete strength for industrial and commercial slabs on ground should not be less than 4000 psi at 28 days. This furnishes satisfactory wear resistance in addition to strength. Generally, in residential construction the slabs on ground will have concrete strengths of 2500 psi or 3000 psi. A minimum of 3000 psi is recommended. The required slab thickness will be a function of the type of loading, magnitude of loading, and contact area of the load.

Reinforcing steel, in the form of welded wire fabric or deformed bars in both directions, is usually placed in the slab on grade for a number of reasons. The reinforcement may add to the strength of the slab, particularly when the slab spans soft spots in the subgrade. It also acts as crack control by minimizing the width of the cracks that may develop between joints. In addition, the use of reinforcement will allow an increased joint spacing. Despite several other relatively minor advantages that result from the use of steel, questions have been raised as to whether reinforcement is always necessary, particularly with uniform support of the slab and short joint spacings. The steel does not prevent cracking nor does it add significantly to the load-carrying capacity of the slab. It is also usually more economical to obtain increased strength in concrete slabs on ground by increasing the thickness of the slab.

Design aids and procedures (based primarily on research done for highway and airport pavements) have been developed and are available in specialized publications. (See references [2] through [9] at the end of this chapter.)

A slab for the very lightest function should not be less than 4 in. thick. This and other slabs may be empirically selected from Table 2-1, which is reprinted from the *CRSI Design Handbook* [10]. These slab thicknesses and associated steel reinforcement suggestions are recommended *minimums* for use when uniform loads rather than wheel loads are the designated load conditions.

In addition to the CRSI recommendations of Table 2-1, it is absolutely essential for the reinforcing steel to be placed in the proper location to function for the purpose intended. The proper position is at or above the middepth of the slab. Both

TABLE 2-1   Slab Thicknesses and Steel Recommended for Slabs on Ground for Various Uniformly Distributed Loads

Uniform loads (PSF)[a]	Minimum slab thickness (in.)	Reinforcement[b]
Less than 100	4	One layer 6 × 6-W1.4 × W1.4 welded wire fabric minimum for ideal conditions, 6 × 6-W2.0 × W2.0 for average conditions
100–200	5	One layer 6 × 6-W2.0 × W2.0 welded wire fabric or one layer 6 × 6-W2.9 × W2.9
Not over 400–500	6	One layer 6 × 6-W2.9 × W2.9 welded wire fabric or one layer 6 × 6-W4.0 × W4.0
600–800	6	Two layers 6 × 6-W2.9 × W2.9 welded wire fabric or two layers 6 × 6-W4.0 × W4.0
1500[c]	7	Two mats of bars (one top, one bottom) each of No. 4 bars at 12 in. o.c. each way
2500[c]	8	Two mats of bars (one top, one bottom) each of No. 5 bars at 12 in. o.c. each way
3000–3500[c]	9	Two mats of bars (one top, one bottom) each of No. 5 bars at 8 to 12 in. o.c. each way

[a]Fill material and compaction should be equivalent to that of ordinary highway practice. If laboratory control of compaction is available, the load capacities can be increased in the ratio of the actual compaction coefficient k to 100.

[b]Place the first layer of reinforcement 2 in. below the top of the slab and the second layer 2 in. up from the bottom of the slab.

[c]For loads in excess of 1500 psf, the subsoil condition should be investigated with extra care.

the CRSI and the Wire Reinforcement Institute (WRI) recommend that for a single reinforcement layer (steel in two directions where the bars are in contact with each other is considered as one layer), the acceptable placement is as follows:

4 in. slab: middle of slab
5 in. slab: 2 in. below top surface
6 in. slab: 2 in. below top surface

REFERENCES

[1]   Charles S. Whitney. "Plastic Theory of Reinforced Concrete Design." *Trans. ASCE,* Vol. 68, 1942.

[2]   Ralph E. Spears. *Concrete Floors on Ground.* Portland Cement Association, 5420 Old Orchard Road, Skokie, IL 60077-1083, 1978.

[3]   Robert G. Packard. *Slab Thickness Design for Industrial Concrete Floors on Grade.* Portland Cement Association, 5420 Old Orchard Road, Skokie, IL 60077-1083, 1976.

[4]   *Thickness Design for Concrete Highway and Street Pavements.* American Concrete Pavement Association, P.O. Box 726, Skokie, IL 60076-0726, 1984.

[5]   *Concrete Floors on Ground.* Portland Cement Association, 5420 Old Orchard Road, Skokie, IL 60077-1083, 1990.

[6]   *Design of Heavy Industrial Pavements.* American Concrete Pavement Association, P.O. Box 726, Skokie, IL 60076-0726, 1988.

[7]   *Concrete Slabs on Grade: Design Specification, Construction, and Problem Resolution.* American Concrete Institute, P.O. Box 9094, Farmington Hills, MI 48333, 1992.

[8]   *Design of Slabs on Grade.* American Concrete Institute, P.O. Box 9094, Farmington Hills, MI 48333, 1992.

[9]   *Guide for Concrete Floor and Slab Construction* (ACI 302-89). American Concrete Institute, P.O. Box 9094, Farmington Hills, MI 48333, 1989.

[10]   *CRSI Design Handbook,* Vol. II, Concrete Reinforcing Steel Institute, 933 North Plum Grove Road, Schaumburg, IL 60173, 1965.

PROBLEMS

In the following problems, consider moment only and tension reinforcing only. For beams, assume $1\frac{1}{2}$ in. cover and No. 3 stirrups. For slabs, assume $\frac{3}{4}$ in. cover. Unless noted otherwise, given loads are superimposed service loads and do not include weights of the members.

2-1.   The beam of cross section shown has $f'_c = 4000$ psi. The bars are A615 grade 40. Find the nominal moment strength (M_n) if:

(a) $d = 14$ in.

(b) $d = 21$ in.

(c) $d = 28$ in.

Compare the results in a plot of M_n versus d .

PROBLEM 2-1   **PROBLEM 2-2**

2-2. Calculate the nominal moment strength (M_n) for the beam of cross section shown. Use $f'_c = 4000$ psi and $f_y = 60,000$ psi. Reinforcement is:

(a) Three No. 8 bars

(b) Three No. 9 bars

(c) Three No. 10 bars

Compare the results in a plot of M_n versus A_s .

2-3. Calculate the nominal moment strength (M_n) for the beam of cross section shown. The steel is A615 grade 40, $b = 12$ in., and there are four No. 9 bars.

(a) $f'_c = 3000$ psi

(b) $f'_c = 4000$ psi

(c) $f'_c = 5000$ psi

Compare the results in a plot of M_n versus f'_c .

2-4. Calculate the practical moment strength ϕM_n for the beam of cross section shown. The beam width $b = 13$ in., and there are four No. 8 bars.

PROBLEMS 2-3 AND 2-4

(a) $f'_c = 4000$ psi, $f_y = 40,000$ psi

(b) $f'_c = 4000$ psi, $f_y = 60,000$ psi

2-5. Determine ϕM_n for a reinforced concrete beam 16 in. wide by 32 in. deep reinforced with seven No. 10 bars (placed in two layers: five in the bottom layer, two in the top layer, with 1 in. clear between layers). Use $f'_c = 4000$ psi and $f_y = 60,000$ psi.

2-6. A reinforced concrete beam having the cross section shown is on a simple span of 28 ft. It carries uniform service loads of 3.60 kips/ft live load and 2.20 kips/ft dead load. Check the adequacy of the beam with respect to moment. Check the steel ratio to ensure that it is within the limitations of the ACI Code. Use $f'_c = 3000$ psi and $f_y = 40,000$ psi.

(a) Reinforcing is six No. 10 bars.

(b) Reinforcing is six No. 11 bars.

PROBLEM 2-6

2-7. A 12-in.-wide by 20-in.-deep concrete beam is reinforced with three No. 8 bars. The beam supports a service live load of 2.5 kips/ft and a service dead load of 0.7 kip/ft on a simple span of 16 ft. Use $f'_c = 4000$ psi and $f_y = 60,000$ psi. Check the adequacy of the beam with respect to moment.

2-8. A rectangular reinforced concrete beam carries *service loads* on a span of 20 ft as shown. Use $f'_c = 3000$ psi and $f_y = 60,000$ psi; $b = 14.5$ in., $h = 26$ in., and reinforcing is three No. 10 bars. Determine whether the beam is adequate with respect to moment.

2-9. A rectangular reinforced concrete beam 14 in. wide by 24 in. deep is to support a service dead load of 0.6 kip/ft and a service live load of 1.4 kips/ft. Reinforcing is A615 grade 60, four No. 9 bars. Use $f'_c = 4000$ psi. Determine the maximum simple span length on which this beam may be utilized.

2-10. A 10-in.-thick one-way slab supports a superimposed service live load of 600 psf on a simple span of 16 ft. Reinforcement is No. 7 at 6 in. on center. Check the adequacy of the slab with respect to moment. Use $f'_c = 3000$ psi and $f_y = 60,000$ psi.

PROBLEM 2-8

2-11. The one-way slab shown spans 12 ft from center of support to center of support. Calculate ϕM_n and determine the *service live load* (psf) that the slab may carry. (Assume that the only dead load is the weight of the slab.) Use $f'_c = 3000$ psi and $f_y = 40,000$ psi.

$\frac{3}{4}$" clear   #8 @ 6" o.c.

Section A–A

PROBLEM 2-11

2-12. An $8\frac{1}{2}$-in.-thick one-way reinforced concrete slab overhangs a simple support. The span of the overhang is 8 ft. Drawings called for the reinforcement to be placed with top cover of 1 in. The steel was misplaced, however, and later was found to be as much as $3\frac{1}{2}$ in. below the top of the concrete. Find ϕM_n for the slab as designed and as built and the percent of reduction in flexural strength. Use $f'_c = 4000$ psi and $f_y = 60,000$ psi. Bars are No. 7 at 11 in. o.c.

2-13. Design a rectangular reinforced concrete beam to resist a total design moment M_u of 133 ft-kips. (This includes the moment due to beam weight.) Architectural considerations require that the width (b) be $11\frac{1}{2}$ in. and the overall depth (h) be 23 in. Use $f'_c = 3000$ psi and $f_y = 60,000$ psi. Sketch your design.

2-14. Rework Problem 2-13 with $M_u = 400$ ft-kips, $b = 16$ in., $h = 28$ in., $f'_c = 4000$ psi, and $f_y = 60,000$ psi.

2-15. For the beam designed in Problem 2-14, if the main reinforcement were incorrectly placed so that the actual effective depth were 24 in., would the beam be adequate? Check by comparing M_u with the ϕM_n resulting from the beam using actual steel, actual b, and $d = 24$ in.

2-16. Design a rectangular reinforced concrete beam (tension steel only) for a simple span of 32 ft. Uniform service loads are 0.85 kip/ft dead load and 1.0 kip/ft live load. The beam is to be $11\frac{1}{2}$ in. wide and 26 in. deep overall (form reuse consideration). Use f'_c = 4000 psi and f_y = 60,000 psi. Calculate ϕM_n for the beam designed.

2-17. Design a simply supported rectangular reinforced concrete beam to span 22 ft and to carry uniform service loads of 1.6 kips/ft dead load and 1.4 kips/ft live load. The assumed dead load includes an estimated beam weight. Use A615 grade 60 steel and f'_c = 3000 psi. Use the recommended ρ from Table A-5. Make the beam width 15 in. and keep the overall depth (h) to full inches. Assume No. 3 stirrups. Check the adequacy of the beam you design by comparing M_u with ϕM_n. Sketch your design.

2-18. Design a rectangular reinforced concrete beam for a simple span of 30 ft. The beam is to carry uniform *service* loads of 1.0 kip/ft dead load and 2.0 kips/ft live load. Because of column sizes, the beam width should not exceed 16 in. Use f'_c = 3000 psi and f_y = 60,000 psi. Sketch your design.

2-19. Rework Problem 2-18 assuming that the total depth h is not to exceed 30 in. and that there is no limitation on the width b.

2-20. Design a rectangular reinforced concrete beam for a simple span of 32 ft. Uniform service loads are 1.5 kips/ft dead load and 2.0 kips/ft live load. The width of the beam is limited to 18 in. Use f'_c = 3000 psi and f_y = 60,000 psi. Sketch your design.

2-21. Rework Problem 2-20 assuming that the total depth h is not to exceed 34 in. and that there is no limitation on the width b.

2-22. Design a rectangular reinforced concrete beam for a simple span of 40 ft. Uniform service loads are 0.8 kip/ft dead load and 1.4 kips/ft live load. Use f'_c = 4000 psi and f_y = 60,000 psi. Sketch your design.

2-23. Design a 28 ft simple span rectangular reinforced concrete beam to support a uniform live load of 0.8 kip/ft and concentrated loads at midspan of 10 kips dead load and 14 kips live load. Use f'_c = 5000 psi and f_y = 60,000 psi.

2-24. Design a simply supported rectangular reinforced concrete beam for the span and *service loads* shown. Use f'_c = 3000 psi and f_y = 60,000 psi.

PROBLEM 2-24

2-25. Rework Problem 2-24 assuming that the beam is to be extended to overhang the right support by 10 ft. The uniform load also extends to the end of the overhang.

2-26. Design a simply supported one-way reinforced concrete floor slab to span 8 ft and carry a service live load of 300 psf. Use $f'_c = 3000$ psi and $f_y = 60,000$ psi. Sketch your design.

2-27. Design a simply supported one-way reinforced concrete floor slab to span 10 ft and carry a service live load of 175 psf and a service dead load of 25 psf. Use $f'_c = 3000$ psi and $f_y = 60,000$ psi. Make the slab thickness to ½ in.
(a) Design the slab for the ACI Code minimum thickness.
(b) Design the thinnest possible slab allowed by the ACI Code.

2-28. Design the simply supported one-way reinforced concrete slab as shown. The service live load is 200 psf. Use $f'_c = 3000$ psi and $f_y = 60,000$ psi. Sketch your design.

Typical Section

PROBLEM 2-28

CHAPTER 3

Reinforced Concrete Beams: T-Beams and Doubly Reinforced Beams

72

3-1

T-BEAMS: INTRODUCTION

Floors and roofs in reinforced concrete buildings may be composed of slabs that are supported so that loads are carried to columns and then to the building foundation. As previously discussed, these are termed *flat slabs* or *flat plates*. The span of such a slab cannot become very large before its own dead weight causes it to become uneconomical. Many types of systems have been devised to allow greater spans without the problem of excessive weight.

One such system, called a *beam and girder system,* is composed of a slab on supporting reinforced concrete beams and girders. The beam and girder framework is, in turn, supported by columns. In such a system, the beams and girders are commonly placed monolithically with the slab. Systems other than the monolithic system do exist, and these may make use of some precast and some cast-in-place concrete. These are generally of a proprietary nature. The typical monolithic system is shown in Figure 3-1. The beams are commonly spaced so that they intersect the girders at the midpoint, third points, or quarter points, as shown in Figure 3-2.

In the analysis and design of such floor and roof systems, it is common practice to assume that the monolithically placed slab and supporting beam interact as a unit in resisting *positive bending moment*. As shown in Figure 3-3, the slab becomes the compression flange, and the supporting beam becomes the web or stem. The interacting flange and stem produce the cross section having the typical T-shape from which the T-beam gets its name. It should be noted that the slab, which comprises the T-beam flange, must itself be designed to span across the supporting beams. Therefore, the slab behaves as a bending member acting in two directions. It should also be noted that should the T-beam cross section be subjected to *negative bending moment* the slab at the top of the stem will be in tension while the bot-

FIGURE 3-1   Beam and girder floor system.

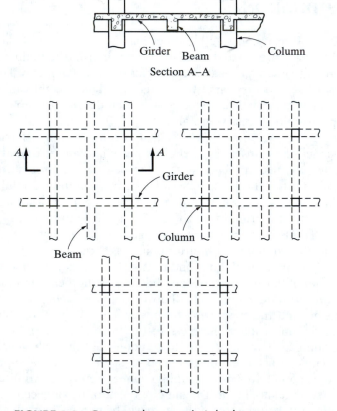

FIGURE 3-2   Common beam and girder layouts.

FIGURE 3-3   T-beam as part of a floor system.

tom of the stem is in compression. It will be seen that this situation will occur at interior supports of continuous beams, which are discussed later.

To simplify the complex two-way behavior of the flange, the ACI Code, for design and analysis purposes, has established criteria whereby the flange, when acting together with the web, will have a limited width that may be considered effective in resisting applied moment. This effective flange width for symmetrical shapes will always be equal to or less than the beam spacing (see Figure 3-3).

3-2

T-BEAM ANALYSIS

For purposes of analysis and design, the ACI Code, Section 8.10, has established limits on the effective flange width as follows:

1. The effective flange width must not exceed one-fourth of the span length of the beam, and the effective overhanging flange width on each side of the web must not exceed eight times the thickness of the slab nor one-half of the clear distance to the next beam. In other words, the effective flange width must not exceed:
    a. One-fourth of the span length *of the beam*
    b. $b_w + 16h_f$
    c. Center-to-center spacing of beams

    The smallest of the three values will control.

2. For beams having a flange on one side only, the effective overhanging flange width must not exceed one-twelfth of the span length of the beam nor six times the slab thickness, nor one-half of the clear distance to the next beam.

3. For isolated beams in which the T-shape is used only for the purpose of providing additional compressive area, the flange thickness must not be less than

one-half of the width of the web, and the total flange width must be not more than four times the web width.

The ductility requirements for T-beams are similar to those for rectangular beams. The maximum steel ratio ρ shall not exceed $0.75\rho_b$. This $0.75\rho_b$, however, is not the same value as that tabulated for rectangular beams because of the T-shaped compressive area. A variation of the rectangular beam approach for $0.75\rho_b$ may be observed in Section 3-3.

The procedure for determining the minimum steel for a T-beam is the same as for rectangular beam when the T-beam flange is in compression (positive moment). Where tensile reinforcement is required by analysis, the steel area A_s shall not be less than that given by

$$A_{s,\min} = \frac{3\sqrt{f'_c}}{f_y}b_w d \geq \frac{200}{f_y}b_w d$$

Note that for T-beams, b_w represents the width of the web. Also note that the first expression controls only if $f'_c > 4440$ psi.

For negative moment (flange in tension),

$$A_{s,\min} = \text{the smaller of } \frac{6\sqrt{f'_c}}{f_y}b_w d \quad \text{or} \quad \frac{3\sqrt{f'_c}}{f_y}bd$$

Because of the relatively large compression area available in the flange of the T-beam, the moment strength is usually limited by the yielding of the tensile steel. Therefore, it is both customary and safe to assume that the tensile steel will yield before the concrete reaches its ultimate strain and crushes. The total tensile force N_T, at the ultimate condition, may then be found by

$$N_T = A_s f_y$$

To proceed with the analysis, the shape of the compressive stress block must be defined. As in our previous analyses, the total compressive force N_C must be equal to the total tensile force N_T. The shape of the stress block must be compatible with the area in compression. Two conditions may exist: the stress block may be completely within the flange, or it may cover the flange and extend into the web. These two conditions will result in what we will term, respectively, a *rectangular T-beam* and a *true T-beam*. In addition to the shape of the stress block, the basic difference between the two is that the rectangular T-beam with effective flange width b is analyzed in the same way as is a rectangular beam of width b, whereas the analysis of the true T-beam must consider the T-shaped stress block.

Example 3-1

The T-beam shown in Figure 3-4 is part of a floor system. Determine the practical moment strength ϕM_n if $f_y = 60,000$ psi (A615 grade 60) and $f'_c = 3000$ psi.

FIGURE 3-4   Sketch for Example 3-1.

Solution:

1. Since the span length is not given, determine the effective flange width in terms of the flange thickness and beam spacing:

$$b_w + 16h_f = 10 + 16(2) = 42 \text{ in.}$$

beam spacing $= 32$ in. o.c.   Use $b = 32$ in.

2. Assume that the steel yields, and find N_T:

$$N_T = A_s f_y = 3.00(60{,}000) = 180{,}000 \text{ lb}$$

3. The flange, if fully stressed to $0.85\, f_c'$, would produce a total compressive force of

$$N_C = (0.85 f_c')h_f b$$

$$= 0.85(3000)(2)(32) = 163{,}200 \text{ lb}$$

4. Since $180{,}000 > 163{,}200$, the stress block must extend below the flange far enough to provide the remaining compression:

$$180{,}000 - 163{,}200 = 16{,}800 \text{ lb}$$

Hence the stress block extends below the flange and the analysis is one for a true T-beam.

5. The remaining compression $(N_T - N_C)$ may be obtained by the additional web area:

$$N_T - N_C = (0.85\, f_c')b_w(a - h_f)$$

Solving for a, we obtain

$$a = \frac{N_T - N_C}{(0.85 f_c')b_w} + h_f = \frac{16{,}800}{0.85(3000)(10)} + 2$$

$$= 2.66 \text{ in.}$$

6.   Check $A_{s,\text{min}}$. From Table A-5:

$$A_{s,\text{min}} = 0.0033b_w d$$

$$= 0.0033(10)(12) = 0.40 \text{ in.}^2$$

$$0.40 \text{ in.}^2 < 3.0 \text{ in.}^2 \qquad\qquad \text{(O.K.)}$$

7.   To calculate the magnitude of the internal couple, it is necessary to know the lever-arm distance between N_C and N_T. The location of N_T is assumed to be at the centroid of the steel area, and we will locate N_C at the centroid of the compression area (see Figure 3-5). Using a reference axis at the top of the section, the centroid may be located a distance $\bar{y}$ below the reference axis, as follows:

$$\bar{y} = \frac{\Sigma (Ay)}{\Sigma A}$$

$$A_1 = 32(2) = 64 \text{ in.}^2, \qquad A_2 = 10(0.66) = 6.6 \text{ in.}^2$$

$$\bar{y} = \frac{64(1) + 6.6(2 + 0.33)}{64 + 6.6} = 1.12 \text{ in.}$$

This locates N_C. Therefore,

$$Z = d - \bar{y}$$

$$= 12 - 1.12 = 10.88 \text{ in.}$$

8.   The nominal (or ideal) moment strength may be found:

$$M_n = N_T Z = \frac{180,000(10.88)}{12,000} = 163 \text{ ft-kips}$$

from which the practical moment strength is

$$\phi M_n = 0.9(163) = 147 \text{ ft-kips}$$

9.   We will now check our assumption of a ductile failure (yielding of steel). In T-beams this is most conveniently accomplished by comparing the actual tension steel area with 75% of the amount of steel required

FIGURE 3-5   T-beam compressive area.

to produce the balanced condition ($0.75A_{sb}$). The location of the balanced neutral axis is found as follows:

$$c_b = \frac{87,000}{f_y + 87,000}(d) \qquad \text{(see Section 2-8)}$$

$$= \frac{87,000}{60,000 + 87,000}(12) = 7.10 \text{ in.}$$

Using the rectangular beam relationship $a = 0.85c$, which is approximate for T-beams,

$$a_b = 0.85(7.10) = 6.035 \text{ in.}$$

Then the total *balanced* compression force N_{Cb} must equal

$$N_{cb} = 0.85f_c'[b(h_f) + b_w(a_b - h_f)]$$

$$= 0.85(3000)[32(2) + 10(6.035 - 2)]$$

$$= 266,093 \text{ lb} = N_{Tb}$$

Also, since $N_{Tb} = A_{sb}f_y$,

$$A_{sb} = \frac{266,093}{60,000} = 4.43 \text{ in.}^2$$

which is the area of steel that makes this beam a balanced beam.

The area of tension steel must not exceed 75% of A_{sb}. We will designate this as $A_{s,max}$:

$$A_{s,max} = 0.75A_{sb}$$

$$= 0.75(4.43) = 3.32 \text{ in.}^2$$

$$3.32 \text{ in.}^2 > 3.0 \text{ in.}^2 \qquad\qquad \text{(O.K.)}$$

3-3

DEVELOPMENT OF T-BEAM $A_{s,max}$

As may be observed, the preceding check in step 9 of Example 3-1 is based on the following relationships:

1. $c_b = \dfrac{87,000}{f_y + 87,000}(d)$

2. $a_b = 0.85c_b$ (where $\beta_1 = 0.85$)

3. $N_{Cb} = 0.85f_c'[b(h_f) + b_w(a_b - h_f)]$

4. $N_{Cb} = N_{Tb} = A_{sb}f_y$

5. $A_{s,\max} = 0.75A_{sb}$

Combining these expressions and solving for $A_{s,\max}$, we arrive at the following expression:

$$A_{s,\max} = \frac{0.75}{f_y}N_{Cb}$$

$$= \frac{0.75}{f_y}(0.85f_c')\left\{bh_f + \left[\beta_1\frac{87{,}000(d)}{87{,}000 + f_y} - h_f\right]b_w\right\}$$

$$= \frac{0.638}{f_y}f_c'h_f\left\{b + b_w\left[\frac{\beta_1}{h_f}\left(\frac{87{,}000(d)}{87{,}000 + f_y}\right) - 1\right]\right\}$$

Substituting for various combinations of f_c' and f_y, $A_{s,\max}$ expressions result as listed in Table 3-1. This development is valid when $a_b \geqslant h_f$, which is the prevalent case. Using these expressions, let us now calculate the $A_{s,\max}$ allowed by the code for Example 3-1:

$$A_{s,\max} = 0.0319h_f\left\{b + b_w\left[\frac{0.503(d)}{h_f} - 1\right]\right\}$$

$$= 0.0319(2)\left\{32 + 10\left[\frac{0.503(12)}{2} - 1\right]\right\}$$

$$= 0.0638(32 + 20.18)$$

$$= 3.33 \text{ in.}^2 \approx 3.32 \text{ in.}^2$$

This represents the maximum permissible area of steel allowed for ductility considerations based on the ACI Code. Since this exceeds the actual furnished A_s (3.33 > 3.00), the ductile failure is assured and the code criterion is satisfied.

▄▄▄▄ **TABLE 3-1   Expressions for $A_{s,\max}$**

f_c' (psi)	f_y (psi)	$A_{s,\max}$ (in.^{2})
3000	40,000	$0.0478h_f\left\{b + b_w\left[\frac{0.582}{h_f}(d) - 1\right]\right\}$
	60,000	$0.0319h_f\left\{b + b_w\left[\frac{0.503}{h_f}(d) - 1\right]\right\}$
4000	40,000	$0.0638h_f\left\{b + b_w\left[\frac{0.582}{h_f}(d) - 1\right]\right\}$
	60,000	$0.0425h_f\left\{b + b_w\left[\frac{0.503}{h_f}(d) - 1\right]\right\}$

For T-beam analysis, this check can be made as soon as b has been determined. If A_s exceeds $A_{s,max}$, then the beam should be analyzed using $A_{s,max}$ as an effective steel area. This approach was demonstrated in Example 2-5.

Example 3-2

For the T-beam shown in Figure 3-6, determine the practical moment strength ϕM_n if $f_c' = 3000$ psi and $f_y = 60,000$ psi. The beam span length is 24 ft.

Solution:

1. Find the effective flange width:

$$\frac{1}{4} \text{ span length} = \frac{24(12)}{4} = 72 \text{ in.}$$

$$b_w + 16h_f = 10 + 16(4) = 74 \text{ in.}$$

$$\text{beam spacing} = 60 \text{ in.}$$

$$\text{Use } b = 60 \text{ in.}$$

2. Check $A_{s,min}$. From Table A-5:

$$A_{s,min} = 0.0033b_w d$$

$$= 0.0033(10)(24) = 0.79 \text{ in.}^2$$

$$0.79 \text{ in.}^2 < 6.00 \text{ in.}^2 \qquad\qquad \text{(O.K.)}$$

3. Check the beam ductility by comparing $A_{s,max}$ with actual A_s:

$$A_{s,max} = 0.0319h_f\left[b + b_w\left(\frac{0.503d}{h_f} - 1\right)\right]$$

$$= 0.0319(4)\left\{60 + 10\left[\frac{0.5033(24)}{4} - 1\right]\right\}$$

$$= 10.23 \text{ in.}^2$$

FIGURE 3-6   Sketch for Example 3-2.

The actual $A_s = 6.00$ in.^{2}. Since $10.23 > 6.00$, the beam is ductile and the steel yields at the ultimate moment.

4.   Knowing that the steel yields, find N_T:

$$N_T = A_s f_y = 6.0(60,000) = 360,000 \text{ lb}$$

5.   The flange itself is capable of furnishing a compression force of

$$N_C = (0.85 f_c')bh_f = 0.85(3000)(60.0)(4) = 612,000 \text{ lb}$$

6.   Since $612,000 > 360,000$, the flange furnishes sufficient compression area and the stress block lies entirely in the flange. Therefore, analyze the T-beam as a rectangular T-beam of width $b = 60$ in. (Note that this beam, although a rectangular T-beam for determination of ϕM_n, will probably be a true T-beam at the balanced condition when maximum A_s is checked.)

7.   The actual steel ratio is

$$\rho = \frac{A_s}{bd} = \frac{6.0}{60(24)} = 0.0042$$

8.   For $\rho = 0.0042$, go to Table A-8 and find the required $\overline{k}$:

$$\text{required } \overline{k} = 0.2395 \text{ ksi}$$

9. $$\phi M_n = \phi bd^2 \overline{k}$$

$$= 0.9(60)(24)^2\left(\frac{0.2395}{12}\right) = 621 \text{ ft-kips}$$

3-4

ANALYSIS OF BEAMS HAVING IRREGULAR CROSS SECTIONS

Beams having other than rectangular and T-shaped cross sections are common, particularly in structures using precast elements. The approach for the analysis of such beams is to use the internal couple in the normal way, taking into account any variation in the shape of the compressive stress block. The method is similar to that used for true T-beam analysis.

Example 3-3

Find the practical moment strength ϕM_n for the beam shown in Figure 3-7. (The ledges in the beam cross section will possibly be used for support of precast slabs.) Use $f_y = 60,000$ psi (A615 grade 60) and $f_c' = 3000$ psi.

FIGURE 3-7   Sketch for Example 3-3.

Solution:

1.   The effective flange width may be considered to be 7 in.

2.   Check $A_{s,\text{min}}$. From Table A-5:

$$A_{s,\text{min}} = 0.0033 b_w d$$

$$= 0.0033(17)(24) = 1.35 \text{ in.}^2$$

$$1.35 \text{ in.}^2 < 5.08 \text{ in.}^2 \qquad\qquad (\text{O.K.})$$

3.   Check the ACI Code requirement for $A_{s,\text{max}}$ (see Table 3-1):

$$A_{s,\text{max}} = 0.0319 h_f \left\{ b + b_w \left[\frac{0.503(d)}{h_f} - 1 \right] \right\}$$

$$= 0.0319(4) \left\{ 7 + 17 \left[\frac{0.503(24)}{4} - 1 \right] \right\}$$

$$= 5.27 \text{ in.}^2$$

$$5.27 \text{ in.}^2 > 5.08 \text{ in.}^2 \qquad\qquad (\text{O.K.})$$

It should be noted in this step that the equation from Table 3-1 applies because the area above the ledges behaves as does the flange of a T-beam.

4.   Knowing that the steel yields, find N_T:

$$N_T = A_s f_y = 5.08(60,000) = 304,800 \text{ lb}$$

5.   Determine the amount of compression that the 7 in. × 4 in. area (above the ledges) is capable of furnishing:

$$N_C = (0.85f_c')h_f b$$

$$= 0.85(3000)(4)(7) = 71,400 \text{ lb}$$

6.   Since 304,800 > 71,400, the compressive stress block must extend below the ledges to provide the remaining compression:

$$304,800 - 71,400 = 233,400 \text{ lb}$$

7.   The remaining compression will be furnished by additional beam area below the ledges. Referring to Figure 3-7,

$$a = \frac{N_T - N_C}{(0.85f_c')b_w} + h_f$$

$$= \frac{233,400}{0.85(3000)(17)} + 4$$

$$= 9.38 \text{ in. from top of beam}$$

8.   Find the location of N_C at the centroid of the compression area. With reference to Figure 3-8, the centroid is located at a distance $\bar{y}$ down from a reference axis at the top of the cross section:

$$\bar{y} = \frac{\Sigma\,(Ay)}{\Sigma\,A}$$

$$A_1 = 7(4) = 28 \text{ in.}^2, \qquad A_2 = 5.38(17) = 91.46 \text{ in.}^2$$

$$\bar{y} = \frac{28(2) + 91.46(4 + 5.38/2)}{28 + 91.46} = 5.59 \text{ in.}$$

from which the lever arm Z may be calculated:

$$Z = d - \bar{y} = 24 - 5.59$$

$$= 18.41 \text{ in.}$$

FIGURE 3-8 Compressive area.

9.   Compute the nominal moment strength M_n and the practical moment strength ϕM_n:

$$M_n = N_T Z = \frac{304{,}800(18.41)}{12{,}000} = 467.6 \text{ ft-kips}$$

$$\phi M_n = 0.9(467.6) = 420.9 \text{ ft-kips}$$

3-5

T-BEAM DESIGN (FOR MOMENT)

The design of the T-sections involves the dimensions of the flange and web and the area of the tension steel, a total of five unknowns. In the normal progression of a design, the flange thickness is determined by the design of the slab, and the web size is determined by the shear and moment requirements at the end supports of a beam in continuous construction. Practical considerations, such as column sizes and forming, may also dictate web width. Therefore, when the T-section is designed for positive moment, most of the five unknowns have been previously determined.

As indicated previously, the ACI Code dictates permissible effective flange width (b). The flange itself generally provides more than sufficient compression area; therefore, the stress block usually lies completely in the flange. Thus most T-beams are only wide rectangular beams with respect to flexural behavior.

The recommended method for design of T-beams will depend on whether the T-beam behaves as a rectangular T-beam or a true T-beam. The first step will be to answer this question. If the T-beam is determined to be a rectangular T-beam, the design procedure is the same as for the tensile reinforced rectangular beam where the size of the cross section is known (see Section 2-15). If the T-beam is determined to be a true T-beam, an approximate design, followed by analysis, may be used.

Example 3-4 _____

Design the T-beam for the floor system shown in Figure 3-9. The floor has a 4-in. slab supported by 22-ft-span-length beams cast monolithically with the slab. Beams are 8 ft 0 in. on center and have a web width of 12 in. and a total depth = 22 in.; $f'_c = 3000$ psi and $f_y = 60{,}000$ psi (A615 grade 60). Service loads are 0.125-ksf live load and 0.200-ksf dead load. The given dead load does not include the weight of the floor system.

FIGURE 3-9 Typical floor section, Example 3-4.

Solution:

1. Establish the design moment:

$$\text{slab weight} = \frac{96(4)}{144}(0.150) = 0.400 \text{ kip/ft}$$

$$\text{stem weight} = \frac{12(18)}{144}(0.150) = \underline{0.225}$$

$$\text{total} = 0.625 \text{ kip/ft}$$

$$\text{service DL} = 8(0.200) = 1.60 \text{ kips/ft}$$

$$\text{service LL} = 8(0.125) = 1.00 \text{ kip/ft}$$

Calculate the factored load and moment:

$$w_u = 1.4(0.625 + 1.60) + 1.7(1.00) = 4.815 \text{ kips/ft}$$

$$M_u = \frac{w_u \ell^2}{8} = \frac{4.815(22)^2}{8} = 291 \text{ ft-kips}$$

2. Assume an effective depth $d = h - 3$ in.:
$$d = 22 - 3 = 19 \text{ in.}$$

3. Determine the effective flange width:

$$\tfrac{1}{4} \text{ span length} = 0.25(22)(12) = 66 \text{ in.}$$

$$b_w + 16h_f = 12 + 16(4) = 76 \text{ in.}$$

$$\text{beam spacing} = 96 \text{ in.}$$

Use an effective flange width $b = 66$ in.

4. Determine whether the beam behaves as a true T-beam or as a rectangular beam by computing the practical moment strength ϕM_n with the complete effective flange assumed to be in compression. This assumes

FIGURE 3-10 T-beam for Example 3-4.

that the bottom of the compressive stress block coincides with bottom of flange as shown in Figure 3-10. Thus

$$\phi M_n = \phi(0.85f_c')bh_f\left(d - \frac{h_f}{2}\right)$$

$$= 0.9(0.85)(3)(66)\frac{4(19 - 4/2)}{12} = 858 \text{ ft-kips}$$

5. Since $858 > 291$, the total effective flange need not be completely utilized in compression, and the T-beam behaves as a wide rectangular beam with a width b of 66 in.

6. Design as a rectangular beam with b and d as known values (see Section 2-15):

$$\text{required } \overline{k} = \frac{M_u}{\phi bd^2} = \frac{291(12)}{0.9(66)(19)^2} = 0.1628 \text{ ksi}$$

7. From Table A-8, select the required steel ratio to provide a $\overline{k}$ of 0.1628 ksi:

$$\text{required } \rho = 0.0028$$

8. Calculate the required steel area:

$$\text{required } A_s = \rho bd$$

$$= 0.0028(66)(19) = 3.51 \text{ in.}^2$$

9. Select the steel bars. Use three No. 10 bars ($A_s = 3.81$ in.^{2}):

$$\text{minimum } b_w = 10.5 \text{ in.} \qquad \text{(O.K.)}$$

Check the actual d:

$$d = 22 - 1.5 - 0.38 - \frac{1.27}{2} = 19.49 \text{ in.}$$

$$19.49 \text{ in.} > 19 \text{ in.} \qquad \text{(O.K.)}$$

FIGURE 3-11   Design sketch for Example 3-4.

10. Check $A_{s,\text{min}}$. From Table A-5:

$$A_{s,\text{min}} = 0.0033b_w d$$

$$= 0.0033(12)(19) = 0.75 \text{ in.}^2$$

$$0.75 \text{ in.}^2 < 3.81 \text{ in.}^2 \qquad\qquad \text{(O.K.)}$$

11. Check $A_{s,\text{max}}$:

$$A_{s,\text{max}} = 0.0319h_f\left[b + b_w\left(\frac{0.503d}{h_f} - 1\right)\right]$$

$$= 0.0319(4)\left\{66 + 12\left[\frac{0.503(19.49)}{4} - 1\right]\right\}$$

$$= 10.64 \text{ in.}^2 > 3.81 \text{ in.}^2 \qquad\qquad \text{(O.K.)}$$

12. Sketch the design (see Figure 3-11).

Example 3-5

Design a T-beam having a cross section as shown in Figure 3-12. Assume that the effective flange width given is acceptable. The T-beam will carry a total design moment M_u of 340 ft-kips. Use $f_c' = 3000$ psi and $f_y = 60,000$ psi. Use 1½-in. cover and No. 3 stirrups.

Solution:

1. The design moment $M_u = 340$ ft-kips (given).
2. Assume an effective depth of

$$d = 22 - 3 = 19 \text{ in.}$$

3. The effective flange width = 27 in. (given).

FIGURE 3-12   Sketch for Example 3-5.

4.   Determine ϕM_n assuming the flange to be completely in compression:

$$\phi M_n = \phi(0.85f_c')bh_f\left(\frac{d - h_f}{2}\right)$$

$$= 0.9(0.85)(3)\frac{(27)(3.5)(19 - 3.5/2)}{12} = 312 \text{ ft-kips}$$

5. $\phi M_n < M_u$; therefore, the beam must behave as a true T-beam.
6.   Find the approximate lever-arm distance for the internal couple:

$$Z = d - \frac{h_f}{2} = 19 - \frac{3.5}{2} = 17.25 \text{ in.}$$

7.   Find the approximate required A_s:

$$A_s = \frac{M_u}{\phi f_y Z} = \frac{340(12)}{0.9(60)(17.25)} = 4.38 \text{ in.}^2$$

8.   Select the bars. Try three No. 11 bars ($A_s = 4.68$ in.^{2}):

$$\text{minimum } b_w = 11 \text{ in.} \qquad \text{(O.K.)}$$

9.   Determine the actual effective depth:

$$d = 22 - 1.5 - 0.38 - \frac{1.41}{2} = 19.42 \text{ in.}$$

Use 19.42 in. Check the beam capacity with an analysis for ϕM_n:
a.   The effective flange width has been established as 27 in.
b.   Check $A_{s,\text{min}}$. From Table A-5:

$$A_{s,\text{min}} = 0.0033b_w d$$

$$= 0.0033(12)(19.42) = 0.77 \text{ in.}^2$$

$$0.77 \text{ in.}^2 < 4.68 \text{ in.}^2 \qquad \text{(O.K.)}$$

c. Check $A_{s,max}$:

$$A_{s,max} = 0.0319h_f\left[b + b_w\left(\frac{0.503d}{h_f} - 1\right)\right]$$

$$= 0.0319(3.5)\left\{27 + 12\left[\frac{0.503(19.42)}{3.5} - 1\right]\right\} = 5.41 \text{ in.}^2$$

$$5.41 > 4.68 \hspace{4cm} \text{(O.K.)}$$

d. The tensile force (steel is at the yield stress) is

$$N_T = A_sf_y = 4.68(60) = 281 \text{ kips}$$

e. The flange compression (assuming full effective flange area is in compression) is

$$N_c = (0.85f_c')bh_f$$
$$= 0.85(3)(27)(3.5) = 241 \text{ kips}$$

f. Since 281 > 241, the compressive stress block must extend below the flange far enough to pick up the remaining compression of

$$281 - 241 = 40 \text{ kips}$$

Hence the analysis is for a true T-beam, as expected.

g. The remaining compression will be obtained by additional web area. Solving for a, the total depth of stress block, as shown in Figure 3-13, yields

$$a = \frac{N_T - N_C}{(0.85f_c')b_w} + h_f$$

$$= \frac{40}{0.85(3)(12)} + 3.5 = 4.81 \text{ in.}$$

h. Locate the centroid of the compressive area from the top of the cross section:

$$\bar{y} = \frac{\Sigma(Ay)}{\Sigma A}$$

$$A_1 = 27(3.5) = 94.5 \text{ in.}^2, \hspace{1cm} A_2 = 12(1.31) = 15.72 \text{ in.}^2$$

FIGURE 3-13   Compressive area, Example 3-5.

FIGURE 3-14   Design sketch for Example 3-5.

$$\bar{y} = \frac{94.5(1.75) + 15.72(4.15)}{94.5 + 15.72} = 2.09 \text{ in.}$$

from which

$$Z = d - \bar{y} = 19.42 - 2.09$$

$$= 17.33 \text{ in.}$$

i. Compute the practical moment strength ϕM_n:

$$\phi M_n = \phi N_T Z = \frac{0.9(281)(17.33)}{12} = 365.2 \text{ ft-kips}$$

It was previously determined that M_u was 340 ft-kips; therefore, the design *for flexure* is adequate, since $\phi M_n > M_u$.

10. Sketch the design (see Figure 3-14).

The approximate method above will work whether the T-beam is a true T-beam or rectangular T-beam. (In fact, the use of an approximate Z to determine an approximate A_s can be used for the design of any beam because the approximate design is to be checked by an analysis anyway.) The method works particularly well for T-beams in which, because of their basic shape, the centroid of the compressive stress block will never be very far from the middepth of the flange, however. An alternative design method for the true T-shape is to design steel for the flange couple and stem couple individually; the total A_s required would then be the sum of the required steel areas for the two individual couples. This is similar to the approach used for the design of beams with compression reinforcement.

3-6

SUMMARY OF PROCEDURE FOR ANALYSIS OF T-BEAMS (FOR MOMENT)

1. Establish the effective flange width based on ACI criteria.
2. Check $A_{s,min}$. Use Table A-5.
3. Check the ACI Code ductility requirement using the proper expression for $A_{s,max}$ from Table 3-1. Note that $A_{s,max}$ must be larger than actual A_s.*
4. Compute the total tension in the steel:

$$N_T = A_s f_y$$

5. Compute the magnitude of the compression that the flange itself is capable of furnishing:

$$N_C = 0.85 f_c' b h_f$$

6. If $N_T > N_C$, the beam will behave as a true T-beam and the remaining compression, which equals $N_T - N_C$, will be furnished by additional web area. If $N_T < N_C$, the beam will behave as a rectangular beam of width b.

True T-Beam

7. Locate the bottom of the compressive stress block in the beam web:

$$a = \frac{N_T - N_C}{0.85 f_c' b_w} + h_f$$

8. Locate the centroid of the total compressive area using the relationship

$$\bar{y} = \frac{\Sigma (Ay)}{\Sigma A}$$

from which

$$Z = d - \bar{y}$$

9. Compute the practical moment strength ϕM_n:

$$\phi M_n = \phi N_C Z \quad \text{or} \quad \phi N_T Z$$

Rectangular T-Beam

7. Compute the actual steel ratio in order to determine $\bar{k}$:

$$\rho = \frac{A_s}{bd}$$

---

*When checking the maximum steel limitation (step 3), if actual $A_s > A_{s,max}$, the practical moment strength ϕM_n must be recalculated using $A_{s,max}$, which may be considered an "effective" A_s.

8.   Consult the proper table in Appendix A and find the required $\overline{k}$ for the ρ value from step 7.

9.   Compute the practical moment strength ϕM_n:

$$\phi M_n = \phi b d^2 \overline{k}$$

A flow diagram of this procedure is presented in Appendix B.

3-7

SUMMARY OF PROCEDURE FOR DESIGN OF T-BEAMS (FOR MOMENT)

1.   Compute the design moment M_u.
2.   Assume that the effective depth $d = h - 3$ in.
3.   Establish the effective flange width based on ACI criteria.
4.   Compute the practical moment strength ϕM_n assuming that the total effective flange is in compression:

$$\phi M_n = \phi(0.85 f_c')bh_f\left(d - \frac{h_f}{2}\right)$$

5.   If $\phi M_n > M_u$, the beam will behave as a rectangular T-beam of width b. If $\phi M_n < M_u$, the beam will behave as a true T-beam.

Rectangular T-Beam

6.   Design as a rectangular beam with b and d as known values. Compute the required $\overline{k}$:

$$\text{required } \overline{k} = \frac{M_u}{\phi b d^2}$$

7.   From the tables in Appendix A, determine the required ρ for the required $\overline{k}$ of step 6.

8.   Compute the required A_s:

$$\text{required } A_s = \rho b d$$

9.   Select bars and check the beam width. Check the actual d and compare it with the assumed d. If the actual d is slightly in excess of the assumed d, the design will be slightly conservative (on the safe side). If the actual d is less than the assumed d, the design may be on the nonconservative side (depending on steel provided) and should be more closely investigated for possible revision.

10. Check $A_{s,\min}$. Use Table A-5.

11. Check the ACI ductility requirement using proper expression for $A_{s,\max}$ from Table 3-1. Note that $A_{s,\max}$ must be larger than actual A_s.
12. Sketch the design.

True T-Beam

6. Assume that $Z = d - h_f/2$.
7. Compute the required A_s based on the assumption of step 6:

$$A_s = \frac{M_u}{\phi f_y Z}$$

8. Select bars and check the beam width.
9. Determine the actual effective depth d and *analyze* the beam. (See the procedure for analysis of T-beams in Section 3-6.)
10. Sketch the design.

A flow diagram of this procedure is presented in Appendix B.

3-8

DOUBLY REINFORCED BEAMS: INTRODUCTION

As indicated in Chapter 2, the practical moment strength of a rectangular reinforced concrete beam reinforced with only tensile steel may be determined by the expression $\phi M_n = \phi b d^2 \overline{k}$, where $\overline{k}$ is a function of the steel ratio ρ, f'_c, and f_y.

The maximum legal limit of ρ in a given cross section (with tensile steel only) has been established by the ACI Code as $\rho_{\max} = 0.75\rho_b$. Therefore, for a given cross section of given material strengths, the maximum practical moment strength ϕM_n may be calculated using the $\overline{k}$ that corresponds to $\rho_{\max}$.

Occasionally, practical and architectural considerations may dictate and limit beam sizes whereby it becomes necessary to develop more moment strength from a given cross section. When this situation occurs, the ACI Code, Section 10.3.4, permits the addition of tensile steel over and above the code maximum provided that compression steel is also added in the compression zone of the cross section. The result constitutes a combined tensile and compressive reinforced beam commonly called a *doubly reinforced beam*.

Where beams span more than two supports (continuous construction), practical considerations are sometimes the reason for the existence of main steel in compression zones. In Figure 3-15, positive moments exist at A and C; therefore, the main tensile reinforcement would be placed in the bottom of the beam. At B, however, a negative moment exists and the bottom of the beam is in compression. The tensile reinforcement must be placed near the top of the beam. It is general prac-

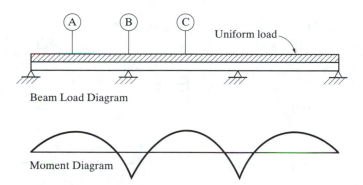

FIGURE 3-15   Continuous beam.

tice that at least some of the tension steel in each of the cases above will be extended the length of the beam and will pass through compression zones. In this case the compression steel may sometimes be used for additional strength. Chapter 7 shows that compression reinforcement will aid significantly in reducing long-term deflections. In fact, the use of compression steel to increase the bending strength of a reinforced concrete beam is an inefficient way to utilize steel. More commonly, deflection control will be the reason for the presence of compression steel.

3-9

DOUBLY REINFORCED BEAM ANALYSIS FOR MOMENT (CONDITION I)

The basic assumptions for the analysis of doubly reinforced beams are similar to those for tensile reinforced beams. One additional significant assumption is that the *compression steel stress* (f'_s) is a function of the strain at the level of the centroid of the compression steel. As discussed previously, the steel will behave elastically up to the point where the strain exceeds the yield strain ϵ_y. In other words, as a limit, $f'_s = f_y$ when the compression steel strain $\epsilon'_s \geq \epsilon_y$. If $\epsilon'_s < \epsilon_y$, the compression steel stress $f'_s = \epsilon'_s E_s$, where E_s is the modulus of elasticity of the steel.

With two different materials, concrete and steel, resisting the compressive force N_C, the total compression will now consist of two forces: N_{C1}, the compression resisted by the concrete, and N_{C2}, the compression resisted by the compressive steel. For analysis, the total resisting moment of the beam will be assumed to consist of two parts or two internal couples: the part due to the resistance of the compressive concrete and tensile steel and the part due to the compressive steel and additional tensile steel. The two internal couples are illustrated in Figure 3-16.

Notation for doubly reinforced beams is as follows:

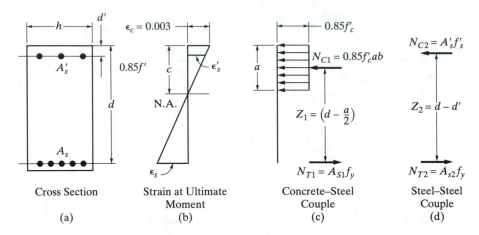

FIGURE 3-16 Doubly reinforced beam analysis.

A_s' = total compression steel cross-sectional area

d = effective depth of tension steel

d' = depth to centroid of compression steel from compression face of beam

A_{s1} = amount of tension steel used by the concrete–steel couple

A_{s2} = amount of tension steel used by the steel–steel couple

A_s = total tension steel cross-sectional area ($A_s = A_{s1} + A_{s2}$)

M_{n1} = nominal moment strength of the concrete–steel couple

M_{n2} = nominal moment strength of the steel–steel couple

M_n = nominal moment strength of the (doubly reinforced) beam

ϵ_s = unit strain at the centroid of the tension steel

ϵ_s' = unit strain at the centroid of the compression steel

The total nominal moment strength may be developed as the sum of the two internal couples, neglecting the concrete that is displaced by the compression steel.

The strength of the steel–steel couple is evaluated as follows:

$$M_{n2} = N_{T2}Z_2$$

Assuming that $f_s = f_y$ (tensile steel yields),

$$M_{n2} = A_{s2}f_y(d - d')$$

Also, since $\Sigma H_F = 0$ and $N_{c2} = N_{T2}$,

$$A_s'f_s' = A_{s2}f_y$$

If we assume that the compression steel yields and that $f'_s = f_y$, then

$$A'_s f_y = A_{s2} f_y$$

from which

$$A'_s = A_{s2}$$

Therefore,

$$M_{n2} = A'_s f_y (d - d')$$

The strength of the concrete–steel couple is evaluated as follows:

$$M_{n1} = N_{T1} Z_1$$

Assuming that the tensile steel yields and $f_s = f_y$,

$$M_{n1} = A_{s1} f_y \left(d - \frac{a}{2} \right)$$

Also, since $A_s = A_{s1} + A_{s2}$, then

$$A_{s1} = A_s - A_{s2}$$

and since $A_{s2} = A'_s$, then

$$A_{s1} = A_s - A'_s$$

Therefore,

$$M_{n1} = (A_s - A'_s) f_y \left(d - \frac{a}{2} \right)$$

Summing the two couples, we arrive at the nominal moment strength of a doubly reinforced beam:

$$M_n = M_{n1} + M_{n2}$$
$$= (A_s - A'_s) f_y \left(d - \frac{a}{2} \right) + A'_s f_y (d - d')$$

The practical moment strength of ϕM_n may then be calculated.

The foregoing expressions are based on the assumption that both tension and compression steels yield prior to concrete strain reaching 0.003. This may be checked by determining the strains that exist at ultimate moment, which depend on the location of the neutral axis. The neutral axis may be located, as previously, by the depth of the compressive stress block and the relationship $a = \beta_1 c$. Thus

$$N_T = N_{C1} + N_{C2}$$
$$A_s f_y = (0.85 f'_c) a b + A'_s f_y$$
$$a = \frac{(A_s - A'_s) f_y}{(0.85 f'_c) b}$$

which may also be expressed as

$$a = \frac{A_{s1}f_y}{(0.85f_c')b}$$

With the calculation of the a distance, the neutral axis location c may be determined and the assumptions checked.

The case where both tensile and compressive steels yield prior to the concrete strain reaching 0.003 will be categorized as *condition I* (see Example 3-6). The case where the tensile steel yields but the compressive steel does not yield prior to the concrete strain reaching 0.003 is categorized as *condition II* (see Example 3-7).

Example 3-6

Compute the practical moment strength ϕM_n for a beam having a cross section as shown in Figure 3-17. Use $f_c' = 3000$ psi and $f_y = 60,000$ psi.

FIGURE 3-17   Sketch for Example 3-6.

Solution:

1.   Assume that all the steel yields

$$f_s' = f_y \quad \text{and} \quad f_s = f_y$$

Therefore, $A_{s2} = A_s'$ [see Figure 3-16d].

2. $$A_s = A_{s1} + A_{s2}$$

$$A_{s1} = A_s - A_s'$$

$$= 6.00 - 2.54 = 3.46 \text{ in.}^2$$

From the concrete–steel couple, the stress block depth can be found:

$$a = \frac{A_{s1}f_y}{(0.85f_c')b} = \frac{3.46(60)}{0.85(3.0)(11)} = 7.40 \text{ in.}$$

3. Assuming that the same relationship $(a = \beta_1 c)$ exists between the depth of the stress block and the beam's neutral axis as existed in singly reinforced beams, the neutral axis may now be located for purposes of checking the steel strains. From Figure 3-16 at the ultimate moment,

$$c = \frac{a}{\beta_1} = \frac{a}{0.85} = \frac{7.40}{0.85} = 8.71 \text{ in.}$$

4. Check the strains to determine whether the assumptions are valid and that both steels yield before concrete crushes (see Figure 3-16b). The strains calculated exist at the ultimate moment:

$$\epsilon_s' = \frac{c - d'}{c}(0.003)$$

$$= \frac{8.71 - 2.5}{8.71}(0.003) = 0.00214$$

$$\epsilon_s = \frac{d - c}{c}(0.003)$$

$$= \frac{20 - 8.71}{8.71}(0.003) = 0.00389$$

$$\epsilon_y = 0.00207 \qquad \text{(from Table A-1)}$$

Since ϵ_s' and ϵ_s both exceed ϵ_y, the compression and tensile steel have reached their yield stress before the concrete reaches a strain of 0.003. Therefore, the assumptions concerning the steel stresses are O.K. ($f_s' = f_y$ and $f_s = f_y$).

5. From the concrete–steel couple:

$$M_{n1} = A_{s1}f_y\left(d - \frac{a}{2}\right)$$

$$= 3.46(60)\left(20 - \frac{7.40}{2}\right) = 3384 \text{ in.-kips}$$

$$\frac{3384}{12} = 282 \text{ ft-kips}$$

From the steel–steel couple:

$$M_{n2} = A_s'f_y(d - d') = 2.54(60)(20 - 2.5)$$

$$= 2667 \text{ in.-kips}$$

$$\frac{2667}{12} = 222 \text{ ft-kips}$$

$$M_n = M_{n1} + M_{n2}$$

$$= 282 + 222 = 504 \text{ ft-kips}$$

6.
$$\phi M_n = 0.9(504)$$

$$= 454 \text{ ft-kips}$$

7.   That both the compressive steel and tensile steel yield prior to the concrete reaching a compressive strain of 0.003 implies a theoretical ductile
beam. Despite this ductile behavior, however, the beam may not satisfy
the ACI Code ductility requirement if the actual ρ is in excess of $0.75\rho_b$;
therefore, a code ductility check should be made.

The ACI Code limitation on ρ (Section 10.3.3) applies to doubly reinforced beams as well as to singly reinforced beams except that in beams
with compression reinforcement the portion of ρ_b equalized by the compression reinforcement need not be reduced by the 0.75 factor. Expressions
for $A_{s,\max}$ for doubly reinforced beams may be developed using a procedure
similar to that used for T-beams. This development and the resulting expressions are found in Appendix B. The intent of the code to ensure a ductile-
type beam is satisfied if the concrete–steel couple has ρ less than $0.75\rho_b$ and
is therefore ductile.

This will usually be satisfactory since the addition of the steel couple
composed of A_s' and A_{s2} will not, of itself, lead to a brittle failure, since this
is a steel couple and has toughness typical of steel. In cases of slabs and
shallow beams where f_s' may be less than f_y, however, simply ensuring that
the concrete–steel couple (with $A_{s1} = A_s - A_s'$) is ductile will not necessarily
ensure that the doubly reinforced beam is ductile. In these cases the expressions of Appendix B should be used.

Checking the concrete–steel couple, we obtain

$$\rho = \frac{A_{s1}}{bd} = \frac{3.46}{11(20)} = 0.0157$$

$$\rho_{\max} = 0.0161$$

Since $0.0157 < 0.0161$, the code criterion for ductile behavior is ensured.

3-10

DOUBLY REINFORCED BEAM ANALYSIS FOR MOMENT (CONDITION II)

As has been pointed out, usually the compression steel (A_s') will reach its yield stress before the concrete reaches a strain of 0.003. Particularly in shallow beams reinforced with the higher-strength steels, this is not necessarily true, however. Referring to Figure 3-16b, if the neutral axis is located relatively high in the cross section, it is possible that $\epsilon_s' < \epsilon_y$ at ultimate moment. The magnitude of ϵ_s' (and therefore f_s') depends on the actual location of the neutral axis. The depth of the compressive stress block a also depends on c, since $a = \beta_1 c$.

The total compressive force must be equal to the total tensile force $A_s f_y$, and an equilibrium equation can be written to solve for the exact required value of c. This turns out to be a quadratic equation.

This situation and its solution may be observed in the following example.

Example 3-7 _____

Compute the practical moment strength ϕM_n for a beam having a cross section as shown in Figure 3-18. Use $f_c' = 5000$ psi and $f_y = 60,000$ psi.

Solution:

1. Assume that all the steel yields. This results in

$$A_{s2} = A_s'$$

FIGURE 3-18   Sketch for Example 3-7.

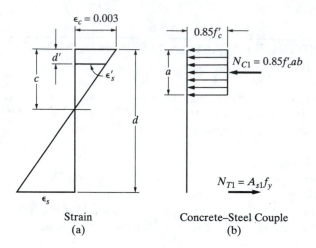

Strain
(a)

Concrete–Steel Couple
(b)

FIGURE 3-19   Compatibility check, Example 3-7.

2.   With reference to Figure 3-19b,

$$a = \frac{(A_s - A_s')f_y}{(0.85f_c')b}$$

$$= \frac{3.10(60)}{0.85(5)(11)}$$

$$= 3.98 \text{ in.}$$

3.   Locate the neutral axis:

$$a = \beta_1 c, \qquad \beta_1 = 0.80 \qquad \text{(reference, ACI Code, Section 10.2.7.3)}$$

$$c = \frac{a}{\beta_1} = \frac{3.98}{0.80} = 4.98 \text{ in.}$$

4.   By similar triangles of Figure 3-19a, check the steel strains:

compressive steel: $\epsilon_s' = \dfrac{0.003(c - d')}{c}$

$$\epsilon_s' = \frac{2.48}{4.98}(0.003) = 0.0015$$

tensile steel: $\epsilon_s = \dfrac{0.003(d - c)}{c}$

$$\epsilon_s = \frac{20 - 4.98}{4.98}(0.003) = 0.00905$$

For grade 60 steel, $\epsilon_y = 0.00207$ (from Table A-1). Since $\epsilon_s > \epsilon_y > \epsilon_s'$, the tensile steel *has* yielded and the compression steel *has not* yielded. Therefore, the assumptions of step 1 are incorrect.

5. With the original assumptions incorrect, a solution for the location of the neutral axis must be established. With reference to Figure 3-16, c will be determined by using the condition that horizontal equilibrium exists. That is, $\Sigma H_F = 0$. Thus

$$N_T = N_{C1} + N_{C2}$$

$$A_s f_y = (0.85\, f_c')ba + f_s' A_s'$$

But

$$a = \beta_1 c$$

and

$$f_s' = \epsilon_s' E_s = \left[\frac{c - d'}{c}(0.003)\right]E_s$$

Then, by substitution,

$$A_s f_y = (0.85 f_c')b\beta_1 c + \left[\frac{c - d'}{c}(0.003)\right]E_s A_s'$$

Multiplying by c and expanding, we obtain

$$A_s f_y c = (0.85 f_c')b\beta_1 c^2 + c(0.003)E_s A_s' - d'(0.003)E_s A_s'$$

Rearranging yields

$$(0.85 f_c' b\beta_1)c^2 + (0.003 E_s A_s' - A_s f_y)c - d'(0.003)E_s A_s' = 0$$

With $E_s = 29{,}000$ ksi, the expression becomes

$$(0.85 f_c' b\beta_1)c^2 + (87 A_s' - A_s f_y)c - 87 d' A_s' = 0$$

where

$A_s = 4.68$ in.^{2}

$f_y = 60$ ksi

$f_c' = 5$ ksi

$b = 11$ in.

$\beta_1 = 0.80$

$A_s' = 1.58$ in.^{2}

$d' = 2.5$ in.

Substitution yields

$$\left[0.85(5)(11)(0.80)\right]c^2 + \left[87(1.58) - 4.68(60)\right]c - 87(2.5)(1.58) = 0$$

$$37.4c^2 - 143.34c - 343.65 = 0$$

$$c^2 - 3.83c - 9.19 = 0$$

This may be solved using the usual formula for the roots of a quadratic equation:

$$\frac{-b \pm \sqrt{b^2 - 4ac}}{2a}$$

where the coefficients are

$$a = 1.0$$

$$b = 3.83$$

$$c = 9.19$$

Or the square may be completed as follows:

$$c^2 - 3.83c = 9.19$$

$$c^2 - 3.83c + \left(\frac{-3.83}{2}\right)^2 = 9.19 + \left(\frac{-3.83}{2}\right)^2$$

$$c^2 - 3.83c + 3.67 = 9.19 + 3.67 = 12.86$$

$$(c - 1.92)^2 = 12.86$$

$$c - 1.92 = \sqrt{12.86} = 3.59$$

$$c = 5.51 \text{ in.}$$

The solution of the quadratic equation for c may be simplified as follows:

$$c = \pm \sqrt{Q + R^2} - R$$

where

$$R = \frac{87A_s' - A_s f_y}{1.7f_c' b\beta_1}$$

$$Q = \frac{87d' A_s'}{0.85 f_c' b\beta_1}$$

Note that basic units are kips and inches, so the value of f_y, for instance, must be in ksi, not in psi.

6.   With this value of c, all the remaining unknowns may be found:

$$f_s' = \frac{c - d'}{c}(87) = \frac{5.51 - 2.50}{5.51}(87)$$

$$= 47.5 \text{ ksi} < 60 \text{ ksi} \qquad \text{(as expected)}$$

7. $\qquad a = \beta_1 c = 0.80(5.51) = 4.41 \text{ in.}$

8. $\qquad N_{C1} = (0.85f_c')ab = 0.85(5)(4.41)(11.0) = 206.2 \text{ kips}$

$$N_{C2} = A_s' f_s' = 47.5(1.58) = 75.1 \text{ kips}$$

$$N_C = 281.3 \text{ kips}$$

$$\text{Check: } N_T = A_s f_y = 4.68(60) = 281 \text{ kips}$$

$$N_T \approx N_C \qquad \text{(O.K.)}$$

9. $\qquad M_{n1} = N_{C1}Z_1 = N_{C1}\left(d - \frac{a}{2}\right) = 206.2\left(20 - \frac{4.41}{2}\right) = 3670 \text{ in.-kips}$

$$M_{n2} = N_{C2}Z_2 = N_{C2}(d - d') = 75.1(20 - 2.5) = 1314 \text{ in.-kips}$$

$$M_n = 4984 \text{ in.-kips} = 415.3 \text{ ft-kips}$$

10. $\qquad\qquad \phi M_n = 0.9(415.3)$

$$= 373.8 \text{ ft-kips}$$

11. Ductility will be checked based on ACI Code requirements. Since $f_s' < f_y$, the amount of tension steel required for the steel–steel couple (A_{s2}) will be less than A_s'. Find the new *effective* A_{s1}:

$$N_{T2} = N_{C2}$$

$$A_{s2}f_y = A_s'f_s'$$

$$A_{s2} = \frac{A_s'f_s'}{f_y} = \frac{1.58(47.5)}{60} = 1.25 \text{ in.}^2$$

Then

$$A_{s1} = A_s - A_{s2} = 4.68 - 1.25 = 3.43 \text{ in.}^2$$

For the concrete–steel couple:

$$\rho = \frac{A_{s1}}{bd} = \frac{3.43}{11(20)} = 0.0156$$

$$0.75\rho_b = 0.0252 \qquad \text{(Table A-5)}$$

$$0.0156 < 0.0252 \qquad\qquad \text{(O.K.)}$$

3-11

SUMMARY OF PROCEDURE FOR ANALYSIS OF DOUBLY REINFORCED BEAMS (FOR MOMENT)

1. Assume that all the steel yields, $f_s = f'_s = f_y$. Therefore,

$$A_{s2} = A'_s$$

2. Using the concrete–steel couple and $A_{s1} = A_s - A'_s$, compute the depth of the compression stress block:

$$a = \frac{A_{s1}f_y}{(0.85f'_c)b} = \frac{(A_s - A'_s)f_y}{(0.85f'_c)b}$$

3. Compute the location of the neutral axis:

$$c = \frac{a}{\beta_1}$$

4. Using the strain diagram, check the strains in both the compressive and tensile steels to determine whether the assumption in step 1 is valid:

$$\epsilon'_s = \frac{0.003(c - d')}{c}$$

$$\epsilon_s = \frac{0.003(d - c)}{c}$$

Assuming that $\epsilon_s \geqslant \epsilon_y$, that is, that the tensile steel has yielded, the two following conditions may exist:

a. Condition I: $\epsilon'_s \geqslant \epsilon_y$. This indicates that the assumption of step 1 is correct and the compression steel has yielded.

b. Condition II: $\epsilon'_s < \epsilon_y$. This indicates that the assumption of step 1 is incorrect and the compression steel has not yielded.

Note that it is possible for two other conditions to exist. These would occur if $\epsilon_s < \epsilon_y$, with the resulting tensile steel stress being at less than the yield stress. This situation would be rare but could occur in the analysis of *existing* overreinforced, doubly reinforced beams and slabs. Conditions I and II assume that $\epsilon_s \geqslant \epsilon_y$.

Condition I

5. If ϵ'_s and ϵ_s both exceed ϵ_y, compute the nominal moment strengths M_{n1} and M_{n2}. For a steel–steel couple:

$$M_{n2} = A'_s f_y (d - d')$$

For a concrete–steel couple:

$$M_{n1} = A_{s1}f_y\left(d - \frac{a}{2}\right)$$

and

$$M_n = M_{n1} + M_{n2}$$

6.   Practical moment strength $= \phi M_n$.
7.   Check the ductility requirement. Ensure that the actual ρ for the concrete–steel couple does not exceed $0.75\rho_b$ (Table A-5) or ensure that the tension steel area is not in excess of $A_{s,\mathrm{max}}$ as determined by expressions found in Appendix B. Note that

$$\text{actual } \rho = \frac{A_{s1}}{bd}$$

Condition II

5.   If ϵ'_s is less than ϵ_y and $\epsilon_s \geqslant \epsilon_y$, compute c using the following formula:

$$(0.85f'_c b\beta_1)c^2 + (87A'_s - A_s f_y)c - 87d'A'_s = 0$$

and solve the quadratic equation for c, or use the simplified formula approach from Example 3-7, step 5. Note that the basic units are kips and inches.
6.   Compute the compressive steel stress (to be less than f_y):

$$f'_s = \frac{c - d'}{c}(87)$$

7.   Solve for a using

$$a = \beta_1 c$$

8.   Compute the compressive forces:

$$N_{C1} = (0.85f'_c)ba$$
$$N_{C2} = A'_s f'_s$$

Check these by computing the tensile force:

$$N_T = A_s f_y$$

Note that N_T should equal $N_{C1} + N_{C2}$.
9.   Compute the ideal resisting moment strengths of the individual couples:

$$M_{n1} = N_{C1}\left(\frac{d - a}{2}\right)$$

and

$$M_{n2} = N_{C2}(d - d')$$

$$M_n = M_{n1} + M_{n2}$$

10. Practical moment strength $= \phi M_n$.

11. Check the ductility requirements. Ensure that the actual ρ for the concrete–steel couple does not exceed $0.75\rho_b$ (Table A-5). Here A_{s1} is computed based on the fact that the compressive steel stress does not reach f_y:

$$A_{s1} = A_s - \frac{A'_s f'_s}{f_y}$$

and

$$\text{actual } \rho = \frac{A_{s1}}{bd}$$

The ductility requirements may also be checked by comparing A_s with $A_{s,\text{max}}$ as determined by expressions found in Appendix B, in which the actual balanced condition is investigated.

3-12

DOUBLY REINFORCED BEAM DESIGN FOR MOMENT

If a check shows that a singly reinforced rectangular section is inadequate and the size of the beam cannot be increased, a doubly reinforced section may be designed using a procedure that consists of the separate design of the two component couples such that their summation will result in a beam of the required strength.

Example 3-8

Design a rectangular reinforced concrete beam to carry service moments of $M_{\text{DL}} = 170$ ft-kips and $M_{\text{LL}} = 270$ ft-kips. Physical limitations require that $b = 14$ in. and $h = 30$ in. If compression steel is needed, $d' = 3$ in. Use $f'_c = 3000$ psi and $f_y = 60,000$ psi. The beam cross section is shown in Figure 3-20.

Solution

1. Assume that $d = h - 4 = 26$ in. (because of the probability of two rows of steel).

2. Calculate the design moment:

$$M_u = 1.4\,M_{\text{DL}} + 1.7 M_{\text{LL}}$$

$$= 1.4(170) + 1.7(270)$$

$$= 238 + 459 = 697 \text{ ft-kips}$$

FIGURE 3-20   Sketch for Example 3-8.

3.   Determine if a singly reinforced beam will work. From Table A-8, using $\rho = 0.0161$,

$$\text{maximum } \overline{k} = 0.7830 \text{ ksi}$$

$$\text{maximum possible } \phi M_n = \phi b d^2 \overline{k}$$

$$= \frac{0.9(14)(26)^2(0.7830)}{12} = 556 \text{ ft-kips}$$

4.   556 ft kips < 697 ft-kips. Therefore, a doubly reinforced beam is required.

5.   Provide a concrete–steel couple having a steel ratio of about 90% of ρ_{max}:

$$\rho = 0.90(0.0161) = 0.0145$$

From Table A-8,

$$\overline{k} = 0.7216 \text{ ksi}$$

6.   The practical moment strength of a concrete–steel couple will then be

$$\phi M_{n1} = \phi b d^2 \overline{k} = \frac{0.9(14)(26)^2(0.7216)}{12}$$

$$= 512 \text{ ft-kips}$$

The required steel area for the concrete–steel couple may now be determined:

$$\text{required } A_{s1} = \rho b d = 0.0145(14)(26)$$

$$= 5.28 \text{ in.}^2$$

7.   The steel–steel couple must be proportioned to have moment strength equal to the remainder of the design moment:

$$\text{required } \phi M_{n2} = M_u - \phi M_{n1} = 697 - 512$$

$$= 185 \text{ ft-kips}$$

8. Considering the steel–steel couple, we have

$$\phi M_{n2} = \phi N_{C2}(d - d')$$

$$N_{C2} = \frac{\phi M_{n2}}{\phi(d - d')} = \frac{185(12)}{0.9(26 - 3)} = 107 \text{ kips}$$

9. Since $N_{C2} = A_s' f_s'$, compute f_s' by using the neutral-axis location of the concrete–steel couple and checking the strain ϵ_s' in the compression steel (see Figure 3-21):

$$a = \frac{A_{s1}f_y}{(0.85f_c')b} = \frac{5.28(60)}{0.85(3)(14)} = 8.87 \text{ in.}$$

$$c = \frac{a}{\beta_1} = \frac{8.87}{0.85} = 10.44 \text{ in.}$$

$$\epsilon_s' = \frac{c - d'}{c}(0.003) = \frac{7.44}{10.44}(0.003) = 0.0021$$

$$\epsilon_y = 0.00207 \qquad \text{(from Table A-1)}$$

Since $\epsilon_y < \epsilon_s'$, the compression steel will yield before the concrete strain reaches 0.003, and $f_s' = f_y$ as a limit.

10. Determine the required compression steel:

$$\text{required } A_s' = \frac{N_{C2}}{f_s'} = \frac{N_{C2}}{f_y} = \frac{107}{60} = 1.78 \text{ in.}^2$$

11. Determine the required tension steel for the steel–steel couple. Since $f_s' = f_y$,

$$A_{s2} = A_s' = 1.78 \text{ in.}^2$$

FIGURE 3-21   Concrete strain diagram for Example 3-8.

FIGURE 3-22   Design sketch for Example 3-8.

12.   Determine the *total* tension steel required:

$$A_s = A_{s1} + A_{s2} = 5.28 \text{ in.}^2 + 1.78 \text{ in.}^2 = 7.06 \text{ in.}^2$$

13.   Select the compression steel (1.78 in.² required). Use two No. 9 bars ($A'_s = 2.00 \text{ in.}^2$).

14.   Select the tension steel (7.06 in.² required). Use six No. 10 bars ($A_s = 7.62 \text{ in.}^2$). Place these in two layers (three bars per layer):

$$\text{required beam width} = 10.5 \text{ in.} \qquad \text{(O.K.)}$$

15.   Assume No. 3 stirrups and determine the actual depth to the centroid of the bar group by considering the total depth (30 in.), required cover (1½ in.), stirrup size (No. 3), tension bar size (No. 10), and required 1 in. minimum clear space between layers:

$$\text{actual } d = 30 - 1.5 - 0.38 - 1.27 - 0.5 = 26.35 \text{ in.}$$

The assumed d was 26 in. Thus

$$26.345 > 26 \qquad \text{(O.K.)}$$

16.   Figure 3-22 is a sketch of the design.

3-13

SUMMARY OF PROCEDURE FOR DESIGN OF DOUBLY REINFORCED BEAMS (FOR MOMENT)

The size of the beam cross section is fixed.

1.   Assume that $d = h - 4$ in.

2. Establish the total design moment M_u.

3. Check to see if doubly reinforced beam is necessary. From the tables in Appendix A, obtain maximum $\overline{k}$ and compute maximum M_R for a singly reinforced beam:

$$\text{maximum } \phi M_n = \phi b d^2 \overline{k}$$

4. If $\phi M_n < M_u$, design the beam as a doubly reinforced beam. If $\phi M_n \geq M_u$, the beam can be designed as a beam reinforced with tension steel only.

For a Doubly Reinforced Beam

5. Provide a concrete–steel couple having the steel ratio

$$\rho = 0.90(\rho_{\max}) = 0.90(0.75\rho_b)$$

With this ρ, enter the appropriate table and determine $\overline{k}$.

6. Determine the moment capacity of the concrete–steel couple:

$$\phi M_{n1} = \phi b d^2 \overline{k}$$

Find the steel required for the concrete–steel couple:

$$\text{required } A_{s1} = \rho b d$$

7. Find the remaining moment that must be resisted by the steel–steel couple:

$$\text{required } \phi M_{n2} = M_u - \phi M_{n1}$$

8. Considering the steel–steel couple, find the required compressive force in the steel (assume that $d' - 3$ in.):

$$N_{C2} = \frac{\phi M_{n2}}{\phi(d - d')}$$

9. Since $N_{C2} = A_s' f_s'$, compute f_s' so that A_s' may eventually be determined. This can be accomplished by using the neutral-axis location of the concrete–steel couple and checking the strain ϵ_s' in the compression steel with ϵ_y from Table A-1. Thus

$$a = \frac{A_{s1} f_y}{(0.85 f_c')b}$$

$$c = \frac{a}{\beta_1}$$

$$\epsilon_s' = \frac{0.003(c - d')}{c}$$

If $\epsilon_s' \geq \epsilon_y$, the compressive steel has yielded at ultimate moment and $f_s' = f_y$. If $\epsilon_s' < \epsilon_y$, then calculate $f_s' = \epsilon_s' E_s$ and use this stress in the following steps.

10. Since $N_{C2} = A_s'f_s'$,

$$\text{required } A_s' = \frac{N_{C2}}{f_s'}$$

11. Determine the required A_{s2}:

$$A_{s2} = \frac{f_s'A_s'}{f_y}$$

12. Find the total tension steel required:

$$A_s = A_{s1} + A_{s2}$$

13. Select the compressive steel (A_s').
14. Select the tensile steel (A_s). Check the required beam width. Preferably, place the bars in one layer.
15. Check the actual d and compare it with the assumed d. If the actual d is slightly in excess of the assumed d, the design will be slightly conservative (on the safe side). If the actual d is less than the assumed d, the design may be on the unconservative side and an analysis and possible revision should be considered.
16. Sketch the design.

3-14

ADDITIONAL CODE REQUIREMENTS FOR DOUBLY REINFORCED BEAMS

The compression steel in beams, whether it is in place to increase flexural strength or to control deflections, will act similarly to all typical compression members in that it will tend to bucile, as shown in Figure 3-23. Should this buckling occur, it will naturally be accompanied by spalling of the concrete cover. To help guard against this type of failure, the ACI Code requires that the compression bars be tied into the beam in a manner similar to that used for reinforced concrete columns (discussed in Chapter 9). Compression reinforcement in beams or girders must be enclosed by ties or stirrups. The size of the ties or stirrups is to be at least No. 3 for No. 10 longitudinal bars or smaller and No. 4 for No. 11 longitudinal bars or larger.

Compression steel

FIGURE 3-23   Possible failure mode for compression steel.

The spacing of the ties or stirrups is not to exceed the smaller of 16 longitudinal bar diameters, 48 tie (or stirrup) bar diameters, or the least dimension of the beam. Alternatively, welded wire fabric of equivalent area may be used. The ties or stirrups are to be used throughout the area where compression reinforcement is required (see the ACI Code, Section 7.11).

PROBLEMS

In the following problems, unless otherwise noted, assume No. 3 stirrups, 1½ in. cover for beams, and 1 in. clear between layers of bars.

3-1. Find ϕM_n for the following T-beam: $b = 36$ in., $b_w = 12$ in., $h_f = 4$ in., $d = 22$ in., $f_c' = 4000$ psi, and $f_y = 60,000$ psi. The reinforcement is four No. 8 bars. Check the steel to ensure that it is within allowable limits.

3-2. Rework Problem 3-1 with $b = 48$ in.

3-3. Rework Problem 3-1 with reinforcement of three No. 11 bars.

3-4. Rework Problem 3-1 with $f_c' = 5000$ psi.

3-5. The simple span T-beam shown is part of a floor system of span length 20 ft 0 in. and beam spacing 45 in. o.c. Use $f_c' = 3000$ psi and $f_y = 60,000$ psi.

   (a) Find the practical moment strength ϕM_n and check the steel to ensure that it is within allowable limits.

   (b) How much steel would be required in this beam cross section to make the compressive stress block just completely cover the flange?

PROBLEM 3-5

3-6. Find the practical moment strength ϕM_n for the T-beam in the floor system shown. The beam span is 31 ft 6 in. Use $f_c' = 4000$ psi and $f_y = 60,000$ psi. Check the steel to ensure that it is within allowable limits.

3-7. The T-beam shown is on a simple span of 30 ft. Use $f_c' = 3000$ psi and $f_y = 60,000$ psi. No dead load exists other than the weight of the floor system.

PROBLEM 3-6

Assume that the slab design is adequate.
(a) Find the practical moment strength ϕM_n.
(b) Compute the permissible service live load that can be placed on the floor (psf).

PROBLEM 3-7

3-8. The simple span T-beam shown is part of a floor system of span length 20 ft 0 in. and beam spacing of 8 ft 0 in. o.c. Find the practical moment strength ϕM_n. Use $f'_c = 3000$ psi and $f_y = 60,000$ psi.

PROBLEM 3-8

3-9. Find ϕM_n for the beams of cross section shown. Assume that the physical dimensions are acceptable.

(a) Spandrel beam with a flange on one side only. Use $f'_c = 4000$ psi and $f_y = 60,000$ psi.

(b) Box beam: $f'_c = 3000$ psi and $f_y = 60,000$ psi.

(a)   (b)

PROBLEM 3-9

3-10. Determine ϕM_n for the cross section that has a rectangular duct cast in it, as shown. Use $f'_c = 3000$ psi, $f_y = 60,000$ psi, 1 in. clear between bar layers, $1\frac{1}{2}$-in. cover, and eight No. 8 bars, as shown.

PROBLEM 3-10

3-11. Design a typical interior tension reinforced T-beam to resist positive moment. A cross section of the floor system is shown. The service loads are 50

PROBLEM 3-11

psf dead load (this does not include the weight of the beam and slab) and 325 psf live load. The beam is on a simple span of 18 ft. Use f_c' = 4000 psi and f_y = 60,000 psi.

3-12. A reinforced concrete floor system consists of a 3 in. concrete slab supported by continuous span T-beams of 24 ft spans. The T-beams are spaced 4 ft 8 in. o.c. The web dimensions, determined by negative moment and shear requirements at the supports, are shown. Select the steel required at midspan to resist a total positive design moment M_u of 575 ft-kips (this includes the weight of the floor system). Use f_c' = 3000 psi and f_y = 60,000 psi.

PROBLEM 3-12

3-13. Select steel for the beams of cross section shown. The positive service moments are 155 ft-kips live load and 80 ft-kips dead load (this includes beam weight). Use f_c' = 3000 psi and f_y = 60,000 psi.

3-14. Find ϕM_n for the beam of cross section shown. Use f_c' = 4000 psi and f_y = 60,000 psi.

3-15. The beam of cross section shown is to span 28 ft on simple supports. The uniform load on the beam (in addition to its own weight) will be composed of equal service dead load and live load. Use f_c' = 4000 psi and f_y = 60,000 psi.

(a)   (b)

PROBLEM 3-13

PROBLEM 3-14

(a) Find the service loads that the beam can carry (in addition to its own weight).

(b) Compare the practical moment strength ϕM_n of the beam as shown with ϕM_n of a beam of similar size reinforced with the maximum allowable area of tension steel only.

3-16. Find ϕM_n for the beam cross section shown. Use $f'_c = 4000$ psi and $f_y = 60,000$ psi.

3-17. Compute the practical moment strength ϕM_n for the beam of cross section shown. How much can ϕM_n be increased if 4 No. 8 bars are added to the top of the beam? Use $d' = 2\frac{1}{2}$ in., $f'_c = 3000$ psi, and $f_y = 60,000$ psi.

3-18. Compute the practical moment strength ϕM_n for the simply supported precast beam shown. Use $f'_c = 3000$ psi and $f_y = 60,000$ psi.

PROBLEM 3-15

PROBLEM 3-16

PROBLEM 3-17

PROBLEM 3-18

3-19. Design a rectangular reinforced concrete beam to resist a total design moment M_u of 780 ft-kips (this includes the moment due to the weight of the beam). The beam size is limited to 15 in. maximum width and 30 in. maximum overall depth. Use $f'_c = 3000$ psi and $f_y = 60,000$ psi. If compression steel is required, make $d' = 2\frac{1}{2}$ in.

3-20. Design a rectangular reinforced concrete beam to resist service moments of 136 ft-kips dead load (includes moment due to weight of beam) and 150 ft-kips due to live load. Architectural considerations require that width be limited to 11 in. and overall depth be limited to 23 in. Use $f'_c = 3000$ psi and $f_y = 60,000$ psi.

3-21. Design a rectangular reinforced concrete beam to carry service loads of 1.05 kips/ft dead load (includes beam weight) and 2.47 kips/ft live load. The beam is a simple span and has a span length of 18 ft. The overall dimensions are limited to width of 10 in. and overall depth of 20 in. Use $f'_c = 3000$ psi and $f_y = 60,000$ psi.

3-22. Redesign the beam of Problem 3-21 for tension reinforcing only and increased width. Keep an overall depth of 20 in.

PROBLEM 3-23

3-23. A simply-supported precast beam having the cross section shown is subjected to a total positive design moment M_u of 280 ft-kips. Select the required reinforcement (both tensile and compressive.) Assume a No. 3 stirrup and 1½ in. cover on the tension side of the beam. Use $f'_c = 4000$ psi and $f_y = 60,000$ psi.

CHAPTER 4

Shear in Beams

4-1

INTRODUCTION

In prior chapters we have been concerned primarily with the bending strength of reinforced concrete beams and slabs. The shear forces create additional tensile stresses that must be considered. In these members, steel reinforcing must be added specifically to provide additional shear strength if the shear is in excess of the shear strength of the concrete itself.

122

The concepts of bending stresses and shearing stresses in homogeneous elastic beams are generally discussed at great length in most strength-of-materials texts. The accepted expressions are

$$f = \frac{Mc}{I} \quad \text{and} \quad v = \frac{VQ}{Ib} \tag{4-1}$$

where f, M, c, and I are as defined in Chapter 1; v is the shear stress; V is the external shear; Q is the statical moment of area about the neutral axis; and b is the width of the cross section.

All points in the length of the beam, where the shear and bending moment are not equal to zero, and at locations other than the extreme fiber or neutral axis are subject to both shearing stresses and bending stresses. The combination of these stresses is of such a nature that maximum normal and shearing stresses at a point in a beam exist on planes that are inclined with respect to the axis of the beam. It can be shown that maximum and minimum normal stresses exist on two perpendicular planes. These planes are commonly called the *principal planes,* and the stresses that act on them are called *principal stresses.* The principal stresses in a beam subjected to shear and bending may be calculated using the following formula:

$$f_{pr} = \frac{f}{2} \pm \sqrt{\frac{f^2}{4} + v^2} \tag{4-2}$$

where f_{pr} is the principal stress and f and v are the bending and shear stresses, respectively, calculated from Equation (4-1).

The *orientation* of the principal planes may be calculated using the following formula:

$$\tan 2\alpha = \frac{2v}{f} \tag{4-3}$$

where α is the angle measured from the horizontal.

The magnitudes of the shearing stresses and bending stresses vary along the length of the beam and with distance from the neutral axis. It then follows that the inclination of the principal planes as well as the magnitude of the principal stresses will also vary. At the neutral axis the principal stresses will occur at a 45° angle. This may be verified by Equation (4-3), substituting $f = 0$, from which $\tan 2\alpha = \infty$ and $\alpha = 45°$.

In Figure 4-1, we isolate a small square unit element from the neutral axis of a beam (where $f = 0$). The vertical shear stresses are equal and opposite on the two vertical faces by reason of equilibrium. If these were the only two stresses present, the element would rotate. Therefore, there must exist equal and opposite horizontal shear stresses on the horizontal faces and of the same magnitude as the vertical shear stresses. (The concept of horizontal shear stresses equal in magnitude to the vertical shear stresses at any point in a beam can also be found in almost any strength-of-materials text.)

If we consider a set of orthogonal planes that are inclined at 45° with respect to the original element and resolve the shear stresses into components that are parallel

Beam under Uniform Load
(a)

Stresses on Unit Element
(b)

FIGURE 4-1   Shear stress relationship.

and perpendicular to these planes, the effect will be as shown in Figure 4-2. Note that the components combine so that one of the inclined planes is in compression while the other is in tension. Concrete is strong in compression but weak in tension, and there is a tendency for the concrete to crack on the plane subject to tension should the stress become large enough. The tensile force resulting from the tensile stress acting on a diagonal plane has historically been designated as *diagonal tension*. When it becomes large enough, it will necessitate that shear reinforcing be provided.

As stated previously, tensile stresses of various inclinations and magnitudes, resulting from either shear alone or the combined action of shear and bending, exist in all parts of a beam and must be taken into consideration in both analysis and design.

The preceding discussion is a fairly accurate conceptual description of what occurs in a plain concrete beam. In the beams with which we are concerned, where the length over which a shear failure could occur (the *shear span*) is in excess of approximately three times the effective depth, the diagonal tension failure would be the mode of failure in shear. Such a failure is shown in Figure 4-3. For shorter spans, the failure mode would actually be some combination of shear, crushing, and

FIGURE 4-2   Effect of shear stresses on inclined planes.

FIGURE 4-3 Typical diagonal tension failure.

splitting. For the longer shear spans in plain concrete beams, cracks due to flexural tensile stresses would occur long before cracks due to the diagonal tension. The earlier flexural cracks would initiate the failure, and shear would be of little consequence. In a concrete beam reinforced for flexure (moment) where tensile strength is furnished by steel, however, tensile stresses due to flexure and shear will continue to increase with increasing load. The steel placed in the beam to reinforce for moment is not located where the large diagonal tension stresses (due to shear) occur. The problem then becomes one of furnishing additional reinforcing steel to resist the diagonal tension stresses.

Considerable research over the years has attempted to establish the exact distribution of the shear stresses over the depth of the beam cross section. Despite extensive studies and ongoing research, the precise shear-failure mechanism is still not fully understood.

As with several previous codes, ACI 318-95 furnishes design guidelines for shear reinforcement based on the vertical shear force V_u that develops at any given cross section of a member. Although it is really the diagonal tension for which shear reinforcing must be provided, diagonal tensile forces (or stresses) are not calculated. Historically, vertical shear force (and in older codes, vertical shear stress) has been taken to be a good indicator of the diagonal tension present.

4-2

SHEAR REINFORCEMENT DESIGN REQUIREMENTS

The design of bending members for shear is based on the assumption that the concrete resists part of the shear, and any excess over and above what the concrete is capable of resisting has to be resisted by shear reinforcement. The basic rationale for the design of the shear reinforcement, or *web reinforcement* as it is usually called in beams, is to provide steel to cross the diagonal tension cracks and subsequently keep them from opening. Visualizing this basic rationale with reference to

Figure 4-3, it is seen that the web reinforcement may take several forms, such as (1) vertical stirrups, (2) inclined or diagonal stirrups, and (3) the main reinforcement bent at ends to act as inclined stirrups.

The ACI Code also permits the use of welded wire fabric (with wires located perpendicular to the axis of the member) and spirals. The most common form of web reinforcement used is the vertical stirrup. The web reinforcement contributes very little to the shear resistance *prior* to the formation of the inclined cracks but appreciably increases the *ultimate* shear strength of a bending member.

For members that are subject to shear and flexure only, the amount of shear force that the concrete alone, unreinforced for shear, can resist is V_c:

$$V_c = 2\sqrt{f'_c}b_w d \qquad \text{ACI Eq. (11-3)}$$

In the expression for V_c, the terms are as previously defined with units for f'_c in psi and units for b_w and d in inches. The resulting V_c will be in units of pounds. For rectangular beams, b_w is equivalent to b. The nominal shear strength of the concrete will be reduced to a dependable shear strength by applying a strength reduction factor ϕ of 0.85 (ACI Code, Section 9.3.2). Should members be subject to other effects of axial tension or compression, other expressions for V_c can be found in Section 11.3 of the code. Also, it is permitted to calculate V_c using a more detailed calculation (ACI 318-95, Section 11.3.2). For most designs, it is convenient and conservative to use ACI Equation 11-3.

The design shear force is denoted V_u and results from the application of factored loads. Values of V_u are most conveniently determined using a typical shear force diagram.

Theoretically, no web reinforcement should be required if $V_u \leq \phi V_c$. The code, however, requires that a minimum area of shear reinforcement be provided in all reinforced concrete flexural members where V_u exceeds $\frac{1}{2}\phi V_c$ except as follows:

1. In slabs and footings
2. In concrete joist construction as defined by the ACI Code, Section 8.11
3. In beams with a total depth of less than 10 in., 2½ times the flange thickness, or one-half the width of the web, whichever is greater

This provision of the code is primarily to guard against those cases where an unforeseen overload would cause failure of the member due to shear. Tests have shown the shear failure of a flexural member to be sudden and without warning. In cases where it is not practical to provide shear reinforcement (footings and slabs) and sufficient thickness is provided to resist V_u, the minimum area of web reinforcement is not required. In cases where shear reinforcement is required for strength or because $V_u > \frac{1}{2}\phi V_c$, the minimum area of shear reinforcement shall be calculated from

$$A_v = \frac{50 b_w s}{f_y} \qquad \text{ACI Eq. (11-13)}$$

In the preceding equation and with reference to Figure 4-4,

A_v = total cross-sectional area of web reinforcement within a distance s; for single-loop stirrups, $A_v = 2A_s$, where A_s is the cross-sectional area of the stirrup bar (in.^{2})

b_w = web width = b for rectangular sections (in.)

s = center-to-center spacing of shear reinforcement in a direction parallel to the longitudinal reinforcement (in.)

f_y = yield strength of web reinforcement steel (psi)

When determining the shear strength of concrete, the 1995 ACI Code, Section 11.1.2, limits the value of $\sqrt{f_c'}$ to 100 psi. This corresponds to a concrete strength of $f_c' = 10,000$ psi. This does not prohibit the use of concrete with $f_c' > 10,000$ psi. The designer cannot count on any strength in excess of 10,000 psi when computing the shear strength provided by the concrete, however. This requirement is not too significant for nonprestressed reinforced concrete members, since 10,000 psi concrete is not commonly used for such members.

The 1995 ACI Code, however, does permit $\sqrt{f_c'} > 100$ psi if a minimum amount of web reinforcement is provided. The required minimum amount would be deter-

FIGURE 4-4   Isometric section showing stirrups partially exposed.

mined using ACI Equation 11-13 multiplied by $f_c'/5000(\leqslant 3)$. This in effect doubles the required amount of minimum web reinforcement when $f_c' = 10,000$ psi.

In any span, that portion in which web reinforcement is theoretically necessary can be determined by using the shear (V_u) diagram. When the applied shear V_u exceeds the capacity of the concrete web ϕV_c, web reinforcement is required. In addition, according to the code, web reinforcement at least equal to the minimum required must be provided elsewhere in the span, where the applied shear is greater than one-half of ϕV_c. The ACI Code, Section 11.1.1, states that the basis for shear design must be

$$\phi V_n \geqslant V_u \qquad\qquad \text{ACI Eq. (11-1)}$$

where

$$V_n = V_c + V_s \qquad\qquad \text{ACI Eq. (11-2)}$$

from which

$$\phi V_c + \phi V_s \geqslant V_u$$

where V_u, ϕ, and V_c are as previously defined; V_n is the total nominal shear strength; and V_s is the nominal shear strength provided by shear reinforcement. For vertical stirrups, V_s may be calculated from

$$V_s = \frac{A_v f_y d}{s} \qquad\qquad \text{ACI Eq. (11-15)}$$

where all terms are as previously defined. The preceding equation may be derived, with reference to Figure 4-5, by assuming that the vertical stirrup resists the vertical component of diagonal tension that acts within the length $s/2$ on either side of the stirrup. The horizontal component is automatically included in the design of the main longitudinal reinforcement. Figure 4-5 shows a stirrup intercepting a typical 45° diagonal tension crack.

FIGURE 4-5   Determination of stirrup spacing based on required strength.

As a limit, the factored shear force (design shear) V_u will equal the shear strength of the concrete plus the shear strength of the web reinforcement. As previously indicated,

$$\phi V_c + \phi V_s \geq V_u$$

Using a *shear stress* concept of the 1971 code and substituting for V_u yields

$$\text{shear stress} = \frac{V_u}{\phi b_w d} \leq \frac{(V_c + V_s)\phi}{\phi b_w d}$$

This may be rewritten as

$$\text{shear stress} \leq \frac{V_c}{b_w d} + \frac{V_s}{b_w d}$$

Here, $V_c / b_w d$ may be considered to be the shear stress capacity of the concrete, and $V_s / b_w d$ may be considered to be the excess shear stress, over and above the concrete capacity, to be resisted by the web reinforcement.

The area contributing stress to be resisted by the web reinforcement is $1.414 s b_w$. Therefore, the diagonal force, as depicted in Figure 4-5, becomes

$$1.414 s b_w \left(\frac{V_s}{b_w d} \right)$$

The vertical component of this force becomes

$$0.707(1.414 s b_w)\left(\frac{V_s}{b_w d} \right) = s b_w \left(\frac{V_s}{b_w d} \right) = \frac{V_s s}{d}$$

Here $A_v f_y$ represents the ultimate tensile capacity of the stirrup. Since vertical equilibrium must exist,

$$A_v f_y = \frac{V_s s}{d}$$

from which

$$V_s = \frac{A_v f_y d}{s} \qquad\qquad \text{ACI Eq. (11-15)}$$

In a similar manner, it can be shown that for inclined stirrups at 45°,

$$V_s = \frac{1.414 A_v f_y d}{s}$$

from ACI Equation (11-16), where s is the horizontal center-to-center distance of stirrups parallel to the main longitudinal steel.

It will be more practical if ACI Equations (11-15) and (11-16) are rearranged as expressions for spacing, since the stirrup bar size, strength, and beam effective depth are usually predetermined. The design is then for stirrup spacing. For vertical stirrups,

$$\text{required } s = \frac{A_v f_y d}{V_s}$$

For 45° stirrups,

$$\text{required } s = \frac{1.414 A_v f_y d}{V_s}$$

Note that these two equations are for *maximum* spacing of stirrups based on *required strength*. The required nominal shear strength V_s may be determined from the factored applied shear (V_u) diagram and ACI Equations (11-1) and (11-2):

$$\phi V_c + \phi V_s \geq V_u$$

Therefore, as a limit,

$$\phi V_c + \phi V_s = V_u$$

from which

$$\text{required } \phi V_s = V_u - \phi V_c$$

4-3

SHEAR ANALYSIS PROCEDURE

The shear analysis procedure involves checking the shear strength in an existing member and verifying that the various code requirements have been satisfied. The member may be reinforced or plain.

Example 4-1

A reinforced concrete beam of rectangular cross section is reinforced for moment only (no shear reinforcement). Beam width $b = 18$ in., $d = 10.25$ in., and the reinforcing is five No. 4 bars. Calculate the maximum factored shear force V_u permitted on the member by the ACI Code. Use $f_c' = 4000$ psi and $f_y = 60,000$ psi.

Solution:

Since no shear reinforcement is provided, the ACI Code, Section 11.5.5.1, requires that

$$\text{maximum } V_u = \tfrac{1}{2}\phi V_c$$

$$= \tfrac{1}{2}\phi(2\sqrt{f_c'} b_w d)$$

$$= 0.5(0.85)(2)(\sqrt{4000})(18)(10.25)$$

$$= 9918 \text{ lb}$$

Example 4-2 _____

A reinforced concrete beam of rectangular cross section is reinforced with seven No. 6 bars in a single layer. Beam width $b = 18$ in., $d = 33$ in., single-loop No. 3 stirrups are placed 12 in. on center, and typical cover is $1\frac{1}{2}$ in. Find V_c, V_s, and the maximum factored shear force V_u permitted on this member. Use $f'_c = 4000$ psi and $f_y = 60,000$ psi.

Solution:

V_c and V_s will be expressed in units of kips.

$$V_c = 2\sqrt{f'_c}\,b_w d = \frac{2\sqrt{4,000}(18)(33)}{1000} = 75.1 \text{ kips}$$

$$V_s = \frac{A_v f_y d}{s} = \frac{2(0.11)(60)(33)}{12} = 36.3 \text{ kips}$$

$$\text{maximum } V_u = \phi V_c + \phi V_s = 0.85(75.1 + 36.3) = 94.7 \text{ kips}$$

_____

In the general case of shear analysis, one must ensure that at all locations in the member, $\phi V_c + \phi V_s \geqslant V_u$. In addition, all other details of the reinforcement pattern must be checked to ensure that they comply with code provisions. (Refer to "Notes on Stirrup Design" in Section 4.4.)

4-4
▬▬▬

STIRRUP DESIGN PROCEDURE

In the design of stirrups for shear reinforcement, the end result is a determination of stirrup size and spacing pattern. A *general procedure* may be adopted as follows:

1. Determine the shear values based on clear span and draw a shear (V_u) diagram.
2. Determine if stirrups are required.
3. Determine the length of span over which stirrups are required (assuming that stirrups *are* required.)
4. On the V_u diagram, determine the area representing "required ϕV_s." This will display the required strength of the stirrups to be provided.
5. Select the size of the stirrup. See item 2a in "Notes on Stirrup Design" below. Find the spacing required at the critical section (a distance d from the face of the support). See "Notes on Stirrup Design" item 3b below.
6. Establish the ACI Code maximum spacing requirements.

7.   Determine the spacing requirements based on shear strength to be furnished by web reinforcing.

8.   Establish the spacing pattern and show sketches.

Notes on Stirrup Design

1.   Materials and maximum stresses

   a.   To reduce excessive crack widths in beam webs subject to diagonal tension, the ACI Code, Section 11.5.2, limits the design yield strength of shear reinforcement to 60,000 psi. This increases to 80,000 psi for deformed welded wire fabric.

   b.   The value of V_s must not exceed $8\sqrt{f'_c}b_w d$ irrespective of the amount of web reinforcement (ACI Code, Section 11.5.6.8).

2.   Bar sizes for stirrups

   a.   The most common stirrup size used is a No. 3 bar. Under span and loading conditions where the shear values are relatively large, it may be necessary to use a No. 4 bar. Rarely is anything larger than a No. 4 bar stirrup ever required, however. In large beams, multiple stirrup sets are sometimes provided in which a diagonal crack would be crossed by four or more vertical bars at one location of a beam. Single-loop stirrups, as shown in Figure 4-4, are generally satisfactory for $b \leq 24$ in.; double-loop stirrups are satisfactory for 24 in. $< b \leq 48$ in.; and triple-loop stirrups are satisfactory for $b > 48$ in.

   b.   When single conventional loop stirrups are used, the web area A_v provided by each stirrup is twice the cross-sectional area of the bar (No. 3 bars, $A_v = 0.22$ in.^{2}; No. 4 bars, $A_v = 0.40$ in.^{2}) since each stirrup crosses a diagonal crack twice.

   c.   If possible, never vary the stirrup bar sizes; use the same bar sizes unless all other alternatives are not reasonable. Spacing should generally be varied and size held constant.

3.   Stirrup spacings

   a.   When stirrups are required, the maximum spacing for vertical stirrups must not exceed $d/2$ or 24 in., whichever is smaller (ACI Code, Section 11.5.4.1). If V_s exceeds $4\sqrt{f'_c}b_w d$, the maximum spacing must not exceed $d/4$ or 12 in., whichever is smaller (ACI Code, Section 11.5.4.3).

   b.   It is usually undesirable to space vertical stirrups closer than 4 in.

   c.   It is generally economical and practical to compute the spacing required at several sections and to place stirrups accordingly in groups of varying spacing. Spacing values should be made to not less than 1 in. increments.

   d.   The code stipulates that when the support reaction introduces a vertical compression into the end region of a member and no concentrated load occurs between the face of support and a distance d from the face of support, the maximum shear will be considered as that at the section a distance d from the face of support (except for brackets, short cantilevers, and special isolated conditions). For stirrup design, the section located a distance d from the face of the support is called the *critical section*. Sections located less than a distance d from the face of the support may be designed for the same V_u as that at the critical section. Therefore, stirrup spacing should be constant from the critical section back to the face of the support based on the spacing requirements *at* the critical section. The first stirrup should be placed at a maximum distance of $s/2$ from the face of the support, where s equals the immediately adjacent required stirrup spacing (a distance of 2 in. is commonly used). For the balance of the span, the stirrup spacing is a function of the shear strength required to be provided by the stirrups or the maximum spacing limitations.

e. The actual stirrup pattern used in the beam is the designer's choice. The choice will be governed by strength requirements and economy. Many patterns will satisfy the strength requirements. In most cases the shear decreases from the support to the center of the span, indicating that the stirrup spacing could be continually increased from the critical section up to the maximum spacing allowed by the code. This would create tedious design, detailing, and bar placing operations but would nevertheless result in the least steel used. This is not warranted economically or within the framework of the philosophy outlined in Appendix B. In the usual uniformly loaded beams, no more than two or three different spacings should be used within a pattern. Longer spans or concentrated loads may warrant more detailed spacing patterns.

Example 4-3

A simply supported rectangular concrete beam shown in Figure 4-6 is 16 in. wide and has an effective depth of 25 in. The beam supports a total factored load (w_u) of 11.5 kips/ft on a clear span of 20 ft. The given load includes the weight of the beam. Design the web reinforcement. Use $f'_c = 4000$ psi and $f_y = 60{,}000$ psi.

Solution:

1. Draw the shear force (V_u) diagram:

$$\text{maximum } V_u = \frac{w_u l}{2} = \frac{11.5(20)}{2} = 115.0 \text{ kips}$$

The quantities at the critical section (2.08 ft from face of support) are designated with an asterisk. Therefore,

$$V_u^* = 115.0 - 2.08(11.5) = 91.1 \text{ kips}$$

2. Determine if stirrups are required. The ACI Code, Section 11.5.5.1, requires that stirrups be supplied if $V_u > \frac{1}{2}\phi V_c$. Thus

FIGURE 4-6   Sketch for Example 4-3.

$$\phi V_c = \phi(2\sqrt{f'_c}b_w d) = 0.85\left[\frac{2\sqrt{4000}(16)(25)}{1000}\right] = 43.0 \text{ kips}$$

$$\tfrac{1}{2}\phi V_c = \tfrac{1}{2}(43.0) = 21.5 \text{ kips}$$

Therefore, since 91.1 kips > 21.5 kips, stirrups are required.

3.   Find the length of span over which stirrups are required. Since stirrups must be provided to the point where $V_u = \tfrac{1}{2}\phi V_c = 21.5$ kips, find where this shear exists on the V_u diagram of Fig. 4-6(c). From the face of support,

$$\frac{115.0 - 21.5}{11.5} = 8.13 \text{ ft}$$

Note this location on the V_u diagram as well as the location at 6.26 ft from the face of support, where $V_u = \phi V_c = 43.0$ kips.

4. Designate as "required ϕV_s" the area enclosed by the ϕV_c line, the V_u^* line, and the sloping V_u line. This shows the required strength of the shear reinforcing at any point along the span and graphically depicts the relationship

$$\phi V_c + \phi V_s \geqslant V_u$$

At any location, the required ϕV_s can be determined from the diagram as the distance between the V_u^* (or V_u) line and the ϕV_c line (the height of the cross-hatched area). For this particular V_u diagram, designating the slope (kips/ft) as m, taking x (ft) from the face of support, and considering the range $2.08 \text{ ft} \leqslant x \leqslant 6.26 \text{ ft}$ we have

$$\text{required } \phi V_s = \text{maximum } V_u - \phi V_c - mx$$

$$= 115.0 - 43.0 - 11.5x$$

$$= 72.0 - 11.5x$$

5. Assume a No. 3 vertical stirrup ($A_v = 0.22 \text{ in.}^2$) and establish the spacing requirement at the critical section based on the required ϕV_s. At this location, the stirrups will be most closely spaced. From ACI Equation (11-15),

$$\text{required } s^* = \frac{\phi A_v f_y d}{\text{required } \phi V_s^*} = \frac{0.85(0.22)(60)(25)}{91.1 - 43.0} = 5.83 \text{ in.}$$

(Note that the denominator in the preceding expression, required ϕV_s^*, is equal to $V_u^* - \phi V_c$.)

We will use a 5 in. spacing. This is the maximum spacing allowed in the portion of the beam between the face of support and the critical section, which lies a distance d from the face of support, and it is based on the amount of shear strength that must be provided by the shear reinforcing. Had the required spacing in this case turned out to be less than 4 in. (see item 3b in "Notes on Stirrup Design" in Section 4-4), a larger bar would have been selected for the stirrups.

6. Establish ACI Code maximum spacing requirements. Recall that if V_s at the critical section is less than $4\sqrt{f_c'}b_w d$, the maximum spacing is $d/2$ or 24 in., whichever is smaller. Therefore, compare V_s^* at the critical section with $4\sqrt{f_c'}b_w d$:

$$4\sqrt{f_c'}b_w d = \frac{4\sqrt{4000}(16)(25)}{1000} = 101.2 \text{ kips}$$

$$V_s^* = \frac{\phi V_s^*}{\phi} = \frac{91.1 - 43.0}{0.85} = 56.6 \text{ kips}$$

Since 56.6 kips < 101.2 kips, the maximum spacing should be the smaller of $d/2$ or 24 in.:

$$\frac{d}{2} = \frac{25}{2} = 12.5 \text{ in.} \qquad \text{Use 12 in.}$$

A second criterion is based on the code minimum area requirement (ACI Code, Section 11.5.5.3). ACI Equation (11-13) may be rewritten in the form

$$s_{max} = \frac{A_v f_y}{50 b_w} = \frac{0.22(60,000)}{50(16)} = 16.5 \text{ in.}$$

where the units of f_y should be carefully noted as psi.

Of the foregoing two maximum spacing criteria, the smaller value will control. Therefore, the 12 in. maximum spacing controls throughout the beam wherever stirrups are required.

7. Determine the spacing requirements based on shear strength to be furnished. At this point, we know that the spacing required at the critical section is 5.83 in. and that the maximum spacing allowed in this beam is 12 in. where stirrups are required.

To establish a spacing pattern for the rest of the beam, the spacing required should be established at various distances from the face of support. This will permit the placing of stirrups in groups, with each group having a different spacing. The number of locations at which the required spacing should be determined is based on judgment and should be a function of the shape of the required ϕV_s portion of the V_u diagram.

To aid in the determination of an acceptable spacing pattern, a plot is developed using the formula

$$\text{required } s = \frac{A_v f_y d}{\text{required } V_s} = \frac{\phi A_v f_y d}{\text{required } \phi V_s}$$

where the denominator can be determined from the expression given in step 4.

For plotting purposes, the required spacing will arbitrarily be found at 1 ft intervals beyond the critical section. At 3 ft from the face of support,

$$\text{required } s = \frac{\phi A_v f_y d}{\text{required } \phi V_s} = \frac{0.85(0.22)(60)(25)}{72.0 - 11.5(3)} = 7.48 \text{ in.}$$

Similarly, required spacing may be found at other points along the beam. The results of these calculations are tabulated and plotted in Figure 4-7. Note that required spacings need not be determined beyond the point where s_{max} (12 in.) has been exceeded.

8.   The plot of Figure 4-7 may be readily used to aid in establishing a final pattern. For example, the 7 in. spacing could be started about 2.75 ft from the face of support, and the maximum spacing of 12 in. could be started at about 4.25 ft from the face of support. The first stirrup will be placed away from the face of support a distance approximately equal to one-half the required spacing at the critical section. The rest of the stirrup pattern may be selected using an approach as shown in the following table.

Spacing (in.)	Theoretical stopping pt.	Length required to cover	Number of spaces to use	Actual length covered	Actual stopping point
2	—	—	1	2″	2″
5	2.75 = 33″	31″	7	35″	37″
7	4.25 = 51″	14″	2	14″	51″
12	120″	69″	5	60″	111″

The spacings and theoretical stopping points for those spacings are determined from Figure 4-7. The 5 in. spacing must run from the end of the 2 in. spacing (2 in. from face of support) to the theoretical stopping point for the 5 in. spacing (33 in.) Therefore, the 5 in. spacings must cover 31 in. For the 5 in. spacing, the required number of spaces is

x (ft)	Req'd s (in.)
3	7.48
4	10.78
5	19.34

FIGURE 4-7   Stirrup spacing requirements for Example 4-3.

FIGURE 4-8   Design sketch for Example 4-3.

$^{31}\!/_5 = 6.20$ spaces; use 7 spaces. This places the last stirrup in the 5 in. spacing group at 37 in. from the face of support. The final pattern for No. 3 single-loop stirrups is one at 2 in., seven at 5 in., two at 7 in., and five at 12 in. This pattern is shown in the design sketch of Figure 4-8. Note that the stirrups, at maximum spacing, have been run all the way to the center of the span. This is common practice and is conservative.

An alternative approach to stirrup spacing is to select a desired spacing (in this case between 5 in. and 12 in.) and to compute the distance from the face of support at which that spacing may begin. This can be accomplished by rewriting the expression

$$\text{required } s = \frac{\phi A_v f_y d}{\text{required } \phi V_s}$$

$$= \frac{\phi A_v f_y d}{(\max V_u - \phi V_c - mx)}$$

in the form

$$x = \frac{\max V_u - \phi V_c - \frac{\phi A_v f_y d}{s}}{m}$$

This expression will furnish the distance x at which any desired stirrup spacing s may commence. Returning to Example 4-3, we can compute where a 7 in. spacing may begin relative to the face of support,

$$x = \frac{115.0 - 43.0 - \frac{0.85(0.22)(60)(25)}{7}}{11.5} = 2.78 \text{ ft}$$

and 12 in. spacing may begin at

$$x = \frac{115.0 - 43.0 - \frac{0.85(0.22)(60)(25)}{12}}{11.5} = 4.23 \text{ ft}$$

Note that Figure 4-7 may be generated equally well with these data.

Example 4-4 _____

A continuous reinforced concrete beam shown in Figure 4-9 is 15 in. wide and has an effective depth of 31 in. The factored loads are shown. (The factored uniform load includes the weight of the beam.) Design the web reinforcement if $f_c' = 4000$ psi and $f_y = 60,000$ psi.

Solution:

1. The shear force (V_u) diagram is shown in Figure 4-10. (Because of symmetry, only the left half is shown.)

FIGURE 4-9   Sketch for Example 4-4.

FIGURE 4-10 V_u diagram for Example 4-4.

2.   Determine if stirrups are required:

$$\phi V_c = \phi 2\sqrt{f_c'}\, b_w d = \frac{0.85(2\sqrt{4000})(15)(31)}{1000} = 50.0 \text{ kips}$$

$$\tfrac{1}{2}\phi V_c = \tfrac{1}{2}(50.0) = 25.0 \text{ kips}$$

Therefore, since 104.9 kips > 25.0 kips, stirrups are required.

3.   Find the length of span over which stirrups are required. Stirrups are required to the point where

$$V_u = \tfrac{1}{2}\phi V_c = 25.0 \text{ kips}$$

From Figure 4-10, the point where V_u is equal to 25.0 kips may be determined by inspection to be at the concentrated load, 5 ft 0 in. from the face of support. No stirrups are required between the two concentrated loads.

4.   Designate "required ϕV_s" on the V_u diagram:

$$\text{required } \phi V_s = \text{maximum } V_u - \phi V_c - mx$$

$$= 107.5 - 50.0 - 1.0x$$

$$= 57.5 - 1.0x \qquad \text{(applies for the range } 2.58 \text{ ft} \leqslant x \leqslant 5.0 \text{ ft)}$$

5.   Assume a No. 3 vertical stirrup ($A_v = 0.22$ in.^{2}):

$$\text{required } s^* = \frac{\phi A_v f_y d}{\text{required } \phi V^*_s} = \frac{0.85(0.22)(60)(31)}{104.9 - 50.0} = 6.3 \text{ in.}$$

Use 6 in.

6.   Establish ACI Code maximum spacing requirements:

$$4\sqrt{f'_c}b_w d = \frac{4\sqrt{4000}(15)(31)}{1000} = 117.6 \text{ kips}$$

$$V^*_s = \frac{\phi V^*_s}{\phi} = \frac{104.9 - 50.0}{0.85} = 64.6 \text{ kips}$$

Since 64.6 kips < 117.6 kips, the maximum spacing should be the smaller of $d/2$ or 24 in.:

$$\frac{d}{2} = \frac{31}{2} = 15.5 \text{ in.}$$

Also check s_{max}:

$$s_{max} = \frac{A_v f_y}{50 b_w} = \frac{0.22(60,000)}{50(15)} = 17.6 \text{ in.}$$

Therefore, use a maximum spacing of 15 in.

7.   Determine the spacing requirements between the critical section and the concentrated load based on shear strength to be furnished. The denominator of the following formula for required spacing uses the expression for required V_s from step 4:

$$\text{required } s = \frac{\phi A_v f_y d}{\text{required } \phi V_s} = \frac{0.85(0.22)(60)(31)}{57.5 - 1.0x}$$

The results of these calculations are tabulated and plotted in Figure 4-11.

x (ft)	Req'd s (in.)
3	6.4
4	6.5
5	6.6

FIGURE 4-11   Stirrup spacing requirements for Example 4-4.

FIGURE 4-12   Design sketches for Example 4-4.

8.   Since no stirrups are required in the distance between the concentrated
loads, it is apparent with reference to Figure 4-11 that the maximum
spacing of 15 in. need not be used in that distance. A spacing of 6 in. will
be used between the face of the support and the concentrated load. The
center portion of the beam will be reinforced with stirrups at a spacing
slightly less than the maximum spacing as a conservative measure and
to create a convenient spacing pattern. The design sketches are shown in
Figure 4-12. Note the symmetry about the span centerline.

4-5

TORSION: INTRODUCTION

Torsion occurs when a member is loaded so that it twists about its longitudinal axis.
This is easily visualized in machines, for instance in the transmission of power
through shafts as is found in electric motors and automotive drivetrains. Structural
members found in buildings may also be subjected to torsional loads. Perhaps the
most common situation is that of the spandrel girder in Figure 4-13.

Beam B-1 frames into the spandrel girder as shown in Figure 4-13a. In Figure
4-13b it is seen that some moment is developed at the supports of beam B-1 as a

FIGURE 4-13   Torsion in beams.

result of their rigidity. The moment developed at the left end of beam B-1 becomes a torsional load on the spandrel girder.

Torsion in noncircular members produces complex behavior in which the member cross section will warp as it twists. Torsional shear will be created in the faces of the member and will tend to produce diagonal tension cracks similar to those produced by flexural shear. The torsional shear will be in opposite directions on opposite sides of the member, however. Since shear and torsion normally occur simultaneously (or interact) within a member, the diagonal tension effects will be additive on one of the faces. When this occurs and when the tensile strength of the concrete is exceeded, a failure at approximately 45° to the horizontal will be initiated, as can be observed in Figure 4-14. Obviously, steel must be introduced to cross any crack that forms so as to prevent a failure. The torsional failure occurring on a warped section may also be observed by twisting a piece of chalk to fracture.

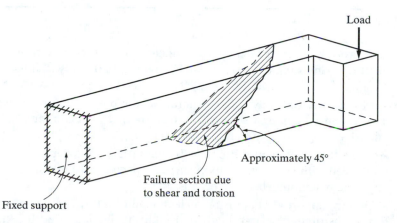

FIGURE 4-14   Beam failure due to combined shear and torsion.

4-6

DESIGN OF TORSION REINFORCEMENT

An approach to the design of torsion reinforcement is furnished in Chapter 11 of the ACI Code (ACI 318-95). The code stipulates in Section 11.6.3.8 that "reinforcement required for torsion shall be added to that required for the shear, moment and axial force that act in combination with the torsion. The most restrictive requirements for reinforcement spacing and placement must be met."

The ACI Code permits the neglect of torsion effects when the factored torsional moment T_u is less than a specified torque limit, which is dependent on concrete strength, the area of the member, and the perimeter of the member. The limit is set at approximately one-quarter of the cracking torque. If T_u does not exceed this limit, it will not cause a structurally significant reduction in either the flexural or shear strength and can therefore be ignored.

Once it is shown that torsion must be included as part of the design, all torsion is assumed to be resisted by closed stirrups and longitudinal steel located near the surface of the member. Under ACI 318-95, the design for torsion is based on a thin-walled tube, space-truss analogy. The basic design expression for torsion is

$$\phi T_n \geqslant T_u \qquad\qquad \text{ACI Eq. (11-20)}$$

Nominal torsional moment strength as well as the requirement for additional longitudinal reinforcement required for torsion may be evaluated using expressions found in the ACI Code, Section 11.6.3. The required details for torsional reinforcement are discussed in Sections 11.6.4 through 11.6.6 of the code.

Since torsional considerations are not common in the analysis and design of traditional reinforced concrete structures, it is the authors' opinion that rigorous treatment of torsion is beyond the scope of this book. The reader is referred to more theoretical texts for design examples and extensive theoretical discussions.

PROBLEMS

4-1. A reinforced concrete beam of rectangular cross section is reinforced for moment only and subjected to a shear V_u of 9000 lb. Beam width $b = 12$ in., $d = 7.25$ in., $f'_c = 3000$ psi, and $f_y = 60,000$ psi. Is the beam satisfactory for shear?

4-2. An 8-in.-thick one-way slab is reinforced for positive moment with No. 6 bars at 6 in. on center. Cover is 1 in. Determine the maximum shear V_u permitted. Use $f'_c = 4000$ psi and $f_y = 60,000$ psi.

4-3. Assume that the beam of Problem 4-1 has an effective depth of 18 in. and is reinforced with No. 3 single-loop stirrups spaced at 10 in. on center. Determine the maximum shear V_u permissible.

4-4. A simply supported beam is on a clear span of 30 ft. The beam carries uniformly distributed service loads of 1.9 kips/ft live load and 0.7 kip/ft dead load (excluding the weight of the beam). Additionally, the beam carries two concentrated service loads of 8 kips dead load each, one load being placed 5 ft in from the face of each support. The beam is reinforced with No. 3 single-loop stirrups placed in the following pattern, starting at the face of the support (symmetry about midspan): one space at 2 in., five spaces at 8 in., four spaces at 10 in., and eight spaces at 12 in. Beam width $b = 15$ in., $h = 28$ in., and $d = 25.4$ in. Use $f'_c = 4000$ psi and $f_y = 60,000$ psi.

(a) Draw an elevation view of the beam showing the stirrup layout.

(b) Draw the V_u diagram.

(c) Calculate $\phi(V_c + V_s)$ for each spacing group (omit the 2 in. spacing).

(d) Superimpose the results from part (c) on the V_u diagram and comment on the results.

4-5. A uniformly loaded beam is subjected to a shear V_u of 60 kips at the face of the support. Clear span is 32 ft. Beam width $b = 12$ in., $d = 22$ in., $f'_c = 4000$ psi, and $f_y = 60,000$ psi. Determine the maximum spacing allowed for No. 3 single-loop stirrups at the critical section.

4-6. A simply supported beam carries a total factored load w_u of 5.0 kips/ft. The span length is 28 ft center to center of supports, and the supports are 12 in. wide. Beam width $b = 14$ in., $d = 20$ in., $f'_c = 4000$ psi, and $f_y = 60,000$ psi. Determine spacings required for No. 3 stirrups and show the pattern with a sketch. (Recall that clear span is used for determining shears.)

4-7. A simply supported rectangular reinforced concrete beam, 13 in. wide and having an effective depth of 20 in., supports a total factored load (w_u) of 4.5 kips/ft on a 30 ft clear span. (The given load includes the weight of the beam.) Design the web reinforcement if $f'_c = 3000$ psi and $f_y = 40,000$ psi.

4-8. A rectangular reinforced concrete beam supports a total factored load (w_u) of 10 kips/ft on a simple clear span of 40 ft. (The given load includes the weight of the beam.) The effective depth $d = 40$ in., $b = 24$ in., $f'_c = 3000$ psi, and $f_y = 60,000$ psi. Design double-loop No. 3 stirrups.

4-9. Design stirrups for the beam shown. The supports are 12 in. wide, and the loads shown are service loads. The dead load includes the weight of the beam. Beam width $b = 16$ in., $d = 20$ in., $f'_c = 4000$ psi, and $f_y = 60,000$ psi. Sketch the stirrup pattern.

PROBLEM 4-9

4-10. For the beam shown, check moment and design single-loop stirrups. The loads shown are factored loads. Assume the supports to be 12 in. wide. Use

$f'_c = 3000$ psi and $f_y = 60,000$ psi. The uniformly distributed load includes the beam weight.

PROBLEM 4-10

4-11. Design stirrups for the beam shown. Service loads are 1.5 kips/ft dead load (includes beam weight) and 1.9 kips/ft live load. The supports are 12 in. wide. Beam width $b = 13$ in. and $d = 24$ in. for both top and bottom steel. Use $f'_c = 3000$ psi and $f_y = 60,000$ psi. Sketch the stirrup arrangement.

PROBLEM 4-11

4-12. Design stirrups for the beam shown. The supports are 12 in. wide, and the loads shown are factored design loads. The dead load includes the weight of the beam. Beam width $b = 14$ in., $d = 24$ in., $f'_c = 3000$ psi, and $f_y = 60,000$ psi. Sketch the stirrup pattern.

PROBLEM 4-12

4-13. The beam shown is supported on pedestals 20 in. wide. The loads are service loads, and the distributed load includes the beam weight. The clear span is 24'-4". Use $f_c' = 4000$ psi; the reinforcing is A615 grade 60 steel. Design shear reinforcing for the beam:

(a) Between the point load and the left reaction

(b) Between the point load and the right reaction

Show design sketches, including the stirrup pattern.

Section A–A

PROBLEM 4-13

4-14. Design the rectangular reinforced concrete beam for *moment and shear.* Use only tension steel for flexure. The loads shown are service loads. The uniform load is composed of 1 kip/ft dead load (does not include beam weight) and 1 kip/ft live load. The concentrated loads are dead load. Assume the supports to be 12 in. wide. Use $f_c' = 4000$ psi and $f_y = 60,000$ psi. Show design sketches, including the stirrup pattern.

PROBLEM 4-14

CHAPTER 5

Development, Splices, and Simple-Span Bar Cutoffs

5-1

DEVELOPMENT LENGTH: INTRODUCTION

One of the fundamental assumptions of reinforced concrete design is that at the interface of the concrete and the steel bars, perfect bonding exists and no slippage occurs. Based on this assumption, it follows that some form of bond stress exists at the contact surface between the concrete and the steel bars. In beams, this bond stress is caused by the change in bending moment along the length of the beam and the accompanying change in the tensile stress in the bars and has historically been

PHOTO 5-1   90° bends for development of No. 18 bars. Seabrook Station, New Hampshire.

termed *flexural bond.* The actual distribution of bond stresses along the reinforcing steel is highly complex, due primarily to the presence of concrete cracks. Research has indicated that large local variations in bond stress are caused by flexural and diagonal cracks, and very high bond stresses have been measured adjacent to these cracks. These high bond stresses may result in small local slips adjacent to the cracks, with resultant widening of cracks as well as increased deflections. Generally, this will be harmless as long as failure does not propagate all along the bar with resultant complete loss of bond. It is possible, if *end anchorage* is reliable, that the bond can be severed along the entire length of bar, excluding the anchorage, without endangering the carrying capacity of the beam. The resulting behavior is similar to that of a tied arch.

End anchorage may be considered reliable if the bar is embedded into concrete a prescribed distance known as the *development length,* ℓ_d, of the bar. If in the beam the actual extended length of a bar is equal to or greater than this required development length, no premature bond failure will occur. That is, the predicted strength of the beam will not be controlled by bond but rather by some other factor.

Hence the main requirement for safety against bond failure is that the length of the bar from any point of given steel stress f_s (or, as a maximum, f_y) to its nearby free end must be at least equal to its development length. If this requirement is satisfied, the magnitude of the flexural bond stress along the beam is of only secondary importance, since the integrity of the member is assured even in the face of possible minor local failures. If the actual available length is inadequate for full development, however, special anchorages, such as hooks, must be provided to ensure adequate strength.

Current design methods based on the ACI Code (318-95) disregard high localized bond stress even though it may result in localized slip between steel and concrete adjacent to the cracks. Instead, attention is directed toward providing adequate length of embedment, past the location at which the bar is fully stressed, which will ensure development of the full strength of the bar.

5-2

DEVELOPMENT LENGTH: TENSION BARS

The ACI Code, Section 12.2.1, specifies that the development length ℓ_d for deformed bars and deformed wires in tension shall be determined using either the tabular criteria of Section 12.2.2 or the general equation of Section 12.2.3, but in either case, ℓ_d shall not be less than 12 in.

The general equation of Section 12.2.3 (ACI Equation 12-1) offers a simple approach that allows the user to see the effect of all variables controlling the development length. The tabular criteria of Section 12.2.2 also offer a simple, conservative approach that recognizes commonly used practical construction situations. Based on a sampling of numerous problems, the authors have found that significantly shorter development lengths are computed using ACI Equation (12-1) of Section 12.2.3. These development lengths were found to compare favorably with the computed ℓ_d values that resulted using the previous ACI 318-89 Code.

Therefore, the development length ℓ_d computation used in this text will be based on ACI Equation (12-1). This equation, when rearranged to solve for ℓ_d, becomes

$$\ell_d = \frac{3}{40}\left(\frac{f_y}{\sqrt{f_c'}}\right)\left[\frac{\alpha\beta\gamma\lambda}{\left(\dfrac{c + K_{TR}}{d_b}\right)}\right]d_b$$

in which the term $(c + K_{TR})/d_b$ shall not be taken greater than 2.5 and where

ℓ_d = development length (in.)

f_y = specified yield strength of nonprestressed reinforcement (psi)

f_c' = specified compressive strength of concrete (psi); the value of $\sqrt{f_c'}$ shall not exceed 100 psi (ACI Code, Section 12.1.2)

d_b = nominal diameter of bar or wire (in.)

The other variables used in Equation (12-1) are defined as follows:

1. Alpha (α) is a reinforcement location factor that accounts for position of the reinforcement in freshly placed concrete.

    Where horizontal reinforcement is so placed that more than 12 in. of fresh concrete is cast in the member below the development length or splice, use $\alpha = 1.3$ (ACI Code, Section 12.2.4.) This is because this condition lends itself to the formation of entrapped air and moisture on the underside of the bars, resulting in partial loss of bond between the concrete and steel.

    For other reinforcement, use $\alpha = 1.0$.

2. Beta (β) is a coating factor reflecting the effects of epoxy coating. Studies of the anchorage of epoxy-coated bars show that bond strength is reduced because the coating prevents adhesion and friction between the bar and the concrete.

    For epoxy-coated reinforcement having cover less than $3d_b$ or clear spacing between bars less than $6d_b$, use $\beta = 1.5$.

    For all other conditions, use $\beta = 1.2$.

    For uncoated reinforcement, use $\beta = 1.0$.

    The product of α and β need not be taken greater than 1.7 (ACI Code, Section 12.2.4.)

3. Gamma (γ) is a reinforcement size factor.

    Where No. 6 and smaller bars are used, use $\gamma = 0.8$.

    Where No. 7 and larger bars are used, use $\gamma = 1.0$

4. Lambda (λ) is a lightweight-aggregate concrete factor.

    For lightweight-aggregate concrete when the average splitting tensile strength f_{ct} is not specified, use $\lambda = 1.3$.

    When f_{ct} is specified, use

    $$\lambda = 6.7 \, \frac{\sqrt{f_c'}}{f_{ct}} \geq 1.0$$

    When normal weight concrete is used, use $\lambda = 1.0$ (ACI Code, Section 12.2.4.)

5. The variable c represents a spacing or cover dimension (in.)

    The value of c will be the smaller of either the distance from the center of the bar to the nearest concrete surface (cover) or one-half the center-to-center spacing of the bars being developed (spacing).

    The bar spacing will be the actual center-to-center spacing between the bars if adjacent bars are all being developed at the same location. If, however, an adjacent bar has been developed at another location, the spacing to be used will be greater than the actual spacing to the adjacent bar. Note in Figure 5-1 that the spacing for bars Y may be taken the same as for bars X, since bars Y are developed in length AB, whereas bars X are developed at a location other than AB.

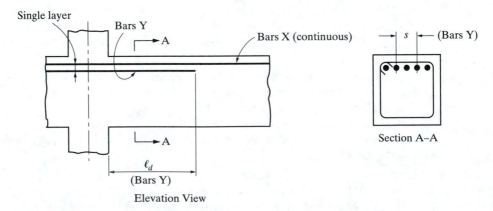

FIGURE 5-1 Spacing criteria for bars being developed.

6.   The transverse reinforcement index K_{TR} is computed from

$$\frac{A_{TR}f_{yt}}{1500sn}$$

where

A_{TR} = total cross-sectional area of all transverse reinforcement that is within the spacing s and that crosses the potential plane of splitting through the reinforcement being developed (in.^{2})

f_{yt} = specified yield strength of transverse reinforcement (psi)

s = maximum center-to-center spacing of transverse reinforcement within ℓ_d (in.)

n = number of bars or wires being developed along the plane of splitting

To simplify the design, the ACI Code permits the use of $K_{TR} = 0$. This is conservative and may be used even if transverse reinforcement is present.

To further simplify development length computations, we designate a portion of ACI Equation (12-1) as K_D, where

$$K_D = \frac{3}{40}\frac{f_y}{\sqrt{f_c'}}$$

Values of K_D as a function of various combinations of f_y and f_c' are tabulated in Table 5-1.

A reduction in the development length ℓ_d is permitted where reinforcement is in excess of that required by analysis (except where anchorage or development for f_y is specifically required or where the design includes provisions for seismic considerations). We designate this reduction factor as K_{ER}. Excess reinforcement factor K_{ER} does not apply for development of positive moment reinforcement at supports (ACI Code, Section 12.11.2) or for development of shrinkage and temperature reinforcement (ACI Code, Section 7.12.2.3).

■■■■■ **TABLE 5-1   Coefficient K_D for ACI Code Equation (12-1)**

$K_D = \dfrac{3}{40}\dfrac{f_y}{\sqrt{f_c'}}$				
f_c' (psi)	$f_y = 40{,}000$ psi	$f_y = 50{,}000$ psi	$f_y = 60{,}000$ psi	$f_y = 75{,}000$ psi
3000	54.8	68.5	82.2	102.7
4000	47.4	59.3	71.2	88.9
5000	42.4	53.0	63.6	79.5
6000	38.7	48.4	58.1	72.6

Although K_{ER} is not reflected in ACI Equation (12-1), it may be calculated from

$$K_{ER} = \frac{A_s \text{ required}}{A_s \text{ provided}}$$

and subsequently applied to the ℓ_d computed from ACI Equation (12-1).

When bundled bars are used, the ACI Code, Section 12.4, stipulates that calculated development lengths are to be made for individual bars within a bundle (either in tension or compression) and then increased by 20% for three-bar bundles and by 33% for four-bar bundles. Bundled bars consist of a group of not more than four parallel reinforcing bars in contact with each other and assumed to act as a unit. For determining the appropriate factors as discussed previously, a unit of bundled bars shall be treated as a single bar of a diameter derived from the equivalent total area. Additional criteria for bundled bars are furnished in the ACI Code, Section 7.6.6.

Summary of Procedures for Calculation of ℓ_d [Using ACI Equation (12-1)]

1. Determine K_D from Table 5-1.
2. Determine multiplying factors (use 1.0 unless otherwise determined).
    a. Use $\alpha = 1.3$ for top reinforcement, when applicable.
    b. Coating factor β applies to epoxy-coated bars. Determine cover and clear spacing as multiples of d_b. Use $\beta = 1.5$ if cover $< 3d_b$ or clear space $< 6d_b$. Use $\beta = 1.2$ otherwise.
    c. Use $\gamma = 0.8$ for No. 6 bars and smaller.
    d. Use $\lambda = 1.3$ for lightweight concrete with f_{ct} not specified. Use $\lambda = 6.7 \sqrt{f_c'}/f_{ct} \geq 1.0$ for lightweight concrete with f_{ct} specified.
3. Check $\alpha\beta \leq 1.7$.
4. Determine c, the smaller of cover or half-spacing (both referenced to the center of the bar).
5. Calculate $K_{TR} = A_{TR}f_{yt}/(1500sn)$, or use $K_{TR} = 0$ (conservative).
6. Check $(c + K_{TR})/d_b \leq 2.5$.
7. Calculate K_{ER} if applicable:

$$K_{ER} = \frac{A_s \text{ required}}{A_s \text{ provided}}$$

8. Calculate ℓ_d:

$$\ell_d = K_D \left[\frac{\alpha\beta\gamma\lambda}{\left(\dfrac{c + K_{TR}}{d_b} \right)} \right] K_{ER} d_b \geq 12 \text{ in.}$$

Example 5-1

Calculate the development length ℓ_d required for No. 8 top bars in tension (more than 12 in. of fresh concrete to be cast below the bars) in a lightweight-aggregate concrete beam. The clear cover is 2 in., and the clear space between bars is 3 in. Use $f_y = 60,000$ psi and $f_c' = 4000$ psi. Stirrups are No. 4 bars.

Solution:

Use ACI (Equation (12-1) and follow the procedural outline that precedes this example.

1.   From Table 5-1, $K_D = 71.2$.
2.   Establish values for the multiplying factors α, β, γ, and λ.
     a. $\alpha = 1.3$ (the bars are top bars).
     b.   The bars are uncoated ("black steel"). $\beta = 1.0$.
     c.   The bars are No. 8. $\gamma = 1.0$.
     d.   Lightweight-aggregate concrete is used. $\lambda = 1.3$.
3.   The product $\alpha \times \beta = 1.3 < 1.7$. (O.K.)
4.   Determine c. Based on cover (center of bar to nearest concrete surface): Consider the clear cover, the No. 4 stirrup diameter and one-half the diameter of the No. 8 bar:

$$c = 2 + 0.5 + 0.5 = 3.0 \text{ in.}$$

Based on bar spacing (one-half the center-to-center distance):

$$c = 0.5[3 + 2(0.5)] = 2.0 \text{ in.}$$

Therefore, use $c = 2.0$ in.

5. K_{TR} may be conservatively taken as zero.
6.   Check $(c + K_{TR})/d_b \leqslant 2.5$:

$$\frac{c + K_{TR}}{d_b} = \frac{2.0 + 0}{1.0} = 2.0 < 2.5 \qquad \text{(O.K.)}$$

7.   The excess reinforcement factor is not applicable and is omitted.
8.   Calculate ℓ_d:

$$\ell_d = K_D \left[\frac{\alpha\beta\gamma\lambda}{\left(\dfrac{c + K_{TR}}{d_b} \right)} \right] d_b$$

$$= 71.2 \left[\frac{1.3(1.0)(1.0)(1.3)}{2.0} \right] (1.0) = 60.2 \text{ in.} > 12 \text{ in.} \qquad \text{(O.K.)}$$

Example 5-2

Calculate the development length required for the No. 9 bars in the top of a 15-in.-thick reinforced concrete slab (see Figure 5-2). Note that these bars are the tension reinforcement for negative moment in the slab at the supporting beam. Since this is a slab, no stirrups are used. Use f_y = 60,000 psi and f_c' = 4000 psi (normal-weight concrete.)

Solution:

1. From Table 5-1, K_D = 71.2.
2. Establish values for the multiplying factors α, β, γ, and λ.
    a. α = 1.3 (the bars are top bars).
    b. The bars are uncoated ("black steel"). β = 1.0.
    c. The bars are No. 9. γ = 1.0.
    d. Normal-weight concrete is used. λ = 1.0.
3. The product $\alpha \times \beta$ = 1.3 < 1.7. (O.K.)
4. Determine c. Based on cover (center of bar to nearest concrete surface): Consider the clear cover and one-half the diameter of the No. 9 bar:

$$c = 0.75 + \frac{1.128}{2} = 1.314 \text{ in.}$$

Based on bar spacing (one-half the center-to-center distance):

$$c = 0.5(8.0) = 4.0 \text{ in.}$$

Section A–A

FIGURE 5-2   Sketch for Example 5-2.

Therefore, use $c = 1.314$ in.

5. K_{TR} is taken as zero. (There is no transverse reinforcement crossing the plane of splitting.)

6.   Check $(c + K_{TR})/d_b \leqslant 2.5$:

$$\frac{c + K_{TR}}{d_b} = \frac{1.314 + 0}{1.128} = 1.165 < 2.5 \qquad \text{(O.K.)}$$

7.   The excess reinforcement factor is not applicable and is omitted.

8.   Calculate ℓ_d:

$$\ell_d = K_D \left[\frac{\alpha\beta\gamma\lambda}{\left(\dfrac{c + K_{TR}}{d_b}\right)} \right] d_b$$

$$= 71.2 \left[\frac{1.3(1.0)(1.0)(1.0)}{1.165} \right](1.128) = 89.6 \text{ in.} > 12 \text{ in.} \qquad \text{(O.K.)}$$

Example 5-3

Calculate the development length required for the interior two No. 7 bars in the beam shown in Figure 5-3. The two No. 7 outside bars are continuous for the full length of the beam. Use $f_y = 60{,}000$ psi and $f'_c = 4000$ psi (normal-weight concrete.)

Solution:

1.   From Table 5-1, $K_D = 71.2$.

2.   Establish values for the multiplying factors α, β, γ, and λ.

     a. $\alpha = 1.3$ (the bars are top bars).

     b.   The bars are uncoated ("black steel"). $\beta = 1.0$.

FIGURE 5-3   Sketch for Example 5-3.

    c.   The bars are No. 7. $\gamma = 1.0$.

    d.   Normal-weight concrete is used. $\lambda = 1.0$.

3.   The product $\alpha \times \beta = 1.3 < 1.7$. (O.K.)

4.   Determine c. Based on cover (center of bar to nearest concrete surface): Consider the clear cover, the No. 4 stirrup diameter, and one-half the diameter of the No. 7 bar:

$$c = 1.5 + 0.5 + \frac{0.875}{2} = 2.44 \text{ in.}$$

Based on bar spacing (one-half the center-to-center distance):

$$c = \frac{13 - 2(1.5) - 2(0.5) - 2\left(\dfrac{0.875}{2}\right)}{3(2)} = 1.355 \text{ in.}$$

Therefore, use $c = 1.355$ in.

5.   Using data on stirrups from Figure 5-3:

$$K_{TR} = \frac{A_{TR}f_{yt}}{1500sn} = \frac{0.40(60,000)}{1500(6)(2)} = 1.333$$

6.   Check $(c + K_{TR})/d_b \leqslant 2.5$:

$$\frac{c + K_{TR}}{d_b} = \frac{1.355 + 1.333}{0.875} = 3.07 > 2.5$$

Therefore, use 2.5.

7.   The excess reinforcement factor is not applicable and is omitted.

8.   Calculate ℓ_d:

$$\ell_d = K_D \left[\frac{\alpha\beta\gamma\lambda}{\left(\dfrac{c + K_{TR}}{d_b}\right)} \right] d_b$$

$$= 71.2 \left[\frac{1.3(1.0)(1.0)(1.0)}{2.5} \right](0.875) = 32.4 \text{ in.} > 12 \text{ in.} \quad \text{(O.K.)}$$

5-3

DEVELOPMENT LENGTH: COMPRESSION BARS

For deformed bars in compression, ℓ_d is computed as the product of the basic development length ℓ_{db} and applicable modification factors and shall not be less than 8 in. The modification factors reflect special conditions. The basic development length is computed as follows:

$$\ell_{db} = 0.02d_b\frac{f_y}{\sqrt{f_c'}}$$

but not less than $0.0003f_yd_b$, according to the ACI Code, Section 12.3 (see Table A-12). The following modification factors may be applied to the basic development length for compression bars:

1.   Reinforcement in excess of that required:

$$\frac{A_s \text{ required}}{A_s \text{ provided}}$$

2.   Bars enclosed within a spiral that is not less than ¼ in. in diameter and not more than 4 in. in pitch or within No. 4 ties in conformance with ACI Section 7.10.5 and spaced at not more than 4 in. on center: Use 0.75.

In summary, a bar must have sufficient anchorage or development length so that the bar can develop its capacity in tension or compression. This is the same as saying that the point of maximum stress can be no closer to the end of the bar than the calculated ℓ_d value.

5-4

DEVELOPMENT LENGTH: STANDARD HOOKS IN TENSION

In the event that the desired development length in tension cannot be furnished, it is necessary to provide mechanical anchorage at the end of the bars. Although the ACI Code (Section 12.6) allows any mechanical device to serve as anchorage if its adequacy is verified by test, anchorage for main or primary reinforcement is usually accomplished by means of a 90° or 180° hook. The dimensions and bend radii for these hooks have been standardized by the ACI Code. Additionally, 90° and 135° hooks have been standardized for stirrups and tie reinforcement. Hooks in compression bars are ineffective and cannot be used as anchorage. Standard reinforcement hooks are shown in Figure 5-4. The bend diameters are measured on the inside of the bar.

The ACI Code, Section 12.5, specifies that the development length ℓ_{dh} (see Figure 5-4) for deformed bars in tension, which terminate in a standard hook, be computed as the product of a basic development length ℓ_{hb} and any applicable modification factors. Mathematically, this may be stated as

$$\ell_{dh} = \ell_{hb} \times \text{MF}$$

FIGURE 5-4   ACI standard hooks.

A.   *Basic development length* (ℓ_{hb})
For a hooked bar with $f_y = 60{,}000$ psi,

$$\ell_{hb} = \frac{1200d_b}{\sqrt{f_c'}}$$

Table A-13 contains values of ℓ_{hb}.

B.   *Modification factors* (to be used if applicable)
1.   Bars with f_y other than 60,000 psi: Use $f_y/60{,}000$.
2.   Concrete cover for No. 3 through No. 11: Side cover (normal to the plane of the hook) $\geqslant 2\frac{1}{2}$ in. and, for 90° hooks, cover on bar extension beyond the bend $\geqslant 2$ in.: Use 0.7.
3.   Ties or stirrups: For Nos. 3 through 11 with the hook enclosed vertically

or horizontally within ties or stirrup ties spaced along the full development length ℓ_{dh} not greater than $3d_b$: Use 0.8.

4. Reinforcement in excess of that required, where anchorage or development for f_y is not specifically required:

$$\frac{A_s \text{ required}}{A_s \text{ provided}}$$

5. Lightweight aggregate concrete: Use 1.3.

6. Epoxy-coated reinforcement: Use 1.2.

The basic development length (ℓ_{hb}) in part A must be modified by the applicable factors of part B. In no case may ℓ_{dh} be less than $8d_b$ or 6 in., whichever is greater.

In addition, the ACI Code, Section 12.5.4, establishes criteria for hooked bars that terminate at the discontinuous ends of members such as simply supported beams, free ends of cantilevers, and ends of members that frame into a joint where the member does not extend beyond the joint. If the full strength (f_y) of the hooked bar must be developed and if both the side cover and the top (or bottom) cover over the hook are less than $2\frac{1}{2}$ in., closed ties or stirrups spaced at $3d_b$ maximum are required over the development length ℓ_{dh}. This does not apply to the discontinuous ends of slabs with concrete confinement provided by the slab continuous on both sides perpendicular to the plane of the hook. Also, the 0.8 MF of preceding item 3 does not apply.

Example 5-4 _____

Determine the anchorage or development length required for the conditions shown in Figure 5-5. Use $f'_c = 3000$ psi (normal-weight concrete) and

FIGURE 5-5   Sketch for Example 5-4.

f_y = 60,000 psi. The No. 8 bars may be categorized as top bars. Assume a side cover on the main bars of 2½ in. minimum.

Solution:

A. Anchorage into the exterior column

1. From Table 5-1, K_D = 82.2
2. Establish values for the multiplying factors α, β, γ, and λ.
    a. α = 1.3 (the bars are top bars).
    b.   The bars are uncoated ("black steel"). β = 1.0.
    c.   The bars are No. 8. γ = 1.0.
    d.   Normal-weight concrete is used. λ = 1.0.
3. The product $\alpha \times \beta$ = 1.3 < 1.7. (O.K.)
4. Determine c. Based on cover (center of bar to nearest concrete surface): Consider the clear cover, the No. 4 stirrup diameter, and one-half the diameter of the No. 8 bar:

$$c = 2.0 + 0.5 + \frac{1.0}{2} = 3.0 \text{ in.}$$

Based on bar spacing (one-half the center-to-center distance):

$$c = \frac{14 - 2(2.0) - 2(0.5) - 2(0.50)}{2(2)} = 2.0 \text{ in.}$$

Therefore, use c = 2.0 in.

5. Using data on stirrups from Figure 5-5,

$$K_{TR} = \frac{A_{TR}f_{yt}}{1500sn} = \frac{0.40(60,000)}{1500(5)(3)} = 1.067$$

6. Check $(c + K_{TR})/d_b \leq 2.5$:

$$\frac{c + K_{TR}}{d_b} = \frac{2.0 + 1.067}{1.0} = 3.07 > 2.5$$

Therefore, use 2.5.

7. The excess reinforcement factor is not applicable and is omitted.
8. Calculate ℓ_d:

$$\ell_d = K_D \left[\frac{\alpha\beta\gamma\lambda}{\left(\dfrac{c + K_{TR}}{d_b} \right)} \right] d_b$$

$$= 82.2 \left[\frac{1.3(1.0)(1.0)(1.0)}{2.5} \right] (1.0) = 42.7 \text{ in.} > 12 \text{ in.} \qquad \text{(O.K.)}$$

FIGURE 5-6   Sketch for Example 5-4.

Since 42.7 in. > 24 in. column width, use a standard hook, either a 90°
hook or a 180° hook.

B. Anchorage using a standard 180° hook

1.   The basic development length ℓ_{hb} for the standard hook shown in Fig-
     ure 5-6 is calculated from

$$\ell_{hb} = \frac{1200d_b}{\sqrt{f_c'}} = \frac{1200(1.0)}{\sqrt{3000}} = 21.9 \text{ in.}$$

(Check this with Table A-13.)

2.   The only applicable modification factor is based on side cover (normal
     to the plane of the hook) of 2½ in. Use an MF of 0.7 (ACI Code Section
     12.5.3.2).

3.   The required development length is then calculated from

$$\ell_{dh} = \ell_{hb} \times \text{MF} = 21.9(0.7) = 15.3 \text{ in.}$$

Check minimum:

$$\text{minimum } \ell_{dh} = 8d_b \geqslant 6 \text{ in.}$$

$$8d_b = 8 \text{ in.} < 15.3 \text{ in.} \qquad\qquad \text{(O.K.)}$$

The minimum width of column required is

$$15.3 + 2.5 = 17.8 \text{ in.} < 24 \text{ in.} \qquad\qquad \text{(O.K.)}$$

Therefore, the hook will fit into the column and the detail is satisfactory.

Anchorage into beam: The development length required if bars are straight
is 42.7 in., as determined previously. Therefore, the bars must extend at least

this distance into the span. The ACI Code has additional requirements for the extension of tension bars in areas of negative moments. These requirements are covered in the discussion on continuous construction in Chapter 6.

5-5

DEVELOPMENT OF WEB REINFORCEMENT

Anchorage of web reinforcement must be furnished in accordance with ACI Code, Section 12.13. Stirrups must be carried as close to the compression and tension surfaces as possible. Close proximity to the compression face is necessary since flexural tension cracks penetrate deeply as ultimate load is approached.

The ACI Code stipulates that ends of single-leg, simple U-, or multiple U-stirrups shall be anchored by one of the following means (see Figure 5-7):

1. For a No. 5 bar or smaller and for Nos. 6, 7, and 8 bars of $f_y = 40,000$ psi or less, anchorage is provided by a standard stirrup hook, bent around a longitudinal bar (ACI Code, Section 12.13.2.1).
2. For Nos. 6, 7, and 8 stirrups with $f_y > 40,000$ psi, anchorage is provided by a standard stirrup hook bent around a longitudinal bar *plus* an embedment between midheight of the member and the outside end of the hook equal to or greater than

$$0.014 d_b \frac{f_y}{\sqrt{f_c'}}$$

A 135° or a 180° hook is preferred, but a 90° hook is acceptable provided that the free end of the hook is extended the full $12d_b$ as required in ACI Code, Section 7.1.3 (ACI Code, Section 12.13.2.2).

It should be noted that the ACI standard hooks for ties and stirrups, as shown in Figure 5-7, include 90° and 135° hooks only. This does not imply that the 180° hook is not acceptable. In the 1977 ACI Code, the 180° hook for stirrup anchorage around a longitudinal bar was reduced to 135° because the 135° hook is easier to fabricate. Many stirrup bending machines now in use are not designed to fabricate a 180° hook. The anchorage strength of either a 135° or 180° hook is approximately the same.

In addition, the ACI Code, Section 12.13.5, establishes criteria with respect to lapping of double U-stirrups or ties (without hooks) to form a closed stirrup. Legs shall be considered properly spliced when lengths of lap are $1.3\ell_d$ as depicted in Figure 5-7c. Each bend of each simple U-stirrup must enclose a longitudinal bar.

If the lap of $1.3\ell_d$ cannot fit within the depth of a shallow member, provided that the depth of the member is at least 18 in., double U-stirrups may be used if each

FIGURE 5-7   Web reinforcement anchorage.

U-stirrup extends the full available depth of the member and the force in each leg does not exceed 9000 lb (that is, $A_b f_y \leq 9000$ lb).

Where torsional reinforcing is required or desired, a commonly used alternative stirrup is the one-piece closed stirrup. Use of the one-piece closed stirrup is disadvantageous, however, in that the entire beam reinforcing (longitudinal steel and stirrups) may have to be prefabricated as a cage and then placed as a unit. This may not be practical if the longitudinal bars have to be passed between column bars. Alternatively, and at a greater cost, the longitudinal bars could be threaded through the closed stirrups and column bars. The use of overlapping U-stirrups (Figure 5-7c) has the advantage of simplifying the placement of the longitudinal

FIGURE 5-8   Closed stirrups.

bars. Two commonly used types of one-piece closed stirrups are shown in Figure 5-8. (See the ACI Code, Section 11.6.4.)

5-6

SPLICES

The need to splice reinforcing steel is a reality due to the limited lengths of steel available. All bars are readily available in lengths up to 60 ft; No. 3 and No. 4 bars will tend to bend in handling when longer than 40 ft, however. Typical stock straight lengths are as follows:

No. 3 bar: 20, 40, 60 ft
No. 4 bar: 30, 40, 60 ft
Nos. 5 to 18 bars: 60 ft

Splicing may be accomplished by welding, by using mechanical connections, or, most commonly for No. 11 bars and smaller, by lapping bars as shown in Figure 5-9. Lap splices may not be used for bars larger than No. 11 except in footings, as provided in the ACI Code, Section 15.8.2.3, and for compression splices of bars of different sizes, as provided in the ACI Code, Section 12.16.2. The splice composed of lapped bars is usually more economical than the other types. The lapped bars are commonly tied in contact with each other. They may, however, be spaced apart up to one-fifth of the lap length, with an upper limit of 6 in. Splices in regions of maximum moment preferably should be avoided.

The ACI Code (Section 1.2.1) requires that the design drawings show the location and length of lap splices and the type and location of welded splices and mechanical connections.

FIGURE 5-9 Stress transfer in tension lap splice.

5-7

TENSION SPLICES

The required length of lap is based on the class in which the splice is categorized. The required lap length increases with increased stress and increased amount of steel spliced in close proximity. Lap length is expressed in terms of the tensile development length ℓ_d for the particular bar, as shown in Section 5-2. The excess reinforcement factor is not considered for tension splices since the splice classification already reflects any excess reinforcement at the splice location.

The ACI Code, Section 12.15, directs that lap splices be class B (lap length = $1.3\ell_d$) except that class A (lap length = $1.0\ell_d$) splices are allowed if (1) the area of reinforcement provided is twice that required for the entire length of the splice *and* (2) not more than 50% of the total reinforcement is spliced within the required lap length.

The minimum length of lap for tension lap splices is 12 in. (ACI Code, Section 12.15.1). Requirements for welded spices and mechanical connections for tensile reinforcement are contained in the ACI Code, Section 12.14.3 and 12.15.

In addition, splices in "tension tie members" must be made with a full welded splice or full mechanical connection, and their locations must be staggered a distance of at least 30 in., in accordance with the ACI Code, Section 12.15.5. Staggering of all tension splices in all types of members is encouraged.

5-8

COMPRESSION SPLICES

The ACI Code, Section 12.16, contains requirements for lap splices for compression bars. For $f'_c = 3000$ psi or more, the following lap lengths, in multiples of bar diameters d_b, are required:

$$f_y = 40,000 \text{ psi}: \quad 20d_b$$

$$f_y = 60,000 \text{ psi}: \quad 30d_b$$

$$f_y = 75,000 \text{ psi}: \quad 44d_b$$

but not less than 12 in. For $f'_c < 3000$ psi, the length of lap should be increased by one-third. Within ties or spirals of specific makeup (ACI Code, Section 12.17.2.4 and 12.17.2.5), these laps may be reduced to 0.83 or 0.75, respectively, of the foregoing values, but must not be less than 12 in.

Compression splices may also be of the end-bearing type, where bars are cut square, then butted together and held in concentric contact by a suitable device. End-bearing splices must not be used except in members containing closed ties, closed stirrups, or spirals. Welded splices and mechanical connections are also acceptable and are subject to the requirements of the ACI Code, Section 12.16. Special splice requirements for columns are furnished by the ACI Code, Section 12.17.

5-9
SIMPLE-SPAN BAR CUTOFFS AND BENDS

The maximum required A_s for a beam is needed only where the moment is maximum. This maximum steel may be reduced at points along a bending member where the bending moment is smaller. This is usually accomplished by either stopping or bending the bars in a manner consistent with the theoretical requirements for the strength of the member, as well as the requirements of the ACI Code.

Bars can theoretically be stopped or bent in flexural members whenever they are no longer needed to resist moment. The ACI Code, Section 12.10.3, however, requires that each bar be extended beyond the point at which it is no longer required for flexure for a distance equal to the effective depth of the member or $12d_b$, whichever is greater, except at supports of simple spans and at free ends of cantilevers. In effect, this prohibits the cutting off of a bar at the theoretical cutoff point, but can be interpreted as permitting bars to be bent at the theoretical cutoff point. If bars are to be bent, a general practice that has evolved is to commence the bend at a distance equal to one-half the effective depth beyond the theoretical cutoff point. The bent bar should be anchored or made continuous with reinforcement on the opposite face of the member. It should be pointed out, however, that the bending of reinforcing bars in slabs and beams to create *truss bars* (see types 3 through 7, Figure 13-4) has fallen into disfavor over the years because of placement problems and the labor involved. It is more common to use straight bars and place them in accordance with the strength requirements.

With simple-span flexural members of constant dimensions, we can assume that the required A_s varies directly with the bending moment and that the shape of a *required A_s curve* is identical with that of the moment diagram. The moment diagram (or curve) may then be used as the required A_s curve by merely changing the vertical scale. Steel areas may be used as ordinates, but it is more convenient to use the required number of bars (assuming that all bars are of the same diameter). The necessary correlation is established by using the maximum ordinate of the curve as the maximum required A_s in terms of the required number of bars. Because of possible variations in the shape of the moment diagram, either a graphical or a math-

FIGURE 5-10   Recommended bar details: one-way simple-span slabs; tensile reinforced simple-span beams similar.

ematical approach may be more appropriate. A graphical approach requires that the moment diagram be plotted to scale. Example 5-5 lends itself to a mathematical solution.

In determining bar cutoffs it should be remembered that the stopping of bars should be accomplished by using a symmetrical pattern so that the remaining bars will also be in a symmetrical pattern. In addition, the ACI Code, Section 12.11.1, requires that for simple spans, at least one-third of the positive moment steel extend into the support a distance of 6 in. In practice, this requirement is generally exceeded. Normally, recommended bar details for single-span solid concrete slabs indicate that all bottom bars should extend into the support. See Figure 5-10 for recommended bar details.

Economy sometimes dictates that reinforcing steel should be cut off in a simple span. Example 5-5 shows one approach to this problem.

Example 5-5 _____

A simple-span, uniformly loaded beam, shown in Figure 5-11a and b, requires six No. 7 bars for tensile reinforcement. If the effective depth d is 18 in., determine where the bars may be stopped. Use $f'_c = 4000$ psi and $f_y = 60,000$ psi. Assume that there is no excess steel (required A_s = furnished $A_s = 3.60$ in.^{2}). Assume normal-weight concrete and that the stirrups extend to the end of the beam at the support.

Solution:

We will try to establish a bar cutoff scheme whereby the two center bars are cut first, followed by the cutting of the other two inside bars. The two corner

w_u

A

A

$\ell = 24'$

Beam Load Diagram
(a)

M_u

$\dfrac{w_u\ell^2}{8}$

M_u Diagram (Second-Degree Curve)
(b)

$16\tfrac{1}{2}''$

Stirrups
#4 @ 9"
(throughout)

$d = 18''$

$1\tfrac{1}{2}''$ clear
(typ.)

6-#7

Section A–A
(c)

℄ span

x_2

x_1

y_1

y_2

Y

6
5
4
3
2
1
0

Number of bars required

$\dfrac{\ell}{2} = 12'$

Required Steel Diagram
(d)

FIGURE 5-11　Sketches for Example 5-5.

bars are to run the full length of the beam. First, we check the minimum steel requirement:

$$A_{s,\min} = \frac{200}{f_y}bd = \frac{200}{60{,}000}(16.5)(18) = 0.99 \text{ in.}^2$$

The two corner bars provide a steel area of 1.20 in.^{2}. Therefore, the minimum steel area requirement is met.

1.　Determine where the first two bars may be cut off. The first two bars may be stopped where only four are required. This distance from the centerline of the span is designated x_1 in Figure 5-11d.

　　Since the moment diagram is a second-degree curve (a parabola), offsets to the line tangent to the curve at the point of maximum moment vary as the squares of the distances from the centerline of the span. The solution for the distance x may be formulated as follows:

$$\frac{(x_1)^2}{\left(\dfrac{\ell}{2}\right)^2} = \frac{y_1}{Y}$$

$$\frac{(x_1)^2}{12^2} = \frac{2}{6}$$

from which $x_1 = 6.93$ ft. This locates the *theoretical* point where two bars may be terminated. Additionally, bars must be extended past this point a distance d or $12d_b$, whichever is larger. Thus

$$12 \text{ bar diameters} = 12(0.875)$$

$$= 10.5 \text{ in.}$$

Since $d = 18$ in., the bars should be extended 18 in. (1.50 ft). Then the minimum distance from the centerline of the span to the cutoff of the first two bars is

$$6.93 + 1.50 = 8.43 \text{ ft}$$

2.   Determine where the next two bars may be cut off. The two remaining bars, which are the corner bars, will continue into the support. With reference to Figure 5-11d:

$$\frac{(x_2)^2}{12^2} = \frac{4}{6}$$

$$x_2 = 9.80 \text{ ft}$$

Therefore, the minimum distance from centerline of span to the cutoff of the next two bars is

$$9.80 + 1.50 = 11.30 \text{ ft}$$

3.   A check must be made of the required development length ℓ_d for the first two bars. Since the bar cutoff occurs 8.43 ft from the centerline of the span, ℓ_d must be less than 8.43 ft for the stress f_y to be developed at the centerline.

a.   From Table 5-1, $K_D = 71.2$.

b.   Establish values for the multiplying factors α, β, γ, and λ.
   (1) $\alpha = 1.0$ (the bars are not top bars).
   (2) The bars are uncoated ("black steel"). $\beta = 1.0$.
   (3) The bars are No. 7. $\gamma = 1.0$.
   (4) Normal-weight concrete is used. $\lambda = 1.0$.

c.   The product $\alpha \times \beta = 1.0 < 1.7$. (O.K.)

d.   Determine c. Based on cover (center of bar to nearest concrete surface): Consider the clear cover, the No. 4 stirrup, and one-half the diameter of the No. 7 bar:

$$c = 1.5 + 0.5 + \frac{0.875}{2} = 2.44 \text{ in.}$$

Based on bar spacing (one-half the center-to-center distance):

$$c = \frac{16.5 - 2(1.5) - 2(0.5) - 2\left(\dfrac{0.875}{2}\right)}{5(2)} = 1.163 \text{ in.}$$

Therefore, use $c = 1.163$ in.

e.   Using data on stirrups from Figure 5-11:

$$K_{TR} = \frac{A_{TR}f_{yt}}{1500sn} = \frac{0.40(60,000)}{1500(9)(2)} = 0.889$$

f.   Check $(c + K_{TR})/d_b \leqslant 2.5$:

$$\frac{c + K_{TR}}{d_b} = \frac{1.163 + 0.889}{0.875} = 2.35 < 2.5 \qquad \text{(O.K.)}$$

g.   The excess reinforcement factor is neglected (conservative).

h.   Calculate ℓ_d:

$$\ell_d = K_D\left[\frac{\alpha\beta\gamma\lambda}{\left(\dfrac{c + K_{TR}}{d_b}\right)}\right]d_b$$

$$= 71.2\left[\frac{1.0(1.0)(1.0)(1.0)}{2.35}\right](0.875) = 26.5 \text{ in.} > 12 \text{ in.} \qquad \text{(O.K.)}$$

26.5 in. = 2.21 ft

Since the required tensile development length of 2.21 ft is much less than the distance from the centerline to the actual cutoff point (8.43 ft), the cutoff for the first two bars is satisfactory. Similarly, if we consider the second two bars, for which ℓ_d can conservatively be taken as 2.21 ft (conservative since the c distance, based on bar spacing, is larger for these two bars than for the first two cut bars), the point at which they are stressed to maximum (the theoretical cutoff point for the first two bars), measured from the centerline, is 6.93 ft. The second two bars must extend at least ℓ_d past this point. Again measured from the centerline, the bars must extend at least

$$6.93 + 2.21 = 9.14 \text{ ft}$$

Since this is less than the actual distance to the cutoff point (11.30 ft), the cutoff for the second pair is satisfactory (see Figure 5-12).

4.   The remaining pair of corner bars, representing one-third of the positive moment steel, must continue into the support. Since the corner bars are stressed to f_y at a distance of 9.80 ft from the centerline of span (where the second pair of bars may be theoretically cut), however, the develop-

FIGURE 5-12   Sketch for Example 5-5.

ment length of these bars must be satisfied from the end of the bar back to the point of maximum stress f_y. The development length required is again conservatively taken as 2.21 ft. The straight development length furnished (or available) is 2.58 ft (see Figure 5-12.) Since 2.58 ft > 2.21 ft, there is adequate development length available. If the development length available were insufficient, either of two solutions could be used: (a) provide a standard 180° hook at the end of each of the two corner bars or (b) extend all four of the outside bars to the end of the beam (thereby cutting only the two center bars.)

Example 5-5 could also be solved by plotting the M_u diagram to scale and superimposing on the M_u diagram the values of ϕM_n for four bars and two bars. The theoretical cut points are established where the ϕM_n lines intersect the M_u curve. For instance, the theoretical cut point for the two center bars is established where the ϕM_n line for four bars intersects the M_u curve. This method has several advantages: (1) any excess flexural steel in the design will result in the two center bars being cut closer to the midpoint of the beam, (2) the calculation of ϕM_n better reflects the available moment strength than does the division of the M_u diagram ordinate into six equal parts (in Example 5-5), and (3) it can be used for any shape M_u diagram.

The bars in Example 5-5 are terminating in a tension zone. When this occurs, the member undergoes a reduction in shear capacity. Therefore, special shear and stirrup calculations must be performed in accordance with the ACI Code, Section 12.10.5, which stipulates that no flexural reinforcement shall be terminated in a tension zone unless *one* of the following conditions is satisfied:

(12.10.5.1) Shear at the cutoff point does not exceed two-thirds of that permitted, including the shear strength of the shear reinforcement provided. This may be written as

$$V_u \leq \tfrac{2}{3}\phi(V_c + V_s)$$

(12.10.5.2) Stirrup area in excess of that required is provided along each bar terminated over a distance equal to $\tfrac{3}{4}d$ from the point of bar cutoff. The excess stirrup area shall not be less than $60b_w s/f_y$. The spacing s shall not exceed $d/(8\beta_b)$, where β_b is the ratio of reinforcement cut off to total area of tension reinforcement at the section.

(12.10.5.3) For No. 11 bars and smaller, the continuing reinforcement provides double the area required for flexure at the cutoff point and shear does not exceed three-quarters of that permitted.

With respect to the preceding conditions, the first is interpreted as a check only. Although the V_s term could be varied, the code is not specific concerning the length of beam over which this V_s must exist. The third condition involves moving the cutoff point to another location. The second condition is a design method whereby additional stirrups may be introduced if the shear strength is inadequate as determined by the ACI Code, Section 12.10.5.1. This condition will be developed further.

It is convenient to determine the *number* of additional stirrups to be added in the length $\tfrac{3}{4}d$ along the end of the bar from the cutoff point. The required excess stirrup area is

$$A_v = \frac{60b_w s}{f_y}$$

Assuming that the size of the stirrup (and therefore A_v) is known, the maximum spacing is

$$s = \frac{A_v f_y}{60b_w}$$

Therefore, the number of stirrups N_s to be added in the length $\tfrac{3}{4}d$ is

$$N_s = \frac{\tfrac{3}{4}d}{s} + 1 = \frac{\tfrac{3}{4}d}{\dfrac{A_v f_y}{60b_w}} + 1 = \left(\frac{45b_w d}{A_v f_y}\right) + 1$$

Also, since maximum $s = d/(8\beta_b)$,

$$N_{s(\min)} = \frac{\tfrac{3}{4}d}{\dfrac{d}{8\beta_b}} + 1 = 6\beta_b + 1$$

The larger resulting N_s controls.

Example 5-6

In the beam shown in Figure 5-13, the location at which the top layer of two No. 9 bars is to be terminated is in a tension zone. At the cutoff point, $V_u = 52$ kips and the No. 3 stirrups are spaced at 11 in. on center. Check shear in accordance with the ACI Code, Section 12.10.5, and redesign the stirrup spacing if necessary. Assume that $f'_c = 3000$ psi and $f_y = 60,000$ psi.

FIGURE 5-13   Sketch for Example 5-6.

Solution:

In accordance with the ACI Code, Section 12.10.5.1, check $V_u \leq \frac{2}{3}\phi(V_c + V_s)$:

$$\frac{2}{3}\phi(V_c + V_s) = \frac{2}{3}(0.85)\left(2\sqrt{f'_c}\,bd + \frac{A_v f_y d}{s}\right)$$

$$= \frac{2}{3}(0.85)\left[2\sqrt{3000}\,(12)(26) + \frac{(0.22)(60,000)(26)}{11}\right]$$

$$= 37,048 \text{ lb}$$

$$= 37.0 \text{ kips} < 52 \text{ kips} \qquad\qquad\qquad\text{(N.G.)}$$

Therefore, add excess stirrups over a length of $\frac{3}{4}d$ along the terminated bars from the cut end in accordance with ACI 12.10.5.2:

$$N_s = \left(\frac{45 b_w d}{A_v f_y} + 1\right) \quad \text{or} \quad (6\beta_b + 1)$$

$$\frac{45(12)(26)}{0.22(60,000)} + 1 = 2.06$$

$$6(\tfrac{1}{3}) + 1 = 3$$

Add three stirrups over a length of $\frac{3}{4}d = 19.5$ in. Find the new spacing required in the 19.5 in. length:

$$\frac{19.5}{11} = 1.77 \text{ stirrups at 11 in. spacing}$$

$$\underline{+\ 3.00} \text{ additional stirrups}$$

$$4.77 \text{ stirrups in 19.5 in. length}$$

The new stirrup spacing is

$$\frac{19.5}{4.77} = 4.09 \text{ in.} \qquad \text{Use 4 in.}$$

The stirrup pattern originally designed should now be altered to include the 4 in. spacing along the last 19.5 in. of the cut bars.

The problems associated with terminating bars in a tension zone may be avoided by extending the bars in accordance with the ACI Code, Section 12.10.5.3, or by extending them into the support.

In summary, a general representation of the bar cutoff requirements for positive moment steel in a simple span may be observed in Figure 5-14. If bars A are to be cut off, they must (1) project ℓ_d past the point of maximum positive moment and (2) project beyond their theoretical cutoff point a distance equal to the effective depth of the member or 12 bar diameters, whichever is greater. The remaining positive moment bars B must extend ℓ_d past the theoretical cutoff point of bars A and extend at least 6 in. into the support.

FIGURE 5-14   Bar cutoff requirements for simple spans (positive moment steel).

5-10

CODE REQUIREMENTS FOR DEVELOPMENT OF POSITIVE MOMENT STEEL AT SIMPLE SUPPORTS

The ACI Code, Section 12.11.3, contains requirements concerning the development of straight, positive moment bars *at simple supports* and at points of inflection. The intent of this code section is the same as the check on the development of the two bars extending into the support in Example 5-5. The method of Example 5-5 may be used if we are working with the actual moment diagram. The code approach does not require the use of a moment diagram. This code section does not apply to reinforcement that terminates in a standard hook beyond the centerline of a simple support.

The ACI Code requirement places a restriction on the size of the bar that may be used such that

$$\ell_d \leq \frac{M_n}{V_u} + \ell_a \qquad \text{ACI Eq. (12-2)}$$

where

M_n = nominal moment strength $\left[A_s f_y \left(d - \dfrac{a}{2} \right) \right]$, assuming all reinforcement

at the section to be stressed to f_y

V_u = total applied design shear force at the section

ℓ_a = (at a support) the embedment length beyond the center of the support

ℓ_a = (at a point of inflection) the effective depth of the member or $12d_b$, whichever is greater

This requirement need not be satisfied for reinforcement terminating beyond the centerline of simple supports by a standard hook or a mechanical anchorage at least equivalent to a standard hook.

The effect of this code restriction is to require that bars be small enough so that they can become fully developed before the applied moment has increased to the magnitude where they *must* be capable of carrying f_y. The M_n/V_u term approximates the distance from the section in question to the location where applied moment M_u exists that is equal to ϕM_n (and where f_y must exist in the bars).

Therefore, the distance from the end of the bar to the point where the bar must be fully developed is $(M_n/V_u) + \ell_a$, and bars must be chosen so that their ℓ_d is less than this distance. The code allows M_n/V_u to be increased by 30% when the ends of the reinforcement are confined by a compressive reaction such as is found in a simply supported beam (a beam supported by a wall).

Example 5-7

At the support of a simply supported beam, a cross section exists as shown in Figure 5-15. Check the bar diameters in accordance with the ACI Code, Section 12.11.3. Assume a support width of 12 in., 1½ in. cover, $f'_c = 4000$ psi, and $f_y = 60,000$ psi. Assume that V_u at the support is 80 kips. Normal-weight concrete is used. The stirrups begin at 3 in. from the face of support.

Solution:

Since this beam has its ends confined by a compressive reaction, we will check ACI (Equation (12-2):

$$\ell_d \leq 1.3\left(\frac{M_n}{V_u}\right) + \ell_a$$

We next calculate the required tensile development length:

1.   From Table 5-1, $K_D = 71.2$.
2.   Establish values for the multiplying factors α, β, γ, and λ.
  a.   α = 1.0 (the bars are not top bars).
  b.   The bars are uncoated ("black steel"). β = 1.0.
  c.   The bars are No. 10. γ = 1.0.
  d.   Normal-weight concrete is used. λ = 1.0.
3.   The product α × β = 1.0 < 1.7. (O.K.)
4.   Determine c. Based on cover (center of bar to nearest concrete surface): Consider the clear cover, the No. 4 stirrup, and one-half the diameter of the No. 10 bar:

FIGURE 5-15   Sketch for Example 5-7.

$$c = 1.5 + 0.5 + \frac{1.27}{2} = 2.64 \text{ in.}$$

Based on bar spacing (one-half the center-to-center distance):

$$c = \frac{15 - 2(1.5) - 2(0.5) - 2\left(\frac{1.27}{2}\right)}{2} = 4.87 \text{ in.}$$

Therefore, use $c = 2.64$ in.

5. K_{TR} is taken as zero since stirrups do not extend to the ends of the bars.
6.   Check $(c + K_{TR})/d_b \leqslant 2.5$:

$$\frac{c + K_{TR}}{d_b} = \frac{2.64 + 0}{1.27} = 2.08 < 2.5 \qquad \text{(O.K.)}$$

7.   The excess reinforcement factor is not applicable and is omitted.
8.   Calculate ℓ_d:

$$\ell_d = K_D \left[\frac{\alpha\beta\gamma\lambda}{\left(\dfrac{c + K_{TR}}{d_b}\right)} \right] d_b$$

$$= 71.2 \left[\frac{1.0(1.0)(1.0)(1.0)}{2.08} \right] (1.27) = 43.5 \text{ in.} > 12 \text{ in.} \qquad \text{(O.K.)}$$

Now check ACI Equation 12-2:

$$\rho = \frac{A_s}{bd} = \frac{2.54}{15(26)} = 0.0065$$

$$\overline{k} = 0.3676 \text{ ksi}$$

$$M_n = bd^2\overline{k} = 15(26)^2(0.3676) = 3727.5 \text{ in.-kips}$$

The maximum permissible required ℓ_d is

$$1.3\frac{M_n}{V_u} + \ell_a = 1.3\left(\frac{3727.5}{80}\right) + 4.5 = 65.1 \text{ in.}$$

$$65.1 \text{ in} > 43.5 \text{ in.} \qquad \text{(O.K.)}$$

Therefore, the bar diameter is adequate (small enough) and the bar can be developed as required. (If the required ℓ_d were in excess of 65.1 in., the use of a standard hook beyond the centerline of support would satisfy the development requirement and this code section would not apply. Also, the use of smaller bars would result in a smaller required ℓ_d.)

PROBLEMS

For the following problems, all concrete is normal weight and all steel is uncoated grade 60 (f_y = 60,000 psi.)

5-1. Determine the tension development length required for the No. 10 bars in the T-beam shown in Figure 3-11 of Example 3-4. Use f_c' = 3000 psi. Assume that the No. 3 stirrups are spaced at 8 in. throughout. Concrete is normal weight. Neglect the compression steel.

5-2. A 12-in.-thick concrete wall is supported on a continuous footing as shown. Use f_c' = 3000 psi. Determine if the development length is adequate if the steel is No. 6 bars at 8 in. o.c. Assume that the critical section for moment (f_y is developed) is at the face of the wall.

PROBLEM 5-2

PROBLEM 5-3

5-3. Calculate the required development length (ℓ_d), indicating where the negative moment steel may be cut off so as to develop the tensile strength of the steel at the face of the column. Required $A_s = 2.75$ in.^{2}, and $f'_c = 4000$ psi.

5-4. Considering the anchorage of the beam bars into the column, determine the largest bar that can be used without a hook. Use $f'_c = 4000$ psi. Clear space between bars is 3 in. (minimum). Side cover is 2 in.

PROBLEM 5-4

5-5. Seven No. 11 vertical compression bars extend from a column into the supporting footing. Use $f'_c = 5000$ psi. The A_s required was 10.2 in.^{2}. There is no lateral reinforcing enclosing the vertical bars in the footing. Determine the required compression development length.

5-6. Determine the development length required in the column for the bars shown. If the available development length is not sufficient to develop the tensile strength of the steel (f_y), design an anchorage using a 180° hook and check its adequacy. Use $f'_c = 4000$ psi. The clear space between the No. 10 bars is 3 in. with a side cover of 2½ in.

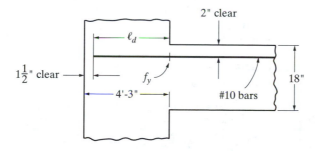

PROBLEM 5-6

5-7. The tension bars in the stem of the reinforced concrete retaining wall are No. 9 at 7 in. o.c. and are to be lap spliced to similar dowels extending up from the footing. Required $A_s = 1.50$ in.^{2}/ft. Use $f'_c = 3000$ psi. Cover on the bars from the rear face of the wall is 2 in., and cover from the end of the wall to the edge bar, measured in the plane of the bars, is 3 in. Calculate the required length of splice.

PROBLEM 5-7

(a)

Section C–C
(b)

PROBLEM 5-8

5-8. Design the tension splices at points A and B in the beam shown, assuming, for purposes of this problem, that the splices must be located as shown. Positive M_u at A is 120 ft-kips; negative M_u at B is 340 ft-kips. Assume that 50% of the steel is spliced at the designated locations. Use $f'_c = 4000$ psi.

5-9. A wall is reinforced with No. 7 bars at 12 in. o.c. in each face as shown. The bars are in compression and are to be spliced to dowels of the same size and spacing in the footing. Use $f'_c = 3000$ psi. Determine the required length of splice.

PROBLEM 5-9

5-10. Number 9 compression bars in a column are to be lap spliced. There is no excess steel, and the bars are enclosed by a spiral of $\frac{3}{8}$-in.-diameter wire having a pitch of 3 in. Use $f'_c = 4000$ psi. Determine the required length of splice.

5-11. For the overhanging beam shown, find the theoretical cutoff point for the center No. 9 bar. Assume the section of maximum moment to be at the face of support. Use $f'_c = 5000$ psi.

Section A–A

PROBLEM 5-11

5-12. A simply supported, uniformly loaded beam carries a total factored load of 4.8 kips/ft (this includes the beam weight) on a clear span of 34 ft. Use $f'_c = 3000$ psi. Assume that the supports are 12 in. wide.

   (a) Design a rectangular beam (tension steel only).

   (b) Determine bar cutoffs.

   (c) Design for shear reinforcement and check whether bar cutoffs in the tension zone satisfy the ACI Code. Redesign the stirrups if necessary.

5-13. The beam shown is to carry a total factored uniform load of 10 kips/ft (includes beam weight) and factored concentrated loads of 20 kips. Use $f'_c = 4000$ psi. Assume that the supports are 12 in. wide.

   (a) Design a rectangular beam (tension steel only).

   (b) Determine bar cutoffs (use the graphical approach).

   (c) Design the shear reinforcement and check bar cutoffs in tension zones if necessary.

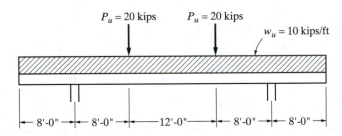

PROBLEM 5-13

CHAPTER 6

Continuous
Construction
Design Considerations

6-1

INTRODUCTION

A common form of concrete cast-in-place building construction consists of a continuous one-way slab cast monolithically with supporting continuous beams and girders. In this type of system, all members contribute in carrying the floor load to the supporting columns (see Figure 3-1). The slab steel runs through the beams, the beam steel runs through the girders, and the steel from both the beams and girders runs through the columns. The result is that the whole floor system is tied together, forming a highly indeterminate and complex type of rigid structure. The behavior of the members is affected by their rigid connections. Not only will loads applied directly *on* a member produce moment, shear, and a definite deflected shape, but loads applied to *adjacent* members will produce similar effects because of the rigidity of the connections. The shears and moments transmitted through a joint will depend on the relative stiffnesses of all the members framing into that joint. With this type of condition, a precise evaluation of moments and shears resulting from a floor loading is excessively time consuming and is outside the scope of this text. Several commercial computer programs are available to facilitate these analysis computations.

In an effort to simplify and expedite the design phase, the ACI Code, Section 8.3.3, permits the use of standard moment and shear equations whenever the span and loading conditions satisfy stipulated requirements. This approach applies to continuous nonprestressed one-way slabs, beams, and girders. It is an approximate method and may be used for buildings of the usual type of construction, spans, and story heights. The ACI moment equations result from the product of a coefficient and $w_u \ell_n^2$. Similarly, the ACI shear equations result from the product of a coefficient and $w_u \ell_n$. In these equations, w_u is the factored design uniform load and ℓ_n is the *clear span* for positive moment (and shear) and the average of two adjacent clear spans for negative moment. The application of the equations is limited to the following:

1. The equations can be used for two or more approximately equal spans (with the larger of two adjacent spans not exceeding the shorter by more than 20%).
2. Loads must be uniformly distributed.
3. The maximum allowable ratio of live load to dead load is 3:1 (based on service loads).
4. Members must be prismatic.

These shear and moment equations generally give reasonably conservative values for the stated conditions. If more precision is required, or desired, for economy or because the stipulated conditions are not satisfied, a more theoretical and precise analysis must be made.

FIGURE 6-1   ACI code coefficients and equations for shear and moment for continuous beams, girders, and one-way slabs.

The moment and shear equations are depicted in Figure 6-1. Their use will be demonstrated later in this chapter.

6-2

CONTINUOUS-SPAN BAR CUTOFFS

Using a design approach similar to that for simple spans, the area of main reinforcing steel required at any given point is a function of the design moment. As the moment varies along the span, the steel may be modified or reduced in accordance with the theoretical requirements of the member's strength and the requirements of the ACI Code.

Bars can theoretically be stopped or bent in flexural members whenever they are no longer needed to resist moment. A general representation of the bar cutoff requirements for continuous spans (both positive and negative moments) is shown in Figure 6-2.

In continuous members the ACI Code, Section 12.11.1, requires that a minimum of one-fourth of the positive moment steel be extended into the support a distance of at least 6 in. The ACI Code, Section 12.12.3, also requires that at least one-third of the negative moment steel be extended beyond the extreme position of the point of inflection a distance not less than one-sixteenth of the clear span, the effective depth of the member d, or 12 bar diameters, whichever is greater. If negative moment bars C (Figure 6-2a) are to be cut off, they must extend at least a full development length ℓ_d beyond the face of support. In addition, they must extend a distance equal to the effective depth of the member or 12 bar diameters, whichever is larger, beyond the theoretical cutoff point defined by the moment diagram. The remaining negative moment bars D (minimum of one-third of total negative steel) must extend at least ℓ_d beyond the theoretical point of cutoff of bars C and, in addition, must extend a distance equal to the effective depth of the member, 12 bar diameters, or one-sixteenth of the clear span, whichever is the greater, past the point of inflection. Where negative moment bars are cut off before reaching the point of inflection, the situation is analogous to the simple beam cutoffs where the reinforcing bars are being terminated in a tension zone. The reader is referred to Example 5-5.

In Figure 6-2b, if positive moment bars A are to be cut off, they must project ℓ_d past the point of maximum positive moment as well as a distance equal to the effective depth of the member or 12 bar diameters, whichever is larger, beyond their theoretical cutoff point. Recall that the location of the theoretical cutoff point depends on the amount of steel to be cut and the shape of the applied moment diagram. The remaining positive moment bars B must extend ℓ_d past the theoretical cutoff point of bars A and extend at least 6 in. into the support. Comments on terminating bars in a tension zone again apply. Additionally, the size of the positive

Negative Moment Steel
(a)

Minimum of one-fourth of positive
moment steel must extend a
distance of at least 6 in. into support

Positive Moment Steel
(b)

FIGURE 6-2 Bar cutoff requirements for continuous slabs (ACI Code).

moment bars at the point of inflection must meet the requirements of the ACI
Code, Section 12.11.3.

Since the determination of cutoff and bend points constitutes a relatively time-
consuming chore, it has become customary to use defined cutoff points that experience has indicated are safe. These defined points may be used where the ACI
moment coefficients have application, but must be applied with judgment where
parameters vary. The recommended bar details and cutoffs for continuous spans
are shown in Figure 6-3.

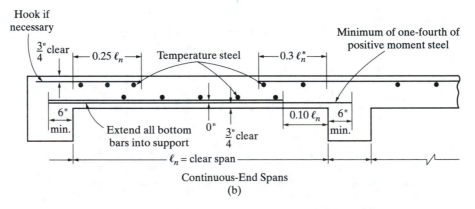

*If adjacent spans have different span lengths, use the larger of the two.

FIGURE 6-3   Recommended bar details and cutoffs, one-way slabs; tensile reinforced beams similar.

DESIGN OF CONTINUOUS FLOOR SYSTEMS

One common type of floor system consists of a continuous cast-in-place one-way reinforced concrete slab supported by monolithic continuous reinforced concrete beams.

Assuming that the floor system parameters and loading conditions satisfy the criteria for application of the ACI Code coefficients, the design of the system may be based on these coefficients. Example 6-1 furnishes a complete design of a typical one-way slab and beam floor system.

Example 6-1

The floor system shown in Figure 6-4 consists of a continuous one-way slab supported by continuous beams. The service loads on the floor are 25 psf dead load (does not include weight of slab) and 250 psf live load. Use $f'_c = 3000$ psi (normal-weight concrete) and $f_y = 60,000$ psi. The bars are uncoated.

A.   Design the continuous one-way floor slab.
B.   Design the continuous supporting beam.

Solution:

The primary difference in this design from previous flexural designs is that, because of continuity, the ACI coefficients and equations will be used to determine design shears and moments.

Partial Plan
(a)

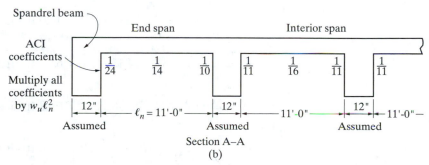

Section A–A
(b)

FIGURE 6-4   Sketches for Example 6-1.

A. Continuous one-way floor slab

1. Determine the slab thickness. The slab will be designed to satisfy the ACI minimum thickness requirements from Table 9.5(a) of the code and this thickness will be used to estimate slab weight.
    With both ends continuous,

$$\text{minimum } h = \frac{1}{28}\ell_n = \frac{1}{28}(11)(12) = 4.71 \text{ in.}$$

    With one end continuous,

$$\text{minimum } h = \frac{1}{24}\ell_n = \frac{1}{24}(11)(12) = 5.5 \text{ in.}$$

    Try a 5½-in.-thick slab. Design a 12-in.-wide segment ($b = 12$ in.).

2. Determine the load:

$$\text{slab dead load} = \frac{5.5}{12}(150) = 68.8 \text{ psf}$$

$$\text{total dead load} = 25.0 + 68.8 = 93.8 \text{ psf}$$

$$w_u = 1.4w_{\text{DL}} + 1.7w_{\text{LL}}$$

$$= 1.4(93.8) + 1.7(250)$$

$$= 131.3 + 425.0$$

$$= 556.3 \text{ psf} \qquad \text{(design load)}$$

    Because we are designing a slab segment that is 12 in. wide, the foregoing loading is the same as 556.3 lb/ft or 0.556 kip/ft.

3. Determine the moments and shears. Moments are determined using the ACI moment equations. Refer to Figures 6-1 and 6-4. Thus

$$+ M_u = \frac{1}{14}w_u\ell_n^2 = \frac{1}{14}(0.556)(11)^2 = 4.81 \text{ ft-kips}$$

$$+ M_u = \frac{1}{16}w_u\ell_n^2 = \frac{1}{16}(0.556)(11)^2 = 4.20 \text{ ft-kips}$$

$$- M_u = \frac{1}{10}w_u\ell_n^2 = \frac{1}{10}(0.556)(11)^2 = 6.73 \text{ ft-kips}$$

$$- M_u = \frac{1}{11}w_u\ell_n^2 = \frac{1}{11}(0.556)(11)^2 = 6.12 \text{ ft-kips}$$

$$- M_u = \frac{1}{24}w_u\ell_n^2 = \frac{1}{24}(0.556)(11)^2 = 2.80 \text{ ft-kips}$$

    Similarly, the shears are determined using the ACI shear equations. In the end span at the face of the first interior support,

$$V_u = 1.15\frac{w_u\ell_n}{2} = 1.15(0.556)\left(\frac{11}{2}\right) = 3.52 \text{ kips}$$

whereas at all other supports,

$$V_u = \frac{w_u\ell_n}{2} = 0.556\left(\frac{11}{2}\right) = 3.06 \text{ kips}$$

4.   Design the slab. Using the assumed slab thickness of 5½ in., find the approximate d. Assume No. 5 bars for main steel and ¾ in. cover for the bars in the slab. Thus

$$d = 5.5 - 0.75 - 0.31 = 4.44 \text{ in.}$$

5.   Design the steel reinforcing. Select the point of maximum moment. This is a negative moment and occurs in the end span at the first interior support, and

$$M_u = \frac{w_u\ell_n^2}{10} = 6.73 \text{ ft-kips}$$

$$\phi M_n = \phi b d^2 \overline{k}$$

Since for design purposes $M_u = \phi M_n$ as a limit, then

$$\text{required } \overline{k} = \frac{M_u}{\phi b d^2} = \frac{6.73(12)}{0.90(12)(4.44)^2}$$

$$= 0.3793 \text{ ksi}$$

From Table A-8,

$$\rho = 0.0069 < \rho_{\max} \qquad \text{(O.K.)}$$

$$\text{required } A_s = \rho b d = 0.0069(12)(4.44)$$

$$A_s = 0.37 \text{ in.}^2$$

Since the steel area required at all other points will be less, the preceding process will be repeated for the other points. The expression

$$\text{required } \overline{k} = \frac{M_u}{\phi b d^2}$$

can be simplified because all values are constant except M_u:

$$\text{required } \overline{k} = \frac{M_u(12)}{0.9(12)(4.44)^2} = \frac{M_u}{17.74}$$

where M_u must be in ft-kips. In the usual manner, the required steel ratio ρ and the required steel area A_s may then be determined. The results of these calculations are listed in Table 6-1.

Minimum reinforcement for slabs of constant thickness is that required for shrinkage and temperature reinforcement:

TABLE 6-1 Slab Steel Area Requirements

Location	Moment equation	$\bar{k}$(ksi)	Required ρ	A_s (in.²/ft)
End span:				
At spandrel	$-\frac{1}{24}w_u\ell_n^2$	0.1578	0.0027	0.14
Midspan	$+\frac{1}{14}w_u\ell_n^2$	0.2771	0.0049	0.26
Interior spans:				
Interior support	$-\frac{1}{11}w_u\ell_n^2$	0.3450	0.0062	0.33
Midspan	$+\frac{1}{16}w_u\ell_n^2$	0.2368	0.0042	0.22

$$\text{minimum required } A_s = 0.0018bh$$
$$= 0.0018(12)(5.5) = 0.12 \text{ in.}^2$$

Also, maximum $\rho = 0.0161$ (see Table A-5). Therefore, the slab steel requirements for flexure as shown in Table 6-1 are within acceptable limits. The shrinkage and temperature steel may be selected based on the preceding calculation:

use No. 3 bars at 11 in. o.c. ($A_s = 0.12$ in.²)

Recall that the maximum spacing allowed is the smaller of $5h$ or 18 in. Since $5h = 5(5.5) = 27.5$ in., the 18 in. would control and the spacing is acceptable.

6. Check the shear strength. From step 3, maximum $V_u = 3.52$ kips at the face of the support. A check of shear at the face of the support, rather than at the critical section which is at a distance equal to the effective depth of the member from the face of the support, is conservative. Slabs are not normally reinforced for shear; therefore,

$$\phi V_n = \phi V_c = \phi 2\sqrt{f_c'}\,b_w d$$
$$= \frac{0.85(2\sqrt{3000})(12)(4.44)}{1000} = 4.96 \text{ kips}$$
$$\phi V_n > \phi V_u$$

Therefore, the thickness is O.K.

7. Select the main steel. Using Table A-4, establish a pattern in which the number of bar sizes and the number of different spacings are kept to a minimum. The maximum spacing for the main steel is 16.5 in. (the smaller of $3h$ or 18 in.). A work sketch (see Figure 6-5) is recommended to establish steel pattern and cutoff points. With regard to the steel selection, note that, in the positive moment areas of both the end span and interior span, No. 4 bars at 9 in. could be used. If alternate bars were terminated, however, the spacing of the bars remaining would exceed the maximum spacing of 16.5 in. The use of No. 4 bars at 8 in. avoids this problem.

Req'd A_s = 0.14 in²   Req'd A_s = 0.37 in²   Req'd A_s = 0.33 in²
Furn. A_s = 0.16 in²   Furn. A_s = 0.37 in²   Furn. A_s = 0.37 in²
#4 @ 15" o.c.   #5 @ 10" o.c.   #5 @ 10" o.c.

Req'd A_s = 0.26 in²   Req'd A_s = 0.22 in²
Furn. A_s = 0.30 in²   Furn. A_s = 0.30 in²
#4 @ 8" o.c.   #4 @ 8" o.c.

←12"→
Assumed

Spandrel beam

Note: Bar cutoffs and temperature steel may be observed in the design sketch, Fig. 6-7.

FIGURE 6-5   Work sketch for Example 6-1.

8. Check anchorage into the spandrel beam. The steel is No. 4 bars at 15 in. o.c. Refer to the procedure for development length calculation in Section 5-2.

   a. From Table 5-1, $K_D = 82.2$.

   b. Establish values for the multiplying factors α, β, γ, and λ.

   (1) $\alpha = 1.3$ (the bars are top bars).

   (2) The bars are uncoated ("black steel"). $\beta = 1.0$.

   (3) The bars are No. 4. $\gamma = 0.8$.

   (4) Normal-weight concrete is used. $\lambda = 1.0$.

   c. The product $\alpha \times \beta = 1.3 < 1.7$. (O.K.)

   d. Determine c. Based on cover (center of bar to nearest concrete surface):

$$c = \frac{3}{4} + \frac{0.5}{2} = 1 \text{ in.}$$

   Based on bar spacing (one-half the center-to-center distance):

$$c = \tfrac{1}{2}(15) = 7.5 \text{ in.}$$

   Therefore, use $c = 1.0$ in.

   e. K_{TR} is taken as zero. There is no transverse steel that crosses the potential plane of splitting.

   f. Check $(c + K_{TR})/d_b \leqslant 2.5$:

$$\frac{c + K_{TR}}{d_b} = \frac{1.0 + 0}{0.5} = 2.0 < 2.5 \qquad\qquad \text{(O.K.)}$$

g. Calculate the excess reinforcement factor:

$$K_{ER} = \frac{A_s \text{ required}}{A_s \text{ provided}} = \frac{0.140}{0.160} = 0.875$$

h. Calculate ℓ_d:

$$\ell_d = K_D\left[\frac{\alpha\beta\gamma\lambda}{\left(\dfrac{c + K_{TR}}{d_b}\right)}\right]d_b$$

$$= 82.2\left[\frac{1.3(1.0)(0.8)(1.0)}{2.0}\right](0.5)$$

$$= 18.7 \text{ in.} > 12 \text{ in.} \qquad\qquad\qquad \text{(O.K.)}$$

Use $\ell_d = 19$ in. (minimum).

9. Since the 19 in. length cannot be furnished, a hook will be provided. Determine if a 180° standard hook will be adequate.

a. From Table A-13, $\ell_{hb} = 11.0$ in.

b. Modification factors (MF) to be used are:

(1) Assume concrete side cover = $2\frac{1}{2}$ in. normal to the plane of the hook; use 0.7.

(2) For excess steel, use

$$\frac{\text{required } A_s}{\text{provided } A_s} = \frac{0.14}{0.16} = 0.875$$

c. The required development length for the hook is

$$\ell_{dh} = \ell_{hb}(\text{MF})$$

$$= 11.0(0.7)(0.875) = 6.74 \text{ in.}$$

Minimum ℓ_{dh} is 6 in. or $8d_b$, whichever is greater:

$$8d_b = 8(\tfrac{1}{2}) = 4 \text{ in.}$$

Therefore, the minimum is 6 in.:

$$6.74 \text{ in.} > 6 \text{ in.} \qquad\qquad\qquad \text{(O.K.)}$$

d. Check the total width of beam required at the discontinuous end (see Figure 6-6):

$$6.74 + 2 = 8.74 \text{ in.} < 12 \text{ in.} \qquad\qquad\qquad \text{(O.K.)}$$

10. Determine the bar cutoff points. For the normal type of construction for which the typical bar cutoff points shown in Figure 6-3 are used, the cutoff points are located so that all bars terminate in compression zones. Therefore, the requirements of the ACI Code, Section 12.10.5, need not

FIGURE 6-6 Hook detail for Example 6-1.

be checked, and the recommended bar cutoff points, as shown in Figure 6-3, are used.

11. Prepare the design sketches. The final design sketch for the slab is shown in Figure 6-7. For clarity, the interior and end spans are shown separately.

B. Continuous supporting beam: The second part of Example 6-1 involves the design of the continuous supporting beam. From Figure 6-4a, it is seen that these beams span between columns. The ACI coefficients to be used for moment determination are shown in Figure 6-8.

1. Determine the loading:

$$\text{service live load} = 250 \text{ psf} \times 12 = 3000 \text{ lb/ft}$$

$$\text{service dead load} = 25 \text{ psf} \times 12 = 300 \text{ lb/ft}$$

$$\text{weight of slab} = \left(\frac{5.5}{12}\right)(150)(12) = 825 \text{ lb/ft}$$

Assuming a beam width of 12 in. and an overall depth of 30 in. for purposes of member weight estimate (see Figure 6-9),

$$\text{weight of beam} = \frac{12(30 - 5.5)}{144}(150) = 306.3 \text{ lb/ft}$$

$$\text{total service live load} = 3000 \text{ lb/ft}$$

$$\text{total service dead load} = 1431.3 \text{ lb/ft} \qquad \text{say, } 1431 \text{ lb/ft}$$

2. Calculate the design load:

$$w_u = 1.4 \, w_{DL} + 1.7 w_{LL}$$

$$= 1.4(1431) + 1.7(3000)$$

Reinforcing-Interior Span
(a)

Reinforcing-End Span
(b)

FIGURE 6-7   Design sketches for Example 6-1.

FIGURE 6-8   Section B–B from Figure 6-4a.

FIGURE 6-9   Sketch for Example 6-1.

$$= 2003 + 5100$$

$$= 7103 \text{ lb/ft} \qquad \text{say, 7.1 kips/ft}$$

The loaded beam is depicted in Figure 6-10.

3.   Calculate the design moments and shears. The design moments and shears are calculated by using the ACI equations:

$$+M_u = \frac{1}{14}w_u\ell_n^2 = \frac{1}{14}(7.1)(22.67)^2 = 260.6 \text{ ft-kips}$$

$$+M_u = \frac{1}{16}w_u\ell_n^2 = \frac{1}{16}(7.1)(22.67)^2 = 228.1 \text{ ft-kips}$$

$$-M_u = \frac{1}{10}w_u\ell_n^2 = \frac{1}{10}(7.1)(22.67)^2 = 364.9 \text{ ft-kips}$$

$$-M_u = \frac{1}{11}w_u\ell_n^2 = \frac{1}{11}(7.1)(22.67)^2 = 331.7 \text{ ft-kips}$$

$$V_u = \frac{w_u\ell_n}{2} = \frac{7.1(22.67)}{2} = 80.5 \text{ kips}$$

$$V_u = 1.15\frac{w_u\ell_n}{2} = 1.15(7.1)\left(\frac{22.67}{2}\right) = 92.6 \text{ kips}$$

FIGURE 6-10   Beam design load and spans.

4. Design the beam. Establish concrete dimensions based on the maximum bending moment. This occurs in the end span at the first interior support where the negative moment $M_u = w_u\ell_n^2/10$. Since the top of the beam is in tension, the design will be that of a rectangular beam.

a. Maximum moment (negative) = 364.9 ft-kips.

b. From Table A-5, assume that $\rho = 0.0090$ (which is less than ρ_{max} of 0.0161). A check of minimum steel required will be made shortly.

c. From Table A-8, $k = 0.4828$ ksi.

d. Assume that $b = 12$ in.:

$$\text{required } d = \sqrt{\frac{M_u}{\phi \bar{b} k}} = \sqrt{\frac{364.9(12)}{0.9(12)(0.4828)}}$$

$$= 29.0 \text{ in.}$$

$$d/b \text{ ratio} = \frac{29.0}{12} = 2.42, \qquad \text{which is within an acceptable range}$$

e. Check the estimated beam weight assuming one layer of No. 11 bars and No. 3 stirrups:

$$\text{required } h = 29.0 + \frac{1.41}{2} + 0.38 + 1.5 = 31.6 \text{ in.}$$

Use $h = 31.5$ in. with an assumed d of 29.0 in. Also, check the minimum h from the ACI Code, Table 9.5(a):

$$\text{minimum } h = \frac{1}{18.5}(22.67)(12) = 14.7 \text{ in.} < 31.5 \text{ in.} \qquad \text{(O.K.)}$$

Note that the estimated beam weight based on $b = 12$ in. and $h = 30$ in. is slightly on the low side but may be considered acceptable.

f. Design the steel reinforcing for points of negative moment as follows.

(1) At the first interior support, based on an assumed ρ of 0.0090 (see the preceding step 4),

$$\text{required } A_s = \rho b d$$

$$= 0.0090(12)(29.0) = 3.13 \text{ in.}^2$$

From Table A-5,

$$A_{s,min} = 0.0033(12)(29.0) = 1.15 \text{ in.}^2$$

$$3.13 \text{ in.}^2 > 1.15 \text{ in.}^2 \qquad \text{(O.K.)}$$

(2) At the other interior supports, $-M_u = 331.7$ ft-kips:

$$\text{required } \bar{k} = \frac{M_u}{\phi b d^2} = \frac{331.7(12)}{0.9(12)(29.0)^2} = 0.4382 \text{ ksi}$$

From Table A-8, $\rho = 0.0081$. Check ρ with ρ_{max}:

$$0.0081 < 0.0161 \qquad \text{(O.K.)}$$

Therefore,

$$\text{required } A_s = \rho bd$$

$$= 0.0081(12)(29.0) = 2.82 \text{ in.}^2$$

Check the required A_s with $A_{s,min}$. From Table A-5,

$$A_{s,min} = 0.0033(12)(29.0) = 1.15 \text{ in.}^2$$

$$2.82 \text{ in.}^2 > 1.15 \text{ in.}^2 \qquad \text{(O.K.)}$$

(3)   At the exterior support (exterior column), $-M_u = 228.1$ ft-kips:

$$\text{required } \bar{k} = \frac{M_u}{\phi bd^2} = \frac{228.1(12)}{0.9(12)(29.0)^2} = 0.3014 \text{ ksi}$$

From Table A-8, $\rho = 0.0054$. Check ρ with ρ_{max}:

$$0.0054 < 0.0161 \qquad \text{(O.K.)}$$

Therefore,

$$\text{required } A_s = \rho bd$$

$$= 0.0054(12)(29.0) = 1.88 \text{ in.}^2$$

Check the required A_s with $A_{s,min}$. From Table A-5,

$$A_{s,min} = 0.0033(12)(29.0) = 1.15 \text{ in.}^2$$

$$1.88 \text{ in.}^2 > 1.15 \text{ in.}^2 \qquad \text{(O.K.)}$$

g.   Design steel reinforcing for points of positive moment as follows. At points of positive moment, the top of the beam is in compression; therefore, the design will be that of a T-beam.

(1)   End-span positive moment:
(a)   Design moment = 260.6 ft-kips = M_u.
(b)   Effective depth d = 29.0 in. (see negative-moment design).
(c)   Effective flange width:

$$\tfrac{1}{4} \text{ span length} = 0.25(22.67)(12) = 68 \text{ in.}$$

$$b_w + 16h_f = 12 + 16(5.5) = 100 \text{ in.}$$

$$\text{beam spacing} = 144 \text{ in.}$$

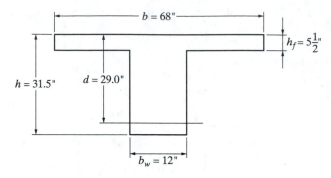

FIGURE 6-11   Beam cross section.

Use an effective flange width $b = 68$ in. (see Figure 6-11).

(d)   Assuming total flange in compression,

$$\phi M_n = \phi(0.85f'_c)bh_f\left(\frac{d - h_f}{2}\right)$$

$$= 0.9(0.85)(3)(68)(5.5)\left(\frac{29.0 - 5.5/2}{12}\right) = 1878 \text{ ft-kips}$$

(e)   Since $1878 > 260.6$, the member behaves as a wide rectangular T-beam with $b = 68$ in. and $d = 29.0$ in.

(f)   required $\bar{k} = \dfrac{M_u}{\phi bd^2}$

$$= \frac{260.6(12)}{0.9(68)(29.0)^2} = 0.0608 \text{ ksi}$$

(g)   From Table A-8,

required $\rho = 0.0011$

(h)   The required steel area is

required $A_s = \rho bd$

$$= 0.0011(68)(29.0) = 2.17 \text{ in.}^2$$

(i)   Use three No. 8 bars ($A_s = 2.37$ in.^{2}):

required $b = 9.0$ in.   (O.K.)

(j)   Check the required A_s with $A_{s,\text{min}}$. From Table A-5,

$$A_{s,\text{min}} = 0.0033(12)(29.0) = 1.15 \text{ in.}^2$$

$$2.37 \text{ in.}^2 > 1.15 \text{ in.}^2 \hspace{3em} \text{(O.K.)}$$

(k)   Check $A_{s,\max}$:

$$A_{s,\max} = 0.0478 h_f \left\{ b + b_w \left[\frac{0.582}{h_f} (d) - 1 \right] \right\}$$

$$= 0.0319(5.5) \left\{ 68 + 12 \left[\frac{0.503(29.0)}{5.5} - 1 \right] \right\}$$

$$= 15.4 \text{ in.}^2 > 2.37 \text{ in.}^2 \qquad \text{(O.K.)}$$

(2)   Interior span positive moment:

   (a)   Design moment = 228.1 ft-kips = M_u.

   (b)   through (e)   See the end-span positive moment computations. Use an effective flange width $b = 68$ in. and an effective depth $d = 29.0$ in. Also, for total flange in compression, $\phi M_n = 1878$ ft-kips $> M_u$. Therefore, this member also behaves as a rectangular T-beam.

   (f) $\qquad$ required $\bar{k} = \dfrac{M_u}{\phi b d^2}$

   $$= \frac{228.1(12)}{0.9(68)(29.0)^2} = 0.0532 \text{ ksi}$$

   (g)   From Table A-8,

   $$\text{required } \rho = 0.0010$$

   (h)   The required steel area is

   $$\text{required } A_s = \rho b d$$

   $$= 0.0010(68)(29.0) = 1.97 \text{ in.}^2$$

   (i)   Use three No. 8 bars ($A_s = 2.37 \text{ in.}^2$):

   $$\text{required } b = 9.0 \text{ in.} \qquad \text{(O.K.)}$$

   (j)   and (k)   The checks for $A_{s,\min}$ and $A_{s,\max}$ are identical to those for the end-span positive moment.

5.   Check the distribution of negative moment steel. The ACI Code, Section 10.6.6, requires that, where flanges are in tension, a part of the main tension reinforcement be distributed over the effective flange width or a width equal to one-tenth of the span, whichever is smaller. The use of smaller bars spread out into part of the flange will also be advantageous where a beam is supported by a spandrel girder or exterior column and the embedment length for the negative moment steel is limited. Thus

$$\frac{\text{span}}{10} = \frac{22.67(12)}{10} = 27 \text{ in.}$$

effective flange width = $b = 68$ in.

Req'd A_s = 1.88 in.^{2}
Use 5-#6
(A_s = 2.20 in.^{2})

Exterior Column
(a)

Req'd A_s = 3.13 in.^{2}
Use 8-#6
(A_s = 3.52 in.^{2})

First Interior Support
(b)

Req'd A_s = 2.82 in.^{2}
Use 7-#6
(A_s = 3.08 in.^{2})

Other Interior Supports
(c)

FIGURE 6-12   Negative moment steel for beam of Example 6-1.

Therefore, distribute the negative moment bars over a width of 27 in. Figure 6-12 shows suitable bars and patterns to use to satisfy the foregoing code requirement and furnish the cross-sectional area of steel required for flexure.

The ACI Code also stipulates that, if the effective flange width exceeds one-tenth of the span, some longitudinal reinforcement shall be provided in the outer portions of the flange. In this design, no additional steel will be furnished. In the authors' opinion, this requirement is satisfied by the slab temperature and shrinkage steel (see Figures 6-7 and 6-19).

6.   Prepare the work sketch. A work sketch is developed in Figure 6-13, which includes the bars previously chosen.

7.   Check the anchorage into the exterior column.

  a.   From Table 5-1, K_D = 82.2

  b.   Establish values for the multiplying factors α, β, γ, and λ.

   (1) α = 1.3 (the bars are top bars).

   (2)   The bars are uncoated ("black steel"). β = 1.0.

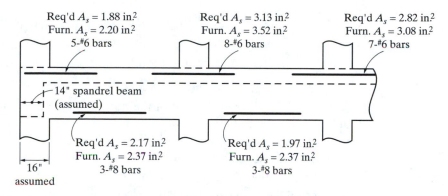

Req'd $A_s = 1.88$ in.^{2}
Furn. $A_s = 2.20$ in.^{2}
5-#6 bars

Req'd $A_s = 3.13$ in.^{2}
Furn. $A_s = 3.52$ in.^{2}
8-#6 bars

Req'd $A_s = 2.82$ in.^{2}
Furn. $A_s = 3.08$ in.^{2}
7-#6 bars

14" spandrel beam
(assumed)

Req'd $A_s = 2.17$ in.^{2}
Furn. $A_s = 2.37$ in.^{2}
3-#8 bars

Req'd $A_s = 1.97$ in.^{2}
Furn. $A_s = 2.37$ in.^{2}
3-#8 bars

16"
assumed

FIGURE 6-13   Work sketch for beam design of Example 6-1.

(3)   The bars are No. 6. $\gamma = 0.8$.

(4)   Normal-weight concrete is used. $\lambda = 1.0$.

c.   The product $\alpha \times \beta = 1.3 < 1.7$. (O.K.)

d.   Determine c. Based on cover (center of bar to nearest concrete surface): Assume $1\frac{1}{2}$ in. clear cover and a No. 3 stirrup:

$$c = 1.5 + 0.375 + \frac{0.75}{2} = 2.25 \text{ in.}$$

Based on bar spacing (one-half the center-to-center distance): Refer to Figure 6-12. Consider the three No. 6 bars that are located within the No. 3 loop stirrup. Here

$$c = \left[\frac{12 - 2(1.5) - 2(0.375) - 0.75}{2} \right]\left(\frac{1}{2}\right) = 1.875 \text{ in.}$$

Therefore, use $c = 1.875$ in.

e. K_{TR} may be conservatively taken as zero.

f.   Check $(c + K_{TR})/d_b \leqslant 2.5$:

$$\frac{c + K_{TR}}{d_b} = \frac{1.875 + 0}{0.75} = 2.5 \ (\leqslant 2.5) \qquad \text{(O.K.)}$$

g.   Determine the excess reinforcement factor:

$$K_{ER} = \frac{A_s \text{ required}}{A_s \text{ provided}} = \frac{1.88}{2.20} = 0.85$$

h.   Calculate ℓ_d:

$$\ell_d = K_D \left[\frac{\alpha\beta\gamma\lambda}{\left(\dfrac{c + K_{TR}}{d_b}\right)} \right] d_b K_{ER}$$

$$= 82.2 \left[\frac{1.3(1.0)(0.8)(1.0)}{2.5} \right] (0.75)(0.85)$$

$$= 21.8 \text{ in.} > 12 \text{ in.} \qquad \text{(O.K.)}$$

Use $\ell_d = 22$ in. (minimum).

With 2.0 in. clear at the end of the bar, the embedment length available in the column is $16.0 - 2.0 = 14.0$ in.

8.   Since 22 in. > 14.0 in., a hook is required. Determine if a 90° standard hook will be adequate.

   a.   From Table A-13, $\ell_{hb} = 16.4$ in.

   b.   Modification factors (MF) to be used are:

   (1)   Assume concrete cover $\geqslant 2\frac{1}{2}$ in. and cover on the bar extension beyond the hook = 2 in.; use 0.7.

   (2)   For excess steel, use

$$\frac{\text{required } A_s}{\text{provided } A_s} = \frac{1.88}{2.20} = 0.85$$

   c.   The required development length for the hook is

$$\ell_{dh} = \ell_{hb} \text{ (MF)}$$

$$= 16.4(0.7)(0.85) = 9.8 \text{ in.}$$

Minimum ℓ_{dh} is 6 in. or $8d_b$, whichever is greater:

$$8d_b = 8(\tfrac{3}{4}) = 6 \text{ in.}$$

$$9.8 \text{ in.} > 6 \text{ in.} \qquad \text{(O.K.)}$$

   d.   Check the total width of column required (see Figure 6-14):

$$9.8 + 2 = 11.8 \text{ in.} < 16 \text{ in.} \qquad \text{(O.K.)}$$

For other points along the continuous beam, use bar cutoff points recommended in Figure 6-3 and as shown in Figure 6-19.

9.   Prepare the stirrup design. Established values are $b_w = 12$ in., effective depth $d = 29.0$ in., $f'_c = 3000$ psi, and $f_y = 60,000$ psi.

   a.   The shear force V_u diagram may be observed in Figure 6-15. Since the diagram is unsymmetrical with respect to the centerline of the span, the stirrup design will be based on the shear in the interior portion of the end span where the maximum values occur. The resulting stirrup pattern will be used throughout the continuous beam. Only the applicable portion of the V_u diagram is shown.

   b.   Determine if stirrups are required:

$$\phi V_c = \phi 2 \sqrt{f'_c} \, b_w d = \frac{0.85(2\sqrt{3000})(12)(29.0)}{1000} = 32.4 \text{ kips}$$

$$\tfrac{1}{2}\phi V_c = \tfrac{1}{2}(32.4) = 16.2 \text{ kips}$$

FIGURE 6-14 Anchorage at column.

FIGURE 6-15 V_u diagram for stirrup design (Example 6-1).

At the critical section d distance (29.0 in.) from the face of support,

$$V_u^* = 92.6 - \frac{29.0}{12}(7.1) = 75.4 \text{ kips}$$

(Quantities at the critical section are designated with an asterisk.) Stirrups are required since $V_u^* > \frac{1}{2}\phi V_c$ (75.4 kips > 16.2 kips).

c. Find the length of span over which stirrups are required. Stirrups are required to the point where

$$V_u = \frac{1}{2}\phi V_c = 16.2 \text{ kips}$$

From Figure 6-15 and referencing from the face of support, $V_u =$ 16.2 kips at

$$\frac{92.6 - 16.2}{7.1} = 10.76 \text{ ft}$$

The distance from the face of support to where $V_u = \phi V_c = 32.4$ kips is

$$\frac{92.6 - 32.4}{7.1} = 8.48 \text{ ft}$$

d. On the V_u diagram, designate the area between the ϕV_c line, the V_u^* line, and the sloping V_u line as "Req'd ϕV_s." At locations between 2.42 ft and 8.48 ft from the face of support, the required ϕV_s varies. Designating the slope of the V_u diagram as m (kips/ft) and taking x (ft) from the face of support $(2.42 \leq x \leq 8.48)$ yields

$$\text{required } \phi V_s = \text{maximum } V_u - \phi V_c - mx$$

$$= 92.6 - 32.4 - 7.1x$$

$$= 60.2 - 7.1x$$

e. Assume a No. 3 vertical stirrup $(A_v = 0.22 \text{ in.}^2)$:

$$\text{required } s^* = \frac{A_v f_y d}{V_s}$$

$$= \frac{\phi A_v f_y d}{\text{required } \phi V_s^*}$$

$$= \frac{\phi A_v f_y d}{V_u^* - \phi V_c}$$

$$= \frac{0.85(0.22)(60)(29)}{75.4 - 32.4} = 7.57 \text{ in.}$$

Use 7½ in. spacing between the critical section and the face of support.

f.   Establish ACI Code maximum spacing requirements:

$$4\sqrt{f_c'}\,b_w d = \frac{4\sqrt{3000}(12)(29)}{1000} = 76.2 \text{ kips}$$

Calculating V_u^* at the critical section yields

$$\phi V_s^* = V_u^* - \phi V_c$$

$$= 75.4 - 32.4 = 43.0 \text{ kips}$$

$$V_s^* = \frac{\phi V_s^*}{\phi} = \frac{43.0}{0.85} = 50.6 \text{ kips}$$

Since 50.6 kips < 76.2 kips, the maximum spacing should be the smaller of $d/2$ or 24 in.:

$$\frac{d}{2} = \frac{29.0}{2} = 14.5 \text{ in.}$$

Also check:

$$s_{\max} = \frac{A_v f_y}{50 b_w} = \frac{0.22(60{,}000)}{50(12)} = 22.0 \text{ in.}$$

Therefore, use a maximum spacing of 14.5 in.

g.   Determine the spacing requirements based on shear strength to be furnished. The denominator of the following formula for required spacing uses the expression for required ϕV_s from step d:

$$\text{required } s = \frac{\phi A_v f_y d}{\text{required } \phi V_s} = \frac{0.85(0.22)(60)(29)}{60.2 - 7.1x} = \frac{325.4}{60.2 - 7.1x}$$

The results for several arbitrary values of x are shown tabulated and plotted in Figure 6-16.

h.   Using Figure 6-16, the stirrup pattern shown in Figure 6-17 is developed. Despite the lack of symmetry in the shear diagram, the stirrup pattern is symmetrical with respect to the centerline of the span. This is conservative and will be used for all spans.

The design sketches are shown in Figure 6-18. As with the slab design, the typical bar cutoff points of Figure 6-3 are used for this beam. Therefore, all bars terminate in compression zones, and the requirements of the ACI Code, Section 12.10.5, need not be checked.

x (ft)	Req'd s (in.)
2.41	7.55
4	10.23
5	13.17
6	18.49

FIGURE 6-16   Stirrup spacing requirements for Example 6-1.

FIGURE 6-17   Stirrup spacing for Example 6-1 end span (interior spans similar).

Main Reinforcing-End Span
(a)

Main Reinforcing-Interior Span
(b)

Section A–A
(c)

FIGURE 6-18   Design sketches for Example 6-1. (Stirrup spacings not shown.)

PROBLEMS

For the following problems, all concrete is normal weight and all steel is grade 60 (f_y = 60,000 psi).

6-1. For the one-way slab shown, determine all moments and shears for service loads of 100 psf dead load (includes the slab weight) and 300 psf live load.

PROBLEM 6-1

6-2. For the continuous beam shown, determine all moments and shears for service loads of 2.00 kips/ft dead load (includes weight of beam and slab) and 3.00 kips/ft live load.

PROBLEM 6-2

6-3. Using the ACI coefficients, design a continuous reinforced concrete beam that will span four supports. The end spans are 24 ft long; the center span is 28 ft long (spans are measured center to center of supports). The exterior support (a spandrel beam) and the interior supporting girders have widths *b* of 18 in. The service loads are 0.75 kip/ft dead load (not including the weight of the beam) and 1.0 kip/ft live load. Use f'_c = 3000 psi. Use only tension reinforcing. Design for moment only. Use the recommended bar cutoffs shown in Figure 6-3.

6-4. A floor system is to consist of beams, girders, and a slab; a partial floor plan is shown. Service loads are to be 30 psf dead load (does *not* include the weight of the floor system) and 150 psf live load. Use f'_c = 4000 psi.

(a) Design the continuous one-way slab.

(b) Design the continuous beam along column line 2.

Be sure to include complete design sketches.

Typical

Partial Floor Plan

PROBLEM 6-4

CHAPTER 7

Serviceability

7-1

INTRODUCTION

The ACI Code, Section 9.1, requires that bending members have structural strength adequate to support the anticipated factored design loads and that they have adequate performance at service load levels. Adequate performance, or *serviceability,* relates to deflections and cracking in reinforced concrete beams and slabs. It is important to realize that serviceability is to be assured at *service load levels,* not at ultimate strength. At service loads, deflections should be held to specified limits because of many considerations, among which are aesthetics, effects on nonstructural elements such as windows and partitions, undesirable vibrations, and proper functioning of roof drainage systems. Any cracking should be limited to hairline cracks for reasons of both appearance and prevention of corrosion of the reinforcing steel.

7-2

DEFLECTIONS

Guidelines for the control of deflections are found in the ACI Code, Section 9.5. In addition, Table 9.5(b) of the code indicates the maximum permissible deflections. For the purpose of following the code guidelines, either of two methods may be used: (1) using the minimum thickness (or depth of member) criteria as established in Table 9.5(a) of the code, which will result in sections that are sufficiently deep and stiff so that deflections will not be excessive; and (2) calculating expected deflections using standard deflection formulas in combination with the code provisions for moment of inertia and the effects of the load/time history of the member.

Minimum thickness (depth) guidelines are simple and direct and should be used whenever possible. Note that the tabulated minimum thicknesses apply to nonprestressed, one-way members that do not support and are not attached to partitions or other construction likely to be damaged by large deflections. For members not within these guidelines, deflections *must* be calculated.

For the second method, in which deflections are calculated, the ACI Code stipulates that the members should have their deflections checked at *service load levels.* Therefore, the *properties* at service load levels must be used. Under service loads, concrete flexural members still exhibit generally elastic-type behavior (see Figure 1-1) but will have been subjected to cracking in tension zones at any point where the applied moment is large enough to produce tensile stress in excess of concrete tensile strength. The cross section for moment-of-inertia determination then has the shape shown in Figure 7-1.

FIGURE 7-1 Typical cracked cross section.

The moment of inertia of the cracked section of Figure 7-1 is designated I_{cr}. It is determined based on the assumption that the concrete is cracked to the neutral axis. In other words, the concrete is assumed to have no tensile strength, and the small tension zone below the neutral axis and above the upper limit of cracking is neglected.

The moment of inertia of the cracked section described represents one end of a range of values that may be used for deflection calculations. At the other end of the range, as a result of a small bending moment and a maximum flexural stress less than the modulus of rupture, the full uncracked section may be considered in determining the moment of inertia to resist deflection. This is termed the *moment of inertia of the gross cross section* and is designated I_g.

In reality, both I_{cr} and I_g occur in a bending member in which the maximum moment is in excess of the cracking moment. The I_{cr} occurs at or near the cracks, whereas the I_g occurs between the cracks. Research has indicated that due to the presence of the two extreme conditions, a more realistic value of a moment of inertia lies somewhere between these values. The ACI Code recommends that deflections be calculated using an *effective moment of inertia I_e*, where

$$I_g > I_e > I_{cr}$$

Once the effective moment of inertia is determined, the member deflection may be calculated by using standard deflection expressions. The effective moment of inertia will depend on the values of the moment of inertia of the gross section and the moment of inertia of the cracked section. The gross (or uncracked) moment of inertia for a rectangular shape may be easily calculated from

$$I_g = \frac{bh^3}{12}$$

This expression neglects the presence of any reinforcing steel.

7-3

CALCULATION OF I_{cr}

The moment of inertia of the cracked cross section can also be calculated in the normal way once the problem of the differing materials (steel and concrete) is overcome. To accomplish this, the steel area will be replaced by an equivalent area of concrete A_{eq} This is a fictitious concrete that *can* resist tension. The determination of the magnitude of A_{eq} is based on the theory (from strength of materials) that when two differing elastic materials are subjected to equal strains the stresses in the materials will be in proportion to their moduli of elasticity.

In Figure 7-2 ϵ_1 is the compressive strain in the concrete at the top of the beam and ϵ_2 is a tensile strain at the level of the steel. Using the notation

$$f_s = \text{tensile steel stress}$$
$$f_{c(\text{tens})} = \text{theoretical tensile concrete stress at the level of the steel}$$
$$E_s = \text{steel modulus of elasticity}$$
$$E_c = \text{concrete modulus of elasticity}$$

the following relationships can be established:

$$\epsilon_2 = \frac{f_s}{E_s} \quad \text{and} \quad \epsilon_2 = \frac{f_{c(\text{tens})}}{E_c}$$

Equating these two expressions and solving for f_s yields

$$\frac{f_s}{E_s} = \frac{f_{c(\text{tens})}}{E_c}$$

$$f_s = \frac{E_s}{E_c}[f_{c(\text{tens})}]$$

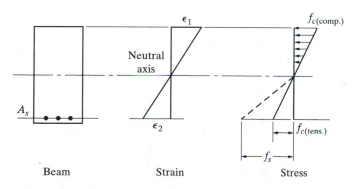

FIGURE 7-2   Beam bending: elastic theory.

The ratio E_s/E_c is normally called the *modular ratio* and is denoted n. Therefore,

$$f_s = nf_{c(\text{tens})}$$

The ACI Code, Section A.5.4, indicates that values of n may be taken as the nearest whole number (but not less than 6). Values of n are tabulated in Table A-6.

Since we are replacing the steel (theoretically) with an equivalent concrete area, the equivalent concrete area A_{eq} must provide the same tensile resistance as that provided by the steel. Therefore,

$$A_{eq}f_{c(\text{tens})} = f_s A_s$$

Substituting, we obtain

$$A_{eq}f_{c(\text{tens})} = nf_{c(\text{tens})}A_s$$

from which

$$A_{eq} = nA_s$$

This defines the equivalent area of concrete with which we are replacing the steel. Another way of visualizing this is to consider the steel to be transformed into an equivalent concrete area of nA_s. The resulting *transformed concrete cross section* is composed of a single (though hypothetical) material and may be dealt with in the normal fashion for neutral-axis and moment-of-inertia determinations. Figure 7-3 depicts the transformed section. Since the steel is normally assumed to be concentrated at its centroid, which is a distance d from the compression face, the replacing equivalent concrete area must also be assumed to act at the same location. Therefore, the representation of this area is shown as a thin rectangle extending out past the beam sides. Recalling that the cross section is assumed cracked up to the neutral axis, the resulting effective area is as shown in Figure 7-4, and the neutral axis will be located a distance $\bar{y}$ down from a reference axis at the top of the section.

The neutral axis may be determined by taking a summation of moments of the effective areas about the reference axis:

FIGURE 7-3 Method of transformed section.

FIGURE 7-4   Effective area.

$$\bar{y} = \frac{\Sigma(Ay)}{\Sigma A} = \frac{(b\bar{y})\dfrac{\bar{y}}{2} + nA_sd}{b\bar{y} + nA_s}$$

$$b(\bar{y}^2) + nA_s\bar{y} = \frac{b(\bar{y}^2)}{2} + nA_sd$$

$$\frac{b(\bar{y}^2)}{2} + nA_s\bar{y} - nA_sd = 0$$

This is a quadratic equation of the form $ax^2 + bx + c = 0$, and it may be solved either by completion of the square, as was done in Example 3-7, or by using the formula for roots of a quadratic equation, which will result in the following useful expression:

$$\bar{y} = \frac{nA_s\left[\sqrt{1 + 2\dfrac{bd}{nA_s}} - 1\right]}{b}$$

Once the neutral axis is located, the moment of inertia (I_{cr}) may be found using the familiar transfer formula from engineering mechanics.

Example 7-1 _____

Find the cracked moment of inertia for the cross section shown in Figure 7-5a. Use $A_s = 2.00$ in.^{2}, $n = 9$ (Table A-6), and $f'_c = 3000$ psi.

Solution:

With reference to the transformed section, shown in Figure 7-5b, the neutral axis is located as follows:

FIGURE 7-5 Sketches for Example 7-1.

$$\bar{y} = \frac{nA_s\left[\sqrt{1 + 2\dfrac{bd}{nA_s}} - 1\right]}{b}$$

$$= \frac{9(2.0)\left[\sqrt{1 + 2\dfrac{(8)(17)}{9(2.0)}} - 1\right]}{8}$$

$$= 6.78 \text{ in.}$$

The moment of inertia of the cracked section may be now be found (all units are inches):

$$I_{cr} = \frac{b\bar{y}^3}{3} + nA_s(d - \bar{y})^2$$

$$= \frac{8(6.78)^3}{3} + 18(17 - 6.78)^2$$

$$= 831.1 + 1880$$

$$= 2711 \text{ in.}^4$$

If the beam cross section contains compression steel, this steel may also be transformed and the neutral-axis location and cracked moment-of-inertia calculations can be carried out as before. Since the compression steel actually displaces concrete that is in compression, it should theoretically be transformed using $(n - 1)A_s'$ rather than nA_s'. For deflection calculations, which are only approximate, however, the use of nA_s' will not detract from the accuracy expected. The resulting transformed section will appear as shown in Figure 7-6.

The neutral axis location may be determined from

$$\frac{b}{2}\bar{y}^2 + nA_s'\bar{y} - nA_s'd' - nA_sd + nA_s\bar{y} = 0$$

FIGURE 7-6   Doubly reinforced beam.

and the moment of inertia with respect to the neutral axis from

$$I_{cr} = \frac{b\bar{y}^3}{3} + nA_s(d - \bar{y})^2 + nA_s'(\bar{y} - d')^2$$

7-4

IMMEDIATE DEFLECTION

Immediate deflection is the deflection that occurs as soon as load is applied on the member. For all practical purposes, the member is elastic. The ACI Code, Section 9.5.2.3, states that this deflection may be calculated using a concrete modulus of elasticity E_c as specified in Section 8.5.1 and an effective moment of inertia I_e computed as follows:

$$I_e = \left\{ \left(\frac{M_{cr}}{M_a}\right)^3 I_g + \left[1 - \left(\frac{M_{cr}}{M_a}\right)^3\right] I_{cr} \right\} \leq I_g$$

where

I_e = effective moment of inertia

I_{cr} = moment of inertia of the cracked section transformed to concrete

I_g = moment of inertia of the gross (uncracked) concrete cross section about the centroidal axis, neglecting all steel reinforcement

M_a = maximum moment in the member at the stage for which the deflection is being computed

M_{cr} = moment that would initially crack the cross section computed from

$$M_{cr} = \frac{f_r I_g}{y_t}$$

where

f_r = modulus of rupture for the concrete. This is $7.5\sqrt{f_c'}$ for normal-weight concrete; values are tabulated in Table A-6; modifications for f_r for lightweight aggregate concretes are indicated in the ACI Code, Sections 9.5.2.3a and b

y_t = distance from the neutral axis of the uncracked cross section (neglecting steel) to the extreme tension fiber

Inspection of the formula for the effective moment of inertia will show that if the maximum moment is low with respect to the cracking moment M_{cr}, the moment of inertia of the gross section I_g will be the dominant factor. If the maximum moment is large with respect to the cracking moment, however, the moment of inertia of the cracked section I_{cr} will be dominant. In any case, I_e will lie somewhere between I_{cr} and I_g. For continuous beams, the use of the average value of the effective moments of inertia existing at sections of critical positive and negative moments is recommended, although some authorities point out that the use of midspan section properties will also give satisfactory results.

The actual calculation of deflections will be made using the standard deflection methods for elastic members. Deflection formulas of the type found in standard handbooks may be suitable, or we may use more rigorous techniques when necessary.

7-5

LONG-TERM DEFLECTION

In addition to deflections that occur immediately, reinforced concrete members are subject to added deflections that occur gradually over long periods. These additional deflections are due mainly to creep and shrinkage and may eventually become excessive. The additional (or long-term) deflections are computed based on two items: (1) the amount of sustained dead and live load and (2) the amount of compression reinforcement in the beam. The additional long-term deflections may be estimated as follows:

$$\Delta_{LT} = \lambda \Delta_i = \left(\frac{\xi}{1 + 50\rho'} \right) \Delta_i$$

where

Δ_{LT} = additional long-term deflection

Δ_i = immediate deflection due to sustained loads

λ = a multiplier for additional long-term deflections (ACI Eq. 9-10)

ρ' = nonprestressed compression reinforcement ratio (A_s'/bd)

ξ = time-dependent factor for sustained loads: 5 years or more   2.0
$\qquad\qquad\qquad\qquad\qquad\qquad\qquad\qquad\qquad$ 12 months   1.4
$\qquad\qquad\qquad\qquad\qquad\qquad\qquad\qquad\qquad$ 6 months   1.2
$\qquad\qquad\qquad\qquad\qquad\qquad\qquad\qquad\qquad$ 3 months   1.0

Some judgment will be required in determining just what portion of the live loads should be considered *sustained*. In a residential application, 20% sustained live load might be a logical estimate, whereas in storage facilities, 100% sustained live load would be reasonable.

The calculated deflections must not exceed the maximum permissible deflections that are found in the ACI Code, Table 9.5(b). This table sets permissible deflections in terms of fractions of span length. These limitations guard against damage to the various parts of the system (both structural and nonstructural parts) as a result of excessive deflection. In the case of attached nonstructural elements, only the deflection that takes place after such attachment needs to be considered.

Example 7-2

Determine which of the ACI Code deflection criteria will be satisfied by the nonprestressed reinforced concrete beam, having a cross section shown in Figure 7-7 and subjected to maximum moments of M_{DL} = 20 ft-kips and M_{LL} = 15 ft-kips. Assume a 50% sustained live load and a sustained load time period of more than 5 years. Assume normal-weight concrete. Use f'_c = 3000 psi and f_y = 60,000 psi. The beam is on a simple span of 30 ft.

Solution:

1.   The maximum *service* moments at midspan are

$$M_{DL} = 20 \text{ ft-kips} \quad \text{and} \quad M_{LL} = 15 \text{ ft-kips}$$

2.   Check the beam depth based on the ACI Code Table 9.5(a):

$$\text{minimum } h = \frac{\ell}{16} = \frac{30(12)}{16} = 22.5 \text{ in.}$$

FIGURE 7-7   Sketch for Example 7-2.

Since 22.5 > 16.5, deflections must be calculated.

3.   The effective moment of inertia will be calculated using

$$I_e = \left\{ \left(\frac{M_{cr}}{M_a} \right)^3 I_g + \left[1 - \left(\frac{M_{cr}}{M_a} \right)^3 \right] I_{cr} \right\}$$

Therefore, we first must compute the various terms within the expression. The moment of inertia of the cracked transformed section will be determined with reference to Figure 7-8. The steel area of 2.37 in.^{2} and a modular ratio n of 9 (see Table A-6) will result in a transformed area of

$$nA_s = 9(2.37) = 21.3 \text{ in.}^2$$

The neutral-axis location is determined as follows:

$$\bar{y} = \frac{nA_s \left[\sqrt{1 + 2\dfrac{bd}{nA_s}} - 1 \right]}{b}$$

$$= \frac{21.3 \left[\sqrt{1 + 2\dfrac{(10)(14)}{21.3}} - 1 \right]}{10}$$

$$= 5.88 \text{ in.}$$

The moment of inertia of the cracked transformed section is then determined:

$$I_{cr} = \frac{10(5.88)^3}{3} + 21.3(14 - 5.88)^2$$

$$= 2082 \text{ in.}^4$$

Determination of the moment of inertia of the gross section results in

$$I_g = \frac{bh^3}{12} = \frac{1}{12}(10)(16.5)^3 = 3743 \text{ in.}^4$$

FIGURE 7-8   Transformed section for Example 7-2.

The moment that would initially crack the cross section may be determined next:

$$M_{cr} = \frac{f_r I_g}{y_t}$$

where

$$y_t = \frac{16.5}{2} = 8.25$$

$$f_r = 7.5\sqrt{f_c'} = 0.411 \text{ ksi} \qquad \text{(from Table A-6)}$$

Therefore,

$$M_{cr} = \frac{0.411(3743)}{8.25(12)} = 15.5 \text{ ft-kips}$$

We will assume that $M_a = 35$ ft-kips on the basis that it is the maximum moment that the beam must carry that will establish the crack pattern. This is not in strict accordance with the ACI Code, which indicates that M_a should be the maximum moment occurring at the stage the deflection is computed. It is logical that, since the cracking pattern is irreversible, the use of the effective moment of inertia based on the full maximum moment is more realistic. This approach is conservative and will furnish a lower I_e, which will subsequently result in a larger computed deflection.

4. Determine the effective moment of inertia:

$$I_e = \left\{ \left(\frac{M_{cr}}{M_a} \right)^3 I_g + \left[1 - \left(\frac{M_{cr}}{M_a} \right)^3 \right] I_{cr} \right\}$$

$$= \left\{ \left(\frac{15.5}{35} \right)^3 3743 + \left[1 - \left(\frac{15.5}{35} \right)^3 \right] (2082) \right\} = 2226 \text{ in.}^4$$

5. Compute the immediate dead load deflection ($M_{\text{DL}} = 20$ ft-kips):

$$\Delta = \frac{5w\ell^4}{384 E_c I_e} = \frac{5M\ell^2}{48 E_c I_e}$$

where M is the moment due to a uniform load and E_c may be found in Table A-6. Thus

$$\Delta = \frac{5(20)(30)^2(1728)}{48(3120)(2226)} = 0.466 \text{ in.}$$

6. Compute the immediate live load deflection ($M_{\text{LL}} = 15$ ft-kips). By proportion,

$$\Delta = \frac{15}{20}(0.466) = 0.35 \text{ in.}$$

TABLE 7-1 Permissible versus Actual Deflections (Example 7-2)

Case	Maximum permissible deflection	Actual computed deflection
1	$\frac{\ell}{180} = \frac{30(12)}{180} = 2$ in.	$\Delta_{LL} = 0.35$ in. (immediate LL)
2	$\frac{\ell}{360} = \frac{30(12)}{360} = 1$ in.	$\Delta_{LL} = 0.35$ in. (immediate LL)
3	$\frac{\ell}{480} = \frac{30(12)}{480} = 0.75$ in.	$\Delta_{LL} + \Delta_{LT} = 0.35 + 1.28 = 1.63$ in.
4	$\frac{\ell}{240} = \frac{30(12)}{240} = 1.5$ in.	$\Delta_{LL} + \Delta_{LT} = 0.35 + 1.28 = 1.63$ in.

7. The total immediate DL + LL deflection is

$$0.466 + 0.35 = 0.816 \text{ in.}$$

8. The long-term deflection (DL + sustained LL) multiplier is

$$\lambda = \frac{\xi}{1 + 50\rho'} = \frac{2.0}{1 + 0} = 2.0$$

Since $M_{DL} = 20$ ft-kips and 50% $M_{LL} = 7.5$ ft-kips, the sustained moment for long-term deflection = 27.5 ft-kips. Then

$$\Delta_{LT} = \frac{27.5}{20}(0.466)(2.0) = 1.28 \text{ in.}$$

9. A comparison of actual deflections to maximum permissible deflections may now be made. In the comparison, made in Table 7-1, the maximum permissible deflections are from the ACI Code, Table 9.5(b). Case 1 in Table 7-1 applies to flat roofs not supporting or attached to nonstructural elements likely to be damaged by large deflections. Case 2 applies to floors not supporting or attached to nonstructural elements likely to be damaged by large deflections. Since the permissible deflection is not exceeded in case 1 or case 2, the beam of Example 7-2 is limited to usage as defined by those two cases.

7-6

DEFLECTIONS FOR CONTINUOUS SPANS

To compute deflections for continuous spans subject to uniformly distributed loads such as the beam in Figure 7-9, the following approximate approach may be used:

$$\Delta = \frac{5w\ell_n^4}{384E_cI_e} - \frac{M\ell_n^2}{8E_cI_e}$$

FIGURE 7-9   Continuous beam.

where

M = negative moment at supports (based on service loads) for span being investigated; if values are different, use average moment

ℓ_n = clear span

E_c = modulus of elasticity for concrete (see Table A-6)

w = uniformly distributed service load

I_e = effective moment of inertia; use the average value of I_e at positive moment area and I_e at negative moment area

In a similar manner, for long-term deflections the long-term deflection multiplier should be averaged for the different locations.

7-7

CRACK CONTROL

With the advent of higher-strength reinforcing steels, where more strain is required to produce the higher stresses, cracking of reinforced concrete flexural members has become more troublesome.

Of primary interest when considering cracking is the width of the cracks that form. Rather than a small number of large cracks, it is more desirable to have only hairline cracks and accept more numerous cracks if necessary. The present ACI Code methods for crack control are based largely on research that has shown that crack width is generally proportional to the amount of stress in the steel and the amount of cover on the steel and that crack width is minimized if the steel is well distributed in the tension zone of the concrete. This problem is discussed in the ACI Code, Section 10.6, and applies to beams and one-way slabs.

The ACI Code directs that only deformed reinforcement is to be used and that the tension reinforcement must be *well distributed* in zones of maximum concrete tension. The problem of flanges in tension (negative moment in T-beams) is specially noted.

Where the design yield strength f_y of the steel exceeds 40,000 psi, a special check must be performed to ensure that there is proper distribution of the tension steel. For a particular beam or slab, a quantity Z is calculated for the check on the steel distribution, with upper limits of Z being set depending on the type of exposure to which the structure will be subjected. Essentially, these limits are values of Z corresponding to crack widths of 0.016 in. for interior exposures and 0.013 in. for exterior exposures, which the ACI committee has judged as reasonable maximums. The ACI has defined Z as

$$Z = f_s \sqrt[3]{d_c A}$$

where

f_s = calculated stress in the steel at service loads (and may be taken as $0.6f_y$) (ksi)

d_c = thickness of concrete cover measured from the extreme tension fiber to the *center of the closest bar* (in.)

A = effective tension area of concrete surrounding the main tension reinforcing bars and having the same centroid as that reinforcement, divided by the number of bars (in.^{2})

Z = quantity limiting distribution of flexural reinforcement, with maximum limits of 175 kips/in. for interior exposures and 145 kips/in. for exterior exposures

Example 7-3

Check the steel distribution for the beam shown in Figure 7-10 to establish whether reasonable control of flexural cracking is accomplished in accordance with the ACI Code, Section 10.6. Use f_y = 60,000 psi.

Solution:

1. The concrete cover from the extreme tension fiber to the center of the closest bar is

$$d_c = 1.5 + 0.38 + \frac{1.128}{2} = 2.44 \text{ in.}$$

FIGURE 7-10 Sketch for Example 7-3.

2.   The effective tension area per bar A may be expressed as follows:

$$A = \frac{bh_T}{\text{number of bars}}$$

where h_T is a linear distance equal to twice the distance from the extreme tension fiber to the centroid of the tensile reinforcement:

$$h_T = (1.5 + 0.38 + 1.128 + 0.5)2 = 7.0 \text{ in.}$$

Therefore,

$$A = \frac{15(7.0)}{8} = 13.13 \text{ in.}^2 \text{ per bar}$$

3. $$Z = f_s\sqrt[3]{d_c A}$$

where

$$f_s = 0.60f_y = 0.60(60) = 36 \text{ ksi}$$
$$Z = 36\sqrt[3]{2.44(13.13)} = 114 \text{ kips/in.}$$
$$114 < 145 \text{ and } 175 \qquad\qquad\qquad\text{(O.K.)}$$

Therefore, the steel distribution is satisfactory for either interior or exterior exposure.

PROBLEMS

7-1.   Locate the neutral axis and calculate the moment of inertia for the cracked transformed cross sections shown. Use $f_c' = 4000$ psi and $f_y = 60,000$ psi.

(a)   (b)   (c)

PROBLEM 7-1

7-2.   Find I_g and I_{cr} for the T-beam shown. The effective flange width is 60 in., and $f_c' = 4000$ psi.

PROBLEM 7-2

7-3.   The beam of cross section shown is on a simple span of 20 ft and carries service loads of 1.5 kips/ft dead load (includes beam weight) and 1.0 kip/ft live load. Use $f_c' = 3000$ psi and $f_y = 60,000$ psi.
   (a)   Compute the immediate deflection due to dead load and live load.
   (b)   Compute the long-term deflection due to the dead load. Assume the time period for sustained loads to be in excess of 5 years.

PROBLEM 7-3

7-4.   Rework Problem 7-3 using a beam on a simple span of 26 ft, service load of 0.8 kip/ft dead load (includes beam weight) over the full span, and a point live load of 12 kips at midspan. Assume tensile reinforcing to be three No. 9 bars and $f_c' = 4000$ psi.

7-5.   The floor beam shown is on a simple span of 16 ft. The beam supports nonstructural elements likely to be damaged by large deflections. The service loads are 0.6 kip/ft dead load (does not include the beam weight) and 1.40

PROBLEM 7-5

kips/ft live load. Assume that the live load is 60% sustained for 6-month periods. Use $f'_c = 3000$ psi and $f_y = 60,000$ psi.

(a) Check the beam for deflections.

(b) If the beam is unsatisfactory, redesign it so that it meets both flexural strength and deflections requirements.

7-6. Calculate the expected long-term deflection due to dead load and sustained live load for (a) the slab and (b) the beam of the floor system designed for Problem 6-4. Assume 10% sustained live load and a time period in excess of 5 years.

7-7. Check the cross sections of Problems 7-1(a) and (b) for acceptability under the ACI Code provisions for distribution of flexural reinforcement (crack control).

7-8. Check the distribution of flexural reinforcement for the members designed in Problems 2-18 and 2-22. If necessary, redesign the steel.

CHAPTER 8

Walls

8-1

INTRODUCTION

Walls are generally used to provide lateral support for an earth fill, embankment, or some other material and to support vertical loads. Some of the more common types of walls are shown in Figure 8-1.

One primary purpose for these walls is to maintain a difference in the elevation of the ground surface on each side of the wall. The earth whose ground surface is at the higher elevation is commonly called the *backfill,* and the wall is said to retain this backfill.

232

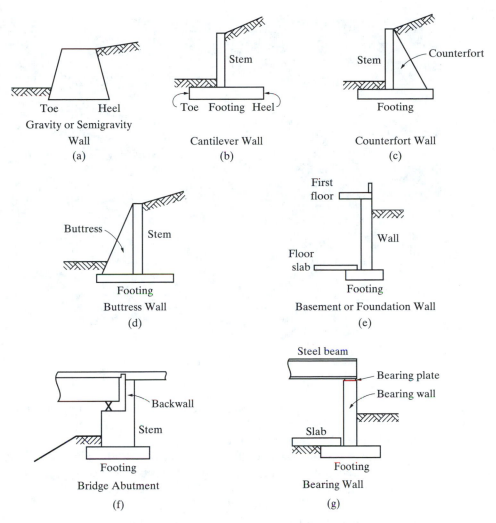

FIGURE 8-1   Common types of walls.

All the walls shown in Figure 8-1 have applications in either building or bridge projects. They do not necessarily behave in an identical manner under load, but still serve the same basic function of providing lateral support for a mass of earth or other material that is at a higher elevation behind the wall than the earth or other material in front of the wall. Hence they all may be broadly termed *retaining structures* or *retaining walls*. Some retaining walls may support vertical loads in addition to the lateral loads from the retained materials.

The gravity wall (Figure 8-1a) depends mostly on its own weight for stability. It is usually made of plain concrete and is used for walls up to approximately 10 ft in height. The semigravity wall is a modification of the gravity wall in which small

PHOTO 8-1   Cantilever retaining wall ($h_w = 12'\text{-}0''$).

amounts of reinforcing steel are introduced. This, in effect, reduces the massiveness of the wall.

The cantilever wall (Figure 8-1b) is the most common type of retaining structure and generally is used for walls in the range from 10 to 25 ft in height. It is so named because its individual parts (toe, heel, and stem) behave as, and are designed as, cantilever beams. Aside from its stability, the capacity of the wall is a function of the strength of its individual parts.

The counterfort wall (Figure 8-1c) may be economical when the wall height is in excess of 25 ft. The counterforts are spaced at intervals and act as tension members to support the stem. The stem is then designed as a continuous member spanning horizontally between the counterforts.

The buttress wall (Figure 8-1d) is similar to the counterfort wall except that the buttresses are located on the side of the stem opposite to the retained material and act as compression members to support the stem. The counterfort wall is more commonly used because it has a clean, uncluttered exposed face and allows for more efficient use of space in front of the wall.

The basement or foundation wall (Figure 8-1e) may act as a cantilever retaining wall. The first floor may provide an additional horizontal reaction similar to the basement floor slab, however, thereby making the wall act as a vertical beam. This wall would then be designed as a simply supported member spanning between the first floor and the basement floor slab.

The bridge abutment (Figure 8-1f) is similar in some respects to the basement wall. The bridge superstructure induces horizontal as well as vertical loads, thus altering the normal cantilever behavior.

The bearing wall (Figure 8-1g) may exist with or without lateral loads. A bearing wall may be defined as a wall that supports any vertical load in addition to its own weight. Depending on the magnitudes of the vertical and lateral loads, the wall may have to be designed for combined bending and axial compression. Bearing walls and basement walls are further discussed later in this chapter.

8-2

LATERAL FORCES ON RETAINING WALLS

The design of a retaining wall must account for all the applied loads. The load that presents the greatest problem and is of primary concern is the lateral earth pressure induced by the retained soil. The comprehensive earth pressure theories evolving from the original Coulomb and Rankine theories can be found in almost any textbook on soil mechanics.

The magnitude and direction of the pressures as well as the pressure distribution exerted by a soil backfill upon a wall are highly indeterminate, due to many variables. These variables include, but are not limited to, the type of backfill used, the drainage of the backfill material, the level of the water table, the slope of the backfill material, added loads applied on the backfill, the degree of soil compaction, and movement of the wall caused by the action of backfill.

An important consideration is that water must be prevented from accumulating in the backfill material. Walls are rarely designed to retain saturated material, which means that proper drainage must be provided. It is generally agreed that the best backfill material behind a retaining structure is a well-drained, cohesionless material. Hence it is the condition that is usually specified and designed for. Materials that contain combinations of types of soil will act like the predominant material.

The lateral earth pressure can exist and develop in three different categories: active state, at rest, and passive state. If a wall is absolutely rigid, earth pressure at rest will develop. If the wall should deflect or move a very small amount away from the backfill, active earth pressure will develop and in effect reduce the lateral earth pressure occurring in the at-rest state. Should the wall be forced to move toward the backfill, for some reason, passive earth pressure will develop and increase the lateral earth pressure appreciably above that occurring in the at-rest state. As indicated, the magnitude of earth pressure at rest lies somewhere between active and passive earth pressures.

Under normal conditions, earth pressure at rest is of such a magnitude that the wall deflects slightly, thus relieving itself of the at-rest pressure. The active pressure

Unit
pressure
(passive state)

Unit
pressure
(active state)

FIGURE 8-2 Analysis of forces acting on walls: level backfill.

results. For this reason, retaining walls are generally designed for active earth pressure due to the retained soil.

Because of the involved nature of a rigorous analysis of an earth backfill and the variability of the material and conditions, assumptions and approximations are made with respect to the nature of lateral pressures on a retaining structure. It is common practice to assume a linear active and passive earth pressure distribution. The pressure intensity is assumed to increase with depth as a function of the weight of the soil in a manner similar to that which would occur in a fluid. Hence this horizontal pressure of the earth against the wall is frequently called an *equivalent fluid pressure*. Experience has indicated that walls designed on the basis of these assumptions and those of the following discussion are safe and relatively economical.

Level Backfill

If we consider a level backfill (of well-drained cohensionless soil), the assumed pressure diagram is shown in Figure 8-2. The unit pressure intensity p_y in any plane a distance y down from the top is

$$p_y = K_a w_e y$$

Therefore, the total active earth pressure acting on a 1 ft width of wall may be calculated as the product of the average pressure on the total wall height h_w and the area on which this pressure acts:

$$H_a = \frac{1}{2} K_a w_e h_w^2 \tag{8-1}$$

where K_a, the *coefficient of active earth pressure,* has been established by both Rankine and Coulomb to be

$$K_a = \frac{1 - \sin \phi}{1 + \sin \phi} = \tan^2\left(45° - \frac{\phi}{2}\right) \qquad (8\text{-}2)$$

and

$$w_e = \text{unit weight of earth (lb/ft}^3)$$

$$\phi = \text{angle of internal friction (soil on soil)}$$

K_a usually varies from 0.27 to 0.40. The term $K_a w_e$ in Equation (8-1) is generally called an *equivalent fluid weight*, since the resulting pressure is identical to that which would occur in a fluid of that weight (units are lb/ft^3).

In a similar manner, the total passive earth pressure force may be established as

$$H_p = \tfrac{1}{2}K_p w_e (h')^2 \qquad (8\text{-}3)$$

where h' is the height of earth and K_p is the *coefficient of passive earth pressure:*

$$K_p = \frac{1 + \sin \phi}{1 - \sin \phi} = \tan^2\left(45° + \frac{\phi}{2}\right) = \frac{1}{K_a}$$

Note that K_p usually varies from 2.5 to 4.0.

The total force in each case is assumed to act at one-third the height of the triangular pressure distribution, as shown in Figure 8-2.

Sloping Backfill

If we consider a sloping backfill, the assumed active earth pressure distribution is shown in Figure 8-3, where $H_s = \tfrac{1}{2}K_a w_e h_b^2$, h_b is the height of the backfill at the back of the footing, and K_a is the coefficient of active earth pressure. Thus

FIGURE 8-3   Analysis of forces acting on walls: sloping backfill.

$$K_a = \cos\theta\left(\frac{\cos\theta - \sqrt{\cos^2\theta - \cos^2\phi}}{\cos\theta + \sqrt{\cos^2\theta - \cos^2\phi}}\right)$$

where θ is the slope angle of the backfill and ϕ is as previously defined. Note that H_s is shown acting parallel to the slope of the backfill.

For walls approximately 20 ft in height or less, it is recommended that the horizontal force component H_H simply be assumed equal to H_s and be assumed to act at $h_b/3$ above the bottom of the footing, as shown in Figure 8-3. The effect of the vertical force component H_V is neglected. This is a conservative approach.

Assuming a well-drained cohensionless soil backfill that has a unit weight of 110 lb/ft^3 and an internal friction angle ϕ of 33°40′, values of equivalent fluid weight for sloping backfill may be determined as listed in Table 8-1.

TABLE 8-1 $K_a w_e$ Values for Sloping Backfill

θ (deg)	$K_a w_e$ (lb/ft^3)
0	32
10	33
20	38
30	54

Level Backfill with Surcharge

Loads are often imposed on the backfill surface behind a retaining wall. They may be either live loads or dead loads. These loads are generally termed a *surcharge* and theoretically may be transformed into an equivalent height of earth.

A uniform surcharge over the adjacent area adds the same effect as an additional (equivalent) height of earth. This equivalent height of earth h_{su} may be obtained by

$$h_{su} = \frac{w_s}{w_e}$$

where

w_s = surcharge load (psf)

w_e = unit weight of earth (lb/ft^3)

In effect, this adds a rectangle of pressure behind the wall with a total lateral surcharge force assumed acting at its midheight, as shown in Figure 8-4. Surcharge loads far enough removed from the wall cause no additional pressure acting on the wall.

$$H_a = \frac{1}{2}K_a w_e h_w^2$$
(due to level backfill)

$$H_{su} = K_a w_e h_{su} h_w$$
(due to surcharge)

FIGURE 8-4   Forces acting on wall: level backfill and surcharge.

8-3

DESIGN OF REINFORCED CONCRETE CANTILEVER RETAINING WALLS

A retaining wall must be stable as a whole, and it must have sufficient strength to resist the forces acting on it. Four possible *modes of failure* will be considered. *Overturning about the toe,* point O, as shown in Figure 8-5, could occur due to lat-

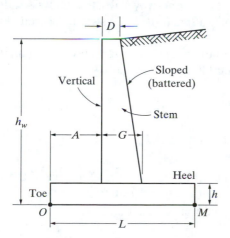

FIGURE 8-5   Cantilever retaining wall proportions.

eral loads. The stabilizing moment must be sufficiently in excess of the overturning moment so that an adequate factor of safety against overturning is provided. The factor of safety should never be less than 1.5 and should preferably be 2.0 or more. *Sliding on the base of the footing,* surface *OM* in Figure 8-5, could also occur due to lateral loads. The resisting force is based on an assumed coefficient of friction of concrete on earth. The factor of safety against sliding should never be less than 1.5 and should preferably be 2.0 or more. *Excessive soil pressure* under the footing will lead to undesirable settlements and possible rotation of the wall. Actual soil pressures should not be allowed to exceed specified maximum pressures, which depend on the characteristics of the underlying soil. The *structural failure of component parts of the wall* such as stem, toe, and heel, each acting as a cantilever beam, could occur. These must be designed to have sufficient strength to resist all anticipated loads.

A *general design procedure* for specific, known conditions may be summarized as follows:

1. Establish the general shape of the wall based on the desired height and function.
2. Establish the site soil conditions, loads, and other design parameters. This includes the determination of allowable soil pressure, earth-fill properties for active and passive pressure calculations, amount of surcharge, and the desired factors of safety.
3. Establish the tentative proportions of the wall.
4. Analyze the stability of the wall. Check factors of safety against overturning and sliding, and compare actual soil pressure with allowable soil pressure.
5. Assuming that all previous steps are satisfactory, design the component parts of the cantilever retaining wall, stem, toe, and heel as cantilever beams.

Using a procedure similar to that used for one-way slabs, the analysis and design of cantilever retaining walls is based on a 12 in. (1 ft) wide strip measured along the length of wall.

The tentative proportions of a cantilever retaining wall may be obtained from the following rules of thumb (see Figure 8-5):

1. Footing width L: Use $\frac{1}{2}h_w$ to $\frac{2}{3}h_w$.
2. Footing thickness h: Use $\frac{1}{10}h_w$.
3. Stem thickness G (at top of footing): Use $\frac{1}{12}h_w$.
4. Toe width A: Use $\frac{1}{4}L$ to $\frac{1}{3}L$.
5. Use a minimum wall batter of $\frac{1}{4}$ in./ft to improve the efficiency of the stem as a bending member and to decrease the quantity of concrete required.
6. The top of stem thickness D should not be less than 10 in.

The given rules of thumb will usually result in walls that can reasonably be designed. Depending on the specific conditions, however, dimensions may have to be adjusted somewhat to accommodate such design criteria as minimum A_s, maximum ρ, shear strength, anchorage, and development. One common alternative design approach is to assume a footing thickness and then immediately design the stem thickness for an assumed steel ratio. Once the stem thickness is established, the wall stability can be checked. Whichever procedure is used, adjustment of dimensions during the design is not uncommon.

Example 8-1 _____

Design a retaining wall for the conditions shown in Figure 8-6. Use $f_c' = 3000$ psi and $f_y = 60,000$ psi.

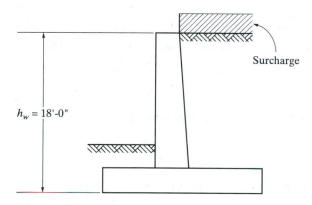

FIGURE 8-6   Sketch for Example 8-1.

Solution:

1. The general shape of the wall, as shown, is that of a cantilever wall, since the overall height of 18 ft is within the range in which this type of wall is normally economical.

2. The design data are unit weight of earth $w_e = 100$ lb/ft^3, allowable soil pressure = 4000 psf, equivalent fluid weight $K_a w_e = 30$ lb/ft^3, and surcharge load $w_s = 400$ psf. The desired factor of safety against overturning is 2.0 and against sliding is 1.5.

3. Establish tentative proportions for the wall.

    a.   Footing width:

$$\tfrac{1}{2} \text{ to } \tfrac{2}{3} \text{ of wall height}$$

$$\tfrac{1}{2}(18) \text{ to } \tfrac{2}{3}(18) = 9 \text{ to } 12 \text{ ft}$$

Use 11 ft.

b.   Footing thickness:

$$\tfrac{1}{10}(18) = 1.8 \text{ ft}$$

Use 1 ft 9 in.

c.   Stem thickness at top of footing:

$$\tfrac{1}{12}(18) = 1.5 \text{ ft}$$

Use 1 ft 6 in.

d.   Toe width:

$$\tfrac{1}{4} \text{ to } \tfrac{1}{3} \text{ footing width}$$

$$\tfrac{1}{4}(11) \text{ to } \tfrac{1}{3}(11) = 2.75 \text{ to } 3.67$$

Use 3 ft 0 in.

e.   Use a batter for the rear face of wall approximately ½ in./ft.

f.   Top of stem thickness, based on G and a batter of ½ in./ft:

$$D = G - (h_w - h)\tfrac{1}{2}$$

$$= 18 - (18 - 1.75)\tfrac{1}{2} = 9.88 \text{ in.}$$

Use 10 in. Therefore, the actual batter is

$$\frac{18 - 10}{18 - 1.75} = 0.492 \text{ in./ft}$$

The preliminary wall proportions are shown in Figure 8-7.

FIGURE 8-7   Tentative wall proportions, Example 8-1.

4.   For the stability analysis, use actual unfactored weights and loads in accordance with the ACI Code, Section 15.2.2.

   a.   *Factor of safety against overturning:* The tendency of the wall to overturn is a result of the horizontal loads acting on the wall. An assumption is made that in overturning, the wall will rotate about the toe and the horizontal loads are said to create an *overturning moment* about the toe. Any vertical loads will tend to create rotation about the toe in the opposite direction and are therefore said to provide a *stabilizing moment.*

   The factor of safety against overturning is then expressed as

$$FS = \frac{\text{stabilizing moment}}{\text{overturning moment}}$$

   The minimum required factor of safety against overturning is normally governed by the applicable building code. A minimum of 1.5 is generally considered to be good practice. (The New York State Building Code requires a minimum of 1.5.) The passive earth resistance of the soil in front of the wall is generally neglected in stability computations because of the possibility of its removal by erosion or excavation.

   As discussed previously, the surcharge may be converted into an equivalent height of earth,

$$h_{su} = \frac{w_s}{w_e} = \frac{400}{100} = 4 \text{ ft}$$

   thus adding a rectangle of earth pressure behind the wall.

   The various vertical and horizontal forces and their associated moments are in Tables 8-2 and 8-3 (see Figure 8-8). Note that soil on the toe is neglected. Both stabilizing and overturning moments are calculated with respect to point O in Figure 8-8.

   In Table 8-2, note that W_2 is the weight of soil and surcharge on the heel from the right-hand edge of the heel to the vertical dashed line in the stem. The weight difference between reinforced concrete and soil (50 lb/ft^3) in the triangular portion that is the back of the stem, is represented by W_3.

   The factor of safety against overturning is

$$FS = \frac{131,661}{48,600} = 2.71 > 2.0 \qquad \text{(O.K.)}$$

   b.   *Factor of safety against sliding:* The tendency of the wall to slide is primarily a result of the horizontal forces, whereas the vertical forces cause the frictional resistance against sliding.

   The total frictional force available (or resisting force) may be expressed as

TABLE 8-2   Stabilizing Moments (Vertical Forces)

Force	Magnitude (lb)	Lever arm (ft)	Moment (ft-lb)
W_1	$0.833(16.25)(150) = 2,030$	3.42	6,944
W_2	$7.17(16.25 + 4.0)(100) = 14,519$	7.42	107,731
W_3	$(\frac{1}{2})(16.25)(0.67)(50) = 272$	4.05	1,102
W_4	$11.0(1.75)(150) = 2,888$	5.5	15,884
	$\Sigma W = 19,709$		$\Sigma M = 131,661$

TABLE 8-3   Overturning Moments (Horizontal Forces)

Force	Magnitude (lb)	Lever arm (ft)	Moment (ft-lb)
H_1	$\frac{1}{2}(30)(18)^2 = 4860$	6.0	29,160
H_2	$4(30)(18) = 2160$	9.0	19,440
	$\Sigma H = 7020$		$\Sigma M = 48,600$

$$F = f(\Sigma W)$$

where f = coefficient of friction between the concrete and soil and ΣW = summation of vertical forces (see Figure 8-8). A typical value for the coefficient of friction is $f = 0.50$. Then the resisting force F can be calculated:

FIGURE 8-8   Stability analysis diagram.

$$F = f(\Sigma W)$$

$$0.50(19{,}709) = 9855 \text{ lb}$$

The factor of safety against sliding may be expressed as

$$FS = \frac{\text{resisting force } F}{\text{actual horizontal force } \Sigma H}$$

$$= \frac{9855}{7020} = 1.40$$

The required factor of safety for this problem is 1.5; hence the resistance against sliding is *inadequate*.

One solution to this problem is to reproportion the wall until the requirements are met. Rather than change the wall, we will use a base shear key to mobilize the passive resistance of the soil and in effect increase the resisting force F and subsequently increase the factor of safety. The design of the base shear key will be one of the last steps in the design of the retaining wall.

c.   *Soil pressures and location of resultant force:* The soil pressure under the footing of the wall is a function of the location of the resultant force, which in turn is a function of the vertical forces and horizontal forces. It is generally desirable and usually required that for walls on soil, the resultant of all the forces acting on the wall must lie within the middle third of the base. When this occurs, the resulting pressure distribution could be either triangular, rectangular, or trapezoidal in shape, with the soil in compression under the entire width of the footing. The resulting maximum foundation pressure must not exceed the safe bearing capacity of the soil.

The first step is to locate the point at which the resultant of the vertical forces ΣW and the horizontal forces ΣH intersects the bottom of the footing. This may be visualized with reference to Figure 8-9. Note that ΣW and ΣH are first combined to form the resultant force R. Since R may be moved anywhere along its line of action, it is moved to the bottom of the footing, where it is then resolved back into its components ΣW and ΣH. The moment about point O due to the resultant force acting at the bottom of the footing must be the same as the moment effect about point O of the components ΣW and ΣH. Therefore, using the components in the plane of the bottom of footing, the location of the resultant that is a distance x from point O may be determined. Note that the moment due to ΣH at the bottom of the footing is zero:

$$\Sigma W(x) = \Sigma Wm - \Sigma Hn$$

As may be observed, ΣWm is the stabilizing moment of the vertical forces with respect to point O and ΣHn is the overturning

FIGURE 8-9   Resultant of forces acting on wall.

moment of the horizontal forces with respect to the same point. Hence this expression may be rewritten as

$$\Sigma W(x) = \text{stabilizing } M - \text{overturning } M$$

$$x = \frac{\text{stabilizing } M - \text{overturning } M}{\Sigma W}$$

With reference to Figure 8-8,

$$x = \frac{131,661 - 48,600}{19,709} = 4.22 \text{ ft from toe}$$

Therefore, the eccentricity e with respect to the centerline of footing is

$$e = 5.5 - 4.22 = 1.28 \text{ ft}$$

With the footing length of 11 ft, the middle third lies 3.67 ft in from each end of footing. Therefore, the resultant does lie within the middle third of the footing.

With an eccentricity of 1.28 ft, the resulting pressure distribution is trapezoidal. If the resultant intersected the base at the edge of the middle third, the pressure distribution would have been triangular, and if $e = 0$, the pressure distribution would have been rectangular, indicating a uniform soil pressure distribution.

The pressures may now be calculated considering ΣW applied as an eccentric load on a rectangular section 11 ft long by 1 ft wide (this is a *typical* 1-ft-wide strip of the wall footing). The pressures are obtained by using the basic equations for bending and axial compression:

$$p = \frac{P}{A} \pm \frac{Mc}{I}$$

where

p = unit soil pressure intensity under the footing

P = total vertical load (ΣW)

A = footing cross-sectional area $[(L)(1.0)]$

M = moment due to eccentric load $[(\Sigma W)(e)]$

c = distance from centerline of footing to outside edge $(L/2)$

I = moment of inertia of footing with respect to its centerline $[(1.0)(L)^3/12]$

The expression given previously may be rewritten as

$$p = \frac{\Sigma W}{(L)(1.0)} \pm \frac{(\Sigma W)(e)(L/2)}{1.0(L)^3/12}$$

Simplifying and rearranging yields

$$p = \frac{\Sigma W}{L}\left(1 \pm \frac{6e}{L}\right)$$

Substituting, we obtain

$$p = \frac{19,709}{11}\left[1 \pm \frac{6(1.28)}{11}\right]$$

$$= 1792(1 \pm 0.698)$$

$$\text{maximum } p = 1792(1.698) = 3043 \text{ psf}$$

$$\text{minimum } p = 1792(0.302) = 541 \text{ psf}$$

The resulting pressures are less than 4000 psf and are therefore satisfactory. The resulting pressure distribution beneath the footing is shown in Figure 8-10.

5. Design the component parts.

   a. *Design of heel:* The load on the heel is primarily earth dead load and surcharge, if any, acting vertically downward. With the assumed straight-line pressure distribution under the footing, the downward load is reduced somewhat by the upward-acting pressure. For design purposes, the heel is assumed to be a cantilever beam 1 ft in width and with a span length equal to 6 ft 6 in. fixed at the rear face of wall (point *A* in Figure 8-10).

FIGURE 8-10   Pressure distribution under footing.

The weight of the footing is

$$1.75(150)(6.50) = 1706 \text{ lb}$$

The earth and surcharge weight is

$$6.50(20.25)(100) = 13{,}163 \text{ lb}$$

The slope of pressure distribution under footing is

$$\frac{3043 - 541}{11} = 227.5 \text{ psf/linear foot}$$

Thus far, all analysis has been based on service (actual) load because allowable soil pressures are determined using a certain factor of safety against reaching pressures that will cause unacceptable settlements. Reinforced concrete, however, is designed on the basis of factored loads. The ACI Code, Section 9.2.4, specifies that where lateral earth pressure H must be included in design, the strength U shall be at least equal to $1.4D + 1.7L + 1.7H$.

A conservative approach to the design of the heel is to use factored loads, as required, and to ignore the relieving effect of the upward pressure under the heel. This is the unlikely condition that would exist if there occurred a lateral force overload (and no associated increased vertical load) causing uplift of the heel.

The *maximum moment* may be obtained by taking a summation of moments about point A (utilizing service loads):

$$M = (13{,}163 + 1706)\frac{6.50}{2} = 48{,}324 \text{ ft-lb}$$

The bending of the heel is such that tension occurs in the top of the footing.

The *maximum shear* may be obtained by taking a summation of vertical forces on the heel side of point A (using service loads):

$$V = 13{,}163 + 1706 = 14{,}869 \text{ lb}$$

The maximum moment and shear must be modified for strength design. Since the loads on the heel are predominantly dead load, a load factor of 1.4 is used. This in effect considers the surcharge to be a dead load. This is acceptable, however, because of the conservative nature of the design. Thus

$$M_u = 48{,}324(1.4) = 67{,}654 \text{ ft-lb}$$

$$V_u = 14{,}869(1.4) = 20{,}817 \text{ lb}$$

The *footing size and reinforcement* (for heel) will be determined next. Since it commonly occurs that shear strength will be the controlling factor with respect to footing thickness, the shear will be checked first. The heel effective depth available, assuming 2 in. cover (ACI 7.7.1) and No. 8 bars, is

$$d = 21 - 2 - 0.5 = 18.5 \text{ in.}$$

The shear strength ϕV_n of the heel, if no shear reinforcing is provided, is the shear strength of the concrete alone:

$$\phi V_n = \phi V_c = \phi \left(2\sqrt{f_c'} \right) bd$$
$$= 0.85(2) \sqrt{3000}(12)(18.5)$$

$$\phi V_n = 20{,}670 \text{ lb}$$

Therefore, $V_u > \phi V_n$ very slightly but close enough to be considered satisfactory.

The *tensile reinforcement* requirement may now be determined in the normal way:

$$\text{required } \overline{k} = \frac{M_u}{\phi bd^2} = \frac{67.65(12)}{0.9(12)(18.5)^2}$$

$$= 0.2196 \text{ ksi}$$

Therefore, from Table A-8, the required $\rho = 0.0039$, from which we can calculate the required steel area:

$$\text{required } A_s = \rho bd = 0.0039(12)(18.5) = 0.87 \text{ in.}^2$$

The minimum area of steel required by the ACI Code, Section 10.5.1, may be obtained using Table A-5:

$$A_{s,\min} = 0.0033(12)(18.5) = 0.73 \text{ in.}^2$$

As discussed in Section 2-8, $A_{s,\min}$ must be provided wherever reinforcement is needed, except where such reinforcement is at least one-third greater than that required by analysis (see the ACI Code, Section 10.5.3).

The ACI Code, Section 10.5.4, also permits the use of a minimum reinforcement equal to that required for shrinkage and temperature steel in structural slabs of uniform thickness as furnished in the ACI Code, Section 7.12. This will always be somewhat less than that required by the ACI Code, Section 10.5.1, but not necessarily less than that specified by the ACI Code, Section 10.5.3. For footings, the shrinkage and temperature steel requirement for slabs of uniform thickness will be used as an absolute minimum in this text.

For the heel reinforcement for this retaining wall, since the required steel area is greater than $A_{s,min}$, we will use the required steel area of 0.87 in.^{2} and select No. 7 bars at 8 in. o.c. (A_s = 0.90 in.^{2}).

b.   *Design of toe:* The load on the toe is primarily a result of the soil pressure distribution on the bottom of the footing acting in an upward direction. For design purposes, the toe is assumed to be a cantilever beam 1 ft in width and with a span length equal to 3 ft 0 in. fixed at the front face of the wall (point *B* in Figure 8-11). The soil on the top of the toe is conservatively neglected. Forces and pressures are calculated with reference to Figure 8-11.

Since the reinforcing steel will be placed in the bottom of the footing, the effective depth available, assuming a 3 in. cover and No. 8 bars, is

$$d = 21 - 3 - 0.5 = 17.5 \text{ in.}$$

The weight of footing for the toe design is

$$1.75(3.0)(150) = 788 \text{ lb}$$

FIGURE 8-11   Pressure distribution for toe design.

The soil pressure directly under point *B,* recalling that the slope of the pressure diagram is 227.5 psf/ft, is

$$3043 - 3.0(227.5) = 2361 \text{ psf}$$

The *design moment* M_u may be obtained by a summation of moments about point *B* in Figure 8-11. Both the moment and the shear must be modified for strength design. According to the ACI Code, Section 9.2.4, a load factor of 1.7 should be used for horizontal earth pressure and for live load, whereas 1.4 should be used for dead load. Since the soil pressure under the toe is primarily the result of horizontal earth pressure, however, a conservative procedure of using 1.7 is recommended. In addition, since the weight of the footing reduces the effect of the horizontal earth pressure, a factor of 0.9 is used for the footing dead load, as recommended by the ACI Code.

The design moment M_u is then calculated as

$$M_u = 1.7(\tfrac{1}{2})(3043)(3.0)^2(\tfrac{2}{3}) + 1.7(\tfrac{1}{2})(2361)(3.0)^2(\tfrac{1}{3})$$

$$- 0.9(788)\left(\frac{3.0}{2}\right)$$

$$= 20{,}476 \text{ ft-lb}$$

The bending of the toe is such that tension occurs in the bottom of the footing.

The *design shear* V_u is obtained by a summation of vertical forces on the toe side of point *B* and applying load factors, as previously discussed:

$$V_u = 1.7(\tfrac{1}{2})(3043)(3.0) + 1.7(\tfrac{1}{2})(2361)(3.0) - 0.9(788)$$

$$= 13{,}071 \text{ lb}$$

Footing size and reinforcement, based on the requirements of the toe, are treated as they were for the heel. The shear strength ϕV_n of the toe is calculated from

$$\phi V_n = \phi V_c = \phi(2\sqrt{f'_c})bd$$

$$= 0.85(2)\ \sqrt{3000}(12)(17.5)$$

$$\phi V_n = 19{,}550 \text{ lb}$$

$$V_u < \phi V_n$$

Therefore, the thickness of the footing is satisfactory.

Based on the determined M_u,

$$\text{required } \overline{k} = \frac{M_u}{\phi b d^2} = \frac{20.476(12)}{0.9(12)(17.5)^2}$$

$$= 0.0743 \text{ ksi}$$

Therefore, from Table A-8,

$$\text{required } \rho = 0.0013$$

from which we can calculate the required steel area:

$$\text{required } A_s = \rho bd = 0.0013(12)(17.5) = 0.27 \text{ in.}^2$$

The minimum area of steel required may be obtained using Table A-5:

$$A_{s,min} = 0.0033(12)(17.5) = 0.69 \text{ in.}^2$$

Since required $A_s < A_{s,min}$, other minimum steel criteria should be checked to establish a controlling minimum value:

(1) Provide one-third additional reinforcing as outlined in the ACI Code, Section 10.5.3:

$$A_{s,min} = 1.33(0.27) = 0.36 \text{ in.}^2$$

(2) Check the required steel area based on the absolute minimum of shrinkage and temperature steel required for structural slabs of uniform thickness (ACI Code, Section 7.12):

$$\text{required } A_s = 0.0018bh$$

$$= 0.0018(12)(21) = 0.45 \text{ in.}^2$$

Since we consider the shrinkage and temperature steel requirement as an absolute minimum, use No. 7 bars at 16 in. o.c. ($A_s = 0.45 \text{ in.}^2$).

c. *Design of stem:* The load on the stem is primarily lateral earth pressure acting (in this problem) horizontally. For design purposes, the stem is assumed to be a vertical cantilever beam 1 ft in width and with a span length equal to 16 ft 3 in. fixed at the top of footing.

The loads acting on the stem from the top of the wall to the top of the footing are depicted in Figure 8-12. The magnitudes of the horizontal forces are

$$H_{s1} = \tfrac{1}{2}(30)(16.25)^2 = 3961 \text{ lb}$$

$$H_{s2} = 4(30)(16.25) = 1950 \text{ lb}$$

The *design moment* M_u in the stem may be obtained by a summation of moments about the top of the footing. Both shears and moments must be modified for strength design. Since the forces are due to lateral earth pressure, a factor of 1.7 should be used. M_u may then be calculated as

$$M_u = 1.7(3961)(5.42) + 1.7(1950)(8.125)$$

$$= 63{,}431 \text{ ft-lb}$$

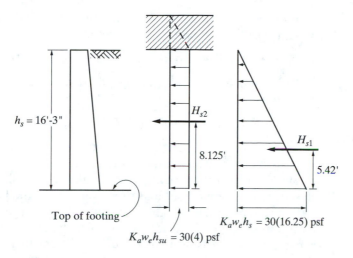

$h_s = 16'\text{-}3''$

H_{s2}

8.125'

H_{s1}

5.42'

Top of footing

$K_a w_e h_s = 30(16.25)$ psf

$K_a w_e h_{su} = 30(4)$ psf

FIGURE 8-12   Forces acting on stem.

The *design shear* V_u is obtained by a summation of the horizontal forces acting on the stem above the top of the footing:

$$V_u = 1.7(3961) + 1.7(1950)$$

$$= 10{,}049 \text{ lb}$$

The *stem size and reinforcement* requirements will be determined next. Because the stem is assumed to be a cantilever slab, V_u as a limit may equal ϕV_n, where $V_n = V_c$. It is not practical to reinforce the stem for shear; therefore, if shear strength is inadequate, stem thickness must be increased. The effective depth available at the top of the footing, assuming 2 in. cover and No. 8 bars, is

$$d = 18 - 2 - 0.5 = 15.5 \text{ in.}$$

The shear strength ϕV_n of the stem (at the top of the footing) if no shear reinforcement is provided is the shear strength of the concrete alone:

$$\phi V_n = \phi V_c = \phi 2\sqrt{f_c'}\,bd$$

$$= 0.85(2)\sqrt{3000}\,(12)(15.5)$$

$$\phi V_n = 17{,}320 \text{ lb}$$

$$V_u < \phi V_n$$

Therefore, the stem thickness need not be increased. Based on M_u at the bottom of the stem,

$$\text{required } \bar{k} = \frac{M_u}{\phi b d^2} = \frac{63.431(12)}{0.9(12)(15.5)^2}$$

$$= 0.2934 \text{ ksi}$$

Therefore, from Table A-8, the required $\rho = 0.0053$, from which we can calculate the required steel area:

$$\text{required } A_s = \rho b d = 0.0053(12)(15.5) = 0.99 \text{ in.}^2$$

The minimum area of steel required may be obtained using Table A-5:

$$A_{s,\text{min}} = 0.0033(12)(15.5) = 0.61 \text{ in.}^2$$

Since required $A_s > A_{s,\text{min}}$, the calculated required A_s controls. Use No. 8 bars at 9 in. o.c. ($A_s = 1.05$ in.^{2}).

The *stem reinforcement pattern* will be investigated more closely. Since the moment and shear vary along the height of the wall, it is only logical that the steel requirements also vary. A pattern is usually created whereby some of the stem reinforcement is cut off where it is no longer required. The actual pattern used is the choice of the designer, based on various practical constraints.

A typical approach to the creation of a stem reinforcement pattern is first to draw the complete M_u diagram for the stem and then to determine bar cutoff points in the same manner as was discussed in Chapter 5. Stem moments due to the external loads will be calculated at 5 ft from the top of the wall and at 10 ft from the top of the wall. These distances are arbitrary and should be chosen so that a sufficient number of points will be available to draw the M_u diagram.

With reference to Figure 8-13, the moment at 5 ft from the top of the wall is calculated by first determining the horizontal forces:

$$H_{s1} = \tfrac{1}{2}(30)(5.0)^2 = 375 \text{ lb}$$

$$H_{s2} = 4(30)(5.0) = 600 \text{ lb}$$

FIGURE 8-13   Stem analysis.

Summing the moments about a plane 5 ft below the top of the wall and introducing the appropriate load factor,

$$M_u = 1.7(375)\left(\frac{5.0}{3}\right) + 1.7(600)\left(\frac{5.0}{2}\right)$$

$$= 3613 \text{ ft-lb}$$

With reference to Figure 8-14, the moment at 10 ft below the top of the wall may be calculated:

$$H_{s1} = \tfrac{1}{2}(30)(10.0)^2 = 1500 \text{ lb}$$

$$H_{s2} = 4(30)(10.0) = 1200 \text{ lb}$$

and

$$M_u = 1.7(1500)\left(\frac{10.0}{3}\right) + 1.7(1200)\left(\frac{10.0}{2}\right)$$

$$= 18{,}700 \text{ ft-lb}$$

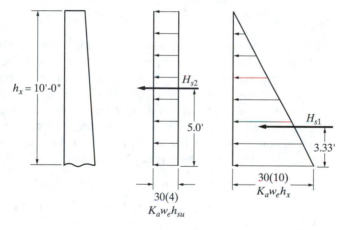

FIGURE 8-14   Stem analysis.

The three M_u values may now be plotted as the dark solid curve in Figure 8-15. This diagram will reflect both the design moment and moment strength with respect to the distance from the top of the wall and must be plotted to scale.

The moment strength ϕM_n of the stem at various locations may be computed from the expression

$$\phi M_n = \phi b d^2 \overline{k}$$

Since we are primarily attempting to establish a cutoff location for some vertical stem reinforcement, the moment strength will be based on a pattern of alternate vertical bars being cut off. With

FIGURE 8-15   Stem steel design.

alternate bars cut off, the remaining reinforcement pattern is No. 8 bars at 18 in. o.c., which furnishes an $A_s = 0.53$ in.^{2}. Caution must be exercised that the spacing of the remaining bars does not exceed three times the wall thickness or 18 in., whichever is less.

The moment strength will be computed at the top of the wall and at the top of the footing, neglecting minimum steel requirements at this time. Since the rear face of the wall is battered, the effective depth varies and may be computed as follows:

$$\text{top of wall: } d = 10 - 2 - 0.5 = 7.5 \text{ in.}$$

$$\text{top of footing: } d = 18 - 2 - 0.5 = 15.5 \text{ in.}$$

At the top of the wall,

$$\rho = \frac{A_s}{bd} = \frac{0.53}{12(7.5)} = 0.0059$$

Therefore, from Table A-8, $\overline{k} = 0.3294$ ksi. Then

$$\phi M_n = \frac{0.9(12)(7.5)^2}{12}(0.3294)$$

$$= 16.7 \text{ ft-kips}$$

At the top of the footing,

$$\rho = \frac{A_s}{bd} = \frac{0.53}{12(15.5)} = 0.0028$$

Therefore, from Table A-8, $\bar{k} = 0.1625$ ksi. Then

$$\phi M_n = \frac{0.9(12)(15.5)^2}{12}(0.1625)$$

$$= 35.1 \text{ ft-kips}$$

These two values (ϕM_n) may now be plotted in Figure 8-15. A straight line will be used to approximate the variation of ϕM_n for No. 8 bars at 18 in. o.c. from the top to the bottom of the wall.

The intersection of the ϕM_n and the M_u curves establishes a theoretical cutoff point for alternate vertical bars based on strength requirements. This location may be determined graphically by scaling on Figure 8-15.

The scaled distance is 12.25 ft below the top of the wall or 4 ft 0 in. above the top of the footing. The No. 8 bar must be extended past this theoretical cutoff point a distance equal to the effective depth of the member or 12 bar diameters, whichever is larger.

Since the effective depth of the stem steel at the top of the footing is 15.5 in. and the wall batter is approximately 0.492 in./ft, the effective depth of the stem steel at 4 ft above the top of footing may be calculated as follows:

$$d = 15.5 - 4(0.492) = 13.5 \text{ in.}$$

$$12d_b = 12(1.00) = 12.0 \text{ in.}$$

Therefore, the required length of bar above the top of the footing would be

$$4 + \frac{13.5}{12} = 5.13 \text{ ft} \qquad \text{Use 5 ft 2 in. (5.17 ft)}$$

Check the required minimum area of steel, $A_{s,\text{min}}$, at the theoretical cutoff point to ensure that discontinuing half of the steel will not violate this code requirement. Once alternate bars have been terminated, the remaining steel will be No. 8 bars at 18 in. ($A_s = 0.53$ in.^{2}). At the theoretical cutoff point 4 ft above the top of the footing, the effective depth $d = 13.5$ in. From Table A-5,

$$A_{s,\text{min}} = 0.0033bd$$

$$= 0.0033(12)(13.5) = 0.53 \text{ in.}^2$$

This is satisfactory ($A_{s,\text{min}} = $ actual $A_s = 0.53$ in.^{2}). Therefore, alternate bars may be stopped 5 ft 2 in. above the top of the footing.

The ACI Code, Section 12.10.5, stipulates that flexural reinforcement must not be terminated in a tension zone unless one of several conditions is satisfied. One of these conditions is that the shear at the cutoff point does not exceed two-thirds of the shear

FIGURE 8-16 Shear at bar cutoff point.

permitted. Therefore, check the shear at the actual cutoff point, 5.17 ft above the top of the footing (11.08 ft below the top of the wall; see Figure 8-16).

For the shear strength calculation, the wall thickness at a height of 5.17 ft above the top of the footing is

$$18.0 - 5.17 \ (0.492) = 15.5 \text{ in.}$$

from which d may be calculated as

$$d = 15.5 - 2 - 0.5 = 13.0 \text{ in.}$$

$$H_{s1} = \tfrac{1}{2}(30)(11.08)^2 = 1841 \text{ lb}$$

$$H_{s2} = 4(30)(11.08) = 1330 \text{ lb}$$

$$\text{total} = 3171 \text{ lb}$$

$$V_u = 3171(1.7) = 5391 \text{ lb}$$

$$\tfrac{2}{3}\phi V_n = \tfrac{2}{3}\phi V_c = \tfrac{2}{3}\phi(2\sqrt{f_c'})bd$$

$$= \tfrac{2}{3}(0.85)(2)\sqrt{3000}(12)(13.0)$$

$$\tfrac{2}{3}\phi V_n = 9684 \text{ lb}$$

$$V_u < \tfrac{2}{3}\phi V_n \hspace{3cm} \text{(O.K.)}$$

In summary, alternate vertical stem reinforcing bars may be stopped at 5 ft 2 in. above the top of the footing (see the typical wall section shown in Figure 8-20 later in this chapter).

d.   *Additional design details:* Check the anchorage requirements for the stem steel (No. 8 bars at 9 in. o.c.).

(1)   From Table 5-1, $K_D = 82.2$.

(2)   Establish values for the multiplying factors α, β, γ, λ.

(a) $\alpha = 1.0$ (the bars are not top bars).

(b)   The bars are uncoated ("black steel"). $\beta = 1.0$.

    (c)   The bars are No. 8. $\gamma = 1.0$.

    (d)   Normal-weight concrete is used. $\lambda = 1.0$.

(3)   The product $\alpha \times \beta = 1.0 < 1.7$. (O.K.)

(4)   Determine c. Based on cover (center of bar to nearest concrete surface): Consider the clear cover and one-half the diameter of the No. 8 bar:

$$c = 2 + 0.5 = 2.5 \text{ in.}$$

Based on bar spacing (one-half the center-to-center distance):

$$c = 0.5(9.0) = 4.5 \text{ in.}$$

Therefore, use $c = 2.5$ in.

(5) K_{TR} is taken as zero. There is no transverse steel crossing the potential plane of splitting.

(6)   Check $(c + K_{TR})/d_b \leqslant 2.5$:

$$\frac{c + K_{TR}}{d_b} = \frac{2.5 + 0}{1.0} = 2.5 \qquad \text{(O.K.)}$$

(7)   Calculate the excess reinforcement factor:

$$K_{ER} = \frac{A_s \text{ required}}{A_s \text{ provided}} = \frac{0.99}{1.05} = 0.94$$

(8)   Calculate ℓ_d.

    (a)   Omitting K_{ER} (this calculated value of ℓ_d will be used shortly for splice length determination):

$$\ell_d = K_D \left[\frac{\alpha\beta\gamma\lambda}{\left(\dfrac{c + K_{TR}}{d_b} \right)} \right] d_b$$

$$= 82.2 \left[\frac{1.0(1.0)(1.0)(1.0)}{2.5} \right] (1.0)$$

$$= 32.9 \text{ in.} > 12 \text{ in.} \qquad \text{(O.K.)}$$

    (b)   Including K_{ER} from step 7, the required anchorage length is

$$\ell_d = 32.9(0.94) = 30.9 \text{ in.} > 12 \text{ in.} \qquad \text{(O.K.)}$$

Use $\ell_d = 31$ in. (minimum).

With the footing thickness equal to 21 in. and a minimum of 3 in. of cover required for the steel at the bottom of the footing, the anchorage length available is $21 - 3 = 18$ in. This anchorage length is not adequate. Rather than hook the bars, however, the bars will be extended into a footing base shear key that will be used to increase the sliding resistance of the wall (see the check on factor of safety against sliding).

The *length of splice* required for main stem reinforcing steel (see the typical wall section shown in Figure 8-20 later in this chapter) may be calculated recognizing that the class B splice is applicable for this condition (see Chapter 5, Section 5-7). Therefore, the required length of the splice is calculated from

$$1.3(32.9) = 42.8 \text{ in.} \qquad \text{Use 43 in.}$$

Note that the preceding calculation omits the effect of excess reinforcement.

Stem face steel in the form of horizontal and vertical reinforcement will be provided as per the ACI Code, Section 14.3. The minimum horizontal reinforcement is specified in Section 14.3.3. Although the minimum vertical reinforcement requirement of Section 14.3.2 does not strictly apply to cantilever retaining walls, it is considered good practice to provide some vertical bars in the exposed face of the wall. The minimum recommended steel for deformed bars not larger than No. 5 with specified yield strength of not less than 60,000 psi is as follows:

horizontal bars (per foot of height of wall): $A_s = 0.0020bt$

vertical bars (per foot of wall horizontally): $A_s = 0.0012bt$

where t = thickness of the wall.

The code also stipulates that walls more than 10 in. thick, except basement walls, must have reinforcement for each direction in each face of the wall. The exposed face must have a minimum of one-half and a maximum of two-thirds the total steel required for each direction. The maximum spacing for the steel must not exceed three times the wall thickness nor 18 in. (ACI Code, Section 14.3.5) for both vertical bars and horizontal bars. For the front face of the wall (exposed face), use two-thirds of the total steel required and an average stem thickness = 14 in.

For horizontal steel,

$$0.0020(12)(14) = 0.34 \text{ in.}^2/\text{ft of height}$$
$$= 0.34(0.67) = 0.23 \text{ in.}^2$$

Use No. 4 bars at 10 in. ($A_s = 0.24$ in.^{2}).

For vertical steel,

$$0.0012(12)(14) = 0.20 \text{ in.}^2/\text{ft of horizontal length}$$
$$= (0.20)(0.67) = 0.14 \text{ in.}^2$$

Use No. 4 bars at 17 in. ($A_s = 0.14$ in.^{2}).

Rear face of wall, not exposed, for horizontal steel,

$$0.34(0.33) = 0.11 \text{ in.}^2$$

Use No. 4 bars at 18 in. ($A_s = 0.13$ in.^{2}).

Longitudinal reinforcement in the footing should provide a steel area equal to that required for shrinkage and temperature in slabs. This is a conservative and acceptable approach since temperature and shrinkage exposure are ordinarily less severe for footings than for slabs. These bars serve chiefly as bar supports and spacers to hold the main steel in place during construction. Thus

$$\text{required } A_s = 0.0018(11)(1.75)(144) = 4.99 \text{ in.}^2$$

Use 12 No. 6 bars ($A_s = 5.28$ in.^{2}), as shown in Figure 8-20 later in this chapter.

Transverse reinforcement in the footing need not run the full width of the footing. Proper anchorage length must be provided from the point of maximum tensile stress, however.

Check anchorage for the top steel in the footing (No. 7 bars at 8 in. o.c.).

(1)   From Table 5-1, $K_D = 82.2$.

(2)   Establish values for the multiplying factors α, β, γ, and λ.

    (a) $\alpha = 1.3$ (the bars are top bars).

    (b)   The bars are uncoated ("black steel"). $\beta = 1.0$.

    (c)   The bars are No. 7. $\gamma = 1.0$.

    (d)   Normal-weight concrete is used. $\lambda = 1.0$.

(3)   The product $\alpha \times \beta = 1.3 < 1.7$. (O.K.)

(4)   Determine c. Based on cover (center of bar to nearest concrete surface): Consider the clear cover and one-half the diameter of the No. 7 bar:

$$c = 2.0 + \frac{0.875}{2} = 2.44 \text{ in.}$$

Based on bar spacing (one-half the center-to-center distance):

$$c = 0.5\,(8.0) = 4.0 \text{ in.}$$

Therefore, use $c = 2.44$ in.

(5) K_{TR} is taken as zero. There is no transverse steel crossing the potential plane of splitting.

(6)   Check $(c + K_{TR})/d_b \leq 2.5$:

$$\frac{c + K_{TR}}{d_b} = \frac{2.44 + 0}{0.875} = 2.79 > 2.5$$

Therefore, use 2.5.

(7)   Calculate the excess reinforcement factor:

$$K_{ER} = \frac{A_s \text{ required}}{A_s \text{ provided}} = \frac{0.87}{0.90} = 0.97$$

(8)   Calculate ℓ_d:

$$\ell_d = K_D \left[\frac{\alpha\beta\gamma\lambda}{\left(\dfrac{c + K_{TR}}{d_b} \right)} \right] (d_b)(K_{ER})$$

$$= 82.2 \left[\frac{1.3(1.0)(1.0)(1.0)}{2.5} \right] (0.875)(0.97)$$

$$= 36.3 \text{ in.} > 12 \text{ in.} \qquad\qquad\qquad\qquad \text{(O.K.)}$$

Use $\ell_d = 37$ in. (minimum).

Check the anchorage of the bottom bars in the footing (No. 7 bars at 16 in. o.c.).

(1)   From Table 5-1, $K_D = 82.2$.

(2)   Establish values for the multiplying factors α, β, γ, and λ.

    (a) $\alpha = 1.0$ (the bars are not top bars).

    (b)   The bars are uncoated ("black steel"). $\beta = 1.0$.

    (c)   The bars are No. 7. $\gamma = 1.0$.

    (d)   Normal-weight concrete is used. $\lambda = 1.0$.

(3)   The product $\alpha \times \beta = 1.0 < 1.7$. (O.K.)

(4)   Determine c. Based on cover (center of bar to nearest concrete surface): Consider the clear cover and one-half the diameter of the No. 7 bar:

$$c = 3.0 + \frac{0.875}{2} = 3.44 \text{ in.}$$

Based on bar spacing (one-half the center-to-center distance):

$$c = 0.5 \,(16.0) = 8.0 \text{ in.}$$

Therefore, use $c = 3.44$ in.

(5) K_{TR} is taken as zero. There is no transverse steel crossing the potential plane of splitting.

(6)   Check $(c + K_{TR})/d_b \leq 2.5$:

$$\frac{c + K_{TR}}{d_b} = \frac{3.44 + 0}{0.875} = 3.93 > 2.5$$

Therefore, use 2.5.

(7)   The excess reinforcement factor K_{ER} is taken as 1.0 since

there is no excess steel.

(8)   Calculate ℓ_d:

$$\ell_d = K_D \left[\frac{\alpha\beta\gamma\lambda}{\left(\dfrac{c + K_{TR}}{d_b} \right)} \right] d_b$$

$$= 82.2 \left[\frac{1.0(1.0)(1.0)(1.0)}{2.5} \right](0.875)$$

$$= 28.8 \text{ in.} > 12 \text{ in.} \qquad\qquad \text{(O.K.)}$$

Use $\ell_d = 29$ in. (minimum).

These details are included in the typical wall section, Figure 8-20.

A *shear key* will be provided between the stem and the footing. We will use a depressed key formed by a 2×6 plank (dressed dimensions $1\frac{1}{2} \times 5\frac{1}{2}$), as shown in Figure 8-20.

The need for a shear key is questionable, since considerable slip is required to develop the key for purposes of lateral force transfer. It may be considered as an added mechanical factor of safety, however.

The shear-friction method of the ACI Code, Section 11.7, should be used to design for horizontal force transfer between the stem and footing. This approach eliminates the need for the shear key, provided that the contact surface is both adequately roughened and crossed by properly anchored reinforcement. According to the code, the surface must be intentionally roughened to an amplitude of $\frac{1}{4}$ in. or more by raking or some other means.

The shear-friction approach assumes a shear plane already cracked. Since the stem is placed against hardened concrete, the plane between the two may be considered analogous to a cracked plane. Sliding along this plane is resisted by the two contact surfaces. As slip begins to occur, the roughness of the contact surfaces forces the two surfaces to separate. This separation is resisted by the reinforcement A_{vf}, which is placed approximately perpendicular to the surfaces. Thus, tension is induced in the reinforcement and contact pressure develops between the stem and the footing.

The nominal shear strength (or friction force that resists sliding) may be computed from

$$V_n = A_{vf} f_y \mu \qquad\qquad \text{ACI Eq. (11-25)}$$

where

A_{vf} = area of shear-friction reinforcement

μ = coefficient of friction in accordance with the ACI Code, Section 11.7.4.3; it may be taken as 1.0 for normal-weight concrete placed against hardened concrete roughened as described previously Note that A_{vf} is steel that is provided for the shear-friction development and that it is in addition to any other steel already provided.

As a limit,

$$V_u = \phi V_n$$

where V_u is shear force applied at the cracked plane. Substituting for V_n,

$$V_u = \phi A_{vf} f_y \mu$$

Solving for A_{vf},

$$\text{required } A_{vf} = \frac{V_u}{\phi f_y \mu}$$

$$= \frac{10{,}049}{(0.85)(60{,}000)(1.0)}$$

$$= 0.20 \text{ in.}^2 \text{ per ft length of wall}$$

Since it is desirable to distribute the shear-friction reinforcement across the width of the contact surface, use two No. 4 dowels per foot, one in each face of the stem. Then

$$\text{provided } A_{vf} = 0.20(2) = 0.40 \text{ in.}^2$$

$$\text{shear strength } V_n = A_{vf} f_y \mu$$

$$= (0.40)(60{,}000)(1.0)$$

$$= 24{,}000 \text{ lb}$$

The ACI Code, Section 11.7.5, stipulates that the maximum V_n shall not exceed

$$0.2 f_c' A_c \quad \text{or} \quad 800 A_c$$

where A_c is the area of the contact surface resisting shear transfer. Thus

$$\text{maximum } V_n = (0.2)(3000)(12)(18) = 129{,}600 \text{ lb}$$

$$\text{maximum } V_n = (800)(12)(18) = 172{,}800 \text{ lb}$$

Therefore, maximum $V_n = 24{,}000$ lb and, since $V_u = 10{,}049$ lb,

$$10{,}049 < (0.85)(24{,}000)$$

$$10{,}049 < 20{,}400 \qquad \qquad \text{(O.K.)}$$

The development length of the No. 4 dowels must be furnished into both the stem and the footing. These are considered to be tension bars. The dowels are 12 in. on centers.

(1)   From Table 5-1, $K_D = 82.2$.

(2)   Establish values for the multiplying factors α, β, γ, and λ.
    (a) $\alpha = 1.0$ (the bars are not top bars).
    (b)   The bars are uncoated ("black steel"). $\beta = 1.0$.
    (c)   The bars are No. 4. $\gamma = 0.8$.
    (d)   Normal-weight concrete is used. $\lambda = 1.0$.

(3)   The product $\alpha \times \beta = 1.0 < 1.7$. (O.K.)

(4)   Determine c. Based on cover (center of bar to nearest concrete surface): Consider the clear cover and one-half the diameter of the No. 4 bar:

$$c = 2.0 + \frac{0.50}{2} = 2.25 \text{ in.}$$

Based on bar spacing (one-half the center-to-center distance):

$$c = 0.5 \,(12.0) = 6.0 \text{ in.}$$

Therefore, use $c = 2.25$ in.

(5) K_{TR} is taken as zero. There is no transverse steel crossing the potential plane of splitting.

(6)   Check $(c + K_{TR})/d_b \leq 2.5$:

$$\frac{c + K_{TR}}{d_b} = \frac{2.25 + 0}{0.50} = 4.50 > 2.5$$

Therefore, use 2.5.

(7)   Calculate the excess reinforcement factor:

$$K_{ER} = \frac{A_s \text{ required}}{A_s \text{ provided}} = \frac{0.20}{0.40} = 0.50$$

(8)   Calculate ℓ_d:

$$\ell_d = K_D \left[\frac{\alpha\beta\gamma\lambda}{\left(\dfrac{c + K_{TR}}{d_b} \right)} \right] (d_b)(K_{ER})$$

$$= 82.2 \left[\frac{1.0(1.0)(0.8)(1.0)}{2.5} \right] (0.50)(0.50) = 6.6 \text{ in.} < 12 \text{ in.}$$

Therefore, use $\ell_d = 12$ in. (required minimum).
The No. 4 dowels are depicted in Figure 8-17.

6.   Design the footing base shear key. The *footing base shear key* (sometimes called a *bearing lug*) is primarily used to prevent a sliding failure. The magnitude of the additional resistance to sliding offered by the key is questionable and is a function of the subsoil material. In addition, the

FIGURE 8-17   Shear-friction reinforcement.

excavation for a key will generally disturb the subsoil during construction and conceivably will do more harm than good. Hence the use of the key for the purpose intended is controversial.

An acceptable design approach is to use the passive earth resistance H_p in front of the key (from the bottom of the footing to the bottom of the key) as the additional resistance to sliding (see Figure 8-18). This neglects any earth in front of the footing and reflects the case where excavation or scour has removed the earth to the level of the bottom of the footing.

The passive earth resistance may be expressed in terms of an equivalent fluid weight. Since $K_a w_e = 30$ lb/ft^3 and $w_e = 100$ lb/ft^3,

$$K_a = \frac{30}{100} = 0.3$$

FIGURE 8-18   Base shear key force analysis.

The coefficient of passive earth resistance is

$$K_p = \frac{1 + \sin \phi}{1 - \sin \phi} = \frac{1}{K_a} = \frac{1}{0.3} = 3.33$$

and

$$K_p w_e = 3.33(100) = 333 \text{ lb/ft}^3$$

$$H_p = \tfrac{1}{2} K_p w_e h_k^2 = \tfrac{1}{2}(333) h_k^2$$

The unfactored actual horizontal force $\Sigma H = 7020$ lb. Therefore, the required resistance to sliding that will furnish a factor of safety of 1.5 is

$$1.5(7020) = 10{,}530 \text{ lb}$$

The actual frictional resistance furnished is 9855 lb (see the discussion of stability analysis). Therefore, the resistance that must be furnished by the base shear key and the passive earth resistance is

$$10{,}530 - 9855 = 675 \text{ lb}$$

With reference to Figure 8-18, the height h_k required to furnish this resistance may be obtained by establishing horizontal equilibrium ($\Sigma H = 0$).

$$\tfrac{1}{2}(333)(h_k)^2 = 675$$

$$h_k^2 = 4.05$$

$$\text{required } h_k = 2.01 \text{ ft} \qquad \text{Use 2 ft 0 in.}$$

The key must be designed for moment and shear. The worst case would be the situation where excavation had *not* taken place and the full height of earth in front of the wall was available to develop passive pressure. This is shown in Figure 8-19. A 1 ft depth of earth has been assumed on top of the footing. Assuming the key as a vertical cantilever

FIGURE 8-19   Base shear key design.

beam, taking a summation of moment about the plane of the bottom of footing, and applying a load factor of 1.7,

$$M_u = 1.7(916)(2.0)(1.0) + 1.7(\tfrac{1}{2})(666)(2.0)(\tfrac{2}{3})(2.0)$$

$$= 4624 \text{ ft-lb}$$

Assume a 10 in. width of key and a No. 8 bar, which provides an effective depth $d = 10 - 3 - 0.5 = 6.5$ in.:

$$\text{required } \overline{k} = \frac{M_u}{\phi bd^2} = \frac{4.624(12)}{0.9(12)(6.5)^2} = 0.1216 \text{ ksi}$$

From Table A-8, the required $\rho = 0.0021$, from which we can calculate the required steel area:

$$\text{required } A_s = \rho bd = 0.0021(12)(6.5) = 0.16 \text{ in.}^2$$

The minimum area of steel required by the ACI Code, Section 10.5.1, may be obtained using Table A-5:

$$A_{s,min} = 0.0033(12)(6.5) = 0.26 \text{ in.}^2$$

Therefore, $A_{s,min}$ of 0.26 in.^{2} controls. This is a very small amount of steel, and it will be more practical to extend some existing stem bars into the key.

A convenient pattern would consist of extending alternate stem bars into the key. This would furnish No. 8 bars at 18 in. o.c. ($A_s = 0.53$ in.^{2}). All stem bars must be extended into the key for anchorage reasons, however. All the bars will be extended to within 3 in. of the bottom of the key. This provides 42 in. of anchorage below the bottom of the stem for the No. 8 bars and exceeds the requirement of 31 in. (see typical wall section in Figure 8-20). The steel furnished in the key, therefore, is No. 8 bars at 9 in. o.c. ($A_s = 1.05$ in.^{2}).

If we conservatively neglect the effect of the greater cover (3.0 in.) in the key, calculations for the required anchorage length at the top of the key are identical to those for the stem, except that the excess reinforcement factor $K_{ER} = 0.26/1.05 = 0.248$, from which the final ℓ_d calculation yields

$$\ell_d = 32.9(0.248) = 8.2 \text{ in.} < 12 \text{ in.}$$

Use $\ell_d = 12$ in. The available anchorage length is $24 - 3 = 21$ in., which exceeds the requirements of 12 in.

The shear strength of the key is

$$\phi V_n = \phi V_c$$

$$= \phi(2\sqrt{f_c'})bd$$

$$= 0.85(2)(\sqrt{3000})(12)(6.5)$$

$$= 7263 \text{ lb}$$

FIGURE 8-20   Typical wall section.

The factored shear is

$$V_u = (1.7)(916)(2.0) + 1.7(\tfrac{1}{2})(666)(2) = 4247 \text{ lb}$$

$$V_u < \phi V_n \tag{O.K.}$$

8-4

DESIGN CONSIDERATIONS FOR BEARING WALLS

Bearing walls (Figure 8-1g) were briefly described at the beginning of this chapter as those walls that carry vertical load in addition to their own weight. Recommendations for the empirical design of such walls are presented in Chapter 14 of the

ACI Code (318-95) and apply primarily to relatively short walls spanning vertically, and subject to vertical loads only, such as those resulting from the reactions of floor or roof systems supported on walls. Walls, other than short walls carrying "reasonably concentric" loads, should be designed as compression members for axial load and flexure in accordance with ACI 318-95, Chapter 10. "Reasonably concentric" implies that the resultant factored load falls within the middle third of the cross section.

The design axial load strength or capacity of such a wall will be

$$\phi P_{nw} = 0.55 \phi f'_c A_g \left[1 - \left(\frac{k\ell_c}{32h} \right)^2 \right] \qquad \text{ACI Eq. (14-1)}$$

where

$\phi = 0.70$

$h =$ thickness of wall (in.)

$\ell_c =$ vertical distance between supports (in.)

$A_g =$ gross area of section (in.^{2})

$k =$ effective length factor

The effective length factor k shall be:

1. For walls braced top and bottom against lateral translation and
   a. Restrained against rotation at one or both ends
      (top and/or bottom)   0.8
   b. Unrestrained against rotation at both ends   1.0
2. For walls not braced against lateral translation   2.0

Where the wall is subject to concentrated loads, the effective length of wall for each concentration must not exceed the center-to-center distance between loads nor exceed the width of bearing plus four times the wall thickness.

The following requirements applicable to bearing walls are prescribed, among others, by the ACI Code, Chapter 14:

1. Reinforced concrete bearing walls must have a thickness of at least $\frac{1}{25}$ of the unsupported height or width, whichever is shorter, and not less than 4 in.
2. Thickness of nonbearing walls shall not be less than 4 in. nor less than $\frac{1}{30}$ times the least distance between members that provide lateral support.
3. The area of horizontal reinforcement must be at least 0.0025 times the area of the wall (0.0025bh per foot) and the area of vertical reinforcement not less than 0.0015 times the area of the wall (0.0015bh per foot), where $b = 12$ in.

and h is the wall thickness. These values may be reduced to 0.0020 and 0.0012, respectively, if the reinforcement is not larger than $\frac{5}{8}$ in. in diameter and consists of either welded wire fabric or deformed bars with f_y of 60,000 psi or greater.

4. Exterior basement walls and foundation walls must not be less than $7\frac{1}{2}$ in. thick.

5. Reinforced concrete walls must be anchored to floors and roofs or to columns, pilasters, buttresses, and intersecting walls.

6. Walls more than 10 in. thick, except for basement walls, must have reinforcement in each direction for each face. The exterior surface shall have a minimum of one-half and a maximum of two-thirds of the total steel required, with the interior surface having the balance of the reinforcement.

7. Vertical reinforcement must be enclosed by lateral ties if in excess of 0.01 times the gross concrete area or when it is required as compression reinforcement.

Example 8-2

Design a reinforced concrete bearing wall to support a series of steel wide-flange beams at 8 ft 0 in. o.c. Each beam rests on a bearing plate 6 in. × 12 in. The wall is braced top and bottom against lateral translation. Assume the bottom end fixed against rotation. The wall height is 15 ft and the design (factored) load P_u from each beam is 125 kips. Use $f'_c = 3000$ psi and $f_y = 60,000$ psi. See Figure 8-21.

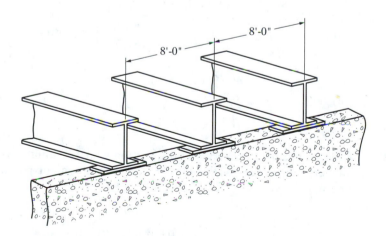

FIGURE 8-21   Bearing wall.

Solution:

1. Assume an 8-in.-thick wall with full concentric bearing.
2. The bearing strength of the concrete under the bearing plate, as governed by the ACI Code, Section 10.15.1, is

$$\phi(0.85)f'_c A_1 = 0.70(0.85)(3000)(6)(12)$$

$$= 128,520 \text{ lb}$$

factored bearing load $P_u = 125,000$ lb

$$128,520 > 125,000 \qquad\qquad\qquad (\text{O.K.})$$

3. The effective length of the wall (ACI Code, Section 14.2.4) must not exceed the center-to-center distance between loads nor the width of bearing plus four times the wall thickness. Beam spacing = 96 in. Thus

$$12 + 4(8) = 44 \text{ in.}$$

Therefore, use 44 in.

4. The minimum thickness required is $\frac{1}{25}$ times the shorter of the unsupported height or width. Assume, for our case, that width does not control. Then

$$h_{\min} = \frac{\ell_c}{25} = \frac{15(12)}{25} = 7.2 \text{ in.}$$

Also, $h_{\min} = 4$ in. Therefore, the 8 in. wall is satisfactory.

5. The capacity of wall is

$$\phi P_{nw} = 0.55\, \phi f'_c A_g\left[1 - \left(\frac{k\ell_c}{32h}\right)^2\right]$$

$$= 0.55(0.70)(3)(44)(8)\left\{1 - \left[\frac{0.8(15)(12)}{32(8)}\right]^2\right\}$$

$$= 406.6(1 - 0.316)$$

$$= 278 \text{ kips}$$

$$\phi P_{nw} > P_u \qquad\qquad\qquad (\text{O.K.})$$

6. The reinforcing steel (ACI Code, Section 14.3), assuming No. 5 bars or smaller, can be found: For the vertical reinforcement per foot of wall length,

$$\text{required } A_s = 0.0012bh$$

$$= 0.0012(12)(8) = 0.12 \text{ in.}^2$$

For the horizontal reinforcement per foot of wall height,

FIGURE 8-22   Section of wall.

$$\text{required } A_s = 0.002bh$$

$$= 0.002(12)(8) = 0.19 \text{ in.}^2$$

The maximum spacing of reinforcement must not exceed three times the wall thickness nor 18 in. (ACI Code, Section 14.3.5). Thus

$$3(8) = 24 \text{ in.} \qquad \text{Use 18 in.}$$

To select reinforcing,

        vertical steel: Use No. 4 bars at 18 in. ($A_s = 0.13$ in.^{2})

     horizontal steel: Use No. 4 bars at 12 in. ($A_s = 0.20$ in.^{2})

The steel may be placed in one layer, since the wall is less than 10 in. thick (see Figure 8-22).

8-5

DESIGN CONSIDERATIONS FOR BASEMENT WALLS

A basement wall is a type of retaining wall in which there is lateral support assumed to be provided at bottom and top by the basement floor slab and first-floor construction, respectively. As previously mentioned, the wall would be designed as a simply supported member with a loading diagram and moment diagram as shown in Figure 8-23.

    If the wall is part of a bearing wall, the vertical load will relieve some of the tension in the vertical reinforcement. This may be neglected since its effect may be small compared with the uncertainties in the assumption of loads. If the vertical load is of a permanent nature and of significant magnitude, its effect should be considered in the design.

FIGURE 8-23   Basement wall with full height backfill: forces and moment diagram.

When a part of the basement wall is above ground, the lateral bending moment may be small and may be computed as shown in Figure 8-24. This assumes that the wall is spanning in a vertical direction. Depending on the type of construction, the basement wall may also span in a horizontal direction and may behave as a slab reinforced in either one or two directions. If the wall design assumes two horizontal reactions as shown, caution must be exercised that the two supports are in place prior to backfilling behind the wall.

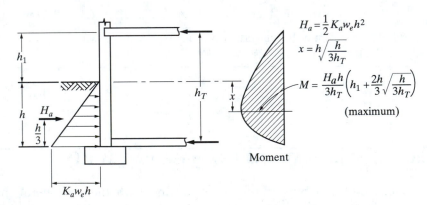

FIGURE 8-24   Basement wall with partial backfill: forces and moment diagram.

PROBLEMS

8-1.   Compute the active earth pressure horizontal force on the wall shown for the following conditions. Use $w_e = 100 \ \text{lb/ft}^3$.

Case	ϕ	θ	W_s (psf)	h_w (ft)
(a)	25	0	400	15
(b)	28	10	0	18
(c)	30	0	200	20
(d)	33	20	0	25

PROBLEM 8-1

8-2. Find the passive earth pressure force in front of the wall for Problem 8-1(a) if $h' = 4$ ft.

8-3. For the wall shown, determine the factors of safety against overturning and sliding and determine the soil pressures under the footing. Use $K_a = 0.3$ and $w_e = 100$ lb/ft³. The coefficient of friction $f = 0.50$.

PROBLEM 8-3

8-4. Same as Problem 8-3, but the toe is 2 ft 0 in.

8-5. In Problem 8-1(c), assume a footing depth of 2 ft. Design the stem steel for M_u at the top of the footing. Check the anchorage into the footing. Disregard other stem steel details. Use $f'_c = 4000$ psi and $f_y = 60,000$ psi. Use thickness at top of stem = 12 in. and thickness at bottom of stem = 1 ft 9 in.

8-6. Completely design the cantilever retaining wall shown. The height of wall h_w is 22 ft, the backfill is level, the surcharge is 600 psf, $w_e = 100$ lb/ft³, $h' = 4$ ft,

$K_a = 0.30$, and the allowable soil pressure is 4 ksf. Use a coefficient of friction of concrete on soil of 0.5, $f'_c = 3000$ psi, and $f_y = 60{,}000$ psi. The required factor of safety against overturning is 2.0 and against sliding is 1.5. The wall batter should be between ¼ and ½ in./ft. The design is to be in accordance with the ACI Code (318-95).

PROBLEM 8-6

8-7. Design a reinforced concrete bearing wall to support a series of precast single tees spaced 7 ft 6 in. on centers. The stem of each tee section is 8 in. wide and bears on the full thickness of wall. The wall is braced top and bottom against lateral translation. Assume the bottom end to be fixed against rotation and the top to be unrestrained against rotation. The wall height is 14 ft, and P_u from each tee is 65 kips. Use $f'_c = 4000$ psi and $f_y = 60{,}000$ psi.

CHAPTER 9

Columns

9-1

INTRODUCTION

The main vertical load-carrying members in buildings are called columns. The ACI Code defines a column as a member used primarily to support axial compressive loads and with a height at least three times its least lateral dimension. The code further defines a *pedestal* as an upright compression member having a ratio of unsupported height to least lateral dimension of 3 or less. The code definition for columns will be extended to include members that are subjected to combined axial compression and bending moment (in other words, eccentrically applied compressive loads), since, for all practical purposes, no column is truly axially loaded.

The three basic types of reinforced concrete columns are shown in Figure 9-1. *Tied columns* (Figure 9-1a) are reinforced with longitudinal bars that are enclosed by horizontal, or lateral, ties placed at specified spacings. *Spiral columns* (Figure 9-1b) are reinforced with longitudinal bars enclosed by a continuous, rather closely spaced, steel spiral. The spiral is made up of either wire or bar and is formed in the shape of a helix. A third type of reinforced concrete column, a *composite column,* is shown in Figure 9-1c. This type of column encompasses compression members reinforced longitudinally with structural steel shapes, pipes, or tubes with or without longitudinal bars. Code requirements for composite compression members are found in Section 10.14. Our discussion is limited to the first two types, tied and spiral columns. Tied columns are generally square or rectangular, whereas spiral columns are normally circular. This is not a hard-and-fast rule, however, since square, spirally reinforced columns and circular tied columns do exist, as do other shapes, such as octagonal and L-shaped columns.

We initially discuss the analysis and design of columns that are *short*. A column is said to be short when its length is such that lateral buckling need not be considered. The ACI Code does, however, require that the length of columns be a design consideration. It is recognized that as length increases, the usable strength of a given cross section is decreased because of the buckling problem. By their very nature, concrete columns are more massive and therefore stiffer than their structural steel counterparts. For this reason, slenderness is less of a problem in reinforced concrete columns. It has been estimated that more than 90% of typical reinforced concrete columns existing in braced frame buildings may be classified as short columns, and slenderness effects may be neglected.

9-2

STRENGTH OF REINFORCED CONCRETE COLUMNS: SMALL ECCENTRICITY

If a compressive load P is applied coincident with the longitudinal axis of a symmetrical column, it theoretically induces a uniform compressive stress over the

FIGURE 9-1   Column types.

PHOTO 9-1   Foundation columns, turbine generator building. Seabrook Station, New Hampshire.

cross-sectional area. If the compressive load is applied a small distance e away from the longitudinal axis, however, there is a tendency for the column to bend due to the moment $M = Pe$. This distance e is called the *eccentricity*. Unlike the zero eccentricity condition, the compressive stress is not uniformly distributed over the cross section but is greater on one side than the other. This is analogous to our previously discussed eccentricity of applied loads with respect to retaining wall footings, where the eccentrically applied load resulted in a nonuniform soil pressure under the footing.

We consider an *axial load* to be a load that acts parallel to the longitudinal axis of a member but *need not* be applied at any particular point on the cross section, such as a centroid or a geometric center. The column that is loaded with a compressive axial load at zero eccentricity is probably nonexistent, and even the axial load/small eccentricity (axial load/small moment) combination is relatively rare. Nevertheless, we first consider the case of columns that are loaded with compressive axial loads at *small eccentricities,* further defining this situation as that in which the induced moments, although they are present, are so small that they are of little significance.

The fundamental assumptions for the calculation of column axial load strength (small eccentricities) are that at ultimate load the concrete is stressed to $0.85f'_c$ and the steel is stressed to f_y. For the cross sections shown in Figure 9-1a and b, the nominal axial load strength at small eccentricity is a straightforward sum of the forces existing in the concrete and longitudinal steel when each of the materials is stressed to its maximum. The following ACI notation will be used:

A_g = gross area of the column section (in.^{2})

A_{st} = total area of *longitudinal* reinforcement (in.^{2})

P_0 = nominal, or theoretical, axial load strength at zero eccentricity

P_n = nominal, or theoretical, axial load strength at given eccentricity

P_u = factored applied axial load at given eccentricity

ρ_g = ratio of total longitudinal reinforcement area to cross-sectional area of column (A_{st}/A_g)

The nominal, or theoretical, axial load strength for the special case of zero eccentricity may be written

$$P_0 = 0.85f'_c(A_g - A_{st}) + f_y A_{st}$$

This theoretical strength must be further reduced to a maximum usable axial load strength using two different strength reduction factors.

Extensive testing has shown that spiral columns are tougher than tied columns, as depicted in Figure 9-2. Both types behave similarly up to the column yield point, at which time the outer shell spalls off. At this point, the tied column fails through crushing and shearing of the concrete and through outward buckling of the bars between the ties. The spiral column, however, has a core area within the spiral that

FIGURE 9-2 Load-strain relationship for columns.

is effectively laterally supported and continues to withstand load. Failure occurs only when the spiral steel yields following large deformation of the column. Naturally, the size and spacing of the spiral steel will affect the final load at failure. Although both columns have exceeded their usable strengths once the outer shell spalls off, the ACI Code recognizes the greater tenacity of the spiral column in Section 9.3.2, where it directs that a strength reduction factor of 0.75 be used for a spiral column, whereas the strength reduction factor for the tied column must be 0.70. In justifying the use of a spirally reinforced column with respect to strength and economics (code requirements for ductility notwithstanding), we should consider that the use of the spiral will increase the usable strength by a factor of $0.75/0.70 = 1.07$, or only 7%.

The code directs that the basic load-strength relationship be

$$P_u \le \phi P_n$$

where P_n is the nominal axial load strength at a given eccentricity and ϕP_n is designated as the *design axial load strength*. Logically, for the case of zero eccentricity, if it could exist, P_n would equal P_0. The ACI Code recognizes that no practical column can be loaded with zero eccentricity, however. Therefore, in addition to imposing the strength reduction factor ϕ, the code directs that the nominal strengths be further reduced by factors of 0.80 and 0.85 for tied and spiral columns, respectively. This results in the following expressions for usable axial load strengths.

For spiral columns,

$$\phi P_{n(\max)} = 0.85\phi[0.85f'_c(A_g - A_{st}) + f_y A_{st}] \qquad \text{ACI Eq. (10-1)}$$

For tied columns,

$$\phi P_{n(\max)} = 0.80\phi[0.85f'_c(A_g - A_{st}) + f_y A_{st}] \qquad \text{ACI Eq. (10-2)}$$

These expressions provide the magnitude of the maximum design axial load strength that may be realized from any column cross section. This will be the design axial load strength at small eccentricity. Should the eccentricity (and the associated moment) become larger, ϕP_n will have to be reduced, as shown in Section 9-9 of this text. It may be recognized that the code equations for $\phi P_{n(\max)}$ provide for an extra margin of axial load strength. This will, in effect, provide some reserve strength to carry small moments.

9-3

CODE REQUIREMENTS CONCERNING COLUMN DETAILS

Main (longitudinal) reinforcing should have a cross-sectional area so that ρ_g will be between 0.01 and 0.08. The minimum number of longitudinal bars is four within rectangular or circular ties, three within triangular ties, and six for bars enclosed by spirals. The foregoing requirements are stated in the ACI Code, Section 10.9. Although not mentioned in the present code, the 1963 code recommended a minimum bar size of No. 5.

The clear distance between longitudinal bars must not be less than 1.5 times the nominal bar diameter nor $1\frac{1}{2}$ in. (ACI Code, Section 7.6.3). This requirement also holds true where bars are spliced. Table A-14 may be used to determine the maximum number of bars allowed in one row around the periphery of circular or square columns.

Cover shall be $1\frac{1}{2}$ in. minimum over primary reinforcement, ties, or spirals (ACI Code, Section 7.7.1).

Tie requirements are discussed in detail in the ACI Code, Section 7.10.5. The minimum size is No. 3 for longitudinal bars No. 10 and smaller; otherwise, minimum tie size is No. 4 (see Table A-14 for a suggested tie size). Usually, No. 5 is a maximum. The center-to-center spacing of ties should not exceed the smaller of 16 longitudinal bar diameters, 48 tie-bar diameters, or the least column dimension. Furthermore, the ties shall be arranged so that every corner and alternate longitudinal bar will have lateral support provided by the corner of a tie having an included angle of not more than 135°, and no bar shall be farther than 6 in. clear on each side from such a laterally supported bar. See Figure 9-3 for typical tie arrangements.

Spiral requirements are discussed in the ACI Code, Section 7.10.4. The minimum spiral size is $\frac{3}{8}$ in. in diameter for cast-in-place construction ($\frac{5}{8}$ in. is usually maximum). Clear space between spirals must not exceed 3 in. or be less than 1 in. The *spiral steel ratio* ρ_s must not be less than the value given by

$$\rho_{s(\min)} = 0.45\left(\frac{A_g}{A_c} - 1\right)\frac{f_c'}{f_y} \qquad \text{(ACI Eq. 10-6)}$$

where

$$\rho_s = \frac{\text{volume of spiral steel in one turn}}{\text{volume of column core in height } (s)}$$

s = center-to-center spacing of spiral (in.) (sometimes called the *pitch*)

FIGURE 9-3 Typical tie arrangements.

A_g = gross cross-sectional area of the column (in.^{2})

A_c = cross-sectional area of the core (in.^{2}) (out-to-out of spiral)

f_y = *spiral* steel yield point (psi) $\leq$ 60,000 psi

f'_c = compressive strength of concrete (psi)

This particular spiral steel ratio will result in a spiral that will make up the strength lost due to the spalling of the outer shell (see Figure 9-2).

An approximate formula for the actual spiral steel ratio in terms of physical properties of the column cross section may be derived from the preceding definition of ρ_s. In Figure 9-4, we denote the overall core diameter (out-to-out of spiral)

FIGURE 9-4 Definition of D_c and D_s.

as D_c and the spiral diameter (center to center) as D_s. The cross-sectional area of the spiral bar or wire is denoted A_{sp}. From the definition of ρ_s, an expression may be written:

$$\text{actual } \rho_s = \frac{A_{sp}\pi D_s}{(\pi D_c^2/4)(s)}$$

If the small difference between D_c and D_s is neglected, then in terms of D_c,

$$\text{actual } \rho_s = \frac{4A_{sp}}{D_c s}$$

9-4

ANALYSIS OF SHORT COLUMNS: SMALL ECCENTRICITY

The analysis of short columns carrying axial loads that have small eccentricities involves checking the maximum design axial load strength and the various details of the reinforcing. The procedure is summarized in Section 9-6.

Example 9-1

Find the maximum design axial load strength for the tied column of cross section shown in Figure 9-5. Check the ties. Assume a short column. Use $f_c' = 4000$ psi and $f_y = 60,000$ psi for both longitudinal steel and ties.

Solution:

1. Check the steel ratio for the longitudinal steel:

$$\rho_g = \frac{A_{st}}{A_g} = \frac{8.00}{(16)^2} = 0.0313$$

$$0.01 < 0.0313 < 0.08 \qquad \text{(O.K.)}$$

FIGURE 9-5   Sketch for Example 9-1.

2.   From Table A-14, using a 13 in. core (column size less cover on each side), the maximum number of No. 9 bars is eight. Therefore, the number of longitudinal bars is satisfactory.

3.   The maximum design axial load strength may now be calculated:

$$\phi P_{n(\text{max})} = 0.80\phi[0.85f_c'(A_g - A_{st}) + f_y A_{st}]$$

$$= 0.80(0.70)[0.85(4)(256 - 8) + 60(8)]$$

$$= 741 \text{ kips}$$

4.   Check the ties. Tie size of No. 3 is acceptable for longitudinal bar size up to No. 10. The spacing of the ties must not exceed the smaller of

$$48 \text{ tie-bar diameters} = 48(\tfrac{3}{8}) = 18 \text{ in.}$$

$$16 \text{ longitudinal-bar diameters} = 16(1.128) = 18 \text{ in.}$$

$$\text{least column dimension} = 16 \text{ in.}$$

Therefore, the tie spacing is O.K. The tie arrangement for this column may be checked by ensuring that the clear distance between longitudinal bars does not exceed 6 in. Clear space in excess of 6 in. would require additional ties in accordance with the ACI Code, Section 7.10.5.3. Thus

$$\text{clear distance} = \frac{16 - 2(1\tfrac{1}{2}) - 2(\tfrac{3}{8}) - 3(1.128)}{2}$$

$$= 4.4 \text{ in.} < 6 \text{ in.}$$

Therefore, no extra ties are needed.

Example 9-2

Determine whether the column of cross section shown in Figure 9-6 is adequate to carry a factored axial load (P_u) of 550 kips. Assume small eccentricity. Check the spiral. Use $f_c' = 4000$ psi and $f_y = 60,000$ psi.

FIGURE 9-6   Sketch for Example 9-2.

Solution:

1. From Table A-2, $A_{st} = 5.53$ in.^{2}, and from Table A-14, a diameter of 15 in. results in a circular area $A_g = 176.7$ in.^{2}. Therefore,

$$\rho_g = \frac{5.53}{176.7} = 0.0313$$

$$0.01 < 0.0313 < 0.08 \qquad\qquad\qquad \text{(O.K.)}$$

2. From Table A-14, using a 12 in. core, seven No. 8 bars are satisfactory.
3. Find the maximum design axial load strength:

$$\phi P_{n(\max)} = 0.85\phi[0.85f'_c(A_g - A_{st}) + f_y A_{st}]$$

$$= 0.85(0.75)[0.85(4)(176.7 - 5.53) + 60(5.53)]$$

$$= 583 \text{ kips}$$

The strength is O.K. since 583 kips > 550 kips.

4. Check the spiral steel: The ⅜-in. diameter is O.K. (ACI Code, Section 7.10.4.2; and Table A-14). The minimum ρ_s is calculated using Table A-14 for the value of A_c:

$$\rho_{s(\min)} = 0.45\left(\frac{A_g}{A_c} - 1\right)\frac{f'_c}{f_y}$$

$$= 0.45\left(\frac{176.7}{113.1} - 1\right)\frac{4}{60} = 0.0169$$

$$\text{actual } \rho_s = \frac{4A_{sp}}{D_c s} = \frac{4(0.11)}{12(2)} = 0.0183$$

$$0.0183 > 0.0169 \qquad\qquad\qquad \text{(O.K.)}$$

The clear distance between spirals must not be in excess of 3 in. nor less than 1 in.:

$$\text{clear distance} = 2.0 - \tfrac{3}{8} = 1\tfrac{5}{8} \text{ in.} \qquad \text{(O.K.)}$$

The column is satisfactory for the specified conditions.

9-5

DESIGN OF SHORT COLUMNS: SMALL ECCENTRICITY

The design of reinforced concrete columns involves the proportioning of the steel and concrete areas and the selection of properly sized and spaced ties or spirals. Since the ratio of steel to concrete area must fall within a given range ($0.01 \leq \rho_g \leq 0.08$), the strength equation given in Section 9-2 is modified to include this term. For a tied column,

$$\phi P_{n(\text{max})} = 0.80\phi[0.85f'_c(A_g - A_{st}) + f_y(A_{st})]$$

$$\rho_g = \frac{A_{st}}{A_g}$$

from which

$$A_{st} = \rho_g A_g$$

Therefore,

$$\phi P_{n(\text{max})} = 0.80\phi[0.85f'_c(A_g - \rho_g A_g) + f_y\rho_g A_g]$$

$$= 0.80\phi A_g[0.85f'_c(1 - \rho_g) + f_y\rho_g]$$

Since

$$P_u \leq \phi P_{n(\text{max})}$$

an expression can be written for required A_g in terms of the material strengths, P_u and ρ_g. For tied columns,

$$\text{required } A_g = \frac{P_u}{0.80\phi[0.85f'_c(1 - \rho_g) + f_y\rho_g]}$$

Similarly for spiral columns,

$$\text{required } A_g = \frac{P_u}{0.85\phi[0.85f'_c(1 - \rho_g) + f_y\rho_g]}$$

It should be recognized that there can be many valid choices as to the size of column that will provide the necessary strength to carry any load P_u. A low ρ_g will result in a larger required A_g and vice versa. Other considerations will normally affect the practical choice of column size. Among them are architectural requirements and the desirability of maintaining column size from floor to floor so that forms may be reused.

The procedure for the design of short columns for loads at small eccentricities is summarized in Section 9-6.

Example 9-3

Design a square tied column to carry axial service loads of 320 kips dead load and 190 kips live load. There is no identified applied moment. Assume that the column is short. Use ρ_g about 0.03, $f_c' = 4000$ psi, and $f_y = 60,000$ psi.

Solution:

1. Material strengths and approximate ρ_g are given.
2. The factored axial load is

$$P_u = 1.7(190) + 1.4(320) = 771 \text{ kips}$$

3. The required gross column area is

$$\text{required } A_g = \frac{P_u}{0.80\phi[0.85f_c'(1 - \rho_g) + f_y\rho_g]}$$

$$= \frac{771}{0.80(0.70)[0.85(4)(1 - 0.03) + 60(0.03)]}$$

$$= 270 \text{ in.}^2$$

4. The required size of the square column would be

$$\sqrt{270} = 16.4 \text{ in.}$$

Use a 16-in.-square column. This choice will require that the actual ρ_g be slightly in excess of 0.03:

$$\text{actual } A_g = (16 \text{ in.})^2 = 256 \text{ in.}^2$$

5. The load on the concrete area (this is approximate since ρ_g will increase slightly) is

$$\text{load on concrete} = 0.80\phi(0.85f_c')A_g(1 - \rho_g)$$

$$= 0.80(0.70)(0.85)(4)(256)(1 - 0.03)$$

$$= 473 \text{ kips}$$

Therefore, the load to be carried by the steel is

$$771 - 473 = 298 \text{ kips}$$

Since the maximum design axial load strength of the steel is $(0.80\phi A_{st}f_y)$, the required steel area may be calculated as

$$\text{required } A_{st} = \frac{298}{0.80(0.70)(60)} = 8.87 \text{ in.}^2$$

We will distribute bars of the same size evenly around the perimeter of the column and must therefore select bars in multiples of four. Use eight No. 10 bars ($A_{st} = 10.2$ in.^{2}). Table A-14 indicates a maximum of eight No. 10 bars for a 13 in. core (O.K.).

6.   Design the ties. From Table A-14, select a No. 3 tie. The spacing must not be greater than

$$48 \text{ tie-bar diameters} = 48(\tfrac{3}{8}) = 18 \text{ in.}$$

$$16 \text{ longitudinal-bar diameters} = 16(1.27) = 20.3 \text{ in.}$$

$$\text{least column dimension} = 16 \text{ in.}$$

Use No. 3 ties spaced 16 in. o.c. Check the arrangement with reference to Figure 9-7. The clear space between adjacent bars in the same face is

$$\frac{16 - 3 - 0.75 - 3(1.27)}{2} = 4.22 \text{ in.} < 6.0 \text{ in.}$$

Therefore, no additional ties are required by the ACI Code, Section 7.10.5.3.

7.   The design sketch is shown in Figure 9-7.

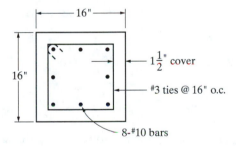

FIGURE 9-7   Design sketch for Example 9-3.

Example 9-4 _____

Redesign the column of Example 9-3 as a circular, spirally reinforced column.

Solution:

1.   Use $f'_c = 4000$ psi, $f_y = 60,000$ psi, and ρ_g approximately 0.03.
2. $P_u = 771$ kips, as in Example 9-3.

3. $$\text{required } A_g = \frac{P_u}{0.85\phi[0.85f'_c(1-\rho_g)+f_y\rho_g]}$$

$$= \frac{771}{0.85(0.75)[0.85(4)(1-0.03)+60(0.03)]}$$

$$= 237 \text{ in.}^2$$

4. From Table A-14, use an 18-in.-diameter column. Thus

$$\text{actual } A_g = 254.5 \text{ in.}^2$$

5. $$\text{load on concrete} = 0.85\phi(0.85)f'_c A_g(1-\rho_g)$$

$$= 0.85(0.75)(0.85)(4)(254.5)(1-0.03)$$

$$= 535 \text{ kips}$$

$$\text{load on steel} = 771 - 535 = 236 \text{ kips}$$

$$\text{required } A_{st} = \frac{236}{0.85\phi f_y}$$

$$= \frac{236}{0.85(0.75)60} = 6.17 \text{ in.}^2$$

Use eight No. 8 bars ($A_{st} = 6.32$ in.^{2}). Table A-14 indicates a maximum of 12 No. 8 bars for a circular core 15 in. in diameter (O.K.).

6. Design the spiral. From Table A-14, select a ⅜-in.-diameter spiral. The spacing will be based on the required spiral steel ratio. Here A_c is from Table A-14. Thus

$$\rho_{s(min)} = 0.45\left(\frac{A_g}{A_c}-1\right)\frac{f'_c}{f_y}$$

$$= 0.45\left(\frac{254.5}{176.7}-1\right)\frac{4}{60} = 0.0132$$

The maximum spiral spacing may be found by setting the actual ρ_s equal to $\rho_{s(min)}$:

$$\text{actual } \rho_s = \frac{4A_{sp}}{D_c s}$$

from which

$$s_{max} = \frac{4A_{sp}}{D_c \rho_{s(min)}}$$

$$= \frac{4(0.11)}{15(0.0132)} = 2.22 \text{ in.}$$

Use a spiral spacing of 2 in. The clear space between spirals must not be less than 1 in. nor more than 3 in.:

FIGURE 9-8   Design sketch for Example 9-4.

$$\text{clear space} = 2 - \tfrac{3}{8} = 1\tfrac{5}{8} \text{ in.} \qquad \text{(O.K.)}$$

7.   The design sketch is shown in Figure 9-8.

9-6

SUMMARY OF PROCEDURE FOR ANALYSIS AND DESIGN OF SHORT COLUMNS WITH SMALL ECCENTRICITIES

Analysis

1.   Check ρ_g within acceptable limits:

$$0.01 \leq \rho_g \leq 0.08$$

2.   Check the number of bars within acceptable limits for the clear space (see Table A-14). The minimum number is four for bars with rectangular or circular ties and six for bars enclosed by spirals.
3.   Calculate the maximum design axial load strength $\phi P_{n(\text{max})}$. See Section 9-2.
4.   Check the lateral reinforcing. For ties, check size, spacing, and arrangement. For spirals, check size, ρ_s, and clear distance.

Design

1.   Establish the material strengths. Establish the desired ρ_g (if any).
2.   Establish the factored axial load P_u.
3.   Determine the required gross column area A_g.
4.   Select the column dimensions. Use full-inch increments.
5.   Find the load carried by the concrete and the load required to be carried by the longitudinal steel. Determine the required longitudinal steel area. Select the longitudinal steel.

6.   Design the lateral reinforcing (ties or spiral).
7.   Sketch the design.

9-7

THE LOAD–MOMENT RELATIONSHIP

The equivalency between an eccentrically applied load and an axial load–moment combination is shown in Figure 9-9. Assume that a force P_u is applied to a cross section at a distance e (eccentricity) from the centroid, as shown in Figure 9-9a and b. Add equal and opposite forces P_u at the centroid of the cross section (Figure 9-9c). The original eccentric force P_u may now be combined with the upward force P_u to form a couple $P_u e$ that is a pure moment. This will leave remaining one force P_u acting downward at the centroid of the cross section. It can therefore be seen that if a force P_u is applied with an eccentricity e, the situation that results is identical to the case where an axial load of P_u at the centroid and a moment of $P_u e$ are simultaneously applied (Figure 9-9d). If we define M_u as the factored moment to be applied on a *compression* member along with a factored axial load of P_u at the centroid, the relationship between the two is

$$e = \frac{M_u}{P_u}$$

We have previously spoken of a column's nominal axial load strength at zero eccentricity P_0. Temporarily neglecting the strength reduction factors that must be applied to P_0, let us assume that we may apply a load P_u with zero eccentricity on a column of nominal axial load strength P_0 (where $P_u = P_0$). If we now move the load P_u away from the zero eccentricity position a distance of e, the column must resist the load P_u and, in addition, a moment $P_u e$. Since $P_u = P_0$ (in our hypothetical case), it is clear that there is no additional strength to carry the moment and

     (a)   (b)   (c)   (d)

FIGURE 9-9   Load–moment–eccentricity relationship.

that the column is overloaded. For this particular column to not be overloaded when subjected to load at eccentricity e, we must reduce P_u to the point where the column can carry both P_u and $P_u e$. The amount of the required decrease in P_u will depend on the magnitude of the eccentricity.

The preceding discussion must be modified because the ACI Code imposes $\phi P_{n(\max)}$ as the upper limit of axial load strength for any column. Nevertheless, the strength of any column cross section is such that it will support a broad spectrum of load and moment (or load and eccentricity) combinations. In other words, we may think of a column cross section as having many different axial load strengths, each with its own related moment strength.

9-8

COLUMNS SUBJECTED TO AXIAL LOAD AT LARGE ECCENTRICITY

The 1971 ACI Code stipulated that compression members must be designed for an eccentricity e of not less than $0.05h$ for spirally reinforced columns or $0.10h$ for tied columns, but at least 1 in. in any case. Here h is defined as the overall dimension of the column. These specified minimum eccentricities were originally intended to serve as a means of reducing the axial load design strength of a section in pure compression. The effect of the minimum eccentricity requirement was to limit the *maximum* axial load strength of a compression member.

Under the 1995 ACI Code, as we have discussed, the maximum design axial load strength $\phi P_{n(\max)}$ is given by ACI Equations (10-1) and (10-2). These two equations apply when eccentricities are not in excess of *approximately* the $0.10h$ and $0.05h$ minimum eccentricity limits of the 1971 Code. Therefore, *small eccentricities* may be considered as those eccentricities up to about $0.10h$ and $0.05h$ for tied and spiral columns, respectively. We will consider cases of *large eccentricities* as those in which ACI Equations (10-1) or (10-2) no longer apply and where ϕP_n must be reduced below $\phi P_{n(\max)}$.

The occurrence of columns subjected to eccentricities sufficiently large so that moment must be a design consideration is common. Even interior columns supporting beams of equal spans will receive unequal loads from the beams due to applied live load patterns. These unequal loads could mean that the column must carry both load and moment, as shown in Figure 9-10a, and the resulting eccentricity of the loads could be appreciably in excess of our definition of small eccentricity. Another example of a column carrying both load and moment is shown in Figure 9-10b. In both cases, the rigidity of the joint will require the column to rotate along with the end of the beam that it is supporting. The rotation will induce moment in the column. A third and very practical example can be found in precast work (Figure 9-10c), where the beam reaction can clearly be seen to be eccentrically applied on the column through the column bracket.

FIGURE 9-10   Eccentrically loaded columns.

9-9

ANALYSIS OF SHORT COLUMNS: LARGE ECCENTRICITY

The first step in our investigation of short columns carrying loads at large eccentricity is to determine the strength of a given column cross section that carries loads at various eccentricities. This may be thought of as an analysis process. For this development, we will find the design axial load strength ϕP_n, where P_n is defined as the nominal axial load strength at a given eccentricity.

Example 9-5

Find the design axial load strength ϕP_n for the tied column for the following conditions: (a) small eccentricity, (b) pure moment, (c) $e = 5$ in., and (d) the balanced condition. The column cross section is shown in Figure 9-11. Assume a short column. Bending is about the Y-Y axis. Use $f'_c = 4000$ psi and $f_y = 60,000$ psi.

FIGURE 9-11   Column cross section for Example 9-5.

Solution:

(a) The analysis of the small eccentricity condition is similar to the analyses of Examples 9-1 and 9-2. We can calculate the design axial load strength from

$$\phi P_n = \phi P_{n(\text{max})}$$
$$= 0.80\phi[0.85f_c'(A_g - A_{st}) + f_y A_{st}]$$
$$= 0.80(0.70)[0.85(4)(280 - 6) + 60(6)]$$
$$= 723 \text{ kips}$$

(b) The analysis of the pure moment condition is similar to the analysis of the case where eccentricity e is infinite, shown in Figure 9-12. We will find the design moment strength M_R, since P_u and ϕP_n will both be zero.

FIGURE 9-12   Column of Example 9-5 loaded with pure moment.

With reference to Figure 9-13d, notice that for pure moment the bars on the load side of the column are in compression, whereas the bars on the side away from the load are in tension. The total tensile and compressive forces must be equal to each other. Since $A_s = A_s'$, A_s' *must* be at a stress less than yield. Assume that A_s is at yield stress. Then

$$C_1 = \text{concrete compressive force}$$
$$C_2 = \text{steel compressive force}$$
$$T = \text{steel tensile force}$$

Referring to the compressive strain diagram portion of Figure 9-13c and noting that the basic units are kips and inches,

$$\epsilon_s' = 0.003\frac{(c - 3)}{c}$$

Since

$$f_c' = E_s \epsilon_s'$$

substituting yields

FIGURE 9-13   Example 9-5b, $e = \infty$.

$$f'_c = 29,000(0.003)\frac{(c-3)}{c}$$

$$= 87\frac{(c-3)}{c}$$

For equilibrium in Figure 9-13d,

$$C_1 + C_2 = T$$

Substituting into the foregoing and accounting for the concrete displaced by the compression steel, we obtain

$$(0.85f'_c)(0.85c)(b) + f'_s A'_s - 0.85f'_c A'_s = f_y A_s$$

$$(0.85)(4)(0.85c)(14) + 87\left(\frac{c-3}{c}\right)(3) - 0.85(4)(3) = 3(60)$$

Solving the preceding equation for the one unknown quantity c yields

$$c = 3.62 \text{ in.}$$

Therefore,

$$f'_s = 87\left(\frac{3.62-3}{3.62}\right) = 14.90 \text{ ksi} \qquad \text{(compression)}$$

Summarizing the forces,

$$C_1 = 0.85f'_c(0.85)cb = 0.85(4)(0.85)(3.62)(14) = 146.5 \text{ kips}$$

$$\text{displaced concrete} = 0.85f'_c A'_s = 0.85(4)(3) = -10.2 \text{ kips}$$

$$C_2 = f'_s A'_s = 14.90(3) = \underline{44.7 \text{ kips}}$$

$$181.0 \text{ kips}$$

$$T = f_y A_s = 60(3.0) = 180 \quad \text{kips}$$

The slight error between T and $(C_1 + C_2)$ will be neglected.
Summarizing the internal couples,

$$M_{n1} = C_1 Z_1$$

$$= \frac{146.5}{12}\left[17 - \frac{0.85(3.62)}{2}\right]$$

$$= 188.8 \text{ ft-kips}$$

$$M_{n2} = C_2 Z_2$$

$$= (44.7 - 10.2)\left(\frac{14}{12}\right)$$

$$= 40.3 \text{ ft-kips}$$

$$M_n = M_{n1} + M_{n2}$$

$$= 188.8 + 40.3$$

$$= 229 \text{ ft-kips}$$

Applying the tied column strength reduction factor ϕ of 0.70 and neglecting, for now, the ACI Code, Section 9.3.2.2(b), the design moment strength becomes

$$\phi M_n = 0.70(229)$$

$$= 160 \text{ ft-kips}$$

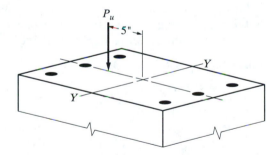

FIGURE 9-14   Example 9-5c, $e = 5$ in.

(c) The situation of $e = 5$ in. is shown in Figure 9-14. In part (a) of this example, all steel was in compression. In part (b), the steel on the side of the column away from the load was in tension. Therefore, there is some value of eccentricity at which this steel will change from tension to compression. Since this value of eccentricity is not known, the strain situation shown in Figure 9-15 is *assumed* and will be verified (or disproved) by calculation.

FIGURE 9-15 Example 9-5c, $e = 5$ in.

The assumptions at ultimate load are:

1. Maximum concrete strain = 0.003.
2. $\epsilon_s' > \epsilon_y$. Therefore, $f_s' = f_y$.
3. ϵ_s is tensile.
4. $\epsilon_s < \epsilon_y$. Therefore, $f_s < f_y$.

The unknown quantities are P_n and c.

Using basic units of kips and inches, the tensile and compressive forces are evaluated. Force C_2 is the force in the compressive steel accounting for the concrete displaced by the steel. With reference to Figure 9-15c:

$$C_1 = 0.85f_c'ab = 0.85(4)(0.85c)(14) = 40.46c$$

$$C_2 = f_y A_s' - 0.85f_c'A_s' = A_s'(f_y - 0.85f_c')$$
$$= 3[60 - 0.85(4)] = 169.8$$

$$T = f_s A_s = \epsilon_s E_s A_s = 87\left(\frac{d-c}{c}\right)A_s$$

$$= 87\left(\frac{17-c}{c}\right)3 = 261\left(\frac{17-c}{c}\right)$$

From Σ forces = 0 in Figure 9-15,

$$P_n = C_1 + C_2 - T$$

$$= 40.46c + 169.8 - 261\left(\frac{17-c}{c}\right)$$

From Σ moments = 0, taking moments about T in Figure 9-15,

$$P_n(12) = C_1\left(d - \frac{a}{2}\right) + C_2(14)$$

$$P_n = \frac{1}{12}[40.46(c)\left(17 - \frac{0.85c}{2}\right) + 169.8(14)] \qquad Eq\ 2$$

The preceding two equations for P_n may be equated and the resulting cubic equation solved for c by trial or by some other iterative method. The solution will yield $c = 14.86$ in., which will result in a value for P_n (from either equation) of 733 kips. Therefore,

$$\phi P_n = 0.70(733)$$

$$= 513 \text{ kips}$$

Check the assumptions that were made:

$$\epsilon'_s = \left(\frac{14.86 - 3}{14.86}\right)(0.003) = 0.0024$$

$$\epsilon_y = 0.00207$$

Since $\epsilon'_s > \epsilon_y$,

$$f'_s = f_y \qquad \text{(O.K.)}$$

Based on the location of the neutral axis, the steel away from the load *is* in tension and

$$f_s = 87\left(\frac{17 - 14.87}{14.86}\right) = 12.53 \text{ ksi} < 60 \text{ ksi} \qquad \text{(O.K.)}$$

All assumptions are verified.

We may also determine the design moment strength for an eccentricity of 5 in. as follows:

$$\phi P_n e = \frac{513(5)}{12}$$

$$= 214 \text{ ft-kips}$$

Therefore, the given column has a design load–moment combination strength of 513 kips axial load and 214 ft-kips moment. This assumes that the moment is applied about the *Y-Y* axis.

(d) The balanced condition exists when the concrete reaches a strain of 0.003 at the same time that the tension steel reaches its yield strain, as shown in Figure 9-16c. Here P_b is defined as nominal axial load strength at the balanced condition, e_b is the associated eccentricity, and c_b is the distance from the compression face to the balanced neutral axis.

From Equation (2-1), we may calculate the value of c_b:

$$c_b = \frac{87,000}{87,000 + f_y}(d) = \frac{87,000}{147,000}(17) = 10.06 \text{ in.}$$

We then may determine ϵ_s':

$$\epsilon_s' = \frac{7.06}{10.06}(0.003) = 0.0021$$

Since $0.0021 > 0.00207$, the compression steel has yielded and $f_s' = f_y = 60$ ksi.

Summarize the forces in Figure 9-16d and let C_2 account for the force in the displaced concrete:

$$C_1 = 0.85(4)(0.85)(10.06)(14) = 407 \text{ kips}$$

$$C_2 = 60(3) - 0.85(4)(3) = 170 \text{ kips}$$

$$T = 60(3) = 180 \text{ kips}$$

$$P_b = C_1 + C_2 - T = 407 + 170 - 180$$

$$= 397 \text{ kips}$$

The value of e_b may be established by summing moments about T:

$$P_b(e_b + 7) = C_1\left(d - \frac{0.85c_b}{2}\right) + C_2(14)$$

$$397(e_b + 7) = 407\left[17 - \frac{0.85(10.06)}{2}\right] + 170(14)$$

from which $e_b = 12.0$ in. Therefore, at the balanced condition,

| | (a) | (b) | (c) Strain | (d) Stress and Force |

FIGURE 9-16   Example 9-5d, balanced condition.

$$\phi P_b = 0.70(397) = 278 \text{ kips}$$

$$\phi P_b e_b = \frac{278}{12}(12) = 278 \text{ ft-kips}$$

The results of the four parts of Example 9-5 are tabulated and plotted in Figure 9-17. All design axial load strengths are denoted ϕP_n, and all design moment strengths are denoted $\phi P_n e$. This plot is commonly called an *interaction diagram.* It applies *only* to the column analyzed, but it is a representation of *all* combinations of axial load and moment strengths for that column cross section.

In Figure 9-17, any point *on* the solid line represents an allowable combination of load and moment. Any point *within* the solid line represents a load–moment combination that is also allowable, but for which this column is *overdesigned.* Any point *outside* the solid line represents an unacceptable load–moment combination or a load–moment combination for which this column is *underdesigned.* The value

e	Axial load strength $(\phi P_n,$ kips)	Moment strength $(\phi P_n e,$ ft-kips)	
Small	723	0–small	
Infinite	0	160	
5"	513	214	
12"	278	278	BALANCED

FIGURE 9-17   Column interaction diagram.

of $\phi P_{n(max)}$, which we calculated in part (a), is superimposed on the plot as a horizontal line.

Radial lines from the origin represent various eccentricities. (Actually, the slopes of the radial lines are equal to $\phi P_n/\phi P_n e$ or $1/e$.) The intersection of the $e = e_b$ line with the solid line represents the balanced condition. Any eccentricity *less* than e_b will result in compression controlling the column, and any eccentricity *greater* than e_b will result in tension controlling the column.

The calculations involved with column loads at large eccentricities are involved and tedious. The previous examples were analysis examples. Design of a cross section using the calculation approach would be a trial-and-error method and would become exceedingly tedious. Therefore, design and analysis aids have been developed that shorten the process to a great extent. These aids may be found in the form of tables and charts. A chart approach is developed in ACI Publication SP-17A(90), *Design Handbook, Volume 2—Columns*. Several charts from SP-17A(90) have been reproduced in Appendix A. The charts take on the basic form of the interaction diagram in Figure 9-17. But, to generalize the charts so that they are applicable to more situations, some new terms are introduced. Referring to Chart A-25, the following definitions will be useful:

$$\rho_g = \frac{A_{st}}{A_g}$$

h = column dimension perpendicular to the bending axis (see sketch included on the chart)

γ = ratio of distance between centroid of outer rows of bars and thickness of the cross section, in the direction of bending

Note that the load (vertical) axis and the moment (horizontal) axis scales are in terms of ϕP_n. The charts may be used to find the design axial load strength of a column along with its associated moment strength. It will be recalled that the primary load-strength relationship for columns is that $P_u \leq \phi P_n$. The charts, then, are basically analysis aids. For design, they may be used for a trial-and-error procedure.

Charts for the three types of cross sections shown in Figure 9-18 are included in Appendix A. These are for material strengths of $f'_c = 4000$ psi and $f_y = 60,000$ psi only. For other combinations, see SP-17A(90). For those columns of the type shown

Charts A-15 to A-18	Charts A-19 to A-22	Charts A-23 to A-26
(a)	(b)	(c)

9-18   Design aid column types.

in Figure 9-18a, the steel is assumed to be distributed equally in each face, that is, one-fourth of the total steel per face. The ϕ factors of 0.70 or 0.75 (as applicable) are reflected in the charts and need not be included in any calculations.

Example 9-6 _____

Using the charts of Appendix A, find the design axial load strength ϕP_n for the column cross section shown in Figure 9-19 at an eccentricity of 5 in. Use $f'_c = 4000$ psi and $f_y = 60{,}000$ psi. Compare the results with Example 9-5c.

FIGURE 9-19   Sketch for Example 9-6.

Solution:

First, determine which chart to use, based on the type of cross section, the material strengths, and the factor γ:

$$\gamma h = 14 \text{ in.}$$

$$\gamma = \frac{14}{20} = 0.70$$

Chart A-24 is for $\gamma = 0.60$, and Chart A-25 is for $\gamma = 0.75$. For purposes of this example, use Chart A-25 rather than an interpolation between the two charts:

$$\rho_g = \frac{A_{st}}{A_g} = \frac{6.00}{20(14)} = 0.0214$$

$$0.01 < 0.0214 < 0.08 \qquad\qquad\qquad \text{(O.K.)}$$

$$\frac{e}{h} = \frac{5.0}{20} = 0.25$$

The quantities ρ_g and e/h are intersected on Chart A-25, as shown in Figure 9-20. From the intersection, reading horizontally to the vertical axis on the left, we read a value of

$$\frac{\phi P_n}{A_g} = 1.85$$

FIGURE 9-20   Use of Chart A-25.

from which

$$\phi P_n = 1.85 A_g = 1.85(14)(20) = 518 \text{ kips}$$

The associated moment strength may be determined:

$$\phi P_n e = (518)(\tfrac{5}{12}) = 216 \text{ ft-kips}$$

This compares favorably with the results of Example 9-5c. The use of interpolation between Charts A-24 and A-25 would produce an even closer correlation with the results of Example 9-5c. The design axial load–moment strengths for other eccentricities for this column may be easily found, since the ρ_g term remains constant.

Example 9-7

Using the column charts, find the value of $\phi P_{n(\max)}$ for the column of Example 9-6.

Solution:

From Example 9-6, $\rho_g = 0.0214$. Interpolating at the left vertical axis ($e/h = 0$), between lines representing $\rho_g = 0.02$ and 0.03 on either Chart A-24 or A-25, results in

$$\frac{\phi P_n}{A_g} = 2.6$$

Therefore,

$$\phi P_{n(\max)} = 2.6 A_g = 2.6(14)(20) = 728 \text{ kips}$$

This compares favorably with 723 kips calculated in Example 9-5a.

Note in Charts A-24 and A-25 that the horizontal lines that represent $\phi P_{n(\max)}$ intersect their respective strength curves at about e/h of 0.10. This confirms that ACI Equations (10-1) and (10-2) give approximately the same

results for maximum design strength as did the minimum eccentricity requirements of the 1971 code.

9-10

ϕ FACTOR CONSIDERATIONS

Columns discussed so far have had strength reduction factors applied in a straightforward manner. That is, $\phi = 0.75$ for spiral columns, and $\phi = 0.70$ for tied columns.
Eccentrically loaded columns, however, carry both axial load and moment. It will
be recalled that beams (flexural members) were subject to a strength reduction factor $\phi = 0.90$ applied to the flexural (moment) strength.

The ACI Code provides for cases where columns are subjected to very small
axial loads and large moments (thereby becoming predominantly bending members, or beams, where $\phi = 0.90$ would be expected). In Section 9.3.2.2(b) of the code,
it is stipulated that for small values of axial load, ϕ may be increased linearly to 0.90
as ϕP_n decreases from $0.10 f'_c A_g$ to zero. Additional restrictions are that f_y does not
exceed 60,000 psi, that the reinforcement be symmetric, and that γ be not less than
0.70. It should be noted that this is a liberalizing stipulation of the code (use of the
original ϕ would result in a conservative design) and that it applies only to cases of
small axial load. In Example 9-5,

$$0.10 f'_c A_g = 0.10(4)(14)(20) = 112 \text{ kips}$$

so that if ϕP_n were 112 kips, then $\phi = 0.70$, whereas if ϕP_n were zero, then $\phi = 0.90$.
For pure moment, as in Example 9-5b, $\phi P_n e$ (or ϕM_n, the design moment strength
of the member) would become

$$\phi P_n e = 160 \left(\frac{0.9}{0.7} \right) = 206 \text{ ft-kips}$$

The strength of the member, as governed by the code, Section 9.3.2.2(b), is
shown by the dashed line on Figure 9-17 for values of ϕP_n between 112 kips and
zero. The allowed increase in ϕ for small axial loads is reflected in Charts A-15
through A-26.

9-11

DESIGN OF ECCENTRICALLY LOADED COLUMNS (ACI CHART APPROACH)

The ACI charts may be used for design of an eccentrically loaded column using a
trial-and-error approach. Recall that the charts are primarily analysis aids.

Example 9-8

Design a short square tied column to carry a factored axial load P_u of 640 kips and a factored moment M_u of 330 ft-kips. Place the reinforcing uniformly in the four faces. Design the ties. Use a 1½-in. cover, $f'_c = 4000$ psi, and $f_y = 60,000$ psi.

Solution:

1.   Determine the eccentricity:

$$e = \frac{M_u}{P_u} = \frac{330(12)}{640} = 6.19 \text{ in.}$$

2.   Estimate the column size required based on the axial load P_u and $\rho_g = 0$. This will be satisfactory for an estimate:

$$\text{required } A_g = \frac{P_u}{0.80\phi(0.85)f'_c} = \frac{640}{0.80(0.70)(0.85)(4)} = 336 \text{ in.}^2$$

Try an 18 in. × 18 in. column ($A_g = 324$ in.^{2}).

3.   Determine e/h and the required $\phi P_n/A_g$ for chart use:

$$\frac{e}{h} = \frac{6.19}{18} = 0.34$$

Since, as a limit, P_u can equal ϕP_n,

$$\text{required } \frac{\phi P_n}{A_g} = \frac{640}{18(18)} = 1.98$$

4.   Determine which chart to use. In Figure 9-21, assuming No. 3 ties and No. 8 main bars,

$$\gamma h = 18 - 2(1.5) - 2(0.38) - 2(0.5) = 13.25 \text{ in.}$$

$$\gamma = \frac{13.25}{18} = 0.736$$

Therefore, by inspection, use Chart A-17 ($\gamma = 0.75$).

FIGURE 9-21   Sketch for Example 9-8.

5.   From the chart, find the required ρ_g that is represented by the curve that passes through the intersection of $\phi P_n / A_g = 1.98$ and $e/h = 0.34$:

$$\text{required } \rho_g = 0.05 \text{ (approximately)}$$

This is a high steel ratio, and it will be difficult to fit the bars in the column. Therefore, try a 20 in. × 20 in. column:

$$\frac{e}{h} = \frac{6.19}{20} = 0.31$$

$$\text{required } \frac{\phi P_n}{A_g} = \frac{640}{(20)(20)} = 1.60$$

$$\gamma h = 20 - 2(1.5) - 2(0.38) - 2(0.5) = 15.25$$

$$\gamma = \frac{15.25}{20} = 0.763$$

Use Chart A-17 ($\gamma = 0.75$):

$$\text{required } \rho_g = 0.027$$

$$\text{required } A_{st} = \rho_g A_g = 0.027(20)(20) = 10.88 \text{ in.}^2$$

6.   Select 12 No. 9 bars with $A_{st} = 12.0$ in.^{2}. Using Table A-14, check to see that 12 No. 9 bars may be used in one row in a 20 in. column. The maximum number of bars is 12 (O.K.).

7.   Design the ties by selecting a No. 4 bar from Table A-14 and determining the spacing as follows:

$$48 \text{ tie-bar diameters} = 48(0.5) = 24 \text{ in.}$$

$$16 \text{ longitudinal-bar diameters} = 16(1.128) = 18 \text{ in.}$$

$$\text{least column dimension} = 20 \text{ in.}$$

FIGURE 9-22   Design sketch for Example 9-8.

Use No. 4 ties at 18 in. o.c.

8.   The design sketch is shown in Figure 9-22.

9-12

THE SLENDER COLUMN

Thus far, our design and analysis has been limited to short columns that require no consideration of necessary strength reduction due to the possibility of buckling. All compression members will experience the buckling phenomenon as they become longer and more flexible. These are sometimes termed *slender columns*. A column may be categorized as *slender* if its cross-sectional dimensions are small in comparison to its unsupported length. The degree of slenderness may be expressed in terms of the *slenderness ratio*

$$\frac{k\ell_u}{r}$$

where

k = effective length factor for compression members (ACI Code, Section 10.12.1)

ℓ_u = the unsupported length of a compression member, which shall be taken as the clear distance between floor slabs, beams, or other members capable of providing lateral support in the direction being considered (ACI Code, Section 10.11.3.1)

r = radius of gyration of the cross section of the compression members, which may be taken as $0.30h$, where h is the overall dimension of a rectangular column in the direction of the moment, or $0.25D$, where D is the diameter of a circular column (ACI Code, Section 10.11.2)

The numerator $k\ell_u$ is termed the *effective length*. It is a function not only of the unsupported length and end conditions of the column but also a function of whether or not *sidesway* exists. Sidesway may be described as a kind of deformation whereby one end of a member moves laterally with respect to the other. Sidesway is also termed *lateral drift*.

The ACI Code, Section 10.12.1, states that for compression members braced against sidesway, k shall be taken as 1.0 unless an analysis shows that a lower value may be used. For compression members not braced against sidesway, the effective length must be greater than 1.0. Therefore, as a rule, compression members free to buckle in a sidesway mode are appreciably weaker than when braced against sidesway.

A simple example is a column fixed at one end and entirely free at the other (cantilever column or flagpole). Such a column will buckle, as shown in Figure 9-23.

FIGURE 9-23   Fixed-free column.

The upper end would move laterally with respect to the lower end. This lateral movement is the sidesway (or lateral drift). In reinforced concrete structures, it is common to deal with indeterminate rigid frames, such as illustrated by the simple portal frame in Figure 9-24. The upper end of the frame can move sideways since it is unbraced. This type of frame is sometimes termed a *sway frame,* and it depends on the rigidity of the joints for stability. The lower ends of the columns may be theoretically pin-corrected, fully restrained, or somewhere in between.

As an example of how the effective length of a column is influenced by sidesway, consider the simple case of a single member, as shown in Figure 9-25. The member braced against sidesway (Figure 9-25a) has an effective length half that of the member without sidesway bracing (Figure 9-25b) and has four times the axial-load capacity based on the Euler critical column load theory.

Frame Unloaded

(a)

Frame Loaded, Unbraced

(b)

FIGURE 9-24   Sidesway on portal frame.

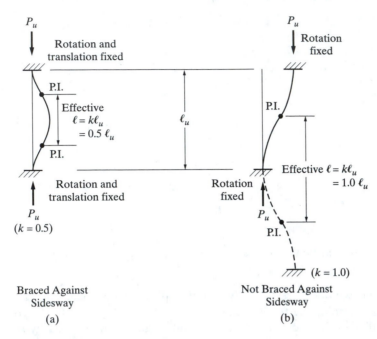

FIGURE 9-25　Sidesway and effective length.

If we consider the column shown in Figure 9-25b to be part of a frame and give the sidesway the notation Δ as shown in Figure 9-26, it is seen that the axial load now acts eccentrically and creates end moments of $P_u\Delta$. This is referred to as the *P-delta effect*. These moments are also referred to as "second-order end moments" since they are in addition to any primary (first-order) end moments that result from applied loads on the frame with no consideration of geometry change (sidesway).

Actual structures are rarely completely braced (nonsway) or completely unbraced (sway). Sidesway may be minimized in various ways. The common approach is to use walls or partitions sufficiently strong and rigid in their own planes to prevent the horizontal displacement. Another method is to use a rigid central core that is capable of resisting lateral loads and lateral displacements due to unsymmetrical loading conditions. For those cases when it is not readily apparent whether a structure is braced or unbraced, the ACI Code (Sections 10.11.4.1 and 10.11.4.2) provides analytical methods to aid in the decision.

For braced columns, slenderness effects may be neglected when

$$\frac{k\ell_u}{r} \leq 34 - 12\left(\frac{M_1}{M_2}\right)$$

where M_1 is the smaller end moment and M_2 is the larger end moment, both obtained by an elastic frame analysis. The ratio M_1/M_2 is positive if the column is bent in single curvature, is negative if bent in double curvature (see Figure 9-27),

FIGURE 9-26   Column subjected to sidesway.

Single-curvature   Double-curvature
bending   bending

FIGURE 9-27   Column curvature.

and must not be taken less than -0.5. For columns not braced against sidesway, slenderness effects may be neglected when $k\ell_u/r$ is less than 22.

Fortunately, for ordinary beam and column sizes and typical story heights of concrete framing systems, effects of slenderness may be neglected in more than 90% of columns in braced (nonsway) frames and in about 40% of columns in unbraced (sway) frames [1].

In cases where slenderness must be considered, the ACI Code gives three methods that can be used. These range from an approximate method in which moments are magnified to account for slenderness to an exact second-order analysis. The approximate method uses a moment magnification factor that amplifies the factored moment computed from a conventional elastic analysis. In turn, the combination of the magnified factored moment and the factored axial load is used in the design of the compression member. Although the approximate analyses have been the traditional design methods of the past, more exact analyses have become possible and practical with the increased availability of sophisticated computer methods. For compression members with $k\ell_u/r$ in excess of 100, the more exact second-order analysis defined in the ACI Code, Section 10.10.1, is required.

The design of slender reinforced concrete columns is one of the more complex aspects of reinforced concrete design and is not within the intended scope of this book. For the more rigorous theoretical background and applications relative to slender columns, the reader is referred to other comprehensive texts on reinforced concrete design that may offer a different emphasis and orientation.

REFERENCE

[1]   Notes on ACI 318-95, "Building Code Requirements for Structural Concrete, with Design Applications." Portland Cement Association, 5420 Old Orchard Road, Skokie, IL 60077-1083, 1996.

PROBLEMS

9-1.   Compute the maximum design axial load strength of the tied columns shown. Assume that the columns are short. Check the tie size and spacing. Use $f'_c = 4000$ psi and $f_y = 60,000$ psi.

9-2.   Compute the maximum design axial load strength for the tied column shown. The column is short. Check the tie size and spacing. Use $f'_c = 4000$ psi and $f_y = 60,000$ psi.

9-3.   Find the maximum axial compressive service loads that the column of cross section shown can carry. The column is short. Assume that the service dead load and live load are equal. Check the ties. Use $f'_c = 4000$ psi and $f_y = 60,000$ psi.

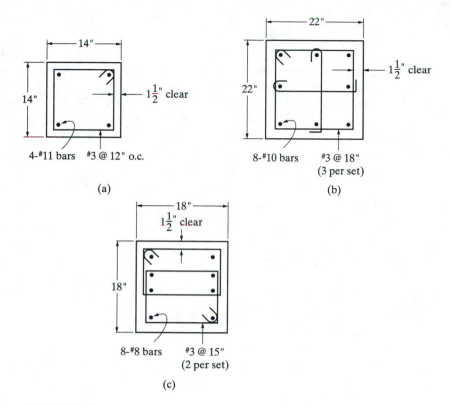

(a)

(c)

(b)

PROBLEM 9-1

PROBLEM 9-2

PROBLEM 9-3

9-4. A short, circular spiral column having a diameter of 18 in. is reinforced with eight No. 9 bars. The cover is 1½ in., and the spiral is ⅜ in. in diameter spaced 2 in. o.c. Find the maximum design axial load strength and check the spiral. Use $f_c' = 3000$ psi and $f_y = 40,000$ psi.

9-5. Same as Problem 9-4, but $f_c' = 4000$ psi and $f_y = 60,000$ psi.

9-6. Compute the maximum axial compressive service live load that may be placed on the column shown. The column is short and is subjected to an axial service dead load of 200 kips. Check the ties. Use $f_c' = 3000$ psi and $f_y = 40,000$ psi.

PROBLEM 9-6

9-7. Design a short, square tied column to carry a total factored design load P_u of 975 kips. Space and practical limitations require a column size of 18 in. × 18 in. Use $f_c' = 4000$ psi and $f_y = 60,000$ psi.

9-8. Design a short, square tied column for service loads of 200 kips dead load and 160 kips live load. Use ρ_g of about 0.04, $f_c' = 3000$ psi, and $f_y = 60,000$ psi. Assume that eccentricity is small.

9-9. Same as Problem 9-8, but use $f_c' = 4000$ psi, $f_y = 60,000$ psi, and a ρ_g of about 0.03.

9-10. Design a short, circular spiral column for service loads of 175 kips dead load and 325 kips live load. Assume that the eccentricity is small. Use $f_c' = 4000$ psi and $f_y = 60,000$ psi. Make ρ_g about 3%.

9-11. The short spiral column of cross section shown is to carry both axial load and moment. Find ϕP_n if $e = 6.0$ in. Use $f_c' = 4000$ psi and $f_y = 60,000$ psi.

PROBLEM 9-11

9-12. For the short column of cross section shown, find ϕP_n and e_b at the balanced condition using basic principles. Check by using the charts. Use $f_c' = 4000$ psi and $f_y = 60,000$ psi. Bending is about the strong axis.

22"
8-#10 bars
16"
$1\frac{1}{2}$" clear
#4 @ 16" o.c.

PROBLEM 9-12

9-13. Design a short, square tied column to carry a factored axial design load P_u of 560 kips and a factored design moment M_u of 280 ft-kips. Place the longitudinal reinforcing uniformly in the four faces. Use $f_c' = 4000$ psi and $f_y = 60,000$ psi.

9-14. Same as Problem 9-13, but design a circular spiral column.

9-15. For the short tied column of cross section shown, find the design axial load strength ϕP_n for an eccentricity of 14 in. Use $f_c' = 4000$ psi and $f_y = 60,000$ psi. Assume that the ties and bracket design are adequate.

14"
P_u
20"
A
A
Elevation

20"
14"
14"
6-#9 bars
Section A–A

PROBLEM 9-15

CHAPTER 10

Footings

10-1

INTRODUCTION

The purpose of the structural portion of every building is to transmit applied loads safely from one part of the structure to another. The loads pass from their point of application into the *superstructure,* then to the *foundation,* and then into the underlying supporting material. We have discussed the superstructure and foundation walls to some extent. The foundation is generally considered to be the entire lowermost supporting part of the structure. Normally, a *footing* is the last, or nearly the last, structural element of the foundation through which the loads pass. A footing has as its function the requirement of spreading out the superimposed load so as not to exceed the safe capacity of the underlying material, usually soil, to which it delivers the load. Additionally, the design of footings must take into account certain practical and, at times, legal considerations. Our discussion is concerned only with spread footings depicted in Figure 10-1. Footings supported on piles will not be discussed.

The more common types of footings may be categorized as follows:

1. *Individual column footings* (Figure 10-1a) are often termed *isolated spread footings* and are generally square. If space limitations exist, however, the footing may be rectangular in shape.

2. *Wall footings* support walls that may be either bearing or nonbearing walls (Figure 10-1b).

3. *Combined footings* support two or more columns and may be either rectangular or trapezoidal in shape (Figure 10-1c and d). If two isolated footings are joined by a *strap beam,* the footing is sometimes called a *cantilever footing* (Figure 10-1e).

4. *Mat foundations* are large continuous footings that support all columns and walls of a structure. They are commonly used where undesirable soil conditions prevail (Figure 10-1f).

5. *Pile caps* or *pile footings* serve to transmit column loads to a group of piles, which will in turn transmit the loads to the supporting soil through friction or to underlying rock in bearing (Figure 10-1g).

10-2

WALL FOOTINGS

Wall footings are commonly required to support direct concentric loads. An exception to this is the footing for a retaining wall. A wall footing may be of either plain or reinforced concrete. Since it has bending in only one direction, it

PHOTO 10-1   Column and wall footings. The Health, Physical Education and Recreation Complex, Hudson Valley Community College, Troy, New York.

is generally designed in much the same manner as a one-way slab, by considering a typical 12-in.-wide strip along the length of wall. Footings carrying relatively light loads on well-drained cohesionless soil are often made of plain concrete.

A wall footing under concentric load behaves similarly to a cantilever beam, where the cantilever extends out from the wall and is loaded in an upward direc-

Individual Column
Footing
(a)

Wall Footing
(b)

Combined Footing
(Rectangular)
(c)

Combined Footing
(Trapezoidal)
(d)

Combined Footing
(Strap or Cantilever)
(e)

Mat Footing
(f)

Pile Footing
(g)

FIGURE 10-1   Footing types.

tion by the soil pressure. The flexural tensile stresses that are induced in the bottom of the footing are acceptable for an unreinforced concrete footing provided that these stresses do not exceed $5\phi\sqrt{f_c'}$ (ACI 318-95, Section 22.5). This same section stipulates that the average shear stress for one-way beam action in an unreinforced concrete footing must not exceed $\frac{4}{3}\phi\sqrt{f_c'}$. These expressions apply only to normal-weight concrete.

In a *reinforced* concrete wall footing, the behavior is identical to that described above. Reinforcing steel is placed in the bottom of the footing in a direction perpendicular to the wall, however, thereby resisting the induced flexural tension, similar to a reinforced concrete beam or slab.

In either case, the cantilever action is based on the maximum bending moment occurring at the face of the wall if the footing supports a concrete wall or at a point halfway between the middle of the wall and the face of the wall if the footing supports a masonry wall. This difference is primarily because a masonry wall is somewhat less rigid than a concrete wall.

For each type of wall, the critical section for shear in the footing may be taken at a distance from face of wall equal to the effective depth of the footing.

Example 10-1

Design a plain concrete wall footing to carry a 12 in. concrete block masonry wall, as shown in Figure 10-2. The service loading may be taken as 10 kips/ft dead load (which includes the weight of the wall) and 20 kips/ft live load. Use $f'_c = 3000$ psi. The allowable soil pressure is 5000 psf (5.0 ksf), and the weight of earth $w_e = 100$ lb/ft³.

Solution:

1. Compute the factored load:

$$w_u = 1.4w_{DL} + 1.7w_{LL}$$

$$= 1.4(10) + 1.7(20)$$

$$= 48 \text{ kips/ft}$$

2. Assume a footing thickness of 3 ft 0 in. This will be checked later in the design. The footing weight is

$$0.150(3) = 0.450 \text{ ksf}$$

Assuming the bottom of footing to be 4 ft 0 in. below the finished ground line, the weight of the soil on top of the footing is

$$(1)(100) = 100 \text{ psf} = 0.100 \text{ ksf}$$

Therefore, the effective allowable soil pressure for superimposed service loads is

$$5.00 - 0.45 - 0.100 = 4.45 \text{ ksf}$$

3. The maximum allowable soil pressure for strength design must now be found. It must be modified in a manner consistent with the modification

FIGURE 10-2 Plain concrete wall footing for Example 10-1.

of the service loads. This may be accomplished by multiplying by the ratio of the total design load (48 kips) to the total service load (30 kips). We then obtain a maximum allowable soil pressure solely for use in the strength design of the footing. This soil pressure should not be construed as an actual allowable soil pressure. Thus

$$4.45\left(\frac{48}{30}\right) = 7.12 \text{ ksf}$$

4. We may now determine the required footing width:

$$\frac{48.0}{7.12} = 6.74 \text{ ft} \qquad \text{Use 6 ft 9 in.}$$

5. Determine the factored soil pressure to be used for the footing design if the footing width is 6 ft 9 in.:

$$\frac{48.0}{6.75} = 7.11 \text{ ksf}$$

6. With the factored soil pressure known, the bending moment in the footing may be calculated. For concrete block masonry walls, the critical section for moment should be taken at the quarter-point of wall thickness (ACI Code, Section 15.4.2b).

    With reference to Figure 10-2, the factored moment is determined as follows:

$$M_u = \frac{7.11(3.125)^2}{2} = 34.7 \text{ ft-kips}$$

7. The unreinforced footing is a homogeneous rectangular section (12 in. in width). Therefore, the concrete tensile stress f_t at the bottom of the footing is

$$f_t = \frac{M_u}{S}$$

where

$$S = \text{section modulus} = \frac{bh^2}{6}$$

$b = 12$ in.

$h = $ total footing thickness (in.)

From the ACI Code, Section 22.5, the maximum tensile stress in a plain concrete footing may not exceed $5\phi\sqrt{f_c'}$, where $\phi = 0.65$ (ACI Code, Section 9.3.5). Therefore,

$$\text{maximum } f_t = 5(0.65)\sqrt{3000} = 178 \text{ psi} = 0.178 \text{ ksi}$$

8. The required footing thickness may now be determined:

$$\text{required } S = \frac{M_u}{f_t}$$

Substituting $bh^2/6$ for S, we obtain

$$\text{required } \frac{bh^2}{6} = \frac{34.7(12)}{0.178}$$

$$\text{required } h^2 = \frac{34.7(12)(6)}{12(0.178)} = 1170 \text{ in.}^2$$

$$\text{required } h = 34.2 \text{ in.}$$

9. It is common practice to assume that the bottom 1 or 2 in. of concrete placed against the ground may be of poor quality and therefore may be neglected for strength purposes. The total required footing thickness may then be determined:

$$34.2 + 2.0 = 36.2 \text{ in.} \qquad \text{say, 36 in.}$$

This checks with our assumed footing thickness and weight. No revisions are necessary.

10. Shear is generally of little significance in plain concrete footings because of the large concrete footing thickness. With reference to Figure 10-3, if the critical section for shear is considered a distance equal to the effective depth of the member from the face of wall and if the effective depth is taken as 34.2 in. (the required h), it may be observed that the critical section is almost at the edge of footing. Therefore, shear may be neglected, since at this section it will be very low. It is checked here for illustrative purposes, however.

   From the ACI Code, Section 22.5, the average shear stress for unreinforced concrete footings on soil must not exceed $^4/_3\phi\sqrt{f_c'}$ for one-way beam action (the behavior exhibited by plain concrete continuous wall footings). Thus

FIGURE 10-3   Plain concrete wall footing for Example 10-1.

$$^4/_3\phi\sqrt{f'_c} = \tfrac{4}{3}(0.65)\sqrt{3000} = 47.5 \text{ psi} = 0.0475 \text{ ksi}$$

Since

$$V_u = 7.11\left(\frac{0.3}{12}\right)(1) = 0.178 \text{ kip}$$

the shear stress may be determined as

$$\text{shear stress} = \frac{3V_u}{2bh} = \frac{3(0.178)}{2(12)(34.2)} = 0.00065 \text{ ksi}$$

which is significantly less than the maximum permitted.

11. It is common practice to use some *longitudinal* steel in continuous wall footings whether or not *transverse* steel is present. This will somewhat enhance the structural integrity by limiting differential movement between parts of the footing should transverse cracking occur. It will also lend some flexural strength in the longitudinal direction. The rationale for this stems from the many uncertainties that exist in both the supporting soil and the applied loads.

   As a guide, this longitudinal steel may be computed in a manner similar to that for temperature and shrinkage steel in a one-way slab, where

$$\text{required } A_s = 0.0018bh \qquad (\text{using } f_y = 60{,}000 \text{ psi})$$

$$= 0.0018(12)(36)$$

$$= 0.78 \text{ in.}^2/\text{ft of width}$$

   Total longitudinal steel required for a 6 ft 9 in. footing width is

$$0.78(6.75) = 5.27 \text{ in.}^2$$

Use 12 No. 6 bars ($A_s = 5.28$ in.^{2}). This would satisfy any longitudinal steel requirement. It is obvious, however, that this large steel requirement does not lend itself to an economical footing design, but rather leads us to conclude that we should question the use of plain concrete wall footings when superimposed loads are heavy.

A redesign using a reinforced concrete wall footing is accomplished in the following problem.

Example 10-2 _____

Design a reinforced concrete wall footing to carry a 12 in. concrete block masonry wall, as shown in Figure 10-4. The service loading is 10 kips/ft dead load (which includes the weight of the wall) and 20 kips/ft live load. Use $f'_c = 3000$ psi, $f_y = 60{,}000$ psi, weight of earth = 100 lb/ft^3, and allowable soil

FIGURE 10-4   Reinforced concrete wall footing for Example 10-2.

pressure = 5000 psf (5.0 ksf). The bottom of the footing is to be 4 ft 0 in. below the finished ground line.

Solution:

1. Compute the factored load:

$$w_u = 1.4w_{DL} + 1.7w_{LL}$$

$$= 1.4(10) + 1.7(20)$$

$$= 48 \text{ kips/ft}$$

2. Assume a total footing thickness = 18 in. Therefore, the footing weight is

$$0.150(1.5) = 0.225 \text{ ksf}$$

Since the bottom of the footing is to be 4 ft below the finished ground line, there will be 30 in. of earth on top of the footing. This depth of earth has a weight of

$$\frac{30(100)}{12} = 250 \text{ psf} = 0.250 \text{ ksf}$$

The effective allowable soil pressure for superimposed service loads is

$$5.00 - 0.225 - 0.250 = 4.53 \text{ ksf}$$

3. As in Example 10-1, we use the ratio of factored load to service load to determine the soil pressure for strength design:

$$\frac{48(4.53)}{30} = 7.25 \text{ ksf}$$

4. The required footing width is

$$\frac{48.0}{7.25} = 6.62 \text{ ft} \qquad \text{Use 6 ft 8 in.}$$

5. The soil pressure to be used for the footing design is

$$\frac{48.0}{6.67} = 7.20 \text{ ksf}$$

6. The assumed effective depth d for the footing is determined by subtracting the concrete cover [see the ACI Code, Section 7.7.1(a)] and one-half of the bar diameter (No. 8 assumed) from the total thickness:

$$d = 18 - 3 - 0.5 = 14.5 \text{ in.}$$

7. Since required thicknesses of reinforced concrete footings are generally controlled by shear requirements, the shear should be checked first.

   With reference to Figure 10-4, since the wall footing carries shear in a manner similar to that of a one-way slab or beam, the critical section for shear will be taken at a distance equal to the effective depth of the footing (14.5 in.) from face of wall (ACI Code, Section 11.1.3):

$$V_u = 1.63(1)(7.20) = 11.74 \text{ kips/ft of wall}$$

   The total nominal shear strength V_n is the sum of the shear strength of the concrete V_c and the shear strength of any shear reinforcing V_s':

$$V_n = V_c + V_s$$

$$\phi V_n = \phi V_c + \phi V_s$$

   Assuming no shear reinforcing,

$$\phi V_n = \phi V_c$$

   In footings, shear reinforcing is not required if

$$\phi V_c > V_u$$

   Computing ϕV_c,

$$\phi V_c = \phi 2\sqrt{f_c'}bd$$
$$= 0.85(2)\sqrt{3000}(12)(14.5)$$
$$= 16.3 \text{ kips/ft of wall}$$
$$16.3 > 11.74$$

   Therefore,

$$\phi V_c > V_u$$

   Thus the assumed thickness of footing is satisfactory for shear, and no revisions are necessary with respect to footing weight.

8. With reference to Figure 10-5, the critical section for moment is taken at the quarter-point of wall thickness (ACI Code, Section 15.4.2b). The maximum factored moment, assuming the footing to be a cantilever beam, is

$$M_u = \frac{7.20(3.08)^2}{2} = 34.2 \text{ ft-kips}$$

9. The required area of tension steel is then determined in the normal way, using $d = 14.5$ in. and $b = 12$ in.:

$$\text{required } \bar{k} = \frac{M_u}{\phi b d^2} = \frac{34.2(12)}{0.9(12)(14.5)^2}$$

$$= 0.1807 \text{ ksi}$$

From Table A-8, the required $\rho = 0.0032$:

$$\text{required } A_s = \rho b d$$

$$= 0.0032(12)(14.5)$$

$$= 0.56 \text{ in}^2/\text{per ft of wall}$$

We will use the ACI Code minimum reinforcement requirement for beams as being applicable for footings. From Table A-5,

$$A_{s,min} = 0.0033(12)(14.5)$$

$$= 0.57 \text{ in.}^2/\text{ft of wall}$$

Finally, as discussed in Chapter 8, the provisions of the ACI Code, Section 10.5.4, for minimum reinforcement in structural slabs of uniform thickness may be considered applicable for footings such as this that transmit vertical loads to the underlying soil. In this text, this will

FIGURE 10-5   Reinforced concrete wall footing for Example 10-2.

be used only as an absolute minimum. Checking the provision of the code for the minimum reinforcement required for grade 60 steel gives us

$$\text{required } A_s = 0.0018bh = 0.0018(12)(18)$$

$$= 0.39 \text{ in.}^2/\text{ft of wall}$$

Therefore, considering the minimum reinforcement ratio for beams as applicable, use required $A_s = 0.57$ in.^{2} per ft of wall and use No. 6 bars at 9 in. o.c. ($A_s = 0.59$ in.^{2}).

10. The development length should be checked for the bars selected.
   a. From Table 5-1, $K_D = 82.2$.
   b. Establish values for the multiplying factors α, β, γ, and λ.
      (1) $\alpha = 1.0$ (the bars are not top bars).
      (2) The bars are uncoated ("black steel"). $\beta = 1.0$.
      (3) The bars are No. 6. $\gamma = 0.8$.
      (4) Normal-weight concrete is used. $\lambda = 1.0$.
   c. The product $\alpha \times \beta = 1.0 < 1.7$. (O.K.)
   d. Determine c. Based on cover (center of bar to nearest concrete surface): Consider the clear cover (3 in. on bottom and sides) and one-half the diameter of the No. 6 bar:

$$c = 3 + 0.375 = 3.38 \text{ in.}$$

Based on bar spacing (one-half the center-to-center distance):

$$c = 0.5(9.0) = 4.50 \text{ in.}$$

Therefore, use $c = 3.38$ in.
   e. K_{TR} is taken as zero. There is no transverse steel crossing the potential plane of cracking.
   f. Check $(c + K_{TR})/d_b \leq 2.5$:

$$\frac{c + K_{TR}}{d_b} = \frac{3.38 + 0}{0.75} = 4.51 > 2.5$$

Therefore, use 2.5.
   g. Calculate the excess reinforcement factor:

$$K_{ER} = \frac{A_s \text{ required}}{A_s \text{ provided}} = \frac{0.57}{0.59} = 0.97$$

   h. Calculate ℓ_d:

$$\ell_d = K_D \left[\frac{\alpha\beta\gamma\lambda}{\left(\dfrac{c + K_{TR}}{d_b}\right)} \right] (d_b)(K_{ER})$$

FIGURE 10-6   Design sketch for Example 10-2.

$$= 82.2\left[\frac{1.0(1.0)(0.8)(1.0)}{2.5}\right](0.75)(0.97)$$

$$= 19.1 \text{ in.} > 12 \text{ in.} \qquad\qquad\qquad\text{(O.K.)}$$

The development length provided, measured from the critical section for moment and allowing for 3 in. end cover, is 34 in. Since 34 in. > 19.1 in., the development length provided is adequate.

11. Although not specifically required in footings by the ACI Code, longitudinal steel will be provided on the same basis as for one-way slabs (Section 7.12). Thus

$$\text{required } A_s = 0.0018bh = 0.0018(12)(18)$$

$$= 0.39 \text{ in.}^2/\text{ft}$$

Total longitudinal steel required for a 6 ft 8 in. footing width is

$$0.39(6.67) = 2.6 \text{ in.}^2$$

Use nine No. 5 bars ($A_s = 2.79$ in.^{2}) spaced equally. The footing design is shown in Figure 10-6.

10-3

WALL FOOTINGS UNDER LIGHT LOADS

A relatively common situation is one in which a lightly loaded wall is supported on average soil. As previously indicated in this chapter, a design would result in a very small footing thickness and width.

In such a situation, experience has shown that for footings carrying plain concrete or block masonry walls, the minimum recommended dimensions shown in

FIGURE 10-7   Recommended minimum footing dimensions for walls carrying light loads.

Figure 10-7 should be used. The minimum depth or thickness of footing should be 8 in. but not less than the wall thickness. The minimum width of footing should equal twice the wall thickness.

10-4

INDIVIDUAL REINFORCED CONCRETE FOOTINGS FOR COLUMNS

An individual reinforced concrete footing for a column, also termed an *isolated spread footing,* is probably the most common, simplest, and most economical of the various types of footings used for structures. Individual column footings are generally square in plan. Rectangular shapes are sometimes used where dimensional limitations exist, however. The footing is a slab that directly supports a column. At times, a pedestal is placed between a column and a footing so that the base of the column need not be set below grade.

The footing behavior under concentric load is that of two-way cantilever action extending out from the column or pedestal. The footing is loaded in an upward direction by the soil pressure. Tensile stresses are induced in each direction in the bottom of the footing. Therefore, the footing is reinforced by two layers of steel perpendicular to each other and parallel to the edges. The required footing-soil contact area is a function of, and determined by, the allowable soil bearing pressure and the column loads being applied to the footing.

Shear

Since the footing is subject to two-way action, two different types of shear strength must be considered: two-way shear and one-way shear. The footing thickness (depth) is generally established by the shear requirements. The two-way shear is commonly termed *punching shear,* since the column or pedestal tends to punch through the footing, inducing stresses around the perimeter of the column or pedestal. Tests have verified that, if failure occurs, the fracture takes the form of a truncated pyramid with sides sloping away from the face of the column or pedestal. The critical section for this two-way shear is taken perpendicular to the plane of the footing and located so that its perimeter b_0 is a minimum but does not come closer to the edge of the column or pedestal than one-half the effective depth of the footing (ACI Code, Section 11.12.1.2).

The design of the footing for two-way action is based on a shear strength V_n, which is not to be taken greater than V_c unless shear reinforcement is provided. V_c may be determined from the ACI Code, Section 11.12.2, and shall be the smallest of

(a) $$V_c = \left(2 + \frac{4}{\beta_c}\right)\sqrt{f_c'}\,b_0 d$$ ACI Eq. (11-35)

(b) $$V_c = \left(\frac{\alpha_s d}{b_0} + 2\right)\sqrt{f_c'}\,b_0 d$$ ACI Eq. (11-36)

(c) $$V_c = 4\sqrt{f_c'}\,b_0 d$$ ACI Eq. (11-37)

where

β_c = ratio of the long side to the short side of the concentrated load or reaction area (loaded area)

b_0 = perimeter of critical section for two-way shear action in footing

α_s = 40 for interior columns, 30 for edge columns, and 20 for corner columns

and V_c, f_c', and d are as previously defined. The introduction of shear reinforcement in footings is impractical and undesirable purely on an economic basis, and it is general practice to design footings based on the shear strength solely of the concrete.

The one-way (or beam) shear may be compared with the shear in a beam or one-way slab. The critical section for this one-way shear is taken on a vertical plane extending across the entire width of the footing and located at a distance equal to the effective depth of the footing from the face of the concentrated load or reaction area (ACI Code, Sections 11.1 and 11.12). As in a beam or one-way slab, the shear strength provided by the footing concrete may be taken as

$$V_c = 2\sqrt{f_c'}\,b_w d$$ ACI Eq. (11-3)

For both one- and two-way action, if we assume no shear reinforcement, the basis for the shear design will be $\phi V_n \geq V_u$, where $V_n = V_c$.

Moment and Development of Bars

The size and spacing of the footing reinforcing steel is primarily a function of the bending moment induced by the net upward soil pressure. The footing behaves as a cantilever beam in two directions. It is loaded by the soil pressure. The fixed end, or critical section for the bending moment, is located as follows (ACI Code, Section 15.4.2):

1.   At the face of the column or pedestal, for a footing supporting a concrete column or pedestal (see Figure 10-8a)
2.   Halfway between the face of the column and the edge of a steel base plate, for a footing supporting a column with a steel base plate (see Figure 10-8b)

The ACI Code, Section 15.6.3, stipulates that the critical section for development length of footing reinforcement shall be assumed to be at the same location as the critical section for bending moment.

(a)

(b)

FIGURE 10-8   Critical sections for design of reinforced concrete footings supporting columns or pedestals.

Transfer of Load from Column into Footing

All loads applied to a column must be transferred to the top of the footing (through a pedestal, if there is one) by compression in the concrete, by reinforcement, or by both.

The bearing strength of the concrete contact area of supporting and supported member cannot exceed $\phi(0.85f'_c A_1)$ as directed by the ACI Code, Section 10.17.1. When the supporting surface is wider on all sides than is the loaded area, the design bearing strength on the loaded area may be multiplied by $\sqrt{A_2/A_1}$, where

A_2 = maximum area of the portion of the supporting
surface that is geometrically similar to
and concentric with the loaded area

A_1 = loaded area

The quantity $\sqrt{A_2/A_1}$ cannot exceed 2.0 (ACI Code, Section 10.17.1). Therefore, in no case can the design bearing strength for the loaded area be in excess of

$$\phi(0.85f'_c A_1)(2)$$

where $\phi = 0.70$ for bearing on concrete and f'_c is as previously defined.

It is common for the footing concrete to be of a lower strength (f'_c) than the supported column concrete. This suggests that both supporting and supported members should be considered in determining load transfer.

Where a reinforced concrete column cannot transfer the load entirely by bearing, the excess load must be transferred by reinforcement where the required A_s = (excess load)/f_y. This may be accomplished by furnishing dowels, one per column bar if necessary but not larger than No. 11 (ACI Code, Section 15.8.2.3).

To provide a positive connection between a reinforced concrete column and footing (whether dowels are required or not), the ACI Code, Section 15.8.2.1, requires a minimum area of reinforcement crossing the bearing surface of 0.005 of the column cross-sectional area. It is generally recommended that a minimum of four bars be used. These four bars should preferably be dowels for the four corner bars of a square column.

The development length of the dowels must be sufficient on both sides of the bearing surface to provide the necessary development length for bars in compression (see Chapter 5).

When the dowel carries excess load into the footing, it must be spliced to the column bar using the necessary compression splice. The same procedure applies where a column rests on a pedestal and where a pedestal rests on a footing.

Where structural steel columns and column base plates are used, the total load is usually transferred entirely by bearing on the concrete contact area. The design bearing strength as stipulated previously also applies in this case. Where a column base detail is inadequate to transfer the total load, adjustments may be made as follows:

1.   Increase column base plate dimensions.
2.   Use higher-strength concrete (f'_c) for the pedestal or footing.

3.   Increase the supporting area with respect to the base plate area until the ratio reaches the maximum allowed by the ACI Code.

In building design, it is common practice to use a concrete pedestal between the footing and the column. The pedestal, in effect, distributes the column load over a larger area of the footing, thereby contributing to a more economical footing design.

Pedestals may be either plain or reinforced. If the ratio of height to least lateral dimension is in excess of three, the member is by definition a column and must be designed and reinforced as a column (see Chapter 9). If the ratio is less than three, it is categorized as a pedestal and theoretically may not require any reinforcement.

The cross-sectional area of a pedestal is usually established by the concrete bearing strength as stipulated in ACI Code, Section 10.17, by the size of a steel column base plate, or by the desire to distribute the column load over a larger footing area.

It is common practice to design a pedestal in a manner similar to a column using a minimum of four corner bars (for a square or rectangular cross section) anchored into the footing and extending up through the pedestal. Ties should be provided in pedestals according to the same requirements as in columns.

10-5

SQUARE REINFORCED CONCRETE FOOTINGS

In isolated square footings, the reinforcement should be uniformly distributed over the width of the footing in each direction. Since the bending moment is the same in each direction, the reinforcing bar size and spacing should be the same in each direction. In reality, the effective depth is not the same in both directions. It is common practice to use the same average effective depth for design computations for both directions, however.

It is also common practice to assume that the minimum tensile reinforcement for beams is applicable to two-way footings for each of the two directions, unless the reinforcement provided is one-third greater than required. As discussed in Section 2-8 (and in the ACI Code, Section 10.5.1), the minimum tensile reinforcement is determined from

$$A_{s,\min} = \frac{3\sqrt{f_c'}}{f_y} b_w d \geqslant \frac{200}{f_y} b_w d$$

The use of this minimum is conservative for footings. The ACI Code, Section 10.5.4, permits the use of a minimum reinforcement equal to that required for shrinkage and temperature steel in structural slabs of uniform thickness. This will always be somewhat less than that required by $A_{s,\min}$, but not necessarily less than that specified by the ACI Code, Section 10.5.3. In this book, the criteria of ACI Code,

Section 10.5.4, will be used in isolated footing cases only as an absolute minimum of steel area to be provided.

Example 10-3 _____

Design a square reinforced concrete footing to support an 18-in.-square tied concrete column, as shown in Figure 10-9. The column is a typical interior column in a building.

FIGURE 10-9   Sketch for Example 10-3.

Solution:

1. The design data are as follows: service dead load = 225 kips, service live load = 175 kips, allowable soil pressure = 5000 psf (5.00 ksf), f_c' for the column = 4000 psi and for the footing = 3000 psi, f_y for all steel = 60,000 psi, and longitudinal column steel consists of No. 8 bars. The weight of earth = 100 lb/ft^3.

2. Assume a total footing thickness of 24 in. The footing weight may then be calculated as

$$0.150(2.0) = 0.300 \text{ ksf}$$

Since the bottom of footing is to be 4 ft below the finished ground line, there will be 24 in. of earth on top of the footing. This depth of earth has a weight of

$$^{24}\!/_{12}(0.100) = 0.200 \text{ ksf}$$

Therefore, the *effective allowable* soil pressure for the superimposed loads becomes

$$5.00 - 0.300 - 0.200 = 4.50 \text{ ksf}$$

The required area of footing may be determined using service loads and allowable soil pressure or by modifying both the service loads and the allowable soil pressure with the ACI load factors. Using the service loads,

$$\text{required } A = \frac{225 + 175}{4.50} = 88.9 \text{ ft}^2$$

Use a 9 ft 6 in. square footing. This furnishes an actual area A of 90.3 ft^2.

3. The factored soil pressure from superimposed loads to be used for the footing design may now be calculated:

$$p_u = \frac{P_u}{A} = \frac{1.4(225) + 1.7(175)}{90.3} = 6.78 \text{ ksf}$$

4. The footing thickness is usually determined by shear strength requirements. Therefore, using the assumed footing thickness, check the shear strength. The thickness h was assumed to be 24 in. Therefore, the effective depth, based on a 3 in. cover for bottom steel and No. 8 bars in each direction, is

$$d = 24 - 3 - 1 = 20 \text{ in.}$$

This constitutes an average effective depth that will be used for design calculations for both directions.

5. The shear strength of individual column footings is governed by the more severe of two conditions: two-way action (punching shear) or one-way action (beam shear). The location of the critical section for each type of behavior is depicted in Figure 10-10. *For two-way action* (Figure 10-10a),

$$B = \text{column width} + \left(\frac{d}{2}\right)2$$

$$= 18 + 20 = 38 \text{ in.} = 3.17 \text{ ft}$$

FIGURE 10-10   Footing shear analysis.

The total factored shear acting on the critical section is

$$V_u = p_u(W^2 - B^2)$$

$$= 6.78(9.5^2 - 3.17^2)$$

$$= 544 \text{ kips}$$

The shear strength of the concrete is taken as the smallest of

(a)
$$V_c = \left(2 + \frac{4}{\beta_c}\right)\sqrt{f_c'}\,b_0 d$$

$$= \left(2 + \frac{4}{1}\right)\sqrt{3000}(38)(4)(20) = 999,000 \text{ lb}$$

(b)   With $\alpha_s = 40$ for an interior column,

$$V_c = \left(\frac{\alpha_s d}{b_0} + 2\right)\sqrt{f_c'}\,b_0 d$$

$$= \left[\frac{40(20)}{38(4)} + 2\right]\sqrt{3000}(38)(4)(20) = 1,209,000 \text{ lb}$$

(c)
$$V_c = 4\sqrt{f_c'}\,b_0 d = 4\sqrt{3000}(4)(38)(20) = 666,000 \text{ lb}$$

from which $V_c = 666,000 \text{ lb} = 666 \text{ kips}$. Thus

$$\phi V_n = \phi V_c = 0.85(666) = 566 \text{ kips}$$

Therefore,

$$\phi V_n > V_u \qquad\qquad \text{(O.K.)}$$

When V_u is relatively close to the shear strength of the concrete (ϕV_c), it indicates that the assumed footing thickness is approximately equal to that required for shear. If these two values were significantly different, the assumed footing thickness should be modified.

For one-way action, the total factored shear acting on the critical section is

$$V_u = p_u W G$$

$$= 6.78(9.5)(2.33)$$

$$= 150 \text{ kips}$$

The shear strength of the concrete is

$$V_c = 2\sqrt{f_c'}\,b_w d$$

$$= 2\sqrt{3000}(9.5)(12)(20)$$

$$= 249,761 \text{ lb}$$

FIGURE 10-11   Footing moment analysis.

$$= 250 \text{ kips}$$

$$\phi V_n = \phi V_c = 0.85(250) = 212.5 \text{ kips}$$

Therefore,

$$\phi V_n > V_u \qquad\qquad \text{(O.K.)}$$

The 24-in.-deep footing is satisfactory with respect to shear. Our assumption of step 2 with regard to weight of the footing and the soil on the footing is satisfactory.

6.   The critical section for bending moment may be taken at the face of column, as depicted in Figure 10-11. Using the factored soil pressure and assuming the footing to act as a wide cantilever beam in both directions, the design moment may be computed:

$$M_u = p_u F\left(\frac{F}{2}\right)(W)$$

$$= 6.78(4)\left(\frac{4}{2}\right)(9.5)$$

$$= 515 \text{ ft-kips}$$

7.   Design the tension steel as follows:

$$\text{required } \bar{k} = \frac{M_u}{\phi b d^2} = \frac{515(12)}{0.9(9.5)(12)(20)^2}$$

$$= 0.1506 \text{ ksi}$$

From Table A-8, the required $\rho = 0.0026$. Therefore,

$$\text{required } A_s = \rho b d$$

$$= 0.0026(9.5)(12)(20)$$

$$= 5.93 \text{ in}^2$$

Check the ACI Code minimum reinforcement requirement. From Table A-5,

$$A_{s,min} = 0.0033(9.5)(12)(20)$$

$$= 7.52 \text{ in.}^2$$

Of the two steel areas, the larger (7.52 in.^{2}) controls.

Since the footing is square and an average effective depth was used, the steel requirements in the other direction may be assumed to be identical. Therefore, use 13 No. 7 bars each way ($A_s = 7.80$ in.^{2} in each direction) and distribute the bars uniformly across the footing in each direction, as shown in Figure 10-12a.

Checking the development length for the No. 7 bars,

a.   From Table 5-1, $K_D = 82.2$.

b.   Establish values for the multiplying factors α, β, γ, and λ.

   (1) $\alpha = 1.0$ (the bars are not top bars).

   (2)   The bars are uncoated ("black steel"). $\beta = 1.0$.

   (3)   The bars are No. 7. $\gamma = 1.0$.

   (4)   Normal-weight concrete is used. $\gamma = 1.0$.

c.   The product $\alpha \times \beta = 1.0 < 1.7$. (O.K.)

d.   Determine c. Based on cover (center of bar to nearest concrete

Plan View   Elevation

(a)   (b)

FIGURE 10-12   Design sketch for Example 10-3.

surface): Consider the clear cover (3 in. on bottom and sides) and one-half the diameter of the No. 7 bar:

$$c = 3 + 0.44 = 3.44 \text{ in.}$$

Based on bar spacing (one-half the center-to-center distance), see Figure 10-12b:

$$c = \frac{1}{2}\left(\frac{114 - 3.44 - 3.44}{12}\right) = 4.46 \text{ in.}$$

Therefore, use $c = 3.44$ in.

e. K_{TR} is taken as zero. There is no transverse steel crossing the potential plane of cracking.

f.   Check $(c + K_{TR})/d_b \leqslant 2.5$:

$$\frac{c + K_{TR}}{d_b} = \frac{3.44 + 0}{0.875} = 3.93 > 2.5$$

Therefore, use 2.5.

g.   Calculate the excess reinforcement factor:

$$K_{ER} = \frac{A_s \text{ required}}{A_s \text{ provided}} = \frac{7.50}{7.80} = 0.96$$

h.   Calculate ℓ_d:

$$\ell_d = K_D\left[\frac{\alpha\beta\gamma\lambda}{\left(\dfrac{c + K_{TR}}{d_b}\right)}\right](d_b)(K_{ER})$$

$$= 82.2\left[\frac{1.0(1.0)(1.0)(1.0)}{2.5}\right](0.875)(0.96)$$

$$= 27.6 \text{ in.} > 12 \text{ in.} \qquad\qquad\qquad\qquad \text{(O.K.)}$$

Use $\ell_d = 27.6$ in. (minimum). The development length provided is 45 in., which is in excess of that required (O.K.).

8.   The concrete bearing strength at the base of the column cannot exceed

$$\phi(0.85f'_c A_1)$$

except where the supporting surface is wider on all sides than the loaded area, for which case the concrete bearing strength of the supporting surface cannot exceed

$$\phi(0.85f'_c A_1)\sqrt{\frac{A_2}{A_1}}$$

but in no case is the bearing strength to exceed

$$\phi(0.85f'_c A_1)(2)$$

Since the supporting surface is wider on all sides, the bearing strength for the *footing* may be computed as follows:

$$\sqrt{\frac{A_2}{A_1}} = \sqrt{\frac{90.3}{2.25}} = 6.3 > 2.0$$

Therefore, use 2.0. Then

$$\textit{footing } \text{bearing strength} = \phi(0.85f_c'A_1)(2.0)$$

$$= 0.70(0.85)(3.0)(18)^2(2.0)$$

$$= 1157 \text{ kips}$$

The *column* bearing strength is computed as follows:

$$\phi(0.85)f_c'A_1 = 0.70(0.85)(4.0)(18)^2 = 771 \text{ kips}$$

The actual design bearing load is

$$P_u = 1.4(225) + 1.7(175)$$

$$= 612.5 \text{ kips}$$

Since $612.5 < 771 < 1157$, the entire column load can be transferred by concrete alone. The ACI Code, however, requires a minimum dowel area of

$$\text{required } A_s = 0.005A_g$$

$$= 0.005(18)^2 = 1.62 \text{ in.}^2$$

Use a minimum of four bars. Four No. 6 bars, $A_s = 1.76$ in.^{2}, is satisfactory. It is general practice in a situation such as this, however, to use dowels of the same diameter as the column steel. Therefore, use four No. 8 dowels, and place one in each corner ($A_s = 3.16$ in.^{2}).

The development length for dowels into the column and footing must be adequate even though full load transfer can be made without dowels.

The bars are in compression. The basic compression development length for No. 8 dowels into the footing is 21.9 in. (from Table A-12). The required development length ℓ_d equals the basic development length times any modification factors. We will use the modification factor for the case where the steel provided is in excess of the steel required:

$$\frac{\text{required } A_s}{\text{provided } A_s} = \frac{1.62}{3.16} = 0.51$$

$$\text{required } \ell_d = 21.9(0.51) = 11.2 \text{ in.}$$

For bars in compression, ℓ_d must not be less than 8 in. Therefore, use ℓ_d of 12 in. into both the column and the footing, since f_c' for the column concrete is higher and the required ℓ_d for the bars into the column would be less than that into the footing. The actual anchorage used may be observed in Figure 10-12b. The dowels should be placed adjacent to the corner longitudinal bars. Generally, these dowels are furnished with a 90° hook at their lower ends and are placed on top of the main footing reinforcement. This will tie the dowel in place and will reduce the possibility of the dowel being dislodged during construction. The hook cannot be considered effective as part of the required development length (ACI Code, Section 12.5.5).

10-6

RECTANGULAR REINFORCED CONCRETE FOOTINGS

Rectangular footings are generally used where space limitations require it. The design of these footings is very similar to that of the square column footing with the one major exception that each direction must be investigated independently. Shear is checked for two-way action in the normal way, but for one-way action, it is checked across the shorter side only. The bending moment must be considered separately for each direction. Each direction will generally require a different area of steel. The reinforcing steel running in the long direction should be placed below the short-direction steel so that it may have the larger effective depth to carry the larger bending moments in that direction.

In rectangular footings, the *distribution* of the reinforcement is different than for square footings (ACI Code, Section 15.4.4). The reinforcement in the long direction should be uniformly distributed over the shorter footing width. A part of the required reinforcement in the short direction is placed in a band equal to the length of the short side of the footing. The portion of the total required steel that should go into this band is

$$\frac{2}{\beta + 1}$$

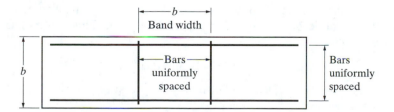

FIGURE 10-13 Rectangular footing plan.

where β is the ratio of the long side to the short side of the footing. The remainder of the reinforcement is uniformly distributed in the outer portions of the footing. This distribution is depicted in Figure 10-13. Other features of the design are similar to those for the square column footing.

Example 10-4

Design a reinforced concrete footing to support an 18 in. square tied interior concrete column, as shown in Figure 10-14. One dimension of the footing is limited to a maximum of 7 ft.

Finished ground line

4'-0"

FIGURE 10-14   Sketch for Example 10-4.

Solution:

1. The design data are as follows: service dead load = 175 kips, service live load = 175 kips, allowable soil pressure = 5000 psf (5.00 ksf), f'_c for both footing and column = 3000 psi, f_y for all steel = 60,000 psi, and longitudinal column steel consists of No. 8 bars. The weight of earth = 100 lb/ft^3.

2. Assume a total footing thickness of 24 in. The footing weight may then be calculated as

$$0.150(2.0) = 0.300 \text{ ksf}$$

Since the bottom of footing is to be 4 ft below the finished ground line, there will be 24 in. of earth on top of the footing. This depth of earth has a weight of

$$^{24}/_{12}(0.100) = 0.200 \text{ ksf}$$

Therefore, the *effective allowable* soil pressure for the superimposed loads becomes

$$5.00 - 0.300 - 0.200 = 4.50 \text{ ksf}$$

Based on service loads, the required area of footing may be calculated:

$$\text{required } A = \frac{175 + 175}{4.50} = 77.8 \text{ ft}^2$$

Use a rectangular footing 7 ft 0 in. by 11 ft 6 in. This furnishes an actual area A of 80.5 ft^2.

3. The factored soil pressure from superimposed loads to be used for the footing design may now be calculated:

$$p_u = \frac{P_u}{A} = \frac{1.4(175) + 1.7(175)}{80.5} = 6.74 \text{ ksf}$$

4. The footing thickness h was assumed to be 24 in. Therefore, the effective depth, based on a 3 in. cover for bottom steel and 1-in.-diameter bars in each direction, will be

$$d = 24 - 3 - 1 = 20 \text{ in.}$$

This constitutes an *average* effective depth, which will be used for design calculations for both directions.

5. Checking the shear strength *for two-way action* (with reference to Figure 10-15a),

Plan View
(a)

Plan View
(b)

FIGURE 10-15 Footing shear analysis.

$$B = \text{column width} + \left(\frac{d}{2}\right)2$$

$$= 18 + 20 = 38 \text{ in.} = 3.17 \text{ ft}$$

The total factored shear acting on critical section is

$$V_u = p_u(A - B^2)$$

$$= 6.74(80.5 - 3.17^2)$$

$$= 475 \text{ kips}$$

The shear strength of the concrete is taken as the smallest of

(a)
$$V_c = \left(2 + \frac{4}{\beta_c}\right)\sqrt{f_c'}b_0 d$$

$$= \left(2 + \frac{4}{1}\right)\sqrt{3000}(38)(4)(20) = 999,000 \text{ lb}$$

(b)   With $\alpha_s = 40$ for an interior column,

$$V_c = \left(\frac{\alpha_s d}{b_0} + 2\right)\sqrt{f_c'}b_0 d$$

$$= \left(\frac{40(20)}{38(4)} + 2\right)\sqrt{3000}(38)(4)(20) = 1,209,000 \text{ lb}$$

(c) $V_c = 4\sqrt{f_c'}b_0 d = 4\sqrt{3000}(38)(4)(20) = 666,000 \text{ lb}$

from which $V_c = 666,000 \text{ lb} = 666 \text{ kips}$. Thus

$$\phi V_n = \phi V_c = 0.85(666) = 566 \text{ kips}$$

Therefore,

$$\phi V_n > V_u \qquad\qquad\qquad \text{(O.K.)}$$

For one-way action, consider shear across the short side only. The critical section is at a distance equal to the effective depth of the member from the face of column (see Figure 10-15b).

The total factored shear acting on the critical section is

$$V_u = p_u W G$$

$$= 6.74(7.0)(3.33)$$

$$= 157.1 \text{ kips}$$

The shear strength of the concrete is

$$V_c = 2\sqrt{f_c'}b_w d$$

$$= 2\sqrt{3000}(7.0)(12)(20)$$

$$= 184{,}034 \text{ lb}$$

$$= 184 \text{ kips}$$

$$\phi V_n = \phi V_c = 0.85(184) = 156.4 \text{ kips}$$

$$\phi V_n < V_u$$

The 24-in.-deep footing is very slightly under strength in shear. We will consider it satisfactory. Our assumption of step 2 with regard to the weight of the footing and the soil on the footing is satisfactory.

6.   For bending moment, each direction must be considered independently with the critical section taken at the face of the column. Using the actual factored soil pressure and assuming the footing to act as a wide cantilever beam in each direction, the design moment may be calculated. With reference to Figure 10-16b, for moment in the long direction,

FIGURE 10-16   Footing moment analysis.

$$M_u = p_u F\left(\frac{F}{2}\right)(W)$$

$$= 6.74(5)\left(\frac{5}{2}\right)(7.0)$$

$$= 590 \text{ ft-kips}$$

For moment in the short direction (Figure 10-16a),

$$M_u = p_u F\left(\frac{F}{2}\right)(L)$$

$$= 6.74(2.75)\left(\frac{2.75}{2}\right)(11.5)$$

$$= 293 \text{ ft-kips}$$

7. Design the tension steel as follows. *For the long direction, where $M_u =$ 590 ft-kips,*

$$\text{required } \overline{k} = \frac{M_u}{\phi b d^2} = \frac{590(12)}{(0.9)(7)(12)(20)^2}$$

$$= 0.2341 \text{ ksi}$$

From Table A-8, the required $\rho = 0.0041$. Therefore,

$$\text{required } A_s = \rho b d$$

$$= 0.0041(7)(12)(20)$$

$$= 6.89 \text{ in.}^2$$

Check the ACI Code minimum reinforcement requirement. From Table A-5,

$$A_{s,min} = 0.0033(7)(12)(20)$$

$$= 5.54 \text{ in.}^2$$

Of the two steel areas, the larger (6.89 in.^{2}) controls; therefore, use 12 No. 7 bars ($A_s = 7.20$ in.^{2}). These bars will run in the long direction and will be distributed uniformly across the 7 ft 0 in. width. They will be placed in the bottom layer where they will have the advantage of slightly greater effective depth. The development length must be checked for these bars.

a. From Table 5-1, $K_D = 82.2$.

b. Establish values for the multiplying factors α, β, γ, and λ.

(1) $\alpha = 1.0$ (the bars are not top bars).

(2) The bars are uncoated ("black steel"). $\beta = 1.0$.

(3)   The bars are No. 7. $\gamma = 1.0$.

(4)   Normal-weight concrete is used. $\lambda = 1.0$.

c.   The product $\alpha \times \beta = 1.0 < 1.7$. (O.K.)

d.   Determine c. Based on cover (center of bar to nearest concrete surface): Consider the clear cover (3 in. on bottom and sides) and one-half the diameter of the No. 7 bar:

$$c = 3 + 0.44 = 3.44 \text{ in.}$$

Based on bar spacing (one-half the center-to-center distance):

$$c = \frac{1}{2}\left(\frac{84 - 3.44 - 3.44}{11}\right) = 3.51 \text{ in.}$$

Therefore, use $c = 3.44$ in.

e. K_{TR} is taken as zero. There is no transverse steel crossing the potential plane of cracking.

f.   Check $(c + K_{TR})/d_b \leq 2.5$:

$$\frac{c + K_{TR}}{d_b} = \frac{3.44 + 0}{0.875} = 393 > 2.5$$

Therefore, use 2.5.

g.   Calculate the excess reinforcement factor:

$$K_{ER} = \frac{A_s \text{ required}}{A_s \text{ provided}} = \frac{6.89}{7.20} = 0.96$$

h.   Calculate ℓ_d:

$$\ell_d = K_D\left[\frac{\alpha\beta\gamma\lambda}{\left(\dfrac{c + K_{TR}}{d_b}\right)}\right](d_b)(K_{ER})$$

$$= 82.2\left[\frac{1.0(1.0)(1.0)(1.0)}{2.5}\right](0.875)(0.96)$$

$$= 27.6 \text{ in.} > 12 \text{ in.} \qquad\qquad (\text{O.K.})$$

Use $\ell_d = 27.6$ in. (minimum).

The development length furnished is $60 - 3 = 57$ in., which is in excess of that required (O.K.).

For the short direction, where $M_u = 293$ ft-kips,

$$\text{required } \overline{k} = \frac{M_u}{\phi b d^2} = \frac{293(12)}{0.9(11.5)(12)(20)^2}$$

$$= 0.0708 \text{ ksi}$$

From Table A-8, the required $\rho = 0.0012$. Therefore,

$$\text{required } A_s = \rho b d$$
$$= 0.0012(11.5)(12)(20)$$
$$= 3.31 \text{ in.}^2$$

Check the ACI Code minimum reinforcement requirement. From Table A-5,

$$A_{s,min} = 0.0033(11.5)(12)(20)$$
$$= 9.11 \text{ in.}^2$$

The $A_{s,min}$ requirement need not be applied if the area of steel provided is at least one-third greater than that required (ACI Code Section 10.5.3), however. Therefore, the required steel area may be calculated from

$$\text{required } A_s = 1.33(3.31) = 4.40 \text{ in.}^2$$

Checking further, using the ACI Code, Section 10.5.4, as an absolute minimum, the required steel area is

$$A_s = 0.0018bh = 0.0018(11.5)(12)(24) = 5.96 \text{ in.}^2$$

Therefore, 5.96 in.² controls. Use 14 No. 6 bars ($A_s = 6.16$ in.²). These bars will run in the short direction but will *not* be distributed uniformly across the 11 ft 6 in. side.

In rectangular footings, a portion of the total reinforcement required in the short direction is placed in a band centered on the column and having a width equal to the short side. The portion of the total required steel that goes into this band is

$$\frac{2}{\beta + 1}$$

where

$$\beta = \frac{\text{long-side dimension}}{\text{short-side dimension}} = \frac{11.5}{7.0} = 1.64$$

from which

$$\frac{2}{\beta + 1} = \frac{2}{1.64 + 1} = 0.757 = 75.7\%$$

Therefore, 75.7% of 14 No. 6 bars must be placed in a band width = 7 ft 0 in. The balance of the required bars will be distributed equally in the outer portions of the footing. Thus

$$(0.757)(14) = 10.6 \text{ bars}$$

Use 11 bars in the 7 ft 0 in. band width. Since reinforcing should be symmetrical with respect to the centerline of the footing, use two bars on each side of the 7 ft 0 in. band width. Therefore, the total steel used in the short direction will be 15 No. 6 bars ($A_s = 6.60$ in.^{2}). The bar arrangement is depicted in Figure 10-17.

The development length will be checked for the No. 6 bars in the center band.

a.   From Table 5-1, $K_D = 82.2$.

b.   Establish values for the multiplying factors α, β, γ, and λ.

   (1) $\alpha = 1.0$ (the bars are not top bars).

   (2)   The bars are uncoated ("black steel"). $\beta = 1.0$.

   (3)   The bars are No. 6. $\gamma = 0.8$.

   (4)   Normal-weight concrete is used. $\lambda = 1.0$.

c.   The product $\alpha \times \beta = 1.0 < 1.7$. (O.K.)

d.   Determine c. Based on cover (center of bar to nearest concrete surface): Consider the clear cover (bottom and sides) and one-half the diameter of the No. 6 bar:

$$c = 3 + 0.38 = 3.38 \text{ in.}$$

Based on bar spacing (one-half the center-to-center distance) in the center band (see Figure 10-17):

$$c = 0.5(8.5) = 4.25 \text{ in.}$$

Therefore, use $c = 3.38$ in.

e. K_{TR} is taken as zero. There is no transverse steel crossing the potential plane of cracking.

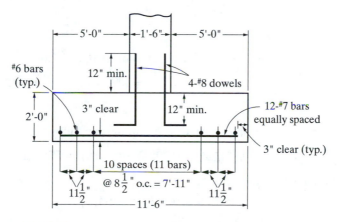

FIGURE 10-17   Design sketch for Example 10-4.

f.   Check $(c + K_{TR})/d_b \leqslant 2.5$:

$$\frac{c + K_{TR}}{d_b} = \frac{3.38 + 0}{0.75} = 4.51 > 2.5$$

Therefore, use 2.5.

g.   Calculate the excess reinforcement factor:

$$K_{ER} = \frac{A_s \text{ required}}{A_s \text{ provided}} = \frac{5.96}{6.60} = 0.903$$

h.   Calculate ℓ_d:

$$\ell_d = K_D \left[\frac{\alpha\beta\gamma\lambda}{\left(\dfrac{c + K_{TR}}{d_b} \right)} \right] (d_b)(K_{ER})$$

$$= 82.2 \left[\frac{1.0(1.0)(0.8)(1.0)}{2.5} \right] (0.75)(0.903)$$

$$= 17.8 \text{ in.} > 12 \text{ in.} \qquad\qquad\qquad \text{(O.K.)}$$

Use ℓ_d = 17.8 in. (minimum). The development length furnished = 33 − 3 = 30 in., which is in excess of that required. (O.K.)

8.   Since the supporting surface is wider on all sides, the bearing strength for the footing may be computed as follows:

$$\text{footing bearing strength} = \phi(0.85 f_c' A_1) \sqrt{\frac{A_2}{A_1}}$$

where

$$\sqrt{\frac{A_2}{A_1}} = \sqrt{\frac{49.0}{2.25}} = 4.67$$

Therefore, use 2.0. Then,

$$\text{footing bearing strength} = \phi(0.85 f_c' A_1)(2.0)$$

$$= 0.70(0.85)(3.0)(18)^2(2.0)$$

$$= 1157 \text{ kips}$$

The column bearing strength is computed as follows:

$$\phi(0.85) f_c' A_1 = 0.70(0.85)(3)(18)^2 = 578 \text{ kips}$$

The factored bearing load is

$$P_u = 1.4(175) + 1.7(175)$$

$$= 542.5 \text{ kips}$$

Since $542.5 < 578 < 1157$, the entire column load can be transferred by concrete alone.

For proper connection between column and footing, use four No. 8 dowels (to match the column steel), one in each corner. The development length requirement for the No.8 dowels is identical to that of Example 10-3.

10-7

ECCENTRICALLY LOADED FOOTINGS

Where footings are subject to eccentric vertical loads or to moments transmitted by the supported column, the design varies somewhat from that of the preceding sections. The soil pressure is no longer uniform across the footing width but may be assumed to vary linearly. The resultant force should be within the middle one-third of the footing base to ensure a positive contact surface between the footing and the soil.

With the soil pressure distribution known, the footing must be designed to resist all moments and shears, as were the concentrically loaded footings.

10-8

COMBINED FOOTINGS

Combined footings are footings that support more than one column or wall. The two-column type of combined footing, which is relatively common, generally results out of necessity. Two conditions that may lead to its use are (1) an exterior column that is immediately adjacent to a property line where it is impossible to use an individual column footing and (2) two columns that are closely spaced, causing their individual footings to be closely spaced. In these situations, a rectangular or trapezoidal combined footing would usually be used. The choice of which shape to use is based on the difference in column loads as well as on physical (dimensional) limitations. If the footing cannot be rectangular, a trapezoidal shape would then be selected.

The physical dimensions (except thickness) of the combined footing are generally established by the allowable soil pressure. In addition, the centroid of the footing area should coincide with the line of action of the resultant of the two column loads. These dimensions are usually determined using service loads in combination with an allowable soil pressure.

352

Example 10-5

Determine the shape and proportions of a combined footing subject to two column loads, as shown in Figure 10-18.

FIGURE 10-18 Sketch for Example 10-5.

Solution:

1. The design data are as follows: service load on the footing from column A is 300 kips and from column B is 500 kips, and the allowable soil pressure is 6.00 ksf.

2. Locate the resultant column load by a summation of moments at point Z in Figure 10-18:

$$\Sigma M_z = 300(2) + 500(18) = 800(x)$$

from which

$$x = 12 \text{ ft-0 in.} \quad \text{(measured from } Z\text{)}$$

3. Assuming a rectangular shape, establish the length of footing L so that the centroid of the footing area coincides with the line of action of resultant force R:

$$\text{required } L = 12(2) = 24 \text{ ft 0 in.}$$

4. Assume a footing thickness of 3 ft 0 in. Therefore, its weight = 0.150(3) = 0.450 ksf, and the allowable soil pressure for superimposed loads = 6.00 − 0.450 = 5.55 ksf. This neglects any soil *on* the footing.

5. The footing area required is

$$\frac{R}{5.55} = \frac{800}{5.55} = 144.1 \text{ ft}^2$$

6.   With a length = 24 ft 0 in., the footing width W required is

$$\frac{144.1}{24} = 6 \text{ ft } 0 \text{ in.}$$

7.   The actual uniform soil pressure is

$$\frac{800}{6(24)} + 0.450 = 6.00 \text{ ksf} \qquad \text{(O.K.)}$$

Example 10-6

Using the design data from Example 10-5, determine the proportions of a combined footing if the footing length is limited to 22 ft.

Solution:

1.   The resultant column load is located as in Example 10-5 at a point 12 ft 0 in. from point Z.
2.   Assume a footing thickness of 3 ft 0 in. Therefore, its weight = 3(0.150) = 0.450 ksf, and the allowable soil pressure for superimposed loads is 6.00 − 0.450 = 5.55 ksf.
3.   The footing area required is then

$$\frac{800}{5.55} = 144.1 \text{ ft}^2$$

4.   Assume a trapezoidal shape. The area A of a trapezoid is (see Figure 10-19)

$$A = \frac{(b + b_1)L}{2}$$

from which

$$b + b_1 = \frac{2A}{L} = \frac{2(144.1)}{22} = 13.1 \text{ ft}$$

5.   The center of gravity of the trapezoid and the resultant force of the column loads are to coincide. The location of the center of gravity, a distance c from point Z, may be written

$$c = \frac{L(2b + b_1)}{3(b + b_1)} = \frac{L(b + b + b_1)}{3(b + b_1)} = 12 \text{ ft}$$

6.   We now have two equations that contain b and b_1. The equation of step 5 may be easily solved for b by substitution of $L = 22$ ft and $(b + b_1) = 13.1$ ft:

FIGURE 10-19   Sketch for Example 10-6.

$$\frac{22(b + 13.1)}{3(13.1)} = 12$$

from which

$$b = \frac{12(3)(13.1)}{22} - 13.1 = 8.34 \text{ ft}$$

and

$$b_1 = 13.1 - 8.34 = 4.76 \text{ ft}$$

Use $b = 8$ ft 4 in. and $b_1 = 4$ ft 9 in. Thus

$$\text{actual } A = \frac{22(4.75 + 8.33)}{2} = 143.9 \text{ ft}^2$$

The footing is very slightly undersized. No revision is warranted.

The structural design of the rectangular and trapezoidal combined footings is generally based on a uniform soil pressure, even though loading combinations will almost always introduce some eccentricity with respect to the centroid of the footing. The determination of the footing thickness and reinforcement must be based on factored loads and soil pressure to be consistent with the ACI strength method approach. The assumed footing behavior, which is briefly described, is a generally used approach to simplify the design of the footing.

In Figure 10-19, the columns are positioned relatively close to the ends of the footing. Assuming the columns as the supports and the footing subjected to an upward uniformly distributed load caused by the uniform soil pressure, moments that create tension in the top of the footing will predominate in the longitudinal direction. Therefore, the principal longitudinal reinforcement will be placed in the top of the footing equally distributed across the footing width. Somewhat smaller moments in the transverse direction will cause compression in the top of the footing. Transverse steel will be placed under each column in the bottom of the footing to distribute the column load in the transverse direction using the provisions for individual column footings. In effect, this makes the combined footing act as a wide rectangular beam in the longitudinal direction, which may then be designed using the ACI Code provisions for flexure.

Pertinent design considerations may be summarized as follows:

1. Main reinforcement (uniformly distributed) is placed in a longitudinal direction in the top of the footing, assuming the footing to be a longitudinal beam.

2. Shear should be checked considering both one-way shear at a distance d from the face of the column and two-way (punching) shear on a perimeter $d/2$ from the face of the column.

3. Stirrups or bent bars are frequently required to maintain an economical footing thickness. This assumes that the shear effect is uniform across the width of the footing.

4. Transverse reinforcement is generally uniformly placed in the bottom of the footing within a band having a width not greater than the column width plus twice the effective depth of the footing. The design treatment in the transverse direction is similar to the design treatment of the individual column footing, assuming dimensions equal to the band width as previously described and the transverse footing width.

5. Longitudinal steel is also placed in the bottom of the footing to tie together and position the stirrups and transverse steel. Although the required steel areas may be rather small, the effects of cantilever moments in the vicinity of the columns should be checked.

10-9

CANTILEVER OR STRAP FOOTINGS

A third type of combined footing is generally termed a *cantilever* or *strap footing*. This is an economical type of footing when the proximity of a property line precludes the use of other types. For instance, an isolated column footing may be too large for the area available, and the nearest column is too distant to allow a rectangular or trapezoidal combined footing to be economical. The strap footing may be regarded as two individual column footings connected by a strap beam.

In Figure 10-20, the exterior footing is placed eccentrically under the exterior column so that it does not violate the property-line limitations. This would produce a nonuniform pressure distribution under the footing, which could lead to footing rotation. To balance this rotational or overturning effect, the exterior footing is connected by a stiff beam, or strap, to the nearest interior footing, and uniform soil pressures under the footings are assumed. The strap, which may be categorized as a flexural member, is subjected to both bending moment and shear, resulting from the forces P_e and R_e acting on the exterior footing. As shown in Figure 10-20, the applied moment is counterclockwise, and the shear will be positive because $R_e > P_e$. At the interior column, there is no eccentricity between the column load P_i and the resultant soil pressure force R_i. Therefore, we will assume that no moment is induced in the strap at the interior column.

We define V as the vertical shear force necessary to keep the strap in equilibrium, as shown in Figure 10-21. Then, with P_e known, V and R_e may be calculated using the principles of statics. A moment summation about R_e yields

$$P_e e = V(L - e)$$

$$V = \frac{P_e e}{L - e}$$

and from a summation of vertical forces,

$$R_e = P_e + V$$

FIGURE 10-20   Cantilever footing.

FIGURE 10-21   Strap beam.

$$R_e = \frac{P_e + P_e e}{L - e} = P_e + \frac{P_e e}{L - e}$$

Note that V acting downward on the strap beam also means that V is an uplift force on the interior footing. Therefore,

$$R_i = P_i - V$$

$$R_i = P_i - \frac{P_e e}{L - e}$$

In summary, R_e becomes greater than P_e by a magnitude of V, whereas R_i becomes less than P_i by a magnitude equal to V.

The footing areas required are merely the reactions R_e and R_i based on service loads divided by the effective allowable soil pressure. These values are based on an assumed trial e and may have to be recomputed until the trial e and the actual e are the same.

The structural design of the interior footing is simply the design of an isolated column footing subject to a load R_i. The exterior footing is generally considered as under one-way *transverse* bending similar to a wall footing with longitudinal steel furnished by extending the strap steel into the footing. The selection of footing thickness and reinforcement should be based on factored loads to be consistent with the ACI strength design approach.

The strap beam is assumed to be a flexural member with no bearing on the soil underneath. Many designers make a further simplifying assumption that the beam weight is carried by the underlying soil; hence the strap is designed as a rectangular beam subject to a constant shearing force and a linearly varying negative bending moment based on factored loads.

Example 10-7 _____

Determine the size of the exterior and interior footings of a strap footing for the conditions and design data furnished in Figure 10-22.

Solution:

1.   The design data are as follows: service load on the footing from column A is 150 kips and from column B is 250 kips, and the allowable soil pressure is 4.00 ksf.

FIGURE 10-22   Sketch for Example 10-7.

2.   Assume that e = 2 ft 6 in. and that the footing thickness is 2 ft 0 in. Therefore, the footing weight = 2(0.150) = 0.300 ksf.
3.   The allowable soil pressure for superimposed loads = 4.0 − 0.300 = 3.70 ksf.
4.   Determine the strap beam shear V:

$$V = \frac{P_e e}{L - e} = \frac{150(2.5)}{17.5} = 21.4 \text{ kips}$$

5.   The footing reactions are

$$R_e = P_e + V = 150 + 21.4 = 171.4 \text{ kips}$$
$$R_i = P_i - V = 250 - 21.4 = 228.6 \text{ kips}$$

6.   For the exterior footing, the required area is

$$\frac{171.4}{3.7} = 46.3 \text{ ft}^2$$

Use a footing 7 ft 0 in. by 7 ft 0 in. (A = 49 ft²). Note in Figure 10-22 that the actual e is then the same as the assumed e, and no revision of calculations is necessary.

For the interior footing, the required area is

$$\frac{228.6}{3.7} = 61.8 \text{ ft}^2$$

Use a footing 8 ft 0 in. by 8 ft 0 in. (A = 64 ft²).

PROBLEMS

10-1. Design a plain concrete wall footing to carry a 12-in.-thick reinforced concrete wall. Service loads are 2.3 kips/ft dead load (includes the weight of the wall) and 2.3 kips/ft live load. Use $f'_c = 3000$ psi and an allowable soil pressure of 4000 psf. Assume that the bottom of the footing is to be 4 ft below grade. The weight of earth $w_e = 100$ lb/ft^3.

10-2. Redesign the footing for the wall of Problem 10-1. Service loads are 8.0 kips/ft dead load and 8.0 kips/ft live load.

10-3. Design a reinforced concrete footing for the wall of Problem 10-1 if the service loads are 6 kips/ft dead load (includes wall weight) and 15 kips/ft live load. Use $f_y = 60,000$ psi.

10-4. Design a square individual column footing (reinforced concrete) to support an 18-in.-square reinforced concrete tied interior column. Service loads are 200 kips dead load and 350 kips live load. Use $f'_c = 3000$ psi and $f_y = 60,000$ psi. The allowable soil pressure is 3500 psf, and $w_e = 100$ lb/ft^3. The column, reinforced with eight No. 8 bars, has $f'_c = 5000$ psi and $f_y = 60,000$ psi. The bottom of the footing is to be 4 ft below grade.

10-5. Design a square individual column footing (reinforced concrete) to support a 16-in.-square reinforced concrete tied interior column. Service loads are 200 kips dead load and 160 kips live load. Both column and footing have $f'_c = 4000$ psi and $f_y = 60,000$ psi. The allowable soil pressure is 5000 psf, and $w_e = 100$ lb/ft^3. The bottom of the footing is to be 4 ft below grade. The column is reinforced with eight No.7 bars.

10-6. Design for load transfer from a 14-in.-square tied column to a 13 ft 0 in. square reinforced concrete footing. Use $P_u = 650$ kips, footing $f'_c = 3000$ psi, column $f'_c = 5000$ psi, and $f_y = 60,000$ psi (all steel). The column is reinforced with eight No. 8 bars.

10-7. Redesign the footing of Problem 10-5 if there is a 7 ft 0 in. restriction on the width of the footing.

10-8. Footings are to be designed for two columns A and B spaced with $D = 16$ ft as shown. There are no dimensional limitations. The service load from column A is 100 kips and from column B is 150 kips. The allowable soil pressure is 4000 psf. Determine the appropriate footing(s) size, type, and layout. Assume thickness and disregard reinforcing.

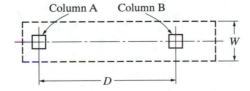

PROBLEMS 10-8 TO 10-11

10-9. Same as Problem 10-8, except service loads are 700 kips from column A and 900 kips from column B, and $D = 14$ ft.

10-10. For the column layout shown, there is a width restriction W of 16 ft. Here $D = 14$ ft. Determine an appropriate footing size and layout if the service load from column A is 700 kips and from column B is 800 kips. Assume thickness and disregard reinforcing. The allowable soil pressure is 4000 psf.

10-11. For the column layout shown, $D = 24$ ft. The footing for the 18-in.-square column A must be placed flush with the left side of the column. Service loads are 200 kips for column A and 300 kips for column B. The allowable soil pressure is 4500 psf. Assume a footing thickness of 2 ft 6 in. and determine an appropriate size, type, and layout for the footing.

CHAPTER 11

Prestressed Concrete Fundamentals

11-1

INTRODUCTION

According to the ACI definition, prestressed concrete is a material that has had internal stresses induced to balance out, to a desired degree, stresses due to externally applied loads. Since tensile stresses are undesirable in concrete members, the object of prestressing is to create compressive stresses (prestress) at the same locations as the tensile stresses within the member so that the tensile stresses will be diminished or will disappear altogether. The diminishing or elimination of tensile stresses within the concrete will result in members that have fewer cracks or are crack-free at service load levels. This is one of the advantages of prestressed concrete over reinforced concrete, particularly in corrosive atmospheres. Prestressed concrete offers other advantages. Because beam cross sections are primarily in compression, diagonal tension stresses are reduced and the beams are stiffer at service loads. In addition, sections can be smaller, resulting in less dead weight.

Despite the advantages, we must consider the higher unit cost of stronger materials, the need for expensive accessories, the necessity for close inspection and quality control, and, in the case of precasting, a higher initial investment in plant.

11-2

DESIGN APPROACH AND BASIC CONCEPTS

Since most of the advantages of prestressed concrete are at service load levels and since permissible stresses in the "green" concrete often control the amount of prestress force to be used, the major part of analysis and design calculations is made using service loads, permissible stresses, and basic assumptions as outlined in Section 18.2 through 18.5 of the ACI Code. The strength requirements of the code must also be met, however. Therefore, at some point, the design must be checked using appropriate load factors and strength reduction factors.

The normal method for applying prestress force to a concrete member is through the use of steel tendons. There are two basic methods of arriving at the final prestressed member: pretensioning and post-tensioning.

Pretensioning may be defined as a method of prestressing concrete in which the tendons are tensioned before the concrete is placed. This operation, which may be performed in a casting yard, is basically a five-step process:

1. The tendons are placed in a prescribed pattern on the casting bed between two anchorages. The tendons are then tensioned to a value not to exceed 94% of the specified yield strength, but not greater than the lesser of 80% of the specified tensile strength of the tendons and the maximum value recommended by the manufacturer of the prestressing tendons or anchorages (ACI

PHOTO 11-1   Precast bridge girder components for post-tensioning.

Code, Section 18.5.1). The tendons are then anchored so that the load in them is maintained.

2.   If the concrete forms are not already in place, they may then be assembled around the tendons.

3.   The concrete is then placed in the forms and allowed to cure. Proper quality control must be exercised, and curing may be accelerated with the use of steam or other methods. The concrete will bond to the tendons.

4.   When the concrete attains a prescribed strength, normally within 24 hours or less, the tendons are cut at the anchorages. Since the tendons are now bonded to the concrete, as they are cut from their anchorages the high prestress force must be transferred to the concrete. As the high tensile force of the tendon creates a compressive force on the concrete section, the concrete will tend to shorten slightly. The stresses that exist once the tendons have been cut are often called the stresses at *transfer*. Since there is no external load at this stage, the stresses at transfer include only those due to prestressing forces and those due to the weight of the member.

5.   The prestressed member is then removed from the forms and moved to a storage area so that the casting bed can be prepared for further use.

Pretensioned members are usually manufactured at a casting yard or plant that is somewhat removed from the job site where the members will eventually be used.

In this case, they are usually delivered to the job site ready to be set in place. Where a project is of sufficient magnitude to warrant it economically, a casting yard may be built on the job site, thus decreasing transportation costs and allowing larger members to be precast without the associated transportation problems.

Figure 11-1 depicts the various stages in the manufacture of a precast, pretensioned member.

Post-tensioning may be defined as a method of prestressing concrete in which the tendons are tensioned *after* the concrete has cured. The operation is commonly a six-step process:

1.   Concrete forms are assembled with flexible hollow tubes (metal or plastic) placed in the forms and held at specified locations.
2.   Concrete is then placed in the forms and allowed to cure to a prescribed strength.
3.   Tendons are placed in the tubes. (In some systems, a complete tendon assembly is placed in the forms prior to the pouring of the concrete.)
4.   The tendons are tensioned by jacking against an anchorage device or end plate that, in some cases, has been previously embedded in the end of the member. The anchorage device will incorporate some method for gripping the tendon and holding the load.
5.   If the tendons are to be bonded, the space in the tubes around the tendons may be grouted using a pumped grout. Some members use unbonded tendons.
6.   The end anchorages may be covered with a protective coating.

Although post-tensioning is sometimes performed in a plant away from the project, it is most often done at the job site, particularly for units too large to be shipped assembled or for unusual applications (Figure 11-2).

Tendon Tensioned between Anchorages

(a)

Forms Assembled and Concrete Placed in Forms

(b)

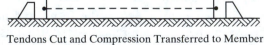

Tendons Cut and Compression Transferred to Member

(c)

FIGURE 11-1   Pretensioned member.

FIGURE 11-2   Post-tensioned member.

The tensioning of the tendons is normally done with hydraulic jacks. Many patented devices are available to accomplish the anchoring of the tendon ends to the concrete.

11-3

STRESS PATTERNS IN PRESTRESSED CONCRETE BEAMS

The stress pattern existing on the cross section of a prestressed concrete beam may be determined by superimposing the stresses due to the loads and forces acting on the beam at any particular time. For our purposes, the following sign convention will be adopted:

Tensile stresses are positive (+).

Compressive stresses are negative (−).

Since we will assume a crack-free cross section at service load level, the entire cross section will remain effective in carrying stress. Also, the entire concrete cross section will be used in the calculation of centroid and moment of inertia.

For purposes of explanation, we will consider a rectangular shape with tendons placed at the centroid of the section, and we will investigate the induced stresses. Although the rectangular shape is used for some applications, it is often less economical than the more complex shapes.

Example 11-1

For the section shown in Figure 11-3, determine the stresses due to prestress immediately after transfer and also the stresses at midspan when the member is placed on a 20 ft simple span. Use $f'_c = 5000$ psi and assume that the concrete has attained a strength of 4000 psi at the time of transfer. Use a central prestressing force of 100 kips.

FIGURE 11-3   Sketches for Example 11-1.

Solution:

1.   Compute the stress in the concrete at the time of initial prestress. With the prestressing force P_s applied at the centroid of the section and assumed acting on the gross section A_c, the concrete stress will be uniform over the entire section. Thus

$$f = \frac{P_s}{A_c} = \frac{-100}{12(18)} = -0.463 \text{ ksi}$$

2.   Compute the stresses due to the beam dead load:

Weight of beam: $w_{DL} = \frac{12(18)}{144}(0.150) = 0.225 \text{ kip/ft}$

Moment due to dead load: $M_{DL} = \frac{w_{DL}\ell^2}{8} = \frac{0.225(20)^2}{8} = 11.25 \text{ ft-kips}$

Compute the moment of inertia I of the beam using the gross cross section and neglecting the transformed area of the tendons (since the steel is at the centroid, it will have no effect on the moment of inertia):

$$I_g = \frac{bh^3}{12} = \frac{12(18)^3}{12} = 5832 \text{ in.}^4$$

Dead load stresses: $f = \frac{Mc}{I} = \frac{11.25(12)(9)}{5832} = \pm 0.208 \text{ ksi}$

3.   Compute the stresses due to prestress plus dead load:

$$f_{(\text{initial prestress + DL})} = -0.463 \pm 0.208$$

$$= -0.671 \text{ ksi} \quad \text{(compression, top)}$$

$$= -0.255 \text{ ksi} \quad \text{(compression, bottom)}$$

These results are shown on the stress summation diagram of Figure 11-4.

FIGURE 11-4   Midspan stresses for Example 11-1.

The tensile stresses due to the DL moment in the bottom of the beam have been completely canceled out and compression exists on the entire cross section. A limited additional positive moment may be carried by the beam without resulting in a net tensile stress in the bottom of the beam. This situation may be further improved on by *lowering the location of the tendon* to induce additional compressive stresses in the bottom of the beam.

Example 11-1 reflects two stages of the prestress process. The transfer stage occurs in a pretensioned member when the tendons are cut at the ends of the member and the prestress force has been transferred to the beam, as shown in Figure 11-1. When the beam in this problem is removed from the forms (picked up by its end points), dead load stresses are introduced, and in this second stage, both the beam weight (dead load) and the prestress force are contributors to the stress pattern within the beam. This stage is important because it occurs early in the life of the beam (sometimes within 24 hours of casting), and the concrete stresses must be held within permissible values as specified in the ACI Code, Section 18.4.

If the prestress force were placed below the neutral axis in Example 11-1, negative bending moment would occur in the member at transfer, causing the beam to curve upward and pick up its dead load. Hence, for a simple beam such as this, where the prestress force is eccentric, the stresses due to the initial prestress would never exist alone without the counteracting stresses from the dead load moment.

11-4

PRESTRESSED CONCRETE MATERIALS

The application of the prestress force both strains or "stretches" the tendons and at the same time induces tensile stresses in them. If the tendon strain is reduced for some reason, the stress will also be reduced. In prestressed concrete, this is known as a *loss of prestress*. This loss occurs after the prestress force has been introduced.

Contributory factors to this loss are creep and shrinkage of the concrete, elastic compression of the concrete member, relaxation of the tendon stress, anchorage seating loss, and friction losses due to intended or unintended curvature in post-tensioning tendons. Estimates on the magnitudes of these losses vary. It is generally known, however, that an ordinary steel bar tensioned to its yield strength (40,000 psi) would lose its entire prestress by the time all stress losses had taken place. Therefore, for prestressed concrete applications, it is necessary to use very high strength steels, where the previously mentioned strain losses will result in a much smaller percentage of change in the original prestress force.

The most commonly used steel for pretensioned prestressed concrete is in the form of a seven-wire, uncoated, stress-relieved strand having a minimum tensile strength (f_{pu}) of 250,000 psi or 270,000 psi, depending on grade. The seven-wire strand is made up of seven cold-drawn wires. The center wire is straight, and the six outside wires are laid helically around it. All six outside wires are the same diameter, and the center wire is slightly larger. This in effect guarantees that each of the outside wires will bear on and grip the center wire.

Prestressing steel does not exhibit the definite yield point characteristic found in the normal ductile steel used in reinforcing steel (see Figure 11-5). The yield strength for prestressing wire and strand is a "specified yield strength" that is obtained from the stress-strain diagram at 1% strain, according to ASTM. Nevertheless, the specified yield point is not as important in prestressing steel as is the yield point in the ductile steels. It is a consideration when determining the ultimate strength of a beam. For more information on prestressing wire and strand, the reader is referred to ASTM Standards A416-94 and A421-91.

In normal reinforced concrete members that are designed to ensure tension failures, the strength of the concrete is secondary in importance to the strength of the steel in the determination of the flexural strength of the member. In prestressed applications, concrete in the range from 4000 to 6000 psi is commonly used. Some of the reasons for this are that (1) volumetric changes for higher-strength concrete are smaller, which will result in smaller prestress losses; (2) bear-

FIGURE 11-5 Comparative stress-strain curves.

ing and development stresses are higher; and (3) higher-strength concrete is more easily obtained in precast work than in cast-in-place work because of better quality control.

In addition, high early strength cement (type III) is normally used to obtain as rapid a turnover time as possible for optimum use of forms.

11-5

ANALYSIS OF RECTANGULAR PRESTRESSED CONCRETE BEAMS

The analysis of flexural stresses in a prestressed member should be performed for different stages of loading, that is, the initial service load stage, which includes dead load plus prestress before losses; the final service load stage, which includes dead load plus prestress plus live load after losses; and finally the ultimate strength stage, which involves load and understrength factors. Generally, checking of prestressed members is accomplished at the service load level based on unfactored loads. The ultimate strength of a member should be checked, however, using the same strength principles as for nonprestressed reinforced concrete members.

Example 11-2

For the beam of cross section shown in Figure 11-6, analyze the flexural stresses at midspan at transfer and in service. Neglect losses. Use a prestressed steel area A_{ps} of 2.0 in.^{2}, use $f'_c = 6000$ psi, and assume that the concrete has attained a strength of 5000 psi at the time of transfer. The initial prestress force = 250 kips. The service dead load = 0.25 kip/ft, which does not include the weight of the beam. The service live load = 1.0 kip/ft. Use $n = 7$.

Assume that the cross section is effective and use the transformed area (neglecting displaced concrete) for the moment of inertia.

Section A–A   Transformed Area

FIGURE 11-6   Sketches for Example 11-2.

Solution:

1. The beam weight is

$$w_{DL} = \frac{20(12)}{144}(0.150) = 0.25 \text{ kip/ft}$$

The moment due to the beam weight is

$$M_{DL} = \frac{w_{DL}\ell^2}{8} = \frac{0.25(30)^2}{8} = 28.1 \text{ ft-kips}$$

The moment due to superimposed loads (DL + LL) is

$$M_{DL+LL} = \frac{w_{(DL+LL)}\ell^2}{8} = \frac{1.25(30)^2}{8} = 140.6 \text{ ft-kips}$$

2. The location of the neutral axis is

$$\bar{y} = \frac{\Sigma(Ay)}{\Sigma A}$$

Using the top of the section as the reference axis,

$$\bar{y} = \frac{12(20)(10) + 14(15)}{12(20) + 14} = 10.28 \text{ in.}$$

The eccentricity e of the strands from the neutral axis is

$$15 - 10.28 = 4.72 \text{ in.}$$

The moment of inertia about the neutral axis is

$$I = \frac{12(20)^3}{12} + 12(20)(0.28)^2 + 14(4.72)^2$$

$$= 8331 \text{ in.}^4$$

3. The stresses may now be calculated. These are summarized in Figure 11-7.

   a. Initial prestress: As a result of the eccentric prestressing force, the induced stress at the initial prestress stage will *not* be uniform but may be computed from

   $$f = -\frac{P_s}{A_c} \pm \frac{Mc}{I}$$

   $$= -\frac{P_s}{A_c} \pm \frac{P_s(e)c}{I}$$

   where P_s/A_c represents the axial effect of the prestress force and $\frac{P_s(e)c}{I}$ is the eccentric, or moment, effect. Then

FIGURE 11-7   Midspan stress summary for Example 11-2.

$$-\frac{P_s}{A_c} = -\frac{250}{12(20)} = -1.04 \text{ ksi} \qquad \text{(compression top and bottom)}$$

$$+\frac{P_s(e)c}{I} = \frac{250(4.72)(10.28)}{8331} = +1.46 \text{ ksi} \qquad \text{(tension in top)}$$

$$-\frac{P_s(e)c}{I} = -\frac{250(4.72)(9.72)}{8331} = -1.38 \text{ ksi} \qquad \text{(compression in bottom)}$$

b.   The stresses due to the beam weight are

$$f = \pm\frac{Mc}{I}$$

$$= +\frac{28.1(12)(9.72)}{8331} = +0.39 \text{ ksi} \qquad \text{(tension in bottom)}$$

$$= -\frac{28.1(12)(10.28)}{8331} = -0.42 \text{ ksi} \qquad \text{(compression in top)}$$

Summarizing the initial service load stage at the time of transfer [prestress plus beam weight (DL)]:

Top of beam: $-1.04 + 1.46 - 0.42 = 0$

Bottom of beam: $-1.04 - 1.38 + 0.39 = -2.03$ ksi   (compression)

The permissible stresses (ACI Code, Section 18.4) immediately after prestress transfer (before losses) are in terms of f'_{ci}, which is the compressive strength (psi) of concrete at the time of initial prestress:

$$\text{compression} = 0.60 f'_{ci}$$

$$= 0.60(5000) = 3000 \text{ psi} = 3.0 \text{ ksi}$$

$$\text{tension} = 3\sqrt{f'_{ci}}$$

$$= 3\sqrt{5000} = 212 \text{ psi} = 0.212 \text{ ksi}$$

Since $2.03 < 3.0$ and $0 < 0.212$, the beam is satisfactory at this stage.

c.   The stresses due to the superimposed loads (DL + LL) are

$$f = \pm \frac{Mc}{I}$$

$$= + \frac{140.6(12)(9.72)}{8331} = +1.97 \text{ ksi} \qquad \text{(tension in bottom)}$$

$$= - \frac{140.6(12)(10.28)}{8331} = -2.08 \text{ ksi} \qquad \text{(compression in top)}$$

Summarizing the second service load stage when the beam has had service loads applied (prestress plus beam dead load plus superimposed loads) gives us

Top of beam: $0 - 2.08 = -2.08$ ksi   (compression)
Bottom of beam: $-2.03 + 1.97 = -0.06$ ksi   (compression)

The permissible stresses in the concrete at the service load level (ACI Code, Section 18.4.2) due to prestress plus total load are:

In compression: $0.60f'_c = 0.60(6000) = 3600 \text{ psi} = 3.60 \text{ ksi}$
In tension: $6\sqrt{f'_c} = 6\sqrt{6000} = 465 \text{ psi} = 0.465 \text{ ksi}$

The permissible stresses given above assume that losses have been accounted for. Our analysis has neglected losses. Aside from this, the stresses in the beam would be satisfactory, since $2.08 < 3.60$. Note in Figure 11-7c that at transfer, no tensile stresses exist on the cross section.

The final stress distribution (Figure 11-7e) in the beam of Example 11-2 shows that the entire beam cross section is under compression. This is the stress pattern that exists at *midspan* (since the applied moments calculated were midspan moments). It is evident that moments will decrease toward the supports of a simply supported beam and that the stress pattern will change drastically. For example, if the eccentricity of the tendon were constant in the beam in question, the net prestress (Figure 11-7a) would exist at the beam ends, where moment due to beam weight and applied loads is zero. Since the tensile stress is undesirable, the location of the tendon is changed in the area of the end of the beam, so that eccentricity is decreased. This results in a *curved* or *draped* tendon within the member, as shown in Figure 11-8. Post-tensioned members may have curved tendons accurately

Pretensioned   Post-tensioned
(a)   (b)

FIGURE 11-8   Draped tendons.

placed to satisfy design requirements, but in pretensioned members, because of the nature of the fabrication process, only approximate curves are formed by forcing the tendon up or down at a few points.

Although shear was not included in the beam analysis, the reader should be aware that the draping of the tendons, in addition to affecting the flexural stresses at the beam ends, produces a force acting vertically upward, which has the effect of reducing the shear force due to dead and live loads. Prestressed concrete flexural members are available in numerous shapes suitable for various applications. A few of the more common ones are shown in Figure 11-9.

Single Tee
(Roofs and Floors)

Double Tee
(Roofs and Floors)

Inverted Tee
(Support Member)

Hollow-Core Slabs
(Roofs and Floors)

Box Beam
(Bridge Members)

I Shape
(Bridge and Roof Girders)

FIGURE 11-9   Typical precast, prestressed flexural members.

11-6

ALTERNATIVE METHODS OF ELASTIC ANALYSIS: INTERNAL COUPLE METHOD

The ACI Code requires that prestressed beams be analyzed elastically to establish whether the stresses developed by the combined action of service loads and prestressing force are within specified allowable stresses. In effect, this limit on the magnitude of stress, specifically at transfer or with service loads in place, controls cracking and subsequently prevents crushing of the concrete.

The analysis method used in Section 11-5 is often designated the *method of superposition* or the *combined loading concept*. Briefly, it is based on superimposing the stresses created by the applied loads with those created by the prestressing force. As previously shown, all these stresses are computed independently and then combined. This method provides the designer a complete picture of stress variation under various loading conditions.

A second method of elastic analysis may be termed the *internal couple method*. In a sense, this is analogous to the internal couple of reinforced concrete beams, discussed in Chapter 2, where steel takes the tension and concrete takes the compression, as shown in Figure 11-10. The two materials form an internal couple resisting the moment due to the external loads. For a prestressed beam, the couple

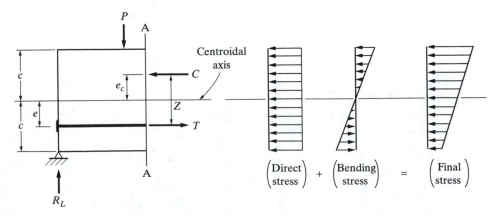

FIGURE 11-10   Internal couple and stress distributions.

consists of the tendon prestress force P_s, which may be designated the tensile force T (therefore, $P_s = T$), and the resultant of the longitudinal compressive stresses in the concrete C.

Note, however, that the internal resisting couple (or moment) in a prestressed concrete beam differs somewhat from that in a reinforced concrete beam. Under service load conditions, the forces C and T in a prestressed concrete beam remain virtually constant, and the lever arm Z increases with increasing moment (see Figure 11-10). In a reinforced concrete beam, the lever arm Z of the internal couple is considered to be essentially constant, whereas the forces C and T increase with increasing moment. If the moment due to the applied loads is M and since the prestress force P_s (which is also the tension T) is essentially constant, it follows that

$$Z = \frac{M}{P_s} = \frac{M}{T}$$

This, in effect, locates the *center of compression* (the location at which C acts). Once the position of C has been found, the stress distribution can be established by combining the direct stress created by C with the bending stress created by C acting at an eccentricity e_c from the centroidal axis of the section, as shown in Figure 11-10.

Since the prestress force is essentially constant as long as the concrete remains uncracked, the position of the resultant compression C on the cross section with respect to the position of the tendon varies directly with the magnitude of the moment. If the moment is zero (which occurs at transfer), the arm Z between C and T will be zero and the resultant of the compressive stresses C will be located at the level of the tendon. Since the location of C varies due to an increasing moment, the stress distribution shape will vary and could be any one of those shown in Figure 11-11.

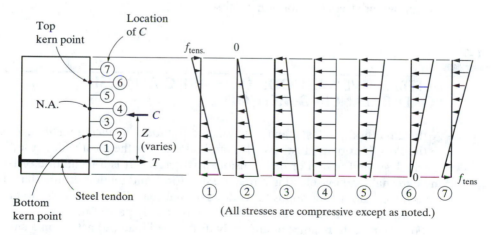

FIGURE 11-11   Stress distribution in concrete for various locations of C (elastic analysis).

Numerically, the stress at any point on a cross section may be obtained using

$$f = \frac{C}{A_g} \pm \frac{Ce_c y}{I_g}$$

where

e_c = eccentricity of C with respect to the centroidal axis

y = distance from the centroidal axis to any point on the cross section (for the outer fibers, $y = c$)

A_g = cross-sectional area of the *gross* concrete section

I_g = moment of inertia with respect to the centroidal axis of the *gross* section

C = total compressive force acting on the cross section

It is common practice in the analysis and design of rectangular-shaped pre-stressed concrete beams to base the stress calculations in the elastic range on the properties of the gross concrete section. This, in effect, neglects the transformed area of the steel tendons as well as any displaced concrete due to the presence of the tendons or ducts. This is an acceptable approach, since the differences in the resulting stresses are quite small.

As the moment due to the applied loads changes and the internal couple lever arm Z changes, small tensile stresses may develop on a given cross section. If no tensile stresses are to be permitted either at transfer or under full service loads, C cannot be located outside the *kern* of the cross section. When a resultant force, act-ing by itself, is located within the kern area, no tensile stress will be produced. When the resultant force acts at the boundary of the kern area, it will produce a tri-angular stress distribution [1]. The boundary of the kern area is referred to as the *kern point*. As shown in Figure 11-11, when C is at the top or bottom kern point, the triangular stress distribution results.

11-7

ALTERNATIVE METHODS OF ELASTIC ANALYSIS: LOAD BALANCING METHOD

A third method of elastic analysis is called the *load balancing method*. According to the Post-Tensioning Institute, this method is by far the most widely used method for analysis and design of post-tensioned structures. It is a technique of balancing the external load by selecting a prestressing force and tendon profile that creates a transverse load acting opposite to the external load. This transverse load may be equal to either the full external applied load or only part of it.

For example, to balance a uniformly distributed load (w) acting on a simply sup-ported beam, a parabolic tendon profile with zero end eccentricities would be selected. The prestressing force P_s needed would be a function of the load to be balanced as well as the acceptable sag of the tendon. If the transverse load created by the tendons exactly balanced the external load, a uniform compressive stress distribution P_s/A_g will develop over the beam cross section, and the beam will remain essentially level with no deflection or camber. To balance the load the end eccentricities should be zero; otherwise, an end moment will be developed that disturbs the uniform stress distribution.

   If only a portion of the external load is balanced, a net moment in the beam at any point will develop from that portion of the load that is *not* balanced by the prestressing. It is only this net moment that must be considered in computing the bending stress. Therefore, the stress acting at any point on a cross section may be expressed as

$$f = \frac{P_s}{A_g} \pm \frac{M_{net}y}{I_g}$$

where

   P_s = prestressing force applied to the member (this is also designated T)

   M_{net} = net unbalanced moment on the section

and A_g, y, and I_g are as previously defined.

   The computed stress due to the uniform compression and the unbalanced moment must then (as in the other methods) be compared with code allowable stresses.

   The externally applied load that will be balanced need not necessarily be uniformly distributed. It can also be a concentrated load or be a combination of both types. For a uniformly distributed load, a shallow parabolic tendon profile is generally selected, whereas a linear profile with a sharp directional change is used for a concentrated load. These are illustrated in Figure 11-12.

   With respect to the balancing of a concentrated load, note the sharp directional change of the tendon under the external load at midspan. This creates an upward component

$$P_p = 2P_s \sin \theta$$

In the case shown, P_p exactly balances the applied load P. Therefore, if we neglect its own weight, the beam is not subject to net *transverse* load. At the ends of the beam, the horizontal components of P_s, which are shown as $P_s\cos \theta$ (and which are collinear with the centroidal axis of the beam) create a uniform compressive stress along the entire length of the beam. Therefore, the stress in the beam at any section may be expressed as

$$f = \frac{P_s\cos \theta}{A_g}$$

and for small values of θ,

$$f = \frac{P_s}{A_g}$$

Balancing of Concentrated Load

(a)

Balancing of Uniformly Distributed Load

(b)

FIGURE 11-12   Load balancing: (a) balancing of concentrated load;
(b) balancing of uniformly distributed load.

If any additional external load is applied, the beam will act as an elastic, homogeneous concrete beam (up to the point of cracking), and a bending stress will
develop, which can be evaluated by

$$f = \frac{M_{\text{net}}c}{I_g}$$

where M_{net} is the moment developed by any load that is applied in addition to P.

With respect to the balancing of the uniformly distributed load, note that the
tendon profile is that of a parabolic curve whose upward transverse component w_p
in lb/ft is given by

$$w_p = \frac{8P_s\delta}{\ell^2} \qquad (11\text{-}1)$$

Assuming that the externally applied load w, including the weight of the beam,
is exactly balanced by the transverse component w_p, there is no bending in the
beam, and the beam is subject to a uniform compressive stress calculated from

$$f = \frac{P_s}{A_g}$$

If the transverse component is different from the applied external load, the bending moment developed will induce a bending stress, which can be evaluated by

$$f = \frac{M_{net}c}{I_g}$$ $f = \frac{P_s}{Ag} \pm \frac{M_{Net}c}{Ig}$

where M_{net} is the moment developed by a load that is applied over and above w.

It is questionable as to what portion of the external load should be balanced by the prestress. If too much of the applied load, such as DL plus ½LL is to be balanced, excessive prestress may be required. The designer must exercise judgment in determining the proper amount of loading to be balanced by prestressing.

Example 11-3

The rectangular prestressed beam shown in Figure 11-13 carries uniformly distributed service loads of 1.0 kip/ft LL and 1.0 kip/ft DL (which includes the weight of the beam). A parabolic tendon will be used that is to furnish a uniformly distributed upward balancing load of 1.5 kips/ft (DL + ½LL). Calculate the required prestressing force and determine the net moment at midspan.

FIGURE 11-13   Sketch for Example 11-3.

Solution:

Solving Equation 11-1 for required P_s:

$$\text{required } P_s = \frac{w_p \ell^2}{8\delta} = \frac{1.5(75)^2}{8(15/12)} = 844 \text{ kips}$$

The net moment at midspan is calculated from

$$M = \frac{w\ell^2}{8} = \frac{(2.0 - 1.5)(75)^2}{8} = 352 \text{ ft-kips}$$

Example 11-4 illustrates the three methods of elastic analysis. In this example, we will neglect the transformed area of the steel as well as any displaced concrete, and we will use the gross properties of the cross section to compute stresses. Note that this varies from the solution of Example 11-2.

Example 11-4 _____

A rectangular prestressed concrete beam shown in Figure 11-14 is simply supported and has a span length of 25 ft 0 in. The beam carries a superimposed service LL of 2.0 kips/ft. The only service DL is the weight of the beam. The parabolic prestressing tendon is located as shown and is subjected to an effective prestress force of 300 kips (neglect any prestress losses). Determine the outer fiber flexural stresses at midspan at transfer (prestress + beam weight) and when the member is under full service load conditions (prestress + beam weight + service LL).

FIGURE 11-14   Sketches for Example 11-4.

Solution:

A. Using the method of superposition

1.   Calculate moments after determining the beam weight:

$$w_{DL} = \frac{28(18)}{144}(0.150) = 0.525 \text{ kip/ft}$$

The moment due to beam weight is

$$M_{DL} = \frac{w_{DL}\ell^2}{8} = \frac{0.525(25)^2}{8} = 41.0 \text{ ft-kips}$$

The moment due to superimposed LL is

$$M_{LL} = \frac{w_{LL}\ell^2}{8} = \frac{2.0(25)^2}{8} = 156.3 \text{ ft-kips}$$

2. Using the gross concrete section and neglecting the transformed steel area, the neutral axis coincides with the centroidal axis. Therefore, the distance from the neutral axis to the outer fiber is 14 in. The eccentricity e of the strands from the neutral axis is found from

$$14 - 8 = 6 \text{ in.}$$

The moment of inertia about the neutral axis is found from

$$I_g = \frac{18(28)^3}{12} = 32,928 \text{ in.}^4$$

3. Calculate the stresses.

a. At transfer, the prestressing stress is determined from

$$f = -\frac{P_s}{A_g} \pm \frac{P_s e c}{I_g}$$

$$= -\frac{300}{18(28)} \pm \frac{300(6)(14)}{32,928}$$

$$= -0.595 \pm 0.765$$

from which

$$\text{stress at top} = -0.595 + 0.765 = 0.170 \text{ ksi} \qquad \text{(tension)}$$

$$\text{stress at bottom} = -0.595 - 0.765 = -1.36 \text{ ksi} \qquad \text{(compression)}$$

The stress due to the service DL (beam weight) is calculated from

$$f = \pm \frac{Mc}{I} = \pm \frac{41.0(12)(14)}{32,928} = \pm 0.209 \text{ ksi}$$

Combining the preceding stresses for the transfer condition gives us

$$\text{stress at top} = +0.170 - 0.209 = -0.039 \text{ ksi} \qquad \text{(compression)}$$

$$\text{stress at bottom} = -1.36 + 0.209 = -1.15 \text{ ksi} \qquad \text{(compression)}$$

b. Under full service load conditions, stress due to superimposed LL is calculated from

$$f = \pm \frac{Mc}{I} = \pm \frac{156.3(12)(14)}{32,928} = \pm 0.797 \text{ ksi}$$

Combining the preceding stresses for the full service load condition gives us

$$\text{stress at top} = -0.039 - 0.797 = -0.836 \qquad \text{(compression)}$$

$$\text{stress at bottom} = -1.15 + 0.797 = -0.353 \text{ ksi} \qquad \text{(compression)}$$

B. Using the internal couple method

1. Given the prestress force of 300 kips and noting that $\Sigma\, H_F = 0$, we see that

$$P_s = T = C = 300 \text{ kips}$$

a. At transfer (with reference to Figure 11-15),

$$\text{lever arm } Z = \frac{M}{T} = \frac{41.0(12)}{300} = 1.64 \text{ in.}$$

The eccentricity of C to the neutral axis is calculated from

$$e_c = 6 - 1.64 = 4.36 \text{ in.} \qquad \text{(below middepth)}$$

$$f = -\frac{C}{A_g} \pm \frac{Ce_c c}{I_g}$$

$$= -\frac{300}{18(28)} \pm \frac{300(4.36)(14)}{32{,}928}$$

$$= -0.595 + 0.556$$

$$\text{stress at top} = -0.595 + 0.556 = -0.039 \text{ ksi} \qquad \text{(compression)}$$

$$\text{stress at bottom} = -0.595 - 0.556 = -1.15 \text{ ksi} \qquad \text{(compression)}$$

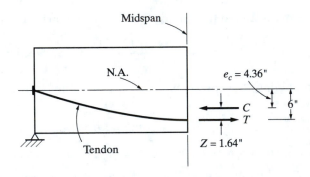

FIGURE 11-15 Location of C.

b. Under full service load (with reference to Figure 11-16),

$$\text{lever arm } Z = \frac{M_{\text{DL}} + M_{\text{LL}}}{T} = \frac{(156.3 + 41.0)(12)}{300} = 7.89 \text{ in.}$$

The eccentricity of C to the neutral axis is calculated from

$$e_c = 7.89 - 6 = 1.89 \text{ in.} \qquad \text{(above middepth)}$$

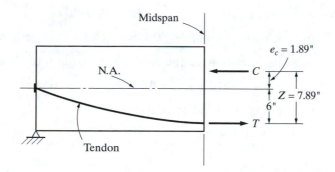

FIGURE 11-16   Location of C.

$$f = -\frac{C}{A_g} \pm \frac{Ce_cc}{I_g}$$

$$= -\frac{300}{18(28)} \pm \frac{300(1.89)(14)}{32,928}$$

$$= -0.595 \pm 0.241$$

$$\text{stress at top} = -0.595 - 0.241 = -0.836 \text{ ksi} \qquad \text{(compression)}$$

$$\text{stress at bottom} = -0.595 + 0.241 = -0.354 \text{ ksi} \qquad \text{(compression)}$$

C. Using the load balancing method

1.   Let $e = \delta = 6$ in. The parabolic tendons produce an upward balancing load of

$$w_p = \frac{8P_s\delta}{\ell^2} = \frac{8(300)(0.5)}{25^2} = 1.92 \text{ kips/ft}$$

a.   At transfer, the unbalanced load on the beam is

$$1.92 - 0.525 = 1.395 \text{ kips/ft} \qquad \text{(upward)}$$

The net moment at midspan is

$$M_{net} = \frac{1.395(25)^2}{8} = 109.0 \text{ ft-kips} \qquad \text{(tension on top)}$$

The bending stress due to the net moment is

$$f = \pm\frac{M_{net}c}{I_g} = \pm\frac{109(12)(14)}{32,928} = \pm 0.556 \text{ ksi}$$

The uniform compressive stress is

$$-\frac{P_s}{A_g} = -\frac{300}{18(28)} = -0.595 \text{ ksi}$$

$$\text{stress at top} = -0.595 + 0.556 = -0.039 \text{ ksi} \qquad \text{(compression)}$$

$$\text{stress at bottom} = -0.595 - 0.556 = -1.15 \text{ ksi} \qquad \text{(compression)}$$

b.   Under full service load, the unbalanced load on the beam is

$$2.0 + 0.525 - 1.92 = 0.605 \text{ kip/ft} \qquad \text{(downward)}$$

The net moment at midspan is

$$M_{\text{net}} = \frac{0.605(25)^2}{8} = 47.3 \text{ ft-kips} \qquad \text{(tension on bottom)}$$

The bending stress due to the net moment is

$$f = \pm\frac{M_{\text{net}}c}{I_g} = \pm\frac{47.3(12)(14)}{32{,}928} = \pm0.241 \text{ ksi}$$

The uniform compressive stress is

$$-\frac{P_s}{A_g} = -\frac{300}{18(28)} = -0.595 \text{ ksi}$$

$$\text{stress at top} = -0.595 - 0.241 = -0.836 \text{ ksi} \qquad \text{(compression)}$$

$$\text{stress at bottom} = -0.595 + 0.241 = -0.354 \text{ ksi} \qquad \text{(compression)}$$

Note that the results agree (with slight round-off error) using the three elastic analysis methods.

The load balancing method offers advantages of simplicity and clarity when dealing with continuous beams and slabs. It is the recommended method for those situations, particularly for preliminary designs. For simple spans, none of the three methods has any particular advantage over the others; all are equally applicable.

11-8

FLEXURAL STRENGTH ANALYSIS

As part of the design and analysis procedure of a prestressed concrete beam, the ACI Code requires that the moment due to factored service loads M_u not exceed the flexural design strength ϕM_n of the member. The design strength of prestressed beams may be computed using strength equations similar to those for reinforced concrete members, discussed in Chapter 2 of this text. The checking of the flexural (ultimate) strength of a prestressed beam ensures that the beam is designed with an adequate factor of safety against failure.

FIGURE 11-17 Equivalent stress block for strength analysis.

The expression for the nominal bending strength of a rectangular-shaped pre-stressed beam is developed from the internal couple of an underreinforced beam at failure, as shown in Figure 11-17.

Assuming failure is initiated by the steel yielding, the magnitude of the internal couple is

$$M_n = A_{ps}f_{ps}\left(d_p - \frac{a}{2}\right)$$

where

A_{ps} = area of prestressed reinforcement in the tension zone

d_p = distance from extreme compression fiber to the centroid of the prestressed reinforcement

a = depth of stress block, determined by equating T and C and calculated from

$$a = \frac{A_{ps}f_{ps}}{0.85f_c'b}$$

f_{ps} = stress in the prestressed reinforcement at nominal strength

For members with bonded prestressing tendons and no nonprestressed tension or compression reinforcement, the value of f_{ps} can be obtained from

$$f_{ps} = f_{pu}\left(1 - \frac{\gamma_p}{\beta_1}\rho_p\frac{f_{pu}}{f_c'}\right) \qquad \text{(Mod. ACI Eq. (18-3))}$$

where

f_{pu} = ultimate tensile strength of the prestressing steel

γ_p = factor based on the type of prestressing steel: 0.40 for ordinary wire and strand when f_{py}/f_{pu} is not less than 0.85; 0.28 for low relaxation wire and strand when f_{py}/f_{pu} is not less than 0.90, where f_{py} is the specified yield stress of the prestressing tendons (psi)

ρ_p = reinforcement ratio A_{ps}/bd_p

and β_1 is as defined in Chapter 2, Section 2-6. The expression for f_{ps} is valid when $f_{se} > f_{pu}/2$, where f_{se} is the effective stress in prestressing steel after losses. Here f_{ps} represents the average stress in the prestressing steel at failure. It is analogous to f_y, but since the high-strength prestressing steels do not have a well-defined yield point, it can be predicted using ACI Equation (18-3).

Example 11-5 _____

Calculate the flexural strength ϕM_n of the prestressed beam of Example 11-4 and compare with M_u. Use $f'_c = 5000$ psi (normal-weight concrete) and seven-wire-strand grade 270 with $f_{pu} = 270{,}000$ psi (ordinary strand with $f_{py} = 0.85 f_{pu}$). Use bonded prestressing tendons and neglect all prestress losses. Therefore, for the purpose of this problem, $f_{se} = f_{pu}$. Use $A_{ps} = 1.224$ in.^{2}. The beam has no nonprestressed tension or compression steel.

Solution:

Since prestress losses are neglected, $f_{se} > f_{pu}/2$. Therefore, ACI Equation (18-3) is applicable. For the given conditions, $\gamma_p = 0.40$ and $\beta_1 = 0.80$. The reinforcement ratio is calculated from

$$\rho_p = \frac{A_{ps}}{bd_p} = \frac{1.224}{18(20)} = 0.00340$$

$$f_{ps} = f_{pu}\left(1 - \frac{\gamma_p}{\beta_1}\rho_p\frac{f_{pu}}{f'_c}\right)$$

$$= 270\left[1 - \frac{0.40}{0.80}(0.00340)\left(\frac{270}{5}\right)\right]$$

$$= 245 \text{ ksi}$$

Check the reinforcement index to verify that the beam is underreinforced and that the steel will yield. The reinforcement index is defined in the ACI Code, Section 18.8.1. Thus

$$w_p = \frac{\rho_p f_{ps}}{f'_c} \leq 0.36\beta_1$$

$$= 0.0034\frac{(245)}{5} = 0.167$$

$$0.36\beta_1 = 0.36(0.80) = 0.288$$

$$0.167 < 0.288 \qquad\qquad \text{(O.K.)}$$

Compute the nominal moment strength:

$$a = \frac{A_{ps}f_{ps}}{0.85f'_c b} = \frac{1.224(245)}{0.85(5)(18)} = 3.92 \text{ in.}$$

$$M_n = A_{ps}f_{ps}\left(d_p - \frac{a}{2}\right)$$

$$= 1.224(245)\left(20 - \frac{3.92}{2}\right)$$

$$= 5410 \text{ in.-kips}$$

$$= 451 \text{ ft-kips}$$

$$\phi M_n = 0.90(451) = 406 \text{ ft-kips}$$

Compute the factored service load moment:

$$M_u = 1.4M_{DL} + 1.7M_{LL}$$

$$= 1.4(41.0) + 1.7(156.3) = 323 \text{ ft-kips}$$

Thus, $M_u < \phi M_n$ (323 ft-kips < 406 ft-kips). Therefore, O.K.

If a prestressed beam is satisfactorily designed based on service loads and then, when checked by the strength equations, is found to have insufficient strength to resist the factored loads, nonprestressed reinforcement may be added to increase the factor of safety. In addition, the ACI Code, Section 18.8.3, requires that the total amount of reinforcement (prestressed and nonprestressed) be sufficient to develop an ultimate moment equal to at least 1.2 times the cracking moment calculated from the modulus of rupture of the concrete.

11-9

NOTES ON PRESTRESSED CONCRETE DESIGN

Since the shape and dimensions of a prestressed concrete member may be established by a trial procedure or even assumed based on physical limitations, the design may be reduced to finding the prestress force, tendon profile, and the amount of the prestress steel area. The design problem then is further reduced to an analysis-type problem whereby service load stresses are checked at various stages and the flexural strength of the member is checked against the moment due to the factored service loads.

The intent of this chapter, however, is to furnish a conceptual approach to prestressed concrete members. Therefore, many significant topics normally considered in an analysis or design problem have been omitted. These include total and practical design procedures, along with shear design, deflection, prestress loss, and end block stresses. This is not meant to imply that these items are of lesser or of no significance, but only that these topics are beyond the scope of our text. They are very adequately covered in other texts that are devoted solely to prestressed concrete (see [2] through [9]).

REFERENCES

[1]   Leonard Spiegel and George F. Limbrunner. *Applied Statics and Strength of Materials,* 2nd ed. Columbus, Ohio: Merrill/Macmillan, 1994, pp. 547–548.

[2]   T. Y. Lin and Ned H. Burns. *Design of Prestressed Concrete Structures,* 3rd ed. New York: John Wiley & Sons, Inc., 1981.

[3]   *Post-Tensioning Manual,* 5th ed. Phoenix, Ariz.: Post-Tensioning Institute 1990.

[4]   H. K. Preston. *Practical Prestressed Concrete.* New York: McGraw-Hill Book Company, 1960.

[5]   B. Bresler, ed. *Reinforced Concrete Engineering,* Vol. I. New York: John Wiley & Sons, Inc., 1974.

[6]   "Notes on ACI 318-95." Portland Cement Association, 5420 Old Orchard Road, Skokie, IL 60077-1083, 1996.

[7]   A. H. Nilson and G. Winter. *Design of Concrete Structures,* 10th ed. New York: McGraw-Hill Book Company, 1986.

[8]   M. Fintel, ed. *Handbook of Concrete Engineering,* 2nd ed. New York: Van Nostrand Reinhold, 1985.

[9]   K. Leet. *Reinforced Concrete Design.* New York: McGraw-Hill Book Company, 1982.

PROBLEMS

11-1.   The *plain concrete* beam shown having a rectangular cross section 10 in. wide and 18 in. deep is simply supported on a single span of 20 ft. Assuming no loads other than the dead load of the beam itself, find the bending stresses that exist at midspan.

11-2.   A beam identical to that of Problem 11-1 is prestressed with a force P_s of 185 kips. The tendons are located at the center of the beam. Use $A_{ps} = 1.23$ in.^{2}. Find the stresses in the beam at midspan at transfer. There is no load other than the weight of the beam. Draw complete stress diagrams.

11-3.   The tendons in the beam of Problem 11-2 are placed 11 in. below the top of the beam at midspan. Assuming that no tension is allowed, determine the maximum service uniform load that the beam can carry in addition to its own weight as governed by the stresses at midspan. Assume that $f'_{ci} = 3500$ psi and $f'_c = 5000$ psi.

11-4. Same as Problem 11-3, except that the tendons are 13 in. below the top of the beam at midspan and permissible stresses are as defined in the ACI Code, Section 18.4.

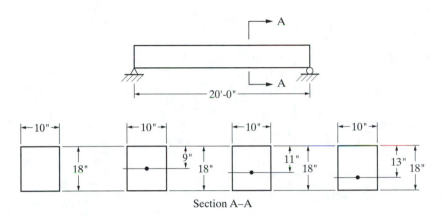

Section A–A

PROBLEMS 11-1 to 11-4

11-5. For the beam shown, calculate the outer fiber stresses at midspan and at the end supports at the following stages: (a) transfer (prestress + beam weight) and (b) under full service load. The beam is simply supported with a span length of 20 ft 0 in. and carries a superimposed live load of 2.7 kips/ft. The tendon is straight and located 9 in. below the neutral axis of the beam. The prestress force is 250 kips. Neglect prestress losses and use the gross concrete section properties. Use the method of superposition for the solution.

PROBLEM 11-5

11-6. Rework Problem 11-5 using the internal couple method.

11-7. The simply supported beam having a midspan cross section as shown is prestressed by a parabolic tendon with an effective prestress force of 233 kips. The beam has a span length of 30 ft and carries a total service load of 1.20 kips/ft, which includes the weight of the beam of 0.21 kip/ft. Calculate the outer fiber stresses at midspan under full service load. Use the gross properties of the cross section. Use the load balancing method.

PROBLEM 11-7

11-8. For the beam of Problem 11-5, calculate the outer fiber stresses at midspan for the following stages: (a) transfer and (b) under full service load. Assume the prestress tendons are parabolically draped with a midspan eccentricity of 9 in. as shown and zero eccentricity at the end supports. Neglect prestress losses and use the gross concrete section properties. The prestress force is still 250 kips. Use the load balancing method.

11-9. Calculate the flexural strength ϕM_n of the prestressed beam shown and compare it with the factored design moment M_u. The service load moments are 125 ft-kips for dead load and 383 ft-kips for live load. Use $f'_c = 5000$ psi (normal-weight concrete) and grade 270 seven-wire strand with $f_{pu} = 270,000$ psi ($f_{py} = 0.85\,f_{pu}$). The tendons are bonded. Neglect all prestress losses.

PROBLEM 11-9

CHAPTER 12

Concrete Formwork

12-1

INTRODUCTION

Forms are temporary structures whose purpose is to provide containment for the fresh concrete and to support it until it can support itself. Forms usually must be *engineered* structures since they are required to support loads composed of the fresh concrete, construction materials, equipment, workers, impact of various kinds, and sometimes wind. The forms must support all the applied loads without collapse or excessive deflection. In addition, the forms must provide for the molding of the concrete to the desired dimensions, shape, and surface finish.

The cost of formwork is significant, generally amounting to anywhere from 40% to 60% of the cost of a concrete structure. Economy in formwork design depends partly on the ingenuity and experiences of the form designer, whether a contractor or an engineer. Judgment with respect to the development of a forming system could both expedite a project and reduce costs. Although forms may be job-built (design examples are presented later in this chapter), many proprietary forming systems are available. Specialty companies will design and construct forms using patented systems. In multiple reuse situations, steel formwork has replaced wood formwork to some degree, although the use of wood is still substantial because of its availability and ease of fabrication.

Whatever the eventual type of forming may be, economy in formwork begins when the architect/engineer, during the design of the structure, examines each member and considers ease of forming and reuse of forms.

12-2

FORMWORK REQUIREMENTS

The essential requirements of good formwork may be categorized as quality, safety, and economy.

Quality in formwork requires that the forms be:

1. *Accurate:* The size, shape, position, and alignment of structural elements will depend on the accuracy with which the forms are built. The designer (engineer or architect) should specify the allowable tolerances in form dimensions for form design and construction, but not make these tolerances finer than necessary, as this could add unnecessarily to formwork cost as well as delay the project.

2. *Rigid:* Forms must be sufficiently rigid to prevent movement, bulging, or sagging during the placing of concrete. Formwork must therefore be adequately propped, braced, and tied. Special consideration may have to be given to such items as corner details and the effect of any uplift pressures.

3.   *Tight jointed:* Joints that are insufficiently tight will leak cement paste. The surface of the concrete will thus be disfigured by fins of the cement paste, and honeycombing may result adjacent to the leaking joint.

4.   *Properly finished:* The formwork in contact with the concrete should be so arranged and jointed as to produce a concrete surface of good appearance. Wires, nails, screws, and form surface flaws must not be allowed to disfigure the concrete surface. In some cases a provision of special form lining may be necessary to achieve the desired surface finish.

Safety in formwork requires that the forms be:

1.   *Strong:* To ensure the safety of the structure and the protection of the workers, it is essential that formwork be designed to carry the full load and side pressures from freshly placed concrete, together with construction traffic and any necessary equipment. On large jobs the design of formwork is usually left to a specialist, but on smaller or routine jobs it may be left to the carpenter supervisor using rule-of-thumb methods.

2.   *Sound:* The materials used to construct the forms must be of the correct size and quantity, of good quality, and sufficiently durable for the job.

Economy in formwork requires that the forms be:

1.   *Simple:* For formwork construction to be economical, it must be designed to be simple to erect and dismantle. Modular dimensions should be used.

2.   *Easily handled:* The sizes of form panels or units should be such that they are not too heavy to handle.

3.   *Standardized:* Comparative ease of assembly and the possibility of reuse will lower formwork costs when sizes are standardized.

4.   *Reusable:* Formwork intended for reuse should be designed for easy removal. If formwork panels have to be ripped down, the concrete may be damaged, materials will be wasted, time will be lost, and expense will be incurred in repairing and replacing damaged panels.

12-3

FORMWORK MATERIALS AND ACCESSORIES

Materials used for forms for concrete structures include lumber, plywood, hardboard, fiberglass, plastic and rubber liners, steel, paper and cardboard, aluminum, fiber forms, and plaster of paris. Additional materials include nails, bolts, screws, form ties, form clamps, anchors, various types of inserts, and various types of form oils and compounds as well as their accessories. Forms frequently involve the use of two or more materials, such as plywood facing attached to steel frames for wall panels.

Form *lumber* generally consists of the softwoods with the species used being the type available in the local area. Various species are usually grouped together for grading and marketing purposes. Some of these groups and their included species commonly used for formwork are:

1. Douglas fir–larch (Douglas fir, western larch)
2. Douglas fir–South (only Douglas fir from southern growth areas)
3. Hem-fir (Western hemlock, California red fir, grand fir, noble fir, white fir, Pacific silver fir)
4. Spruce-pine-fir (alpine fir, balsam fir, black spruce, Englemann spruce, jack pine, lodgepole pine, red spruce, white spruce)
5. Southern pine (loblolly pine, longleaf pine, shortleaf pine, slash pine)

Form lumber is made up of standard sizes, either rough or dressed, with the grading quality of *construction grade* or *No. 2 grade* usually specified. Shoring or falsework requiring greater capacity should be of *select structural grade* lumber. Partially seasoned wood should be used because it has been found to be the most stable. Green lumber will warp and crack, whereas kiln-dried lumber will swell excessively when it becomes wet. Boards of various thicknesses may be used for sheathing when the imprint of the boards on the concrete surface is desired for architectural reasons.

Plywood is available as flat panels (4 ft × 8 ft sheets) made of thin sheets of wood (called plies) with a total thickness ranging from ¼ in. to 1⅛ in. It is commonly used for sheathing or lining forms because it gives smooth concrete surfaces that require a minimum of hand finishing and because the relatively large sheets are economical and easy to use. U.S. plywood is built up of an odd number of plies with the grain of adjacent layers perpendicular. The plies are dried and joined under pressure with glues that make the joints as strong or stronger than the wood itself. The alternating direction of the grains of adjoining layers equalizes strains and thus minimizes shrinkage and warping of the plywood panels. Generally, the grain direction of the outer layers is parallel to the long dimension of the panel. For maximum strength, the direction of the grain in the face layers should be placed parallel to the span.

The plywood should be the exterior grade because of its waterproof glue. It should also be factory treated with a form oil or parting compound. With proper care, plywood can be reused many times.

Coated plywood is occasionally used. Called *overlaid* or *plastic coated,* it is ordinary exterior plywood with a resin-impregnated fiber facing material fused to one or both sides of the plywood sheet. The overlay covers the grain of the wood, resulting in a smoother and more durable forming surface. The resins used in overlay production are hard and resist water, chemicals, and abrasion. Two grades, high density and medium density, are available, and their difference is in the density of the surfacing material. Coated plywood is generally reused considerably more than the plain plywood form.

Nearly any exterior-type of plywood can be used for concrete forming. A special panel called *plyform* is manufactured specifically for that purpose, however. Plyform is exterior-type plywood limited to certain wood species and veneer grades to ensure high performance and is manufactured in two classes, class I and class II. Class I is the strongest, stiffest, and most widely available type. Both classes have smooth, solid surfaces and can have many reuses. They are mill-oiled unless otherwise specified. Plyform is manufactured in thicknesses ranging from $\frac{15}{32}$ in. to $1\frac{1}{8}$ in., and the most commonly used thicknesses are $\frac{5}{8}$ in. and $\frac{3}{4}$ in.

Plyform can also be manufactured with a *high-density overlaid (HDO) surface* (on one side or both sides). HDO plyform has an exceptionally smooth, hard surface for the smoothest possible concrete finishes and the maximum number of reuses. The HDO surface is a hard, semiopaque resin-fiber overlay heat-fused to panel faces. It can have as many as 200 reuses, and light oiling between pours is recommended.

Structural I plyform is stronger and stiffer than plyform class I or II and is sometimes used when the face grain must be parallel to supports and there is a heavy loading against the forms. It is also available with HDO faces.

Hardboard (fiberboard) is made up of wood particles that have been impregnated, pressed, and baked. When used as a form liner, which is generally the case, hardboard must be backed with sheathing of some kind because it does not have the strength that plywood has. Tempered hardboard, which is preferred for formwork, has been impregnated with drying oil or other material that makes the board less absorbent and improves its strength. Hardboard has limited reuse capability.

Fiberglass is a glass-fiber-reinforced plastic. It is especially suitable for repetitive production of complicated shapes, particularly precast elements. The initial cost is high, but the extensive reuse of one mold without evidence of wear contributes to economy. Suitable reinforcement and backing must be provided so that the mold will not be deformed when it is handled. Molds can be used with or without form oil. Wear of the mold surface will be slightly less if an oil is used.

Plastic and rubber form liners generally come in sheets, either flexible or rigid, and are attached to the solid form sheathing. The term *form liners* includes any sheet, plate, or layer of material attached directly to the inside face of forms to improve or alter the surface texture and quality of the finished concrete. Substances that are applied by brushing, dipping, mopping, or spraying to preserve the form material and to make form stripping easier are referred to as *form coatings*. Some of these coatings are so effective as to approximate the form liner in function. Repetitive use, a great variety of textures and patterns, and ease of stripping are among the advantages of these form liners.

Various types of rigid insulation board are used as form liners and attached to the form sheathing. The boards are generally left in place, either bonded to the concrete or held in place by form plank clips.

Steel forms have been widely used as special-purpose forms. Steel panel systems have been fabricated and used, and steel framing and bracing are important in the construction of many wood and plywood panel systems. Patented steel pans and dome components form the underside of waffle slabs and pan joists. Corrugated steel sheets serve as permanent bottom forms for decks; that is, they remain in place after the concrete has been placed. Fabricated steel form systems are extensively used in the precast and prestressed concrete industries due to their suitability of being reused extensively.

Earth as a form is used in subsurface construction where the soil is stable enough to retain the desired shape of the concrete structure. With the resulting rough surface finish, the use of earth as a form is generally limited to footings and foundations.

Fiber forms are composed of multiple layers of heavy paper bonded together and impregnated with waxes and resins to create a water-repellent cardboard. These are generally single-use, cylindrical-shape molds for columns or other applications where preformed shapes are desirable. "Sonotube" fiber forms are patented lightweight units that can be adapted to various applications.

Form accessories consist of a multitude of items necessary for form planning and construction. Types, availability, and detailed information can usually be obtained from manufacturers' catalogs as well as local concrete construction specialties distributors.

Some of the more common types of accessories are fasteners, spreaders, ties, anchors, hangers, clamps, and inserts. Typical examples of some of the many types available are shown in Figure 12-1. The most common *fastener* used is the double-headed nail, which may be withdrawn with a minimum of effort and little damage to the forms. *Spreaders* are braces that are inserted in forms to keep the faces a proper distance apart until the concrete is placed. Preferably, they are removed during or after the placement of the concrete so that they are not cast in the concrete. They may be wood blocks or proprietary metal pieces. *Ties* are tensile units adapted to holding concrete forms secure against the lateral pressure of the fresh concrete, with or without provision for spacing the forms a definite distance apart. They pass through the concrete and are fastened on each side. Various types of ties are available, many of which are patented items. *Anchors* are devices used to secure formwork to previously placed concrete of adequate strength, normally embedded in concrete during placement. There are two basic parts, the embedded anchoring device and the external fastener, which is removed after use. *Hangers* are devices used for suspending one object from another, such as the hardware attached to a building frame to support forms. *Inserts* are of many designs and are attached to the forms in such a way that they remain in the concrete when the forms are stripped. They provide for anchorage of brick or stone veneers, pipe hangers, suspended ceilings, duct work, and any building hardware or components that must be firmly attached to the concrete. *Clamps* consist of many varied devices, but serve a similar purpose to that of the tie. Beam form clamps firmly hold the beam sides and bottom together with a minimum of nailing required. Column clamps or yokes encircle

Plank Spreaders for Footing Forms

Spreader

Taper Tie

She-Bolt Tie

Beam Form Clamp

Coil Tie System

Column Form Clamp

Coil Tie Hanger

Wedge Insert

Hanger Insert

FIGURE 12-1 Typical form accessories. (Courtesy of A. H. Harris and Sons, Inc.)

PHOTO 12-1   Wall forms and bracing.

column forms and hold them together securely, withstanding the lateral pressure
of the freshly placed concrete.

12-4

LOADS AND PRESSURES ON FORMS

The concrete form is a structure. Like all structures, it must be designed and constructed with due regard to the effects of the imposed loads. A well-designed form must have adequate strength to resist failure and in addition must have sufficient stiffness so that deflection will not be excessive. Efficient and economical use of the material of which the forms are built is also an integral part of the design process.

The first consideration in the design of a form for concrete is the load to be supported. The loads may be considered in two categories, vertical loads and lateral loads, where the lateral loads may be further categorized as externally applied load (such as wind) and internally applied pressure due to the contained fresh concrete. These loads must be carried to the ground by the formwork system or resisted by in-place construction that has adequate strength for the purpose.

ACI Committee Report 347R-94, *Guide to Formwork for Concrete* [1], states:

Vertical loads consist of dead load and live load. The weight of formwork plus the weight of freshly placed concrete is dead load. The live load includes the weight of workmen, equipment, material storage, runways and impact.

Vertical loads assumed for shoring and reshoring design for multistory construction must include all loads transmitted from the floors above as dictated by the proposed construction schedule. Vertical supports and horizontal framing should be designed for a minimum live load of 50 psf of horizontal projection. When motorized carts are used the minimum live load should be 75 psf. The minimum design load for combined dead and live loads should be 100 psf, or 125 psf if motorized carts are used.

These vertical loads would be applicable for the design of the formwork for floor and roof slabs (with the exception of slabs on ground).

Lateral pressure is exerted on all nonhorizontal surfaces that contain the fresh concrete. The pressures are imposed on wall and column forms and in essence are hydraulic loadings. The amount of lateral pressure is influenced by the weight of the concrete, temperature of the concrete, vertical rate of placement, height of the form, and method of consolidation (hand spaded or mechanically vibrated). Variations in mixture, the size and shape of forms, and the amount and location of reinforcing also affect lateral pressure, but are usually neglected since their effects are small. ACI 347R-94 establishes the lateral pressure created by fresh concrete made with type I cement, weighing 150 pcf, containing no pozzolans or admixtures, having a slump 4 in. or less, and having normal internal vibration to a depth of 4 ft or less, as follows, where

p = lateral pressure (psf)

R = rate of placement (ft/hr)

T = temperature of concrete in the forms (°F)

h = height of fluid or plastic concrete above point considered (ft)

w = unit weight of fresh concrete (pcf)

1.   For columns,

$$p = 150 + \frac{9000R}{T}$$ ACI Eq. (2-2)

with a maximum of 3000 psf, a minimum of 600 psf, but in no case greater than 150h.

2.   For walls, with rate of placement less than 7 ft/hr,

$$p = 150 + \frac{9000R}{T}$$ ACI Eq. (2-2a)

with a maximum of 2000 psf, a minimum of 600 psf, but in no case greater than 150h.

3. For walls, with a rate of placement of 7 to 10 ft/hr,

$$p = 150 + \frac{43,400}{T} + \frac{2800R}{T} \qquad \text{ACI Eq. (2-3)}$$

with a maximum of 2000 psf, a minimum of 600 psf, but in no case greater than 150h.

4. Unless the conditions of items 1, 2, and 3 are met, formwork should be designed for the lateral pressure of the newly placed concrete calculated by

$$p = wh \qquad \text{ACI Eq. (2-1)}$$

For columns or other forms that may be filled rapidly before any stiffening of the concrete takes place, h should be taken as the full height of the form or the distance between construction joints when more than one placement of concrete is to be made.

5. If concrete is pumped from the base of the form, the form should be designed for full hydrostatic head of concrete wh plus a minimum allowance of 25% for pump surge pressure. Pressure may be as high as the face pressure of the pump piston.

6. Caution must be taken when using external vibration or concrete made with shrinkage-compensating or expansive cements. Pressures in excess of equivalent hydrostatic pressure may occur. Although not specified in ACI 347R-94, it is not uncommon for form designers to use a design load twice that given by the formulas in items 1, 2, and 3 when forms are vibrated externally.

Formwork should also be designed to resist all foreseeable *lateral loads,* such as seismic forces, wind, cable tensions, inclined supports, dumping of concrete, and impact due to equipment. ACI 347R-94 recommends for slabs a minimum horizontal design load of 100 lb per lineal foot of floor edge or 2% of the total dead load of the floor, whichever is greater. Wall forms exposed to the elements should be designed for a minimum wind load of 15 psf, and bracing for wall forms should be designed for a lateral load of at least 100 lb per lineal foot of wall applied at the top.

In addition, formwork should be designed for any special loads likely to occur, such as unsymmetrical placement of concrete and uplift. Form designers must be alert to provide for any and all special loading conditions.

12-5

THE DESIGN APPROACH

The design of job-built forms may be considered largely as beam and post design. The bending members usually span several supports and are therefore indeterminate. Assumptions and approximations are made that simplify the calculations and facilitate the design process.

After establishing the appropriate design loads, the sheathing and supporting members are analyzed or designed in sequence. Bending members (sheathing, joists, studs, stringers, or wales) are considered to be uniformly loaded and supported on (1) a single span, (2) two spans, or (3) three or more spans. The uniform load assumption is common practice unless the spacing of point loads exceeds one-third to one-half of the span between supports, in which case the worst loading condition is investigated.

Each bending member should be analyzed or designed for bending moment, shear, and deflection. In addition, vertical supports (shoring) and lateral bracing (if applicab!e) must be analyzed or designed for either compressive or tensile loads. Bearing stresses at supports must be investigated (except for the sheathing).

In the analysis or design of the component parts the traditional stress equations are used (see any strength of materials text). These expressions for stress are as follows.

For bending stress:

$$f_b = \frac{M}{S}$$

For shear stress:

$$f_v = \frac{1.5V}{A} \qquad \text{(for rectangular wood members)}$$

$$f_v = \frac{VQ}{Ib} \quad \text{or} \quad \frac{V}{Ib/Q} \qquad \text{(for plywood)}$$

For compression stress (both parallel and perpendicular to the grain):

$$f_{comp} = \frac{P}{A}$$

For tension stress:

$$f_{tens} = \frac{P}{A}$$

where

f_b = calculated unit stress in bending (psi)

f_v = calculated unit stress in shear (psi)

f_{comp} = calculated unit stress in compression (either parallel or perpendicular to the grain) (psi)

f_{tens} = calculated unit stress in tension (psi)

M = maximum bending moment (in.-lb)

S = section modulus (in.^{3})

P = concentrated load (lb)

V = maximum shear (lb)

A = cross-sectional area (in.^{2})

Ib/Q = rolling shear constant (in.^{2}/ft)

If we equate allowable unit stresses to the maximum unit stresses developed in a beam subjected to a uniformly distributed load w (lb/ft), expressions can be derived for the maximum allowable span length. Therefore, knowing the design loads and member section properties, a maximum allowable span length can be computed.

Table 12-1 contains expressions for maximum allowable span length as governed by moment, shear, and deflection. The reader may wish to derive these expressions from basic principles. The moment expressions are based on the maximum positive or negative moment. The maximum shear considered is the shear that exists at d distance from the support, where d is the depth of the member. Shear considerations for plywood vary from those accorded sawn lumber because of the cross-directional way in which the plies of the plywood are assembled. When plywood is loaded in flexure, the plies with the grain perpendicular to the direction of the span are the weakest aspect of the plywood with respect to shear. The wood fibers in these plies roll at stresses below the fiber shear strength parallel to the grain, hence the name *rolling shear*. For a discussion, of the properties of plywood with respect to shear, see Reference 2. Deflection of forms must be limited to minimize unsightly bulges in the resulting concrete surface. The deflection limit may be specified as a fraction of span (that is, $\ell/240$), as a limit ($\frac{1}{8}$ in.), or as the smaller of the two. The architect/engineer must decide on the deflection limits for the formwork based on bulging and sagging that can be tolerated in the surfaces of the finished structure. The casting of test panels may be warranted in some cases. Limiting deflection to $\frac{1}{360}$ of the span is acceptable in many cases where surfaces are coarse-textured and there is little reflection of light. Three design equations for deflection are given in Table 12-1. Alternatively, the designer may wish to compute the required size of the members when the design loads and span lengths are known. The same basic principles apply.

Section properties for selected thicknesses of plyform are given in Table 12-2. These section properties reflect that various species of wood used in manufacturing plywood have different stiffness and strength properties. Those species with similar properties are assigned to a species group. To simplify plywood design, the effects of using different species groups in a given panel as well as the effects of the cross-banded construction of the panel have been taken into consideration in establishing the section properties.

In calculating these section properties, all plies were transformed to properties of the face ply. As a result, the designer need not be concerned with the actual panel layup but only with the allowable stresses for the face ply and the given section properties of Table 12-2.

██████ **TABLE 12-1   Concrete Form Design Equations (To Determine Allowable Span Length)**

	One span	Two spans	Three or more spans
Bending moment	$\ell = 9.8\sqrt{\dfrac{F_bS}{w}}$	$\ell = 9.8\sqrt{\dfrac{F_bS}{w}}$	$\ell = 10.95\sqrt{\dfrac{F_bS}{w}}$
Shear	$\ell = \dfrac{16F_vA}{w} + 2d$	$\ell = \dfrac{12.8F_vA}{w} + 2d$	$\ell = \dfrac{13.3F_vA}{w} + 2d$
	$\ell^a = \dfrac{24F_v(Ib/Q)}{w} + 2d$	$\ell^a = \dfrac{19.2F_v(Ib/Q)}{w} + 2d$	$\ell^a = \dfrac{20F_v(Ib/Q)}{w} + 2d$
Deflection $\Delta_{all.} = \dfrac{\ell}{240}$	$\ell = 1.57\sqrt[3]{\dfrac{EI}{w}}$	$\ell = 2.10\sqrt[3]{\dfrac{EI}{w}}$	$\ell = 1.94\sqrt[3]{\dfrac{EI}{w}}$
Deflection $\Delta_{all.} = \dfrac{\ell}{360}$	$\ell = 1.37\sqrt[3]{\dfrac{EI}{w}}$	$\ell = 1.83\sqrt[3]{\dfrac{EI}{w}}$	$\ell = 1.69\sqrt[3]{\dfrac{EI}{w}}$
When deflection Δ (in.) is specified	$\ell = 5.51\sqrt[4]{\dfrac{\Delta EI}{w}}$	$\ell = 6.86\sqrt[4]{\dfrac{\Delta EI}{w}}$	$\ell = 6.46\sqrt[4]{\dfrac{\Delta EI}{w}}$

Notes: ℓ, span length (center to center of supports) (in.); F_b, allowable bending stress (psi); S, section modulus (in.^{3}); w, uniform load (lb/ft); F_v, allowable shear stress (psi); A, cross-sectional area (in.^{2}); d, depth of member (in.); E, modulus of elasticity (psi); I, moment of inertia (in.^{4}); Ib/Q, rolling shear constant for plywood (in.^{2}/ft); Δ, deflection (in.).

^{a}For plywood only.

The section properties of Table 12-2 are generally the minimums that can be expected. Hence the actual panel obtained in the marketplace will usually have a section property greater than that represented in the table.

The plyform design values presented in Table 12-2 are based on wet strength and 7-day load duration, so no further adjustment in these values is required except for the modulus of elasticity. The modulus shown is an adjusted value based on the assumption that shear deflection is computed separately from bending deflection. These values should be used for bending deflection calculations (which is the usual case). To calculate shear deflection, the modulus should be reduced to 1,500,000 psi for Class I and structural plyform and to 1,300,000 for Class II plyform.

Section properties for selected members of standard dressed (S4S) sawn lumber are given in Table 12-3.

Typical base design values for visually graded dimension lumber are furnished in Table 12-4. This table is simplified and brief and is primarily intended as a resource to accompany the examples and problems of this text. Those who require more detailed information with respect to section properties and design values should obtain Reference 4.

■■■■   **TABLE 12-2**   Section Properties and Design Values for Plyform

Thickness *t* (in.)	Approx. weight (psf)	Properties for stress applied parallel with face grain			Properties for stress applied perpendicular to face grain		
		Moment of inertia *I* (in.⁴/ft)	Effective section modulus *KS* (in.³/ft)	Rolling shear const. *Ib/Q* (in.²/ft)	Moment of inertia *I* (in.⁴/ft)	Effective section modulus *KS* (in.³/ft)	Rolling shear const. *Ib/Q* (in.²/ft)
Class I							
1/2	1.5	0.077	0.268	5.153	0.024	0.130	2.739
5/8	1.8	0.130	0.358	5.717	0.038	0.175	3.094
3/4	2.2	0.199	0.455	7.187	0.092	0.306	4.063
7/8	2.6	0.296	0.584	8.555	0.151	0.422	6.028
1	3.0	0.427	0.737	9.374	0.270	0.634	7.014
Class II							
1/2	1.5	0.075	0.267	4.891	0.020	0.167	2.727
5/8	1.8	0.130	0.357	5.593	0.032	0.225	3.074
3/4	2.2	0.198	0.454	6.631	0.075	0.392	4.049
7/8	2.6	0.300	0.591	7.990	0.123	0.542	5.997
1	3.0	0.421	0.754	8.614	0.220	0.812	6.987
Structural I							
1/2	1.5	0.078	0.271	4.908	0.029	0.178	2.725
5/8	1.8	0.131	0.361	5.258	0.045	0.238	3.073
3/4	2.2	0.202	0.464	6.189	0.108	0.418	4.047
7/8	2.6	0.317	0.626	7.539	0.179	0.579	5.991
1	3.0	0.479	0.827	7.978	0.321	0.870	6.981

	Design values		
	Plyform class I	Plyform class II	Structural I plyform
Modulus of elasticity (psi)	1,650,000	1,430,000	1,650,000
Bending stress (psi)	1,930	1,330	1,930
Rolling shear stress (psi)	72	72	102

Source: APA—The Engineered Wood Association [3].

Note: All properties adjusted to account for reduced effectiveness of plies with grain perpendicular to applied stress.

■■■■   **TABLE 12-3   Properties of Structural Lumber**

Nominal size (in.)	Standard dressed size (S4S) (in.)	Area of section, A (in.^{2})	Moment of inertia,[a] I (in.^{4})	Section Modulus,[a] S (in.^{3})	Weight[b] (lb/ft)
2 × 4	1½ × 3½	5.25	5.36	3.06	1.28
2 × 6	1½ × 5½	8.25	20.80	7.56	2.01
2 × 8	1½ × 7¼	10.88	47.63	13.14	2.64
2 × 10	1½ × 9¼	13.88	98.93	21.39	3.37
2 × 12	1½ × 11¼	16.88	178.0	31.64	4.10
3 × 6	2½ × 5½	13.75	34.66	12.60	3.34
3 × 8	2½ × 7¼	18.13	79.39	21.90	4.41
3 × 10	2½ × 9¼	23.13	164.9	35.65	5.62
3 × 12	2½ × 11¼	28.13	296.6	52.73	6.84
4 × 4	3½ × 3½	12.25	12.51	7.15	2.98
4 × 6	3½ × 5½	19.25	48.53	17.65	4.68
4 × 8	3½ × 7¼	25.38	111.1	30.66	6.17
4 × 10	3½ × 9¼	32.38	230.8	49.91	7.87
4 × 12	3½ × 11¼	39.38	415.3	73.83	9.57
6 × 6	5½ × 5½	30.25	76.26	27.73	7.35
6 × 8	5½ × 7½	41.25	193.4	51.56	10.03
6 × 10	5½ × 9½	52.25	393.0	82.73	12.70
6 × 12	5½ × 11½	63.25	697.1	121.2	15.37

[a]I and S are about the strong axis.
[b]Weight in lb/ft when the unit weight of wood is 35 lb/ft^3.

The base design values in Table 12-4 must be modified by applicable adjustment factors that are appropriate for the conditions under which the wood is used. Among the adjustment factors itemized in Reference 4 are

C_D = load duration factor
C_M = wet service factor
C_t = temperature factor
C_F = size factor (not applicable to southern pine)
C_{fu} = flat use factor
C_r = repetitive member factor
C_L = beam stability factor
C_P = column stability factor
C_H = shear stress factor
C_b = bearing area factor

■■■■ **TABLE 12-4** **Base Design Values for Visually Graded Dimension Lumber (Normal Load Duration and Dry Service Condition)**

No. 2 grade (2″–4″ thick, 2″ and wider)

Species	Design values (psi)					
	F_b	F_t	F_v	$F_{c\perp}$	F_c	E
Douglas fir-larch	875	575	95	625	1300	1,600,000
Douglas fir–south	825	525	90	520	1300	1,200,000
hem-fir	850	500	75	405	1250	1,300,000
Spruce-pine-fir	875	425	70	425	1100	1,400,000

Construction grade (2″–4″ thick, 2″–4″ wide)

Species	Design values (psi)					
	F_b	F_t	F_v	$F_{c\perp}$	F_c	E
Douglas fir-larch	1000	650	95	625	1600	1,500,000
Douglas fir–south	925	600	90	520	1550	1,200,000
hem-fir	975	575	75	405	1500	1,300,000
Spruce-pine-fir	975	475	70	425	1350	1,300,000

Southern pine (2″–4″ thick)

No. 2 grade	Design values (psi)					
	F_b	F_t	F_v	$F_{c\perp}$	F_c	E
2″–4″ wide	1500	825	90	565	1650	1,600,000
5″–6″ wide	1250	725	90	565	1600	1,600,000
8″ wide	1200	650	90	565	1550	1,600,000
10″ wide	1050	575	90	565	1500	1,600,000
12″ wide	975	550	90	565	1450	1,600,000
Construction grade 4″ wide	1100	625	100	565	1800	1,500,000

Adjustment factors	F_b	F_t	F_v	$F_{c\perp}$	F_c	E
Load duration C_D[a]	1.25	1.25	1.25	—	1.25	—
Wet service C_M	0.85	1.0	0.97	0.67	0.80	0.90

Source: Courtesy of American Forest & Paper Association, Washington, D.C. [4]

[a] Values shown are typical for forming applications.

The product of the base design value (F_b for moment or F_v for shear) and any applicable adjustment factors provides an allowable unit stress for use in the design and analysis of wood members. The allowable unit stress is denoted as a primed value (e.g., F_b'), which indicates that it is an adjusted design value calculated for specific conditions. For instance, for allowable shear stress,

$$F'_v = F_v C_D C_M C_t C_H$$

If no adjustment factors apply, then the allowable unit stress will be equal to the tabulated base design value (e.g., $F'_v = F_v$). One required value that is not an allowable stress is modulus of elasticity E. It will be determined in a similar fashion as the product of a base design value and applicable adjustment factors.

Determination of Allowable Bending Stress F'_b

Applicable adjustment factors for allowable bending stress are load duration, wet service, temperature, size, flat use, repetitive member, and beam stability.

The load duration factor C_D for 7 days or less duration of load (common for form design) is given in Table 12-4.

The wet service factor C_M is applicable when the moisture content of the wood is more than 19% (which would occur in a wet service situation such as when the wood is in contact with fresh concrete) and the wood is at ordinary temperature. Table 12-4 shows C_M factors.

The temperature factor C_t is generally not applicable in form design and may be disregarded.

The size factor C_F is based on member size and is shown in Table 12-5. Construction-grade material allowable stresses are not adjusted for the size of the member. Southern pine base design values shown in Table 12-4 have size adjustments already included. The size factor C_F applies only to visually graded sawn lumber members.

The flat use factor C_{fu} is also shown in Table 12-5 and is applicable when dimension lumber 2 in. to 4 in. thick is loaded on the wide face.

The repetitive member factor C_r applies only to F_b and to members 2 in. to 4 in. thick. ACI Committee 347, however, recommends against application of C_r for cases where base stresses have already been increased the 25% permitted for short-duration loads [5].

■■■■■ **TABLE 12-5 Size and Flat Use Factors for Bending Stress F_b**

Width of lumber	Size factor C_F [a]		Flat use factor C_{fu} [b]	
	2″–3″ thick	4″ thick	2″–3″ thick	4″ thick
2″–3″	1.5	1.5	1.0	—
4″	1.5	1.5	1.1	1.0
5″	1.4	1.4	1.1	1.05
6″	1.3	1.3	1.15	1.05
8″	1.2	1.3	1.15	1.05
10″	1.1	1.2	1.2	1.1
12″	1.0	1.1	1.2	1.1

Source: Courtesy of American Forest & Paper Association, Washington, D.C. [4].

[a] Applicable to No. 2 grade.

[b] Applicable to No. 2 grade and construction grade.

The beam stability factor C_L is essentially a reduction factor for F_b where insufficient lateral restraint is furnished for the bending member. Since formwork assemblies are usually designed to meet lateral support criteria as prescribed by the "National Design Specification for Wood Construction" [4], the use of C_L is generally not applicable. For the purpose of this text, all form bending-members are assumed to have adequate lateral support.

Determination of Allowable Shear Stress F_v'

Applicable adjustment factors for allowable shear stress are wet service, load duration, temperature, and shear stress.

The wet service factor C_M and the load duration factor C_D are furnished in Table 12-4. The temperature factor is generally not applicable in form design.

The shear stress factor C_H is a function of wood imperfections. Conservative practice suggests that $C_H = 1.0$ be used whenever there is no information on splits, checks, and shakes for the lumber in question [5]. For the examples and problems of this chapter, the value of C_H will be taken as 1.0.

Determination of Allowable Stress for Compression Perpendicular to the Grain $F_{c\perp}'$

Applicable adjustment factors for allowable stress perpendicular to the grain are wet service, temperature, and bearing area. Note that the stress increase for short-term loading does not apply to $F_{c\perp}$.

The wet service factor C_M is furnished in Table 12-4. Again, the temperature factor is generally not applicable in form design.

The bearing area factor C_b is applicable where the bearing length is less than 6 in. long and at least 3 in. from the end of the member. It may be calculated from

$$C_b = \frac{\ell_b + 0.375}{\ell_b}$$

where ℓ_b is the length of the bearing (in.) measured parallel to the grain. For bearing at the end of a member and lengths of bearing equal to 6 in. or more, use $C_b = 1.0$. Note that C_b will never be less than 1.0. Therefore, it is conservative to omit it.

Determination of Modulus of Elasticity E'

The only applicable adjustment factor for modulus of elasticity in form design is the wet service C_M. It is shown in Table 12-4.

12-6

DESIGN OF FORMWORK FOR SLABS

Figure 12-2 shows a typical structural system for job-built forms for elevated slabs. The sequence of design is first to consider a strip of sheathing of the specified thickness and 12 in. in width. The maximum allowable span may then be determined based on the allowable values of bending stress, shear stress, and deflection for the sheathing. The lower of the computed values will determine the maximum spacing of the joists. This span value, usually rounded down to some lower modular value, becomes the spacing of the joists.

FIGURE 12-2   Typical job-built form for elevated slab.

Based on the joist spacing used, the joist itself is analyzed to determine its maximum allowable span. Each joist must support the load from the sheathing halfway over to the adjacent joist on either side. Therefore, the *width* of the load area carried by the joist is equal to the spacing of the joists. The joist span selected becomes the spacing of the stringers. Again, a modular value is selected for stringer spacing.

Based on the selected stringer spacing, the process is repeated to determine the maximum stringer span (distance between vertical supports or shores). Notice in the design of the stringers that the joist loads are actually applied to the stringer as a series of concentrated loads at the points where the joists rest on the stringer. It is simpler and sufficiently accurate to treat the load on the stringer as a uniformly distributed load, however. Again, the width of the uniform design load applied to the stringer is equal to the stringer spacing. The calculated stringer span must next be checked against the capacity of the shores used to support the stringers. The load on each shore is equal to the shore spacing multiplied by the load per foot of stringer. Thus the maximum shore spacing (or stringer span) is limited to the lower span length as governed by stringer strength or shore strength. In addition, it is necessary to check the bearing at the point where each joist rests on the stringer. This

TABLE 12-6 Effective Length Factor K_e

Buckling modes						
Theoretical K_e value	0.5	0.7	1.0	1.0	2.0	2.0
Recommended design K_e when ideal conditions approximated	0.65	0.80	1.2	1.0	2.10	2.4

End condition code	Rotation fixed, translation fixed
	Rotation free, translation fixed
	Rotation fixed, translation free
	Rotation free, translation free

Source: Courtesy of American Forest & Paper Association, Washington, D.C. [4].

is done by dividing the load at this point by the bearing area and comparing the resulting stress with the allowable unit stress in compression *perpendicular* to the grain. A similar procedure is applied at the point where each stringer rests on a vertical support.

The stringer shown in Figure 12-2 is supported by solid, rectangular wood shores that are columns (which we will assume are axially loaded). As with all axially loaded columns, the allowable load is a function of the slenderness ratio ℓ/d, the ratio of the unbraced length of the member to its least lateral dimension (not to exceed 50).

The slenderness ratio ℓ/d is further modified and expressed as ℓ_e/d, where ℓ_e represents an effective unbraced column length and is defined as

$$\ell_e = K_e\ell$$

where K_e is an effective length factor based on column end conditions that affect rotation and translation. Factor K_e can be obtained from Table 12-6.

The following design approach applies for the determination of the allowable stress for compression parallel to the grain for simple, solid-sawn lumber columns, as recommended in Reference 4.

Determination of Allowable Stress for Compression Parallel to the Grain F_c'

Applicable adjustment factors for allowable stress for compression parallel to the grain are load duration, wet service, temperature, size, and column stability. This may be expressed as

$$F_c' = F_c C_D C_M C_t C_F C_P$$

where

F_c = base design value for compression parallel to the grain (psi)

C_P = column stability factor

and all other quantities have been previously defined. This allowable stress is applicable to all values of slenderness ratio (≤ 50) and replaces the previously used short-, intermediate-, and long-column equations of earlier design specifications. Note that although the slenderness ratio ℓ_e/d for solid columns shall not exceed 50, during construction this limit is increased to 75.

Since wood shores (columns) are generally reused repeatedly, ACI Committee 347 does not recommend the use of any adjustment factor that provides increased stresses for short load duration [5]. In addition, temperature and wet service adjustments for wood shores are generally not required or considered. Therefore, only the column size factor and the column stability factor are normally considered in shore design.

The size factor C_F for compression parallel to the grain for the two grades indicated can be taken from Table 12-7.

■■■■ **Table 12-7   Size Factor C_F for Compression Parallel
to the Grain**

Width of lumber	Size factor C_F	
	No. 2 grade	Const. grade
2"–4"	1.15	1.0
5"	1.10	—
6"	1.10	—
8"	1.05	—
10"	1.0	—

Source: Courtesy of American Forest & Paper Association,
Washington, D.C. [4].

The column stability factor C_P is a function of the effective slenderness ratio ℓ_e/d of the shore, the adjusted modulus of elasticity E', and the adjusted base value of compression parallel to the grain before C_P is applied.

The unadjusted modulus of elasticity is normally used for wood shore design since shores are rarely in the wet service condition. Therefore, $E' = E$.

The column stability factor C_P for solid-sawn lumber can be calculated from Equation 3.7-1 in Reference 4. For convenience, this equation is modified and written as

$$C_P = \frac{1+\alpha}{1.6} - \sqrt{\left(\frac{1+\alpha}{1.6}\right)^2 - \frac{\alpha}{0.8}}$$

where

$$\alpha = \frac{0.3E'}{\left(\frac{\ell_e}{d}\right)^2 F_c^*}$$

and F_c^* is the adjusted base value of compression stress parallel to the grain before application of C_P.

Various tables are available to simplify the design approach and to expedite the selection of the formwork structural members [5]. These should be used with caution because of job-specific conditions and possible tabular limitations.

Example 12-1 _____

Design the formwork for a 6 in. structural concrete floor slab. The floor system is of the type shown in Figure 12-2. Use ¾ in. class I plyform for the sheathing and No. 2 Douglas fir–larch for the rest of the lumber. The maximum deflection for the sheathing may be taken as ¹⁄₂₄₀ of the span. The maximum deflection for other bending members is taken as ¹⁄₃₆₀ of the span. Based on end conditions, the effective unbraced length of the shores may be taken as 10 ft. The following conditions for design have been established:

1.   Joists and stringers will be designed based on adequate lateral support.
2.   Joists, stringers, and shores are used under dry service conditions.

Solution:

1.   *Sheathing design* (find the joist spacing): Consider a 12-in.-wide strip of sheathing perpendicular to the supporting joists. The sheathing acts as a beam and is continuous over three or more supports. Determine the maximum allowable span for the sheathing. This becomes the maximum spacing for the joists (which support the sheathing).

   a.   The design values for ¾ in. Class I plyform (see Table 12-2) are

$$E = 1,650,000 \text{ psi} \quad \text{(modulus of elasticity)}$$

$$F_b = 1930 \text{ psi} \quad \text{(bending stress)}$$

$$F_v = 72 \text{ psi} \quad \text{(rolling shear stress)}$$

   The plyform properties with face grain parallel to span (perpendicular to the joists) are

$$I = 0.199 \text{ in.}^4/\text{ft}$$

$$S = 0.455 \text{ in.}^3/\text{ft}$$

$$Ib/Q = 7.187 \text{ in.}^2/\text{ft} \quad \text{(rolling shear constant)}$$

$$w_s = 2.2 \text{ psf (weight of sheathing; for a 12 in.}$$
$$\text{strip, this will be lb/ft)}$$

   b.   The loading on the sheathing is

DL (slab): (6/12)(150)	= 75 psf
LL (min.):	= 50 psf
Neglect sheathing weight	_____
	125 psf = w

   c.   The maximum joist spacing based on bending moment formula (from Table 12-1) is

$$\ell = 10.95 \sqrt{\frac{F_b S}{w}}$$

$$= 10.95 \sqrt{\frac{1930(0.455)}{125}} = 29 \text{ in.}$$

d.   The maximum joist spacing based on shear is

$$\ell = \frac{20F_v(Ib/Q)}{w} + 2d$$

$$= \frac{20(72)(7.187)}{125} + 2(0.75) = 84.3 \text{ in.}$$

e.   The maximum joist spacing based on deflection (maximum deflection is $\frac{1}{240}$ of the span) is

$$\ell = 1.94 \sqrt[3]{\frac{EI}{w}}$$

$$= 1.94 \sqrt[3]{\frac{1,650,000(0.199)}{125}}$$

$$= 26.8 \text{ in.}$$

Deflection controls. The maximum spacing of supporting joists should not exceed 26.8 in. Use joists at 24 in. o.c.

2.   *Joist design* (find the stringer spacing): Assume 2×8 (S4S) joists and a 7-day maximum duration of load. Consider the joists as uniformly loaded beams continuous over three or more spans (the supports are the stringers).

a.   Obtain allowable stresses using base design values from Table 12-4 and appropriate adjustment factors.

(1)   Bending: $F_b = 875$ psi. Adjustment factors:

(a)   Load duration factor from Table 12-4: $C_D = 1.25$.

(b)   Size factor from Table 12-5: $C_F = 1.2$.

Therefore,

$$F_b' = F_b C_D C_F$$

$$= 875(1.25)(1.2) = 1313 \text{ psi}$$

(2)   Shear: $F_v = 95$ psi. Adjustment factor:

(a)   Load duration factor from Table 12-4: $C_D = 1.25$.

Therefore,

$$F_v' = F_v C_D = 95(1.25) = 118.8 \text{ psi}$$

(3)   Modulus of elasticity: $E = 1,600,000$ psi. No adjustment factors apply. Thus

$$E' = E = 1,600,000 \text{ psi}$$

Properties for the 2×8 (S4S) from Table 12-3 are

$$S = 13.14 \text{ in.}^3$$

$$I = 47.63 \text{ in.}^4$$

$$A = 10.88 \text{ in.}^2$$

b.   Loading: Since joists support a 2 ft width of sheathing, the loading on the joist is

$$w = 125 \text{ psf } (2) = 250 \text{ lb/ft}$$

Assume the weight of the sheathing and joists to be 5 psf. Then

$$w = 250 + 5(2) = 260 \text{ lb/ft}$$

c.   The maximum stringer spacing based on bending moment is

$$\ell = 10.95 \sqrt{\frac{F'_b S}{w}}$$

$$= 10.95 \sqrt{\frac{1313(13.14)}{260}} = 89.2 \text{ in.}$$

d.   The maximum stringer spacing based on shear is

$$\ell = \frac{13.3 F'_v A}{w} + 2d$$

$$= \frac{13.3(118.8)(10.88)}{260} + 2(7.25)$$

$$= 80.6 \text{ in.}$$

e.   The maximum stringer spacing based on deflection (maximum deflection is $\frac{1}{360}$ of the span) is

$$\ell = 1.69 \sqrt[3]{\frac{E'I}{w}}$$

$$= 1.69 \sqrt[3]{\frac{1,600,000(47.63)}{260}}$$

$$= 112.3 \text{ in.}$$

Shear governs. Therefore, the maximum spacing of supporting stringers cannot exceed 80.6 in. Use a stringer spacing of 6 ft 6 in. (78 in.).

3.   *Stringer design* (find the shore spacing): Use 4 in. × 8 in. (S4S) stringers and a 7-day maximum duration of load. Consider the stringers to be uniformly loaded beams continuous over three or more supports. The supports are the shores. The loads from the joists are concentrated loads, but for simplicity, we will assume a uniformly distributed load.

a.   Obtain allowable stresses using base design values from Table 12-4 and appropriate adjustment factors.

(1)   Bending: $F_b = 875$ psi. Adjustment factors:

(a)   Load duration factor from Table 12-4: $C_D = 1.25$.

(b)   Size factor from Table 12-5: $C_F = 1.3$.

Therefore,

$$F'_b = F_b C_D C_F$$

$$= 875(1.25)(1.3) = 1422 \text{ psi}$$

(2)   Shear: $F_v = 95$ psi. Adjustment factor:
    (a)   Load duration factor from Table 12-4: $C_D = 1.25$.
    Therefore,

$$F'_v = F_v C_D = 95(1.25) = 118.8 \text{ psi}$$

(3)   Modulus of elasticity: $E = 1{,}600{,}000$ psi. No adjustment factors apply. Thus

$$E' = E = 1{,}600{,}000 \text{ psi}$$

Properties for the 4×8 (S4S) from Table 12-3 are

$$S = 30.66 \text{ in.}^3$$

$$I = 111.1 \text{ in.}^4$$

$$A = 25.38 \text{ in.}^2$$

b.   Loading: Each stringer supports a 6 ft 6 in.–wide strip of design load. Assuming a formwork weight of 5 psf, the uniformly distributed load on a stringer is calculated from

$$w = 6.5(125 + 5) = 845 \text{ lb/ft}$$

c.   The maximum shore spacing based on bending (of the stringers) is

$$\ell = 10.95 \sqrt{\frac{F'_b S}{w}}$$

$$= 10.95 \sqrt{\frac{1422(30.66)}{845}} = 78.7 \text{ in.}$$

d.   The maximum shore spacing based on shear is

$$\ell = \frac{13.3 F'_v A}{w} + 2d$$

$$= \frac{13.3(118.8)(25.38)}{845} + 2(7.25) = 62.0 \text{ in.}$$

e.   The maximum shore spacing based on deflection is

$$\ell = 1.69 \sqrt[3]{\frac{EI}{w}}$$

$$= 1.69 \sqrt[3]{\frac{1{,}600{,}000(111.1)}{845}} = 100.5 \text{ in.}$$

Shear governs. Therefore, the maximum spacing of supporting shores cannot exceed 62.0 in. Use a shore spacing of 5 ft 0 in. (60.0 in.).

4.   *Design of shores:* The stringers are spaced at 6 ft 6 in. on center and are supported by shores at 5 ft 0 in. on center. Therefore, each shore must support a floor area of

$$6.5(5.0) = 32.5 \text{ ft}^2$$

Again, assuming formwork weight of 5 psf, the load per shore is calculated as

$$32.5(125 + 5) = 4225 \text{ lb}$$

Although commercial shores are usually readily available to support this load, we will design 4 × 4 wood shores. The effective unbraced length of the shore ℓ_e is 10 ft 0 in. in each direction. The capacity of the 4 × 4 (S4S) shore is calculated using the recommendations of Reference 4, as discussed previously.

a.   The base design value for compression parallel to the grain from Table 12-4 is $F_c = 1300$ psi.

b.   Adjustment factors:

(1)   Size factor from Table 12-7: $C_F = 1.15$.

(2)   For the column stability factor C_P, initially the following items must be established:

(a)   For modulus of elasticity, there is no adjustment factor:

$$E' = E = 1,600,000 \text{ psi}$$

(b)   Find F_c^*:

$$F_c^* = F_c C_F = 1300(1.15) = 1495 \text{ psi}$$

(c) $$\frac{\ell_e}{d} = \frac{10(12)}{3.5} = 34.3 < 50 \qquad \text{(O.K.)}$$

(d)   Solve for α:

$$\alpha = \frac{0.3E'}{\left(\dfrac{\ell_e}{d}\right)^2 F_c^*}$$

$$= \frac{0.3(1,600,000)}{34.3^2(1495)}$$

$$= 0.273$$

Solve for C_P:

$$C_P = \frac{1+\alpha}{1.6} - \sqrt{\left(\frac{1+\alpha}{1.6}\right)^2 - \frac{\alpha}{0.8}}$$

$$= \frac{1+0.273}{1.6} - \sqrt{\left(\frac{1+0.273}{1.6}\right)^2 - \frac{0.273}{0.8}}$$

$$= 0.255$$

c.   Compute the allowable stress F'_c:

$$F'_c = F_c C_F C_P = 1300(1.15)(0.255) = 381 \text{ psi}$$

Therefore, the allowable load is

$$P = F'_c A = 381(3.5)^2 = 4667 \text{ lb}$$

$$4667 \text{ lb} > 4225 \text{ lb} \qquad\qquad\qquad\qquad \text{(O.K.)}$$

Use 4×4 (S4S) shores.

5.   *Bearing stresses:*

a.   Where stringers bear on shores (4×8 stringers on 4×4 shores),

$$\text{contact area} = 3.5(3.5) = 12.25 \text{ in.}^2$$

$$\text{total load on shore} = 4225 \text{ lb}$$

The actual bearing stress perpendicular to grain of stringer is

$$\frac{4225}{12.25} = 345 \text{ psi}$$

Determine the allowable bearing stress perpendicular to the grain of the stringer. From Table 12-4, $F_{c\perp} = 625$ psi. The adjustment factor applicable in this case is C_b, since the length of bearing ℓ_b is 4 in.:

$$C_b = \frac{\ell_b + 0.375}{\ell_b} = \frac{4.375}{4} = 1.094$$

Therefore,

$$F'_{c\perp} = 625(1.094) = 684 \text{ psi}$$

$$345 \text{ psi} < 684 \text{ psi} \qquad\qquad\qquad\qquad \text{(O.K.)}$$

b.   Where joists bear on stringers (2×8 joists on 4×8 stringers),

$$\text{contact area} = 1.5(3.5) = 5.25 \text{ in.}^2$$

Recalling from the design of the joists that the loading on each joist was 260 lb/ft, the load on the stringer from each joist is

$$260(6.5) = 1690 \text{ lb}$$

The actual bearing stress perpendicular to the grain is

$$\frac{1690}{5.25} = 322 \text{ psi}$$

Determine the allowable bearing stress perpendicular to the grain. Since the actual bearing stress is low relative to the 625 psi base design value for $F'_{c\perp}$, the increase in $F'_{c\perp}$ due to C_b may be disregarded. Thus

$$322 \text{ psi} < 625 \text{ psi} \qquad\qquad \text{(O.K.)}$$

6. *Lateral bracing:* For floor systems, the minimum load to be used in designing lateral bracing is the greater of 100 lb per lineal foot of floor edge or 2% of the total dead load of the floor. We will assume the slab to be 80 ft × 100 ft and placed in one operation. Guy wire bracing capable of carrying a load of 4000 lb each will be used on all four sides of the slab area attached at slab elevation and making a 45° angle with the ground. Guy wires can resist only tensile forces.

   Calculating lateral load H as 2% of the dead load of the floor, again assuming the formwork to be 5 psf, yields

$$H = 0.02(75 + 5)(80)(100) = 12,800 \text{ lb}$$

Distributing this load along the long side yields

$$\frac{12,800}{100} = 128 \text{ lb/ft} > 100 \text{ lb/ft}$$

and along the short side yields

$$\frac{12,800}{80} = 160 \text{ lb/ft} > 100 \text{ lb/ft}$$

These results are shown in Figure 12-3a. For determination of the guy wire spacing, the 160 lb/ft lateral load will be used. From Figure 12-3b,

Plan View

(a)

Guy Wire Diagram

(b)

FIGURE 12-3   Floor slab lateral bracing design.

the tension in the guy wire T is calculated as

$$\frac{T}{1.414} = \frac{160}{1}$$

$$T = 226.2 \text{ lb per ft of slab being braced}$$

The maximum spacing for the guy wires is

$$\frac{4000}{226.2} = 17.7 \text{ ft}$$

Use guy wires spaced at 15 ft (max.) on center on all sides.

12-7

DESIGN OF FORMWORK FOR BEAMS

Figure 12-4 shows one of several common types of beam forms. The usual design procedure involves consideration of the vertical loads, with the following components to be designed: the beam bottom, the ledger that supports joists, and the supporting shores. Bearing stresses must also be checked.

FIGURE 12-4 Typical beam formwork.

For the deeper beams (24 in. and more), consideration should also be given to the lateral pressure produced by the fresh concrete, which must be resisted by the beam sides. The beam sides would be designed in much the same way as the sheathing in a wall form. Also of importance in Figure 12-4 are the *kickers*, which hold the beam sides in place against the pressure of the concrete, and *blocking*, which serves to transmit the slab load from the ledgers to the T-head shores.

Beam bottoms (or soffits) are usually made to the exact width of the beam. They may be composed of one or more 2 in. planks, or they may be of plywood backed by 2 × 4s. In the following example, the soffit is made of a 2 × 12, which is finished on two sides (S2S), giving it final dimensions of 1½ in. × 12 in.

Example 12-2

Design forms to support the 12 in. × 20 in. beam shown in Figure 12-5. The beam is to support a 4-in.-thick reinforced concrete slab. Use Douglas fir–larch No. 2 grade. The maximum allowable deflection is to be $\frac{1}{360}$ of the span for bending members. The unsupported shore height will be based on an assumed floor-to-floor height of 10 ft, from which the depth of the beam will be subtracted. All bending members are to be designed based on adequate lateral support.

Solution:

1. *Beam bottom design* (compute the maximum spacing between shores): Assume a 7-day maximum duration of load. Assume the plank to be continuous over three or more supports.

    a. Obtain allowable stresses using base design values from Table 12-4 and appropriate adjustment factors from Tables 12-4 and 12-5.

        (1) Bending: F_b = 875 psi. Adjustment factors: C_D = 1.25, C_M = 0.85, and C_{fu} = 1.2. Therefore,

        $$F_b' = F_b C_D C_M C_{fu}$$

        $$= 875(1.25)(0.85)(1.2) = 1116 \text{ psi}$$

        (2) Shear: F_v = 95 psi. Adjustment factors: C_D = 1.25 and C_M = 0.97. Therefore,

        $$F_v' = F_v C_D C_M = 95(1.25)(0.97) = 115.2 \text{ psi}$$

        (3) Modulus of elasticity: E = 1,600,000 psi. Adjustment factor: C_M = 0.9. Therefore,

        $$E' = E C_M = 1,600,000(0.9) = 1,440,000 \text{ psi}$$

        Properties for the 2 × 12 (S2S) are

        $$S = \frac{bh^2}{6} = \frac{12(1.5)^2}{6} = 4.5 \text{ in.}^3$$

Typical Beam Forms

(a)

Alternate Beam Bottom

(b)

FIGURE 12-5   Beam form design.

$$I = \frac{bh^2}{12} = \frac{12(1.5)^3}{12} = 3.38 \text{ in.}^4$$

b.   The loading on the beam soffit is calculated as:

DL (reinforced concrete beam): $\frac{12(20)}{144}(150) = 250 \text{ lb/ft}$

LL (use 50 psf): $\frac{12}{12}(50) = 50 \text{ lb/ft}$

total load = 250 + 50 = 300 lb/ft

c.   The maximum shore spacing based on bending is

$$\ell = 10.95 \sqrt{\frac{F_b' S}{w}}$$

$$= 10.95 \sqrt{\frac{1116(4.5)}{300}}$$

$$= 44.8 \text{ in.}$$

d.   The maximum shore spacing based on shear is

$$\ell = \frac{13.3 F_v' A}{w} + 2d$$

$$= \frac{13.3(115.2)(12)(1.5)}{300} + 2(1.5)$$

$$= 94.9 \text{ in}$$

e.   The maximum shore spacing based on deflection is

$$\ell = 1.69 \sqrt[3]{\frac{E'I}{w}}$$

$$= 1.69 \sqrt[3]{\frac{1,440,000(3.38)}{300}}$$

$$= 42.8 \text{ in.}$$

Deflection governs. Try shore spacing at 42 in. o.c.

2.   *Ledger design:* Use ¾ in. plyform sheathing (vertically) for the beam sides and 2 × 4 kickers as shown. The ledger is supported at each shore by a blocking piece. Since the shores are to be 42 in. o.c., the ledger will be continuous over three or more spans. Use 2 × 4s (S4S) for the ledger as shown. Compute the required spacing for the ledger supports and compare with the 42 in. spacing previously determined. Neglect the connection of the ledger to the vertical sheathing.

   a.   Obtain allowable stresses using base design values from Table 12-4 and appropriate adjustment factors from Tables 12-4 and 12-5.

   (1)   Bending: F_b = 875 psi. Adjustment factors: C_D = 1.25 and C_F = 1.5. Therefore,

$$F_b' = F_b C_D C_F$$

$$= 875(1.25)(1.5) = 1641 \text{ psi}$$

   (2)   Shear: F_v = 95 psi. Adjustment factor: C_D = 1.25. Therefore,

$$F_v' = F_v C_D = 95(1.25) = 118.8 \text{ psi}$$

   (3)   Modulus of elasticity: E = 1,600,000 psi. No adjustment factors apply. Thus

$$E' = E = 1,600,000 \text{ psi}$$

Properties for the 2×4 (S4S) from Table 12-3 are

$$A = 5.25 \text{ in.}^2$$

$$I = 5.36 \text{ in.}^4$$

$$S = 3.06 \text{ in.}^3$$

b. Loading: The 2×4 joists are supported by the ledger, as shown in Figure 12-5. Although the ledger is loaded with point loads, a uniform load will be assumed for simplicity. The loading on the slab sheathing is

$$\text{DL (slab): } \left(\frac{4}{12}\right)(150) = \quad 50 \text{ psf}$$

$$\text{LL (min.)} = \quad 50 \text{ psf}$$

$$\text{assume sheathing weight} = \quad \underline{5 \text{ psf}}$$

$$105 \text{ psf}$$

Since the span of the joists from the ledger to the adjacent stringer is 4 ft 0 in., the load to the ledger is calculated as

$$w = \tfrac{1}{2}(4)(105) = 210 \text{ lb/ft}$$

c. The maximum blocking spacing based on bending is

$$\ell = 10.95 \sqrt{\frac{F_b'S}{w}}$$

$$= 10.95 \sqrt{\frac{1641(3.06)}{210}}$$

$$= 53.5 \text{ in.}$$

d. The maximum blocking spacing based on shear is

$$\ell = \frac{13.3F_v'A}{w} + 2d$$

$$= \frac{13.3(118.8)(5.25)}{210} + 2(3.5)$$

$$= 46.5 \text{ in.}$$

e. The maximum blocking spacing based on deflection is

$$\ell = 1.69 \sqrt[3]{\frac{E'I}{w}}$$

$$= 1.69 \sqrt[3]{\frac{1{,}600{,}000(5.36)}{210}}$$

$$= 58.2 \text{ in.}$$

Since all the three foregoing spacings *exceed* 42 in., the 2 × 4 ledgers supported by blocking at 42 in. on center are satisfactory.

3. *Design of the shores:* The shores are spaced 42 in. (or 3.5 ft) on center, and each must support a loading of

$$\text{from beam bottom: } 300(3.5) = 1050 \text{ lb}$$

$$\text{from slab forms (two sides): } 210(3.5)(2) = 1470 \text{ lb}$$

$$\text{total load per shore} = 1050 + 1470 = 2520 \text{ lb}$$

Assume 4 × 4 (S4S) wood shores. The unsupported shore height will be based on an assumed floor-to-floor height of 10 ft 0 in., from which the depth of the beam will be subtracted. The unsupported height is

$$\ell = 10(12) - 20 = 100 \text{ in.} = 8.33 \text{ ft}$$

We will assume the shores are pin-connected. From Table 12-6, $K_e = 1.0$. Therefore, the effective unbraced length is

$$\ell_e = K_e\ell = 1.0(8.33) = 8.33 \text{ ft}$$

a. The base design value for compression parallel to the grain from Table 12-4 is $F_c = 1300$ psi.

b. Adjustment factors:

(1) Size factor from Table 12-7: $C_F = 1.15$.

(2) For the column stability factor C_P, initially the following items must be established:

(a) For modulus of elasticity, there is no adjustment factor:

$$E' = E = 1{,}600{,}00 \text{ psi}$$

(b) Find F_c^*:

$$F_c^* = F_cC_F = 1300(1.15) = 1495 \text{ psi}$$

(c) $\qquad\qquad \dfrac{\ell_e}{d} = \dfrac{8.33(12)}{3.5} = 28.6 < 50 \qquad\qquad \text{(O.K.)}$

(d) Solve for α:

$$\alpha = \frac{0.3E'}{\left(\dfrac{\ell_e}{d}\right)^2 F_c^*}$$

$$= \frac{0.3(1,600,000)}{28.6^2(1495)}$$

$$= 0.393$$

Solve for C_P:

$$C_P = \frac{1+\alpha}{1.6} - \sqrt{\left(\frac{1+\alpha}{1.6}\right)^2 - \frac{\alpha}{0.8}}$$

$$= \frac{1+0.393}{1.6} - \sqrt{\left(\frac{1+0.393}{1.6}\right)^2 - \frac{0.393}{0.8}}$$

$$= 0.354$$

c.   Compute the allowable stress F_c':

$$F_c' = F_c C_F C_P = 1300(1.15)(0.354) = 529 \text{ psi}$$

Therefore, the allowable load is

$$P = F_c' A = 529(3.5)^2 = 6480 \text{ lb}$$

$$6480 \text{ lb} > 2520 \text{ lb} \hspace{4cm} \text{(O.K.)}$$

Use 4×4 (S4S) shores spaced 42 in. on center.

4.   *Bearing stresses:*

a.   Assume 4×4 (S4S) T-heads on the 4×4 (S4S) shores. Actual bearing stress perpendicular to the grain of the T-head is calculated as

$$\frac{\text{shore load}}{\text{contact area}} = \frac{2520}{12.25} = 206 \text{ psi}$$

From Table 12-4, the base design value for $F_{c\perp}$ is 625 psi. We will neglect the adjustment factor for bearing area (due to $C_b > 1.0$ since $3\frac{1}{2}$ in. < 6 in.). Therefore, use $F_{c\perp}' = 625$ psi. Thus

$$206 \text{ psi} < 625 \text{ psi} \hspace{4cm} \text{(O.K.)}$$

b.   Check bearing stress between the 2×4 ledger and the 2×4 blocking. The load from the ledger to the blocking is $210 (3.5) = 735$ lb. The actual bearing stress perpendicular to the grain of the ledger is

$$\frac{\text{load}}{\text{contact area}} = \frac{735}{1.5(3.5)} = 140 \text{ psi}$$

The allowable bearing stress, from the preceding step 4, part a is 625 psi. Thus

$$140 \text{ psi} < 625 \text{ psi} \hspace{4cm} \text{(O.K.)}$$

c.   Check bearing stress between the 2×4 joists and the 2×4 ledger. The joist loading is $(105 \text{ psf})(2 \text{ ft}) = 210$ lb/ft, and the span of the joist is 4 ft. Therefore, the load from the joist to the ledger is (210 lb/ft)(2 ft) = 420 lb. The actual bearing stress perpendicular to the grain of the ledger (and the joists) is

$$\frac{\text{load}}{\text{contact area}} = \frac{420}{1.5(1.5)} = 186.7 \text{ psi}$$

The allowable bearing stress is determined as in step 4, part a (the bearing area adjustment factor C_b is not applicable since this is end bearing):

$$186.7 \text{ psi} < 625 \text{ psi} \qquad\qquad \text{(O.K.)}$$

d.   Check the bearing of the beam soffit on the 4 × 4 (S4S) T-heads. The load from the beam soffit is (300 lb/ft)(3.5 ft) = 1050 lb. The actual bearing stress perpendicular to the grain of the T-head is

$$\frac{\text{load}}{\text{contact area}} = \frac{1050}{12(3.5)} = 25 \text{ psi}$$

For the allowable bearing stress, we will neglect the bearing area adjustment factor. The contact surface may be subjected to a wet condition so this adjustment factor ($C_M = 0.67$ from Table 12-4) will be used:

$$F'_{c\perp} = F_{c\perp}C_M = 625(0.67) = 419 \text{ psi}$$

$$25 \text{ psi} < 419 \text{ psi} \qquad\qquad \text{(O.K.)}$$

12-8

WALL FORM DESIGN

The design procedure for wall forms is similar to that used for slab forms, substituting studs for joists, wales for stringers, and ties for shores. See Figure 12-6 for locations of these members.

The maximum lateral pressure against the sheathing must be determined first. With the sheathing thickness specified, the maximum allowable span for the sheathing is computed based on bending, shear, and deflection. This will be the maximum stud spacing. (An alternative approach would be to establish the stud spacing and then calculate the required thickness of the sheathing.)

Next, the maximum allowable stud span is calculated based on stud size and loading, considering bending, shear, and deflection. This will be the maximum wale spacing. (An alternative approach would be to establish the wale spacing and then calculate the required size of the studs.)

The next step is to determine the maximum allowable spacing of wale supports (tie spacing). This is calculated based on wale size and loading. (An alternative approach

FIGURE 12-6 Typical wall forms.

would be to preselect the tie spacing and then calculate the wale size.) Double wales are commonly used to avoid the necessity of drilling wales for tie insertion.

The load supported by each tie must be computed and compared with the tie capacity. The load on each tie is calculated as the design load (psf) multiplied by the tie spacing (ft) and wale spacing (ft). If the load exceeds the tie strength, a stronger tie must be used or the tie spacing must be reduced.

Bearing stresses must also be checked where the studs bear on the wales and where the tie ends bear on the wales. Maximum bearing stress must not exceed the allowable compression stress perpendicular to the grain or crushing will result.

Finally, lateral bracing must be designed to resist any expected lateral loads, such as wind loads.

Example 12-3

Design formwork for an 8-ft-high wall. Refer to Figure 12-6. The concrete is to be placed at a rate of 4 ft/hr and will be internally vibrated. Temperature is expected to be 90°F. The maximum allowable deflection of bending members is to be $\frac{1}{360}$ of the span. Use $\frac{3}{4}$ in. class I plyform for the sheathing and No. 2 Douglas fir–larch for the rest of the lumber. Assume all bending members to be supported on three or more spans. The following conditions for design have been established:

1. Studs and wales are to be designed based on adequate lateral support.
2. Studs, wales, and bracing are to be used under dry service conditions.

Solution:

1. *Sheathing design.* (find the stud spacing): Consider a 12-in.-wide strip of sheathing perpendicular to the supporting studs and acting as a beam continuous over three or more spans. The sheathing spans horizontally. Place the face grain perpendicular to studs.

    a.   The design values for $\frac{3}{4}$ in. class I plyform (see Table 12-2) are

    $$E = 1,650,000 \text{ psi}$$

    $$F_b = 1930 \text{ psi}$$

    $$F_v = 72 \text{ psi}$$

    Plyform properties for face grain parallel to the span are

    $$I = 0.199 \text{ in.}^4$$

    $$S = 0.455 \text{ in.}^3$$

    $$Ib/Q = 7.187 \text{ in.}^2/\text{ft}$$

    b.   Loading: The sheathing will be designed for concrete pressure, which is the lesser of $150h$ (where h will be taken as 8 ft), 2000 psf, or as determined by formula (noting that $R < 7$ ft/hr):

$$p = 150 + \frac{9000R}{T} = 150 + \frac{9000(4)}{90} = 550 \text{ psf} < 600 \text{ psf}$$

$$150(h) = 150(8) = 1200 \text{ psf}$$

Use the ACI recommended minimum of 600 psf for the sheathing design load, although the pressure could be decreased near the top of the form where $150(h)$ controls. The length in which the decreased pressure could be used may be calculated as

$$\frac{600}{150} = 4.0 \text{ ft} \quad \text{(from the top of the form)}$$

It is conservative to design the full height for 600 psf, however.

c.   The maximum stud spacing based on bending is

$$\ell = 10.95 \sqrt{\frac{F_b S}{w}}$$

$$= 10.95 \sqrt{\frac{1930(0.455)}{600}} = 13.25 \text{ in.}$$

d.   The maximum stud spacing based on shear is

$$\ell = \frac{20 F_v (Ib/Q)}{w} + 2d$$

$$= \frac{20(72)(7.187)}{600} + 2(0.75) = 18.75 \text{ in.}$$

e.   The maximum stud spacing based on deflection is

$$\ell = 1.69 \sqrt[3]{\frac{EI}{w}}$$

$$= 1.69 \sqrt[3]{\frac{1,650,000(0.199)}{600}} = 13.82 \text{ in.}$$

Bending is critical. Use a stud spacing of 12 in. o.c.

2.   *Stud design* (compute the wale spacing): Assume 2 × 4 (S4S) studs and a 7-day maximum duration of load.

a.   Obtain allowable stresses using base design values from Table 12-4 and appropriate adjustment factors from Tables 12-4 and 12-5.

(1)   Bending: $F_b = 875$ psi. Adjustment factors: $C_D = 1.25$ and $C_F = 1.5$. Therefore,

$$F_b' = F_b C_D C_F$$

$$= 875(1.25)(1.5) = 1641 \text{ psi}$$

(2)   Shear: $F_v = 95$ psi. Adjustment factor: $C_D = 1.25$. Therefore,

$$F'_v = F_v C_D = 95(1.25) = 118.8 \text{ psi}$$

(3)   Modulus of elasticity: $E = 1{,}600{,}000$ psi. No adjustment factors apply. Thus

$$E' = E = 1{,}600{,}000 \text{ psi}$$

For the 2×4 lumber, from Table 12-3,

$$A = 5.25 \text{ in.}^2$$

$$I = 5.36 \text{ in.}^4$$

$$S = 3.06 \text{ in.}^3$$

b.   Loading: Since the stud spacing is 12 in. o.c., the load w will be 600 lb/ft (see step 1, part b).

c.   The maximum wale spacing based on bending is

$$\ell = 10.95 \sqrt{\frac{F'_b S}{w}}$$

$$= 10.95 \sqrt{\frac{1641(3.06)}{600}} = 31.7 \text{ in.}$$

d.   The maximum wale spacing based on shear is

$$\ell = \frac{13.3 F'_v A}{w} + 2d$$

$$= \frac{13.3(118.8)(5.25)}{600} + 2(3.5) = 20.8 \text{ in.}$$

e.   The maximum wale spacing based on deflection is

$$\ell = 1.69 \sqrt[3]{\frac{E' I}{w}}$$

$$= 1.69 \sqrt[3]{\frac{1{,}600{,}000(5.36)}{600}} = 41.0 \text{ in.}$$

Therefore, shear governs. Use a wale spacing of 20 in. o.c. (maximum). The bottom wale and the top wale may be placed, respectively, 4 in. up from the bottom and 4 in. down from the top.

3.   *Wale design* (compute the tie spacing): Double 2×4 (S4S) wales will be assumed, and the allowable stresses will be adjusted for a 7-day maximum duration of load.

a.   Design values: Allowable stresses and E will be the same as for the studs. Properties for the wales will be twice those for the studs because the wales are doubled. Thus

$$A = 10.5 \text{ in.}^2$$

$$I = 10.72 \text{ in.}^4$$

$$S = 6.12 \text{ in.}^3$$

b.   Loading: Each wale will support a strip of wall form that has a height equal to the spacing of the wales:

$$w = \frac{20}{12}(600) = 1000 \text{ lb/ft}$$

c.   The maximum tie spacing based on bending is

$$\ell = 10.95 \sqrt{\frac{F_b' S}{w}}$$

$$= 10.95 \sqrt{\frac{1641(6.12)}{1000}} = 34.7 \text{ in.}$$

d.   The maximum tie spacing based on shear is

$$\ell = \frac{13.3 F_v' A}{w} + 2d$$

$$= \frac{13.3(118.8)(10.5)}{1000} + 2(3.5) = 23.6 \text{ in.}$$

e.   The maximum tie spacing based on deflection is

$$\ell = 1.69 \sqrt[3]{\frac{E' I}{w}}$$

$$= 1.69 \sqrt[3]{\frac{1{,}600{,}000(10.72)}{1000}} = 43.6 \text{ in.}$$

Shear governs. A modular spacing of 24 in. would be desirable, and 23.6 in. ≈ 24 in. Use tie spacing of 24 in. o.c. (Recall that the loading is conservative.)

4.   Check the load on the ties (P_{tie}) with the capacity of the ties. Assume the tie capacity to be 3000 lb (ties of various capacities are widely available). Also assume that the ties have 1½ in. wedges bearing on the wales. Then

$$P_{\text{tie}} = (\text{wale spacing}) \times (\text{tie spacing}) \times (\text{pressure})$$

$$= \frac{20}{12}\left(\frac{24}{12}\right)(600) = 2000 \text{ lb}$$

2000 lb < 3000 lb

Therefore, the capacity of the tie is satisfactory.

5.   Check bearing stresses.

a.   Where tie wedges bear on wales (wedges are 1½ in. wide),

$$P_{\text{tie}} = 2000 \text{ lb}$$

$$\text{bearing contact area} = (2)(1.5)(1.5) = 4.5 \text{ in.}^2$$

$$\text{bearing stress (actual)} = \frac{2000}{4.5} = 444 \text{ psi}$$

Here $F'_{c\perp} = 625$ psi (neglect bearing area adjustment factor). Thus

$$444 < 625 \qquad\qquad\qquad\qquad \text{(O.K.)}$$

b.   Where studs bear on wales (double wales),

$$\text{bearing contact area} = (2)(1.5)(1.5) = 4.5 \text{ in.}^2$$

The load on the wale from the stud is

$$P = (\text{load/ft on stud}) \times (\text{wale spacing})$$

$$= 600\left(\frac{20}{12}\right) = 1000 \text{ lb}$$

$$\text{actual bearing stress} = \frac{1000}{4.5} = 222 \text{ psi}$$

Here $F'_{c\perp} = 625$ psi (as in part a). Thus

$$222 < 625 \qquad\qquad\qquad\qquad \text{(O.K.)}$$

6.   Lateral bracing should be designed for wall forms based on the greater of wind load (using 15 psf as a minimum) or 100 lb/ft applied at the top of the wall. Calculate wind load on wall forms using the minimum 15 psf:

$$\text{wind load} = (15 \text{ psf})(1 \text{ ft})(8 \text{ ft}) = 120 \text{ lb per ft of wall}$$

This load would be considered to act at midheight of the wall, 4 ft above the base, and would create an overturning moment about the base of

$$M_{OT} = 120 \text{ lb/ft}(4 \text{ ft}) = 480 \text{ ft-lb} \qquad (\text{per ft of wall})$$

The equivalent force, acting at the top of the wall, that would create the same overturning moment is

$$\text{force} = \frac{480 \text{ ft-lb}}{8 \text{ ft}} = 60 \text{ lb} \qquad (\text{per ft of wall})$$

$$60 \text{ lb/ft} < 100 \text{ lb/ft}$$

Therefore, use 100 lb/ft. This load, assumed to act at the top of the wall, can act in either direction. If *guy wires* are used, they must be placed on *both* sides of the wall. If *wooden strut bracing* is used, it can resist tension or compression and therefore *single side* bracing may be used.

In this problem use single-side strut bracing, as shown in Figure 12-7, and design for compression. The horizontal load H on the strut at point A is calculated from

FIGURE 12-7   Lateral bracing for wall form.

$$H(6.5) = 100(8)$$

$$H = 123 \text{ lb}$$

The force F in the strut, using the slope triangle shown, is determined from

$$\frac{F}{8.2} = \frac{123}{5}$$

Therefore, $F = 202$ lb (per foot of wall).

Use double 2×4 (S4S) lumber for the strut and compute the capacity as a compression member. (This will be adequate for tension also.) For No. 2 grade Douglas fir–larch:

a.   The base design value for compression parallel to the grain from Table 12-4 is $F_c = 1300$ psi.

b.   Adjustment factors:

(1)   Size factor from Table 12-7: $C_F = 1.15$.

(2)   For the column stability factor C_P, initially the following items must be established:

(a)   For modulus of elasticity, there is no adjustment factor:

$$E' = E = 1,600,000 \text{ psi}$$

(b)   Find F_c^*:

$$F_c^* = F_c C_F = 1300(1.15) = 1495 \text{ psi}$$

(c)   Assume that the ends are pin-connected. Therefore, $K_e = 1.0$ and $\ell_e = 8.2$ ft. Then

$$\frac{\ell_e}{d} = \frac{8.2(12)}{3.0} = 32.8 < 50 \qquad \text{(O.K.)}$$

(d)   Solve for α:

$$\alpha = \frac{0.3E'}{\left(\dfrac{\ell_e}{d}\right)^2 F_c^*}$$

$$= \frac{0.3(1,600,000)}{32.8^2(1495)}$$

$$= 0.298$$

Solve for C_P:

$$C_P = \frac{1+\alpha}{1.6} - \sqrt{\left(\frac{1+\alpha}{1.6}\right)^2 - \frac{\alpha}{0.8}}$$

$$= \frac{1+0.298}{1.6} - \sqrt{\left(\frac{1+0.298}{1.6}\right)^2 - \frac{0.298}{0.8}}$$

$$= 0.277$$

c.   Compute the allowable stress F_c':

$$F_c' = F_c C_F C_P = 1300(1.15)(0.277) = 414 \text{ psi}$$

Therefore, the allowable load is

$$P = F_c'A = 414(2)(5.25) = 4347 \text{ lb}$$

The maximum allowable strut spacing is calculated from

$$\frac{4347 \text{ lb}}{202 \text{ lb/ft}} = 21.5 \text{ ft}$$

Use struts at 21 ft 0 in. on center.

Single 2×4 struts could have been used if an intermediate brace were used to reduce the unbraced length.

12-9

FORMS FOR COLUMNS

Concrete columns are usually one of five shapes: square, rectangular, L-shaped, octagonal, and round. Forms for the first four shapes are generally made of sheathing, consisting of vertical planks or plywood, with wood yokes and steel bolts, patented steel clamps, or steel bands used to resist the concrete pressure acting on the sheathing. Forms for round columns may be wood, steel plate, or patented fiber tubes.

Since forms for columns are usually filled rapidly, frequently in less than 60 min, the pressure on the sheathing will be high, especially for tall columns.

The ACI recommendations for lateral concrete pressure in column forms were discussed in Section 12-4. ACI limits the pressure to a maximum value of 3000 psf, with the equation for internal pressure applicable to concrete consolidated with an internal vibrator. The pressure, however, should not exceed 150*h*, where *h* is the depth in feet below the upper surface of freshly placed concrete. Thus the *maximum* pressure at the bottom of a form 10 ft high should be taken as 150(10) = 1500 psf regardless of the rate of filling the form or concrete temperature.

It is suggested that the pressure be conservatively calculated using the equation

$$p = 150h$$

with a maximum value of 3000 psf.

Figure 12-8 illustrates a typical column form using sheathing and patented column clamps. If the thickness of the sheathing is selected, the design consists of determining the maximum safe spacing of the column clamps considering the pressure from the concrete as well as the permissible deflection, allowable bending stress, and allowable shearing stress.

The sheathing span length ℓ may be calculated for moment, shear, and deflection, with the shortest of these span lengths being the controlling value.

Since the pressure against the forms varies with height, however, the determination of the optimum clamp spacing becomes laborious. As a result, tables have been developed that aid in quick determination of support (clamp) spacing. Table 12-8 is an example of one such table specifically set up for plywood sheathing. The tabular values are based on the assumption that the lateral pressure is uniform between clamps and of an intensity equal to that at the lower clamp.

Clamps must also be investigated to determine if they can resist the applied loads. The manufacturer usually has recommended capacities for steel column clamps. Wood-yoke-type clamps with tie rods must be designed.

Generally, the type of forming system is a function of column size and height. As column size increases, either the thickness of the sheathing must be increased or vertical stiffeners must be added to prevent sheathing deflection. If vertical supports or stiffeners are used (see Figure 12-8) in combination with a plywood sheathing, the sheathing should span between the vertical supports and the plywood face grain should be horizontal (in the direction of the span) for maximum strength. The clamp spacing is then a function of the vertical support member strength. If plywood sheathing spans between clamps (without vertical supports), the face grain should be vertical (in the direction of the span) for maximum strength.

Chamfer strip

Plywood column sides
stiffened by vertical
2" × 4"s

Adjustable
column clamps

ℓ

Cleanout door

Template for
positioning
form

Cleanout detail

Column Forms Using Vertical Stiffeners

(a)

Column Forms Using Sheathing and Clamps

(b)

FIGURE 12-8 Typical column forms: (a) column forms using vertical stiffeners, (b) column forms using sheathing and clamps. (Ronald D. Smith, *Principles and Practices of Heavy Construction,* 2nd ed., © 1976, p. 227. Reprinted by permission of Prentice Hall, Englewood Cliffs, N.J.)

TABLE 12-8   Safe Span in Inches for Class I Plyform, Continuous over Four or More Supports

Pressure (psf)	Stress parallel to grain				Stress perpendicular to grain			
	1/2 in.	5/8 in.	3/4 in.	1 in.	1/2 in.	5/8 in.	3/4 in.	1 in.
75	20	24	26	32	14	16	21	28
100	18	22	24	30	12	14	19	26
125	17	20	23	28	12	13	18	25
150	16	19	22	27	11	13	17	24
175	15	18	21	26	10	12	16	23
200	15	17	20	25	10	11	15	22
300	13	15	17	22	9	10	13	19
400	12	14	16	20	8	9	12	18
500	11	13	15	18	7	8	11	16
600	10	12	13	17	7	8	11	15
700	9	11	12	16	6	8	10	14
800	9	10	11	15	6	7	9	14
900	8	10	11	14	5	6	8	13
1000	8	9	10	13	5	6	7	12
1100	8	9	10	12	5	5	7	11
1200	7	8	9	12	4	5	6	10
1300	7	8	9	11	4	5	6	10
1400	6	7	9	11	4	4	6	9
1500	6	7	8	11	4	4	5	9
1600	6	6	8	10	—	4	5	8
1700	5	6	8	10	—	4	5	8
1800	5	6	7	9	—	4	5	8
1900	5	6	7	9	—	4	5	7
2000	5	5	7	9	—	—	4	7
2200	4	5	6	8	—	—	4	7
2400	4	5	6	8	—	—	4	6
2600	4	4	5	7	—	—	4	6
2800	4	4	5	7	—	—	4	6
3000	—	4	5	6	—	—	—	5

Notes: F_b = 1930 psi; F_v = 72 psi; E = 1,650,000 psi; allowable deflection = span/360 but not greater than $1/16$ in. Safe spans less than 4 in. are not shown. Tabulated spans are rounded to the nearest inch.

Example 12-4 _____

Determine a clamp spacing pattern for column form sheathing made up of 3/4-in.-thick plywood. The column height is to be 12 ft 0 in. Assume the sheathing continuous over four or more supports and its face grain parallel to the span (vertical). Use class I plyform design values of

$$F_b = 1930 \text{ psi}$$

$$F_v = 72 \text{ psi}$$

$$E = 1{,}650{,}000 \text{ psi}$$

with allowable deflection of span/360 but not greater than $\frac{1}{16}$ in.

Solution:

1. Table 12-8 is used to determine the maximum span of the plywood between clamps. This depends on the pressure on the form, which is determined from

$$p = wh$$

where

w = unit weight of concrete (pcf)

h = depth of fresh concrete (ft)

2. Denoting the vertical distance from the bottom of the form as y (ft), the pressure is determined from

$$p = wh = 150(12 - y)$$

For some arbitrary values of y, the calculated pressures and the maximum spans (clamp spacings) from Table 12-8 are shown in Table 12-9.

3. A plot of maximum clamp spacing as a function of distance above top-of-footing is shown in Figure 12-9. The final clamp layout, also shown in Figure 12-9, is determined by trial and error. This procedure is similar to stirrup design (Chapter 4). One should attempt to minimize the number of clamps without having too many different-size spacings.

■■■■ **Table 12-9   Clamp Spacing Determination**

y[a] (ft)	Pressure (psf)	Maximum clamp spacing (in.)[b]
0	1800	7
3	1350	9
6	900	11
9	450	15
11.5	75	26

[a]Quantity y is measured upward from the bottom of the form.
[b]From Table 12-8.

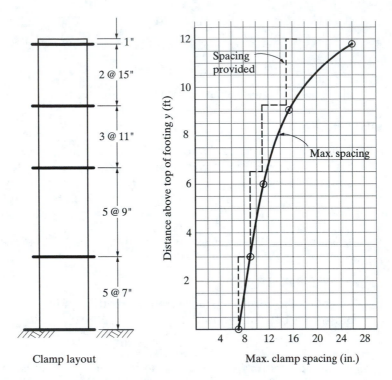

FIGURE 12-9 Sketch for Example 12-4.

REFERENCES

[1] "Guide to Formwork for Concrete" (ACI 347R-94). American Concrete Institute, P.O. Box 9094, Farmington Hills, MI 48333.

[2] "Plywood Design Specification." APA—The Engineered Wood Association, P.O. Box 11700, Tacoma, WA 98411, 1995.

[3] "Concrete Forming." APA—The Engineered Wood Association, P.O. Box 11700, Tacoma, WA 98411, 1994.

[4] "National Design Specification for Wood Construction" ANSI/NFoPA NDS-1991, revised 1991 edition, with supplements and commentary. American Forest & Paper Association, 1111 19th Street, N.W., Suite 800, Washington, D.C. 20036.

[5] M. K. Hurd, *Formwork for Concrete,* SP-4, 6th ed. American Concrete Institute, P.O. Box 9094, Farmington Hills, MI 48333, 1995.

PROBLEMS

Where applicable in these problems, and unless otherwise noted, *assume:*

1.   The vertical live load is to be 75 psf (motorized carts).
2.   Bending members are continuous over three or more spans and are assumed to have adequate lateral support.
3.   There is a 7-day duration of load.
4.   Lumber is No. 2 grade hem-fir.
5.   The forming weight is 5 psf; neglect sheathing weight.
6.   The maximum deflection is $\frac{1}{360}$ of the span.
7.   All lumber is (S4S).
8.   Plywood is placed with the face grain perpendicular to the supports.
9.   No available information exists with respect to wood splits, checks, and shakes. Assume $C_H = 1.0$.

12-1.   Using basic principles, derive the equations of Table 12-1 for allowable span length ℓ as governed by moment, shear, and deflection. Handbooks (such as the AISC *Manual*) may be helpful for moment, shear, and deflection equations. Show load diagrams.
(a) One span
(b) Two spans
(c) Three spans

12-2.   A slab form is to be built for an 8-in.-thick concrete slab. The plywood sheathing face grain is perpendicular to the joists. The maximum allowed deflection is to be the smaller of $\frac{1}{360}$ of the span or $\frac{1}{8}$ in. Compare the maximum allowable joist spacing for class II plyform $\frac{1}{2}$ in. thick and 1 in. thick. Draw a sectional view showing slab, sheathing, and joists.

12-3.   A 6-in.-thick concrete slab is to be formed using plywood supported on 2×8 (S4S) joists that are spaced 1 ft 6 in. on center. Find the maximum allowable stringer spacing if maximum allowable deflection is $\frac{1}{240}$ of the span. Draw a sketch of the formwork.

12-4.   For the slab of Problem 12-3, assume that double 2×10 stringers spaced 5 ft 0 in. on center will support the joists. Determine the maximum shore spacing. Draw a sketch of the formwork. (Neglect shore capacity.)

12-5.   In Problem 12-4, if the shores were to be spaced 6 ft 0 in. on center, select a new stringer size. The stringer may be either doubled 2-in.-thick planks or a single wood beam.

12-6.   Compare the capacities of 6 ft 0 in. and 12 ft 0 in. 4×4 (S4S) wooden shores. What are the capacities if the shores are full nominal size (4 in. $\times$ 4 in.)?

12-7. Design a soffit (beam bottom) for an $11\frac{1}{4}$ in. × 24 in. reinforced concrete beam form. Use a 2 × 12. Determine the maximum shore spacing. Draw a sectional view through the beam.

12-8. Design a plywood beam bottom form shown as an alternative in Figure 12-5. The beam will be 14 in. × 24 in. First design the class I plyform to span the clear span between 2 × 4s (single span, maximum deflection of $\frac{1}{16}$ in.). Then determine maximum shore spacing assuming that the weight of the beam is supported by the 2 × 4s, which back the beam bottom.

12-9. In Problem 12-8, replace the 2 × 4s with 2 × 6s and determine the new maximum shore spacing.

12-10. A 12-ft-high concrete wall is to be placed at a rate of 6 ft/hr, and the temperature is expected to be 90°F. What is the *maximum* lateral pressure due to fresh concrete for which the wall forms must be designed? Draw a diagram showing lateral pressure versus distance from the bottom of the wall for the full 12 ft height of wall.

12-11. Design the formwork for an 8-in.-thick reinforced concrete floor slab. Use $\frac{3}{4}$ in. class II plyform and No. 2 grade Douglas fir–larch for the other lumber. Use 2 × 8 joists and double 2 × 8 stringers. Use 4 × 4 shores with an unsupported height of 10 ft. Assume that the slab will be 120 ft × 120 ft in plan. Use guy wire bracing (at 45° to the 10 ft height) that has a tensile capacity of 4400 lb.

12-12. Design forms to support reinforced concrete beams as shown in Figure 12-5a with the following changes. The beam will be $11\frac{1}{4}$ in. × 22 in., joists are 1 ft 8 in. on center, and stringers are spaced 7 ft 0 in. on center. Shores will be full nominal size 4 × 4s with an unsupported height of 10 ft. All lumber will be No. 2 grade southern pine.

12-13. Design the formwork for a 12-ft-high reinforced concrete wall. Concrete will be placed at a rate not to exceed 5 ft/hr and will be internally vibrated. Temperature is expected to be 80°F. Use $\frac{3}{4}$ in. class I plyform for the sheathing and No. 2 grade Douglas fir–larch for the rest of the lumber. Use 2 × 4s for studs and doubled 2 × 6s for wales. Ties will have a capacity of 5000 lb (2-in.-wide wedges). For lateral bracing design, assume the wind to be 15 psf and use a guy wire (at 45° to the 10 ft height) that has a tensile capacity of 4400 lb.

12-14. Determine a clamp spacing pattern for a column form that has sheathing of 1-in.-thick plywood. The column height is to be 14 ft 0 in. Use Table 12-8. Assume that $F_b = 1930$ psi, $F_v = 72$ psi, and $E = 1,650,000$ and that the face grain is parallel to the span between clamps.

CHAPTER 13

Detailing Reinforced Concrete Structures

13-1

INTRODUCTION

The contract documents package for a typical building as developed by an architect/engineer's office commonly includes both drawings and specifications. The drawings typically concern the following areas: site, architectural, structural, mechanical, and electrical. The specifications supplement and amplify the drawings. The contract documents package is the product that results from what may be categorized as the planning and design phase of a project.

The next sequential phase may be categorized as the *construction phase*. It includes many subcategories for reinforced concrete structures, two of which are *detailing* and *fabricating* of the reinforcing steel. As described in the ACI *Detailing Manual-1994,* [SP-66(94)] [1], detailing consists of the preparation of placing drawings, reinforcing bar details, and bar lists that are used for the fabrication and placement of the reinforcement in a structure. Fabricating consists of the actual shopwork required for the reinforcing steel, such as cutting, bending, bundling, and tagging.

Most bar fabricators not only supply the reinforcing steel but also prepare the placing drawings and bar lists, fabricate the bars, and deliver to the project site. In some cases the bar fabricator may also act as the placing subcontractor.

PHOTO 13-1   Reactor containment foundation mat. Seabrook Station, New Hampshire.

It is general practice in the United States for all reinforced concrete used in building projects to be designed, detailed, and fabricated in accordance with the ACI Code (ACI 318-95). In addition, the Concrete Reinforcing Steel Institute regularly publishes its *Manual of Standard Practice* [2], which contains the latest recommendations of the reinforcing steel industry for standardization of materials and practices.

Techniques have also been developed that make use of electronic computers and other data-processing equipment to facilitate the generation of bar lists and other components of the detailing process. This not only aids in standardization and accuracy of the documents produced, but can also be readily incorporated into the stock control system and the shopwork planning of the reinforcing steel fabricator.

13-2

PLACING DRAWINGS

The *placing drawing* (commonly called a *shop drawing*) consists of a plan view with sufficient sections to clarify and define bar placement. As such, it is the guide that the ironworkers will use as they place the reinforcing steel on the job. In addition, the placing drawing will contain typical views of beams, girders, joists, columns, and other members as necessary. Frequently, tabulations called *schedules* are used to list similar members, which vary in size, shape, and reinforcement details. A bar list, bending details, or both may or may not be shown on the placing drawing, as some fabricators not only have their own preferred format but prefer the list to be prepared as a separate entity.

The preparation of the placing drawing is based on the complete set of contract documents and generally contains only the information necessary for bar fabrication and placing. Building dimensions are not shown unless they are necessary to locate the steel properly.

The *engineering drawing* (Figure 13-1), which is a part of the structural plans of the contract documents, is the drawing on which the placing drawing is based. Figure 13-2 shows a placing drawing of the same system shown in Figure 13-1. This building is an example of a framing system using girders between columns to support beams, which in turn support one-way slabs. The girders support only two-thirds of the beams; the remainder frame directly into the columns.

The engineering drawing, as may be observed, shows the floor plan view locating and identifying the structural elements, along with views of typical beams, girders, and slabs and their accompanying schedules. The placing drawing supplements the engineering drawing by furnishing all the information necessary for bar fabrication and placement. The precise size, shape, dimensions, and location of each bar are furnished, using a marking system discussed later in this chapter. Information relative to bar supports may also be included. Figure 13-2 illustrates a placing drawing that includes placing data for bar supports, as well as a bending details schedule.

FIGURE 13-1 Engineering drawing for beam and girder framing. (Courtesy of the American Concrete Institute [1].)

FIGURE 13-2 Placing drawing for beam and girder framing. (Courtesy of the American Concrete Institute [1].)

Placing drawings, in addition to controlling the placement of the steel in the forms, serve as the basis for ordering the steel. Therefore, a proper interpretation of the contract documents by the fabricator is absolutely essential. Generally, all placing drawings are submitted to the architect or engineer for checking and approval before shop fabrication begins.

13-3

MARKING SYSTEMS AND BAR MARKS

With respect to buildings, two identification systems are required. The first involves the identification of the various structural members, whereas the second involves the identification of the individual bars within the members. The marking system for the structural members may consist of an alphabetical-numerical identification for each beam, girder, and slab, with the columns designated numerically as used in Figures 13-1 and 13-2. Also used is a system of alphabetical and numerical coordinates in which the centerlines of columns are numbered consecutively in one direction and lettered consecutively in the other. A coordinate system may be observed in the foundation-engineering drawing of Figure 13-3, where a column may have a coordinate designation such as B2 or C3. The system is generally established on the architectural and structural drawings and adopted by the detailer, unless the detailer requires a more precise identification system.

Footings, as may be observed in Figure 13-3, are generally designated with an F prefix followed by a number, such as F1 and F3, without regard to a coordinate system. Footing piers or pedestals may be identified using the coordinate system, such as B2 or D4, or may be designated with a P prefix followed by a number, such as P1 or P3. Beams, joists, girders, lintels, slabs, and walls are generally given designations that indicate the specific floor in the building, the type of member, and an identifying number. For example, 1G2 indicates a first-floor girder numbered 2, and RB4 indicates a roof beam numbered 4.

In some cases the floor designation is omitted, as shown in Figures 13-1 and 13-2. The beams and girders are then designated with a prefix B or G, respectively, followed by a number (for example, B4 or G2). In some cases suffixes have been added, such as G2A, indicating that there is a difference in the member.

Along with a marking system established for the structural members, a system of identifying and marking the reinforcing bars must be established.

In buildings, only bent bars are furnished with a mark number or designation. The straight bar has its own identification by virtue of its size and length. Numerous systems are in use throughout the industry, with the system choice generally a function of the building type, size, and complexity as well as the standards of each fabricator.

One commonly used system is the use throughout the project of an arbitrary letter such as K followed by consecutive numbers, without regard to bar location or

FIGURE 13-3 Engineering drawing for foundations. (Courtesy of the American Concrete Institute [1].)

shape. This system may be observed in the placing drawing of Figure 13-2. The letter is prefixed with the size of the bar. For example, 8K19 represents a No. 8 bar whose shape and dimensions may be observed in the bending details schedule and whose location, in this case, may be established by the beam and girder schedule as being the top reinforcing at the noncontinuous end of the B6 members.

An alternative system is to use many letters rather than one arbitrary letter. Column bars may be designated with a C and footing bars with an F. For example, a 7F5 would be a No. 7 footing bar, whose shape and dimensions would be established in a bending details schedule and whose location would be observed in a footing schedule, typical footing details, or the foundation plan.

Other acceptable systems are currently being used. Of primary importance in any system that is chosen is that it should be simple, logical, easy to understand, and not lead to ambiguity or confusion.

13-4

SCHEDULES

Schedules generally appear both on engineering drawings and placing drawings. Typical schedules may be observed in Figures 13-1, 13-2, and 13-3. On the engineering drawings (Figure 13-1), it is a tabular form indicating a member mark number, concrete dimensions, and the member reinforcing steel size and location. Specific design details pertinent to the member reinforcing may also be furnished in the schedule. On the engineering drawing, the schedule must be correlated with a typical section and plan view to be meaningful. Schedules are generally used for the typical members, among which are slabs, beams, girders, joists, columns, footings, and piers. Typical footing and pier schedules may be observed in Figure 13-3, and typical beam, girder, and slab schedules may be observed in Figure 13-1.

Similar schedules are used on the placing drawings, but added information is furnished. The placing drawing schedule is more detailed and generally indicates the number of bars, member mark number, and physical dimensions of member reinforcing steel. In addition, it indicates size and length of straight bars, mark numbers (if bent bars), location of bars, and spacing, along with all specific notes and comments relative to the reinforcing bars. This schedule must also be worked together with typical sections and plan views. The schedules are generally accompanied by a bar list, indicating bending details that may or may not be presented on the placing drawing. There is no standard format for either engineering drawing or placing drawing schedules. They are merely a convenient technique of presenting information for a group of similar items, such as groups of beams, girders, columns, and footings. The schedule format will vary somewhat to conform to the requirements of a particular job.

A schedule for all structural components may not be necessary on a placing drawing. In Figure 13-2 the slab reinforcement is shown directly on the plan, so there is no need for a slab schedule.

13-5

FABRICATING STANDARDS

The fabrication process consists of cutting, bending, bundling, and tagging the reinforcing steel. Our discussion will primarily be limited to the cutting and bending because of their effect on a member's structural capacity. Bending, which includes the making of standard hooks, is generally accomplished in accordance with the requirements of the ACI Code (ACI 318-95), the provisions of which have been discussed in Chapter 5.

In the fabricating shop, bars to be bent are first cut to length as stipulated and then sent to a special bending department, where they are bent as designated in the bending details schedule or bar lists. The common types of bent bars have been standardized throughout the industry, and applicable configurations are generally incorporated onto the placing drawing or bar lists in conjunction with the bending details (see Figure 13-2). Each configuration, sometimes called a bar type, has a designation such as 7, 8, or 9 and S1 or T1, with each dimension designated by a letter. Typical bar bends are shown in Figure 13-4. In addition, standards have been established with respect to the details of the hooks and bends. The ACI Code (Sections 7.1, 7.2, and 7.3) establishes minimum requirements and is graphically portrayed in Figure 13-5. This table also shows the extra length of bar needed for the hook (A or G), which must be added to the sum of all other detailed dimensions to arrive at the total length of bar. It is common practice to show all bar dimensions as *out to out* (meaning outside to outside) of bar. The ACI Code also stipulates that bars must be bent cold unless indicated otherwise by the engineer/architect. Field bending of bars partially embedded in concrete is not allowed unless specifically permitted by the engineer/architect (ACI Code, Section 7.3).

Straight bars are cut to the prescribed length from longer stock-length bars, which are received in the fabricating shop from the mills. Tolerances in fabrication of reinforcing steel are generally standardized and are given in Figure 13-6. For instance, the cutting tolerance for straight bars is the specified length ±1 in., unless special tolerances are called for. Due consideration for these tolerances must be made by both the engineer and contractor in the design and construction phases.

13-6

BAR LISTS

The bar list serves several purposes. It is used for fabrication, including cutting, bending, and shipping, as well as placement and inspection. It represents a bill of materials indicating complete descriptions of the various bar items. The information in a bar list is obtained from the placing drawing or while the placing drawing

Notes:

1. All dimensions are out-to-out of bar except *A* or *G* on standard 180-deg and 135-deg hooks.

2. The *J* dimension on 180-deg hooks to be shown only when necessary to restrict hook size; otherwise standard hooks are to be used.

3. Where *J* is not shown, *J* will be kept equal to or less than *H* on Types 3, 5, and 22. Where *J* can exceed *H*, it should be shown.

4. The *H* dimension on stirrups to be shown where necessary to fit within concrete.

5. Where bars are to be bent more accurately than standard bending tolerances, bending dimensions which require closer fabrication should have limits indicated.

6. Figures in the circles show types.

7. For minimum bend diameters, see Sections 3.7.1 of this standard; for recommended hook dimensions, see Table 1.

8. Types S1-S6, S11, T1-T3, T6-T9 apply to bar sizes #3-#8 inclusive only.

Unless otherwise noted diameter D is the same for all bends and hooks on a bar.

Where slope differs from 45° dimensions "H" and "K" must be shown.

ENLARGED VIEW SHOWING BAR BENDING DETAILS

FIGURE 13-4 Typical bar bends. (Courtesy of the American Concrete Institute [1].)

452

		180-deg hooks		90-deg hooks
Bar Size	Finished* bend diameter D, in.	A or G	J	A or G
#3	2¼	5"	3"	6"
#4	3	6"	4"	8"
#5	3¾	7"	5"	10"
#6	4½	8"	6"	1'-0"
#7	5¼	10"	7"	1'-2"
#8	6	11"	8"	1'-4"
#9	9½	1'-3"	11¾"	1'-7"
#10	10¾	1'-5"	1'-1¼"	1'-10"
#11	12	1'-7"	1'-2¾"	2'-0"
#14	18¼	2'-3"	1'-9¾"	2'-7"
#18	24	3'-0"	2'-4½"	3'-5"

Recommended end hooks, all grades

		General use			Seismic use	
		90-deg hook	135-deg hook		135-deg hook	
Bar size	D,* in.	A or G	A or G	H, approx.	A or G	H, approx.
#3	1½	4"	4"	2½"	4¼"	3"
#4	2	4½"	4½"	3"	4½"	3"
#5	2½	6"	5½"	3¾"	5½"	3¾"
#6	4½	1'-0"	8"	4½"	8"	4½"
#7	5¼	1'-2"	9"	5¼"	9"	5¼"
#8	6	1'-4"	10½"	6"	10½"	6"

Stirrup and tie hooks, all grades

d_b = nominal diameter of bar, in.
* Finished bend diameters include "spring back" effect when bars straighten out slightly after being bent and are slightly larger than minimum bend diameters in 3.7.1

FIGURE 13-5 Standard hook details (Courtesy of the American Concrete Institute [1].)

FIGURE 13-6 Standard fabricating tolerances for bar sizes No. 3 through No. 11. (Courtesy of the American Concrete Institute [1].)

Notes: Entire shearing and bending tolerances are customarily absorbed in the extension past the last bend in a bent bar.

All tolerances single plane and as shown. Tolerances for types S1 through S6, S11, T1 through T3, and T6 through T9 apply only to bar sizes #3 through #8.

* Dimensions on this line are to be within tolerance shown, but are not to differ from opposite parallel dimension more than ½ in.

Angular deviation—Maximum plus or minus 2½ deg or plus or minus ½ in. per ft, but not less than ½ in., on all 90-deg hooks and bends.

Tolerance symbols:
1. Bar sizes #3, #4, #5:
   = plus or minus ½ in. when gross bar length < 12 ft
   = plus or minus 1 in. when gross bar length ≥ 12 ft
   Bar sizes #6 through #11:
   = plus or minus 1 in.
2. Plus or minus 1 in.
3. Plus 0, minus ½ in.
4. Plus or minus ½ in.
5. Plus or minus ½ in. for diameter ≤ 30 in.
   Plus or minus 1 in. for diameter > 30 in.
6. Plus or minus 1.5 percent of o dimension ≥ plus or minus 2 in. minimum. If application of positive tolerance to Type 9 results in a chord length equal to or greater than the arc or bar length, the bar may be shipped straight.

ABC PRODUCTS COMPANY
CHICAGO, ILLINOIS

CUSTOMER	Jones Bros. Construction Co.
PROJECT	Fieldcrest Apt. Bldg.
LOCATION	Smithville, N.C.
MATERIAL FOR	Basement Columns

JOB NO.	27693
DWG. NO.	Figs. 18-4a, 18-6a
SHEET	1 OF 2
DATE	3-17-87 REVISED 4-7-87
DRAWN BY	H.N.H.

Item	No. Pcs.	Size	Length	Mark	Type	A	B	C	D	E	F	G	H	J	K	O	R
1	STRAIGHT																
2	4	18	23-11														
3	4	18	18-11														
4	12	18	8-11														
5																	
6	8	14	23-11														
7	4	14	8-11														
8																	
9	12	9	12-8														
10	6	9	4-1														
11	6	9	4-1														
12																	
13	STRAIGHT SAW CUT BOTH ENDS																
14	8	18	23-11	18W1													
15	8	18	11-5	18W2													
16																	
17	HEAVY BENDING																
18	4	11	20-0	11BC5	5		16-0	1-0	3-0				3		1-0		
19	64	11	13-6	11C16	5		3-0	1-3	9-3				4		1-3		
20																	
21	18	9	12-8	9C4	5		1-11	1-8	9-1				4½		1-8		
22																	
23	LIGHT BENDING																
24	22	3	8-4	3T6	T2	4	2-1	1-9	2-1	1-9			4				
25	22	3	7-8	3T9	T2	4	1-11	1-7	1-11	1-7			4				
26	50	3	6-3	3BT1	T2	4	1-4¾	1-4¾	1-4¾	1-4¾			4				
27	26	3	6-3	3BT3	T2	4	1-0¾	1-8¾	1-0¾	1-8¾			4				
28	44	3	3-4	3T10	S10		1-3½	9	1-3½								
29	22	3	2-10	3T23	T5	5	2-1	4									
30	52	3	2-10	3BT4	S10		1-0¼	9¼	1-0¼								
31	22	3	2-8	3T8	T5	5	1-11	4									
32	22	3	2-6	3T20	T5	5	1-9	4									
33																	
34	SPIRALS																
35	No. Pcs.	Size	Length	Mark	Diam.	Pitch	Turns	Splices									
36	4	½Φ	8-9	SP5	21	3	38	3									

ALL DIMENSIONS ARE OUT TO OUT
ALL STEEL ASTM   A 615   GRADE   60

FOR TYPICAL BEND TYPES REFER TO
ACI DETAILING MANUAL

Note: Fig. 13-4 identifies typical bend types. All dimensions less than 12 in. are given in inches.
   Dimensions 12 in. or greater are given in feet and inches, e.g., 1-3 (except diameter of spirals which is given in inches).

FIGURE 13-7 Typical bar lists for buildings. (Courtesy of the American Concrete Institute [1].)

is being prepared. A typical bar list form is shown in Figure 13-7, and its similarity to the bending details schedule of Figure 13-2 is apparent.

The bar list generally includes both straight and bent bars and indicates all bar dimensions and bends as well as the grade of steel and the number of pieces. A bar list of this type may be used in addition to a bending detail schedule on the placing drawing. Some fabricators, however, prefer not to use a bending detail schedule. With this system the detailers will use sketches until the drawing is complete and then transfer the information to separate bar lists. Two bar lists are prepared, one for straight bars and one for bent bars. Dimensions less than 12 in. are given in inches; over 12 in. they are given in feet and inches.

13-7

EXTRAS

Bars are sold on the basis of weight. To a base price are added various extra charges (extras) dependent principally on the amount of effort required to produce the final product. Among these extras are *bending extras* and *special fabrication extras*.

Bent bars are generally classified as *heavy bending* or *light bending*. Extra charges are made for all shop bending, with the charge a function of the classification. Due to the increased amount of handling and number of bends per pound of steel, light bending charges per pound are appreciably more than the charges for heavy bending. According to the ACI, *heavy bending* is defined as bar sizes No. 4 to through No. 18, which are bent at not more than six points, radius bent to one radius, and bending not otherwise defined. *Light bending* includes all No. 3 bars; all stirrups and column ties; and all bars No. 4 to through No. 18 that are bent at more than six points, bent in more than one plane, radius bent with more than one radius in any one bar, or a combination of radius and other bending. Special fabrication includes fabrication of bars specially suited to conditions for a given project. This may include special tolerances and variations from minimum standards as well as unusual bends and spirals.

13-8

BAR SUPPORTS AND BAR PLACEMENT

Bar supports are used to hold the bars firmly at their designated locations before and during the placing of concrete. These supports may be of metal, plastic, precast concrete, or other approved materials. Standard specifications for steel wire bar supports as well as the placing of bar supports have been established by the Con-

TYPICAL TYPES AND SIZES OF WIRE BAR SUPPORTS

SYMBOL	BAR SUPPORT ILLUSTRATION	BAR SUPPORT ILLUSTRATION PLASTIC CAPPED OR DIPPED	TYPE OF SUPPORT	TYPICAL SIZES
SB		CAPPED	Slab Bolster	¾, 1, 1½, and 2 inch heights in 5 ft. and 10 ft. lengths
SBU*			Slab Bolster Upper	Same as SB
BB		CAPPED	Beam Bolster	1, 1½, 2, over 2" to 5" heights in increments of ¼" in lengths of 5 ft.
BBU*			Beam Bolster Upper	Same as BB
BC		DIPPED	Individual Bar Chair	¾, 1, 1½, and 1¾" heights
JC		DIPPED　　　　DIPPED	Joist Chair	4, 5, and 6 inch widths and ¾, 1 and 1½ inch heights
HC		CAPPED	Individual High Chair	2 to 15 inch heights in increments of ¼ inch
HCM*			High Chair for Metal Deck	2 to 15 inch heights in increments of ¼ in.
CHC		CAPPED	Continuous High Chair	Same as HC in 5 foot and 10 foot lengths
CHCU*			Continuous High Chair Upper	Same as CHC
CHCM*			Continuous High Chair for Metal Deck	Up to 5 inch heights in increments of ¼ in.
JCU**		DIPPED	Joist Chair Upper	14" Span Heights – 1" thru +3½" vary in ¼" increments
CS			Continuous Support	1½" to 12" in increments of ¼" in lengths of 6'-8"

*Usually available in Class 3 only, except on special order.
**Usually available in Class 3 only, with upturned or end bearing legs.

FIGURE 13-8　Standard types and sizes of wire bar supports. (Courtesy of the Concrete Reinforcing Steel Institute.)

crete Reinforcing Steel Institute (CRSI). Standard types and sizes of wire bar supports are shown in Figure 13-8. It is a general practice that unless the engineers' drawings or specifications show otherwise, bar supports will be furnished in accordance with CRSI standards. More detailed information relative to bar supports may be found in the CRSI publications *Placing Reinforcing Bars* [3] and *Manual of Standard Practice* [2].

13-9

COMPUTER DETAILING

The term *computer detailing* is somewhat of a misnomer. Although computers and other electronic data-processing equipment have been used in the bar-fabricating industry for many years, it has not been until recently that the actual detailing has been done with computers. The generation of the placing drawings is well within the capability of currently available computer-aided design and drafting (CADD) software, but only the larger steel bar companies, which can afford to dedicate staff to this function, use CADD in this way. The most beneficial aspect of the use of computers in the bar-fabrication business concerns the handling and manipulation of data and *fabrication management* in the shop. Several commercially available programs perform at various levels of sophistication, and bar fabricators sometimes create their own in-house software to perform unique functions geared to their own needs. Each package and each in-house program is different, and the person entering the field can expect to receive training on the particular equipment and software that the company is using. The development and availability of increasingly sophisticated software can be expected.

The functions most widely performed by computers in the bar-fabricating business involve the generation and printing of notes and labels, schedules (beam, column, slab, pier, footing, joist, and the like), bending details, bar tags, and weight summaries. The software will also optimize the cutting schedule to minimize waste (which is very important in the high-volume, low-margin, rebar fabricating business). In addition, information can be generated that will limit bar bundles based on maximum weight and configuration.

The process begins with the placing drawing being prepared, whether using CADD or manual drafting. For ease of use, it is preferable to furnish the labels on the placing drawing. If the drawing is complex, the detailer will label a reinforcing bar or a group of bars with a single letter or number, which is then keyed to a label list. Part of the output will then be the label list printed on a material that can be attached to and be a part of the reproducible placing drawing. Data are keyed directly into the computer or recorded on a standard input form, which is then followed by the keyboarding operation. Older systems used punched tape or punched cards.

FIGURE 13-9 Computer-aided detailing: placing drawing. (Courtesy of the American Concrete Institute [1].)

```
DIMENSION FABRICATORS, INC.                                              REBAR SHEARING SCHEDULE
CUTTING BATCH: 68H        SHEAR STATION: 1    MATERIAL GRADE: 60         TAG LIST: 02        PAGE  1
Items 1 thru 8 Inclusive
===*============================* ================================================================
 *  SZ     PCS  =LENGTH=  *  NO.  =====CUT=====   YLD  SEC-BIN    JOB  BAR LIST NO. ITEM =MARK=  ----TAG---  STOCK/
 *                        *  CUT  ====LENGTH===   PCS                                                      SCRAP
===*============================* ================================================================
 1) #4    19  60' 0  *  2  30' 0        38    7 1  NTE  768   8          1           ST 68H-1
 *----------------------*
 2) #4     1  60' 0  *  1  23' 8         1    7 1   N   768   8          2
 *                    *  7   4' 7  (-1)  7    2 1   N   768   8          7   4S1
 *                    *  1   3'11         1    2 2   N   768   8          8   4S3             0' 4 SCRAP
 *----------------------*
 3) #4     6.
 *
 *
 *------
 4) #4
 *
 *------
 5) #4
 *----
 6) #4
 *
 *
 *----
 7) #4
 *
 *
 *----
 8) #4
 *----
 9) #4
 *
 *----
10) #4
 *----
11) #4
 *----
12) #4
 *----
 *
 * #4
 *----
 *----
```

REBAR SHEARING SCHEDULE SUMMARY

```
CUTTING BATCH: 68H               SHEAR STATION: 1   MATERIAL GRADE: 60
Items 1 thru 8 Inclusive                TAG LIST: 02  PAGE 2
=========================================================

#4 Rebar   STOCK REQUIRED               2,405 LBS.
           SHEARED WEIGHT               2,375 LBS.
           RE-STOCK 20' or OVER  0.64 %    15 LBS.
           RE-STOCK UNDER 20     0.00 %     0 LBS.
           SCRAP                 0.60 %    14 LBS.
           NOT PROCESSED                   41 LBS.

TOTAL      STOCK REQUIRED               2,405 LBS.
           SHEARED WEIGHT               2,375 LBS.
           RE-STOCK 20' or OVER  0.64 %    15 LBS.
           RE-STOCK UNDER 20 '   0.00 %     0 LBS.
           SCRAP                 0.60 %    14 LBS.
           NOT PROCESSED                   41 LBS.
```

FIGURE 13-10   Rebar shearing schedule and rebar shearing schedule summary. (Courtesy of Dimension Fabricators, Inc., Schenectady, N.Y.)

The data become part of a database, which then provides information for the various other operations. A bill of material, or *bar list,* is commonly generated on which the bars are segregated by grade and size in descending order. Some programs allow the merging of rebar requirements for several jobs; lower-level (and less expensive) programs may not have this capability. It is not difficult to imagine the complexities involved. The bar shop must keep orderly track of bars that vary in grade (40 or 60), type (uncoated, epoxy coated, galvanized), shape (see Figure 13-4), length, and size.

JOB NO. 768		QTY. 24	SIZE 4	LENGTH 4 0		MARK 4S3	
PROJECT COLONIE MUNICIPAL FACILITIES						GRADE 60	
MATERIAL FOR LATHAM WATER "BLACK" DWG.5							
TYPE 17	A	B 2 0	C 2 0	D		E	
FR	G	H	J	K		O	
FT	IN	FT IN	FT IN	FT IN	FT IN	FT IN	
BAR LIST NO. 8			ITEM 8	BUNDLE 1/1		BUNDLE WT. 64	
		TAG NO 8					
DIMENSION FABRICATORS							

FIGURE 13-11   Bar tag. (Courtesy of Dimension Fabricators, Inc., Schenectady, N.Y.)

Several illustrations provide examples of the types of documents that are commonly used in the bar-fabricating business. Figure 13-9 shows a placing drawing in which each item is identified by the use of a label enclosed within an oval. The label list, generated by computer, lists the associated information for each label. For instance, the bars labeled "36" on the south wall elevation view are vertical bars on the inside face (V.I.F.). The label list entry is [36   50   #5 × 11-07 @ 8"] indicating that there are 50 of these No. 5 bars, each 11 ft 7 in. long, and spaced at 8 in. on center. At the lower center of the drawing is a computer-generated bending schedule.

The computer can also generate a rebar shearing schedule and a rebar shearing schedule summary (weight summary). Typical printouts are shown in Figure 13-10. Note how the cutting of the 60-ft-long bars is optimized to minimize the scrap.

Figure 13-11 shows a computer-generated bar tag for bar 4S3, which also appears on the shearing schedule. The bar tag indicates that this is an ACI type 17 bar (refer to Figure 13-4).

Computers have become an indispensable tool in the bar-fabricating business. They allow for more productive use of the detailer's talents, freeing the detailer from tedious and repetitive clerical tasks.

REFERENCES

[1]   *ACI Detailing Manual,* 1994 [SP-66(94)]; includes "Details and Detailing of Concrete Reinforcement" (ACI 315-92), "Manual of Engineering and Placing Drawings for Reinforced Concrete Structures" (ACI 315R-94), and "Supporting Reference Data." American Concrete Institute, P.O. Box 9094, Farmington Hills, MI 48333-9094.

[2]   *Manual of Standard Practice,* 26th ed. Concrete Reinforcing Steel Institute, 933 North Plum Grove Road, Schaumburg, IL 60173-4758, 1996.

[3]   *Placing Reinforcing Bars,* 7th ed. Concrete Reinforcing Steel Institute, 933 North Plum Grove Road, Schaumburg, IL 60173-4758, 1996.

Tables and Charts

TABLE A-1 Reinforcing Steel

Type of steel and ASTM specification number	Sizes available	Grade	Minimum tensile strength (psi)	f_y (psi)	ϵ_y
Billet steel, A615	Nos. 3–6	40	70,000	40,000	0.00138
	Nos. 3–11 Nos. 14 and 18	60	90,000	60,000	0.00207
	Nos. 11, 14, and 18	75	100,000	75,000	0.00259
Rail steel, A616	Nos. 3–11	50	80,000	50,000	0.00172
		60	90,000	60,000	0.00207
Axle steel, A617	Nos. 3–11	40	70,000	40,000	0.00138
		60	90,000	60,000	0.00207
Low-alloy steel, A706	Nos. 3–11 Nos. 14 and 18	60	80,000 (min.: 1.25f_y)	60,000 (Max.: 78,000)	0.00207

Bar number	3	4	5	6	7	8	9	10	11	14	18
Unit weight per foot (lb)	0.376	0.668	1.043	1.502	2.044	2.670	3.400	4.303	5.313	7.65	13.60
Diameter[a] (in.)	0.375	0.500	0.625	0.750	0.875	1.000	1.128	1.270	1.410	1.693	2.257
Area (in.^{2})	0.11	0.20	0.31	0.44	0.60	0.79	1.00	1.27	1.56	2.25	4.00

[a]The nominal dimensions of a deformed bar (diameter and area) are equivalent to those of a plain round bar having the same weight per foot as the deformed bar.

■■■■ **TABLE A-2   Areas of Multiples of Reinforcing Bars (in.^{2})**

Number of bars	Bar number								
	#3	#4	#5	#6	#7	#8	#9	#10	#11
1	0.11	0.20	0.31	0.44	0.60	0.79	1.00	1.27	1.56
2	0.22	0.40	0.62	0.88	1.20	1.58	2.00	2.54	3.12
3	0.33	0.60	0.93	1.32	1.80	2.37	3.00	3.81	4.68
4	0.44	0.80	1.24	1.76	2.40	3.16	4.00	5.08	6.24
5	0.55	1.00	1.55	2.20	3.00	3.93	5.00	6.35	7.80
6	0.66	1.20	1.86	2.64	3.60	4.74	6.00	7.62	9.36
7	0.77	1.40	2.17	3.08	4.20	5.53	7.00	8.89	10.9
8	0.88	1.60	2.48	3.52	4.80	6.32	8.00	10.2	12.5
9	0.99	1.80	2.79	3.96	5.40	7.11	9.00	11.4	14.0
10	1.10	2.00	3.10	4.40	6.00	7.90	10.0	12.7	15.6
11	1.21	2.20	3.41	4.84	6.60	8.69	11.0	14.0	17.2
12	1.32	2.40	3.72	5.28	7.20	9.48	12.0	15.2	18.7
13	1.43	2.60	4.03	5.72	7.80	10.3	13.0	16.5	20.3
14	1.54	2.80	4.34	6.16	8.40	11.1	14.0	17.8	21.8
15	1.65	3.00	4.65	6.60	9.00	11.8	15.0	19.0	23.4
16	1.76	3.20	4.96	7.04	9.60	12.6	16.0	20.3	25.0
17	1.87	3.40	5.27	7.48	10.2	13.4	17.0	21.6	26.5
18	1.98	3.60	5.58	7.92	10.8	14.2	18.0	22.9	28.1
19	2.09	3.80	5.89	8.36	11.4	15.0	19.0	24.1	29.6
20	2.20	4.00	6.20	8.80	12.0	15.8	20.0	25.4	31.2

■■■■ **TABLE A-3   Minimum Required Beam Widths (in.)**

Number of bars in one layer	Bar number							
	#3 and #4	#5	#6	#7	#8	#9	#10	#11
2	6.0	6.0	6.5	6.5	7.0	7.5	8.0	8.0
3	7.5	8.0	8.0	8.5	9.0	9.5	10.5	11.0
4	9.0	9.5	10.0	10.5	11.0	12.0	13.0	14.0
5	10.5	11.0	11.5	12.5	13.0	14.0	15.5	16.5
6	12.0	12.5	13.5	14.0	15.0	16.5	18.0	19.5
7	13.5	14.5	15.0	16.0	17.0	18.5	20.5	22.5
8	15.0	16.0	17.0	18.0	19.0	21.0	23.0	25.0
9	16.5	17.5	18.5	20.0	21.0	23.0	25.5	28.0
10	18.0	19.0	20.5	21.5	23.0	25.5	28.0	31.0

Note: Tabulated values based on No. 3 stirrups, minimum clear distance of 1 in., and a 1$\frac{1}{2}$ in. cover.

■■■■■■ TABLE A-4   Areas of Reinforcing Bars per Foot of Slab (in.^{2})

Bar spacing (in.)	Bar number								
	#3	#4	#5	#6	#7	#8	#9	#10	#11
2	0.66	1.20	1.86						
2½	0.53	0.96	1.49	2.11					
3	0.44	0.80	1.24	1.76	2.40	3.16	4.00		
3½	0.38	0.69	1.06	1.51	2.06	2.71	3.43	4.35	
4	0.33	0.60	0.93	1.32	1.80	2.37	3.00	3.81	4.68
4½	0.29	0.53	0.83	1.17	1.60	2.11	2.67	3.39	4.16
5	0.26	0.48	0.74	1.06	1.44	1.90	2.40	3.05	3.74
5½	0.24	0.44	0.68	0.96	1.31	1.72	2.18	2.77	3.40
6	0.22	0.40	0.62	0.88	1.20	1.58	2.00	2.54	3.12
6½	0.20	0.37	0.57	0.81	1.11	1.46	1.85	2.34	2.88
7	0.19	0.34	0.53	0.75	1.03	1.35	1.71	2.18	2.67
7½	0.18	0.32	0.50	0.70	0.96	1.26	1.60	2.03	2.50
8	0.16	0.30	0.46	0.66	0.90	1.18	1.50	1.90	2.34
9	0.15	0.27	0.41	0.59	0.80	1.05	1.33	1.69	2.08
10	0.13	0.24	0.37	0.53	0.72	0.95	1.20	1.52	1.87
11	0.12	0.22	0.34	0.48	0.65	0.86	1.09	1.39	1.70
12	0.11	0.20	0.31	0.44	0.60	0.79	1.00	1.27	1.56
13	0.10	0.18	0.29	0.41	0.55	0.73	0.92	1.17	1.44
14	0.09	0.17	0.27	0.38	0.51	0.68	0.86	1.09	1.34
15	0.09	0.16	0.25	0.35	0.48	0.64	0.80	1.02	1.25
16	0.08	0.15	0.23	0.33	0.45	0.59	0.75	0.95	1.17
17	0.08	0.14	0.22	0.31	0.42	0.56	0.71	0.90	1.10
18	0.07	0.13	0.21	0.29	0.40	0.53	0.67	0.85	1.04

TABLE A-5   Design Constants

f'_c (psi)	$\left[\dfrac{3\sqrt{f'_c}}{f_y} \geqslant \dfrac{200}{f_y}\right]^a$	$0.75\rho_b{}^b$	Recommended design ρ
	$f_y = 40{,}000$ psi		
3000	0.0050	0.0278	0.0135
4000	0.0050	0.0372	0.0180
5000	0.0053	0.0436	0.0225
6000	0.0058	0.0490	0.0270
	$f_y = 50{,}000$ psi		
3000	0.0040	0.0206	0.0108
4000	0.0040	0.0275	0.0144
5000	0.0042	0.0324	0.0180
6000	0.0046	0.0364	0.0216
	$f_y = 60{,}000$ psi		
3000	0.0033	0.0161	0.0090
4000	0.0033	0.0214	0.0120
5000	0.0035	0.0252	0.0150
6000	0.0039	0.0283	0.0180
	$f_y = 75{,}000$ psi		
3000	0.0027	0.0116	0.0072
4000	0.0027	0.0155	0.0096
5000	0.0028	0.0182	0.0120
6000	0.0031	0.0206	0.0144

[a]Does not apply to T-beams with flanges in tension (see Section 3-2). To compute $A_{s,min}$, see Section 2-8.
[b]See Equation 2-3 for ρ_b.

TABLE A-6   Properties and Constants for Concrete

	f'_c (psi)			
	3000	3500	4000	5000
E_c (psi)[a]	3,120,000	3,370,000	3,605,000	4,030,000
n[b]	9	9	8	7
$7.5\sqrt{f'_c}$ (ksi)[c]	0.411	0.444	0.474	0.530

[a]E_c for normal-weight concrete = $57{,}000\sqrt{f'_c}$.
[b]Nearest whole number.
[c]Modulus of rupture (f_r).

TABLE A-7   Coefficient of Resistance ($\bar{k}$) versus Reinforcement Ratio (ρ)
(f'_c = 3000 psi; f_y = 40,000 psi; Units of $\bar{k}$ Are ksi)

ρ	$\bar{k}$	ρ	$\bar{k}$	ρ	$\bar{k}$
0.0010	0.0397	0.0056	0.2142	0.0102	0.3754
0.0011	0.0436	0.0057	0.2178	0.0103	0.3787
0.0012	0.0476	0.0058	0.2214	0.0104	0.3821
0.0013	0.0515	0.0059	0.2251	0.0105	0.3854
0.0014	0.0554	0.0060	0.2287	0.0106	0.3887
0.0015	0.0593	0.0061	0.2323	0.0107	0.3921
0.0016	0.0632	0.0062	0.2359	0.0108	0.3954
0.0017	0.0671	0.0063	0.2395	0.0109	0.3987
0.0018	0.0710	0.0064	0.2431	0.0110	0.4020
0.0019	0.0749	0.0065	0.2467	0.0111	0.4053
0.0020	0.0788	0.0066	0.2503	0.0112	0.4086
0.0021	0.0826	0.0067	0.2539	0.0113	0.4119
0.0022	0.0865	0.0068	0.2575	0.0114	0.4152
0.0023	0.0903	0.0069	0.2611	0.0115	0.4185
0.0024	0.0942	0.0070	0.2646	0.0116	0.4218
0.0025	0.0980	0.0071	0.2682	0.0117	0.4251
0.0026	0.1019	0.0072	0.2717	0.0118	0.4283
0.0027	0.1057	0.0073	0.2753	0.0119	0.4316
0.0028	0.1095	0.0074	0.2788	0.0120	0.4348
0.0029	0.1134	0.0075	0.2824	0.0121	0.4381
0.0030	0.1172	0.0076	0.2859	0.0122	0.4413
0.0031	0.1210	0.0077	0.2894	0.0123	0.4445
0.0032	0.1248	0.0078	0.2929	0.0124	0.4478
0.0033	0.1286	0.0079	0.2964	0.0125	0.4510
0.0034	0.1324	0.0080	0.2999	0.0126	0.4542
0.0035	0.1362	0.0081	0.3034	0.0127	0.4574
0.0036	0.1399	0.0082	0.3069	0.0128	0.4606
0.0037	0.1437	0.0083	0.3104	0.0129	0.4638
0.0038	0.1475	0.0084	0.3139	0.0130	0.4670
0.0039	0.1512	0.0085	0.3173	0.0131	0.4702
0.0040	0.1550	0.0086	0.3208	0.0132	0.4733
0.0041	0.1587	0.0087	0.3243	0.0133	0.4765
0.0042	0.1625	0.0088	0.3277	0.0134	0.4797
0.0043	0.1662	0.0089	0.3311	0.0135	0.4828
0.0044	0.1699	0.0090	0.3346	0.0136	0.4860
0.0045	0.1736	0.0091	0.3380	0.0137	0.4891
0.0046	0.1774	0.0092	0.3414	0.0138	0.4923
0.0047	0.1811	0.0093	0.3449	0.0139	0.4954
0.0048	0.1848	0.0094	0.3483	0.0140	0.4985
0.0049	0.1885	0.0095	0.3517	0.0141	0.5016
0.0050	0.1922	0.0096	0.3551	0.0142	0.5047
0.0051	0.1958	0.0097	0.3585	0.0143	0.5078
0.0052	0.1995	0.0098	0.3619	0.0144	0.5109
0.0053	0.2032	0.0099	0.3653	0.0145	0.5140
0.0054	0.2069	0.0100	0.3686	0.0146	0.5171
0.0055	0.2105	0.0101	0.3720	0.0147	0.5202

TABLE A-7 (CONT.)   Coefficient of Resistance ($\bar{k}$) versus Reinforcement Ratio (ρ) ($f'_c = 3000$ psi; $f_y = 40,000$ psi; Units of $\bar{k}$ Are ksi)

ρ	$\bar{k}$	ρ	$\bar{k}$	ρ	$\bar{k}$
0.0148	0.5233	0.0192	0.6523	0.0236	0.7693
0.0149	0.5263	0.0193	0.6551	0.0237	0.7718
0.0150	0.5294	0.0194	0.6579	0.0238	0.7743
0.0151	0.5325	0.0195	0.6607	0.0239	0.7768
0.0152	0.5355	0.0196	0.6635	0.0240	0.7793
0.0153	0.5386	0.0197	0.6662	0.0241	0.7818
0.0154	0.5416	0.0198	0.6690	0.0242	0.7843
0.0155	0.5446	0.0199	0.6718	0.0243	0.7867
0.0156	0.5477	0.0200	0.6745	0.0244	0.7892
0.0157	0.5507	0.0201	0.6773	0.0245	0.7917
0.0158	0.5537	0.0202	0.6800	0.0246	0.7941
0.0159	0.5567	0.0203	0.6827	0.0247	0.7966
0.0160	0.5597	0.0204	0.6854	0.0248	0.7990
0.0161	0.5627	0.0205	0.6882	0.0249	0.8015
0.0162	0.5657	0.0206	0.6909	0.0250	0.8039
0.0163	0.5686	0.0207	0.6936	0.0251	0.8063
0.0164	0.5716	0.0208	0.6963	0.0252	0.8088
0.0165	0.5746	0.0209	0.6990	0.0253	0.8112
0.0166	0.5775	0.0210	0.7016	0.0254	0.8136
0.0167	0.5805	0.0211	0.7043	0.0255	0.8160
0.0168	0.5835	0.0212	0.7070	0.0256	0.8184
0.0169	0.5864	0.0213	0.7097	0.0257	0.8208
0.0170	0.5893	0.0214	0.7123	0.0258	0.8232
0.0171	0.5923	0.0215	0.7150	0.0259	0.8255
0.0172	0.5952	0.0216	0.7176	0.0260	0.8279
0.0173	0.5981	0.0217	0.7203	0.0261	0.8303
0.0174	0.6010	0.0218	0.7229	0.0262	0.8326
0.0175	0.6039	0.0219	0.7255	0.0263	0.8350
0.0176	0.6068	0.0220	0.7282	0.0264	0.8373
0.0177	0.6097	0.0221	0.7308	0.0265	0.8397
0.0178	0.6126	0.0222	0.7334	0.0266	0.8420
0.0179	0.6155	0.0223	0.7360	0.0267	0.8443
0.0180	0.6184	0.0224	0.7386	0.0268	0.8467
0.0181	0.6212	0.0225	0.7412	0.0269	0.8490
0.0182	0.6241	0.0226	0.7438	0.0270	0.8513
0.0183	0.6269	0.0227	0.7463	0.0271	0.8536
0.0184	0.6298	0.0228	0.7489	0.0272	0.8559
0.0185	0.6326	0.0229	0.7515	0.0273	0.8582
0.0186	0.6355	0.0230	0.7540	0.0274	0.8605
0.0187	0.6383	0.0231	0.7566	0.0275	0.8627
0.0188	0.6411	0.0232	0.7591	0.0276	0.8650
0.0189	0.6439	0.0233	0.7617	0.0277	0.8673
0.0190	0.6467	0.0234	07642	0.0278	0.8695
0.0191	0.6495	0.0235	0.7667		

TABLE A-8   Coefficient of Resistance ($\bar{k}$) versus Reinforcement Ratio (ρ)
(f'_c = 3000 psi; f_y = 60,000 psi; Units of $\bar{k}$ Are ksi)

ρ	$\bar{k}$	ρ	$\bar{k}$	ρ	$\bar{k}$	ρ	$\bar{k}$
0.0010	0.0593	0.0048	0.2717	0.0086	0.4638	0.0124	0.6355
0.0011	0.0651	0.0049	0.2771	0.0087	0.4686	0.0125	0.6397
0.0012	0.0710	0.0050	0.2824	0.0088	0.4733	0.0126	0.6439
0.0013	0.0768	0.0051	0.2876	0.0089	0.4781	0.0127	0.6482
0.0014	0.0826	0.0052	0.2929	0.0090	0.4828	0.0128	0.6524
0.0015	0.0884	0.0053	0.2982	0.0091	0.4875	0.0129	0.6565
0.0016	0.0942	0.0054	0.3034	0.0092	0.4923	0.0130	0.6607
0.0017	0.1000	0.0055	0.3086	0.0093	0.4970	0.0131	0.6649
0.0018	0.1057	0.0056	0.3139	0.0094	0.5016	0.0132	0.6690
0.0019	0.1115	0.0057	0.3191	0.0095	0.5063	0.0133	0.6731
0.0020	0.1172	0.0058	0.3243	0.0096	0.5109	0.0134	0.6773
0.0021	0.1229	0.0059	0.3294	0.0097	0.5156	0.0135	0.6814
0.0022	0.1286	0.0060	0.3346	0.0098	0.5202	0.0136	0.6854
0.0023	0.1343	0.0061	0.3397	0.0099	0.5248	0.0137	0.6895
0.0024	0.1399	0.0062	0.3449	0.0100	0.5294	0.0138	0.6936
0.0025	0.1456	0.0063	0.3500	0.0101	0.5340	0.0139	0.6976
0.0026	0.1512	0.0064	0.3551	0.0102	0.5386	0.0140	0.7017
0.0027	0.1569	0.0065	0.3602	0.0103	0.5431	0.0141	0.7057
0.0028	0.1625	0.0066	0.3653	0.0104	0.5477	0.0142	0.7097
0.0029	0.1681	0.0067	0.3703	0.0105	0.5522	0.0143	0.7137
0.0030	0.1736	0.0068	0.3754	0.0106	0.5567	0.0144	0.7176
0.0031	0.1792	0.0069	0.3804	0.0107	0.5612	0.0145	0.7216
0.0032	0.1848	0.0070	0.3854	0.0108	0.5657	0.0146	0.7255
0.0033	0.1903	0.0071	0.3904	0.0109	0.5701	0.0147	0.7295
0.0034	0.1958	0.0072	0.3954	0.0110	0.5746	0.0148	0.7334
0.0035	0.2014	0.0073	0.4004	0.0111	0.5790	0.0149	0.7373
0.0036	0.2069	0.0074	0.4053	0.0112	0.5835	0.0150	0.7412
0.0037	0.2123	0.0075	0.4103	0.0113	0.5879	0.0151	0.7451
0.0038	0.2178	0.0076	0.4152	0.0114	0.5923	0.0152	0.7489
0.0039	0.2233	0.0077	0.4202	0.0115	0.5967	0.0153	0.7528
0.0040	0.2287	0.0078	0.4251	0.0116	0.6010	0.0154	0.7566
0.0041	0.2341	0.0079	0.4299	0.0117	0.6054	0.0155	0.7604
0.0042	0.2395	0.0080	0.4348	0.0118	0.6097	0.0156	0.7642
0.0043	0.2449	0.0081	0.4397	0.0119	0.6140	0.0157	0.7680
0.0044	0.2503	0.0082	0.4445	0.0120	0.6184	0.0158	0.7718
0.0045	0.2557	0.0083	0.4494	0.0121	0.6227	0.0159	0.7756
0.0046	0.2611	0.0084	0.4542	0.0122	0.6269	0.0160	0.7793
0.0047	0.2664	0.0085	0.4590	0.0123	0.6312	0.0161	0.7830

TABLE A-9   Coefficient of Resistance ($\bar{k}$) versus Reinforcement Ratio (ρ)
(f'_c = 4000 psi; f_y = 40,000 psi; Units of $\bar{k}$ Are ksi)

ρ	$\bar{k}$	ρ	$\bar{k}$	ρ	$\bar{k}$	ρ	$\bar{k}$
0.0010	0.0398	0.0057	0.2204	0.0104	0.3906	0.0151	0.5504
0.0011	0.0437	0.0058	0.2241	0.0105	0.3941	0.0152	0.5536
0.0012	0.0477	0.0059	0.2278	0.0106	0.3976	0.0153	0.5569
0.0013	0.0516	0.0060	0.2315	0.0107	0.4011	0.0154	0.5602
0.0014	0.0555	0.0061	0.2352	0.0108	0.4046	0.0155	0.5635
0.0015	0.0595	0.0062	0.2390	0.0109	0.4080	0.0156	0.5667
0.0016	0.0634	0.0063	0.2427	0.0110	0.4115	0.1057	0.5700
0.0017	0.0673	0.0064	0.2464	0.0111	0.4150	0.0158	0.5733
0.0018	0.0712	0.0065	0.2501	0.0112	0.4185	0.0159	0.5765
0.0019	0.0752	0.0066	0.2538	0.0113	0.4220	0.0160	0.5798
0.0020	0.0791	0.0067	0.2574	0.0114	0.4254	0.0161	0.5830
0.0021	0.0830	0.0068	0.2611	0.0115	0.4289	0.0162	0.5863
0.0022	0.0869	0.0069	0.2648	0.0116	0.4323	0.0163	0.5895
0.0023	0.0908	0.0070	0.2685	0.0117	0.4358	0.0164	0.5927
0.0024	0.0946	0.0071	0.2721	0.0118	0.4392	0.0165	0.5959
0.0025	0.0985	0.0072	0.2758	0.0119	0.4427	0.0166	0.5992
0.0026	0.1024	0.0073	0.2795	0.0120	0.4461	0.0167	0.6024
0.0027	0.1063	0.0074	0.2831	0.0121	0.4495	0.0168	0.6056
0.0028	0.1102	0.0075	0.2868	0.0122	0.4530	0.0169	0.6088
0.0029	0.1140	0.0076	0.2904	0.0123	0.4564	0.0170	0.6120
0.0030	0.1179	0.0077	0.2941	0.0124	0.4598	0.0171	0.6152
0.0031	0.1217	0.0078	0.2977	0.0125	0.4632	0.0172	0.6184
0.0032	0.1256	0.0079	0.3013	0.0126	0.4666	0.0173	0.6216
0.0033	0.1294	0.0080	0.3049	0.0127	0.4701	0.0174	0.6248
0.0034	0.1333	0.0081	0.3086	0.0128	0.4735	0.0175	0.6279
0.0035	0.1371	0.0082	0.3122	0.0129	0.4768	0.0176	0.6311
0.0036	0.1410	0.0083	0.3158	0.0130	0.4802	0.0177	0.6343
0.0037	0.1448	0.0084	0.3194	0.0131	0.4836	0.0178	0.6375
0.0038	0.1486	0.0085	0.3230	0.0132	0.4870	0.0179	0.6406
0.0039	0.1524	0.0086	0.3266	0.0133	0.4904	0.0180	0.6438
0.0040	0.1562	0.0087	0.3302	0.0134	0.4938	0.0181	0.6469
0.0041	0.1600	0.0088	0.3338	0.0135	0.4971	0.0182	0.6501
0.0042	0.1638	0.0089	0.3374	0.0136	0.5005	0.0183	0.6532
0.0043	0.1676	0.0090	0.3409	0.0137	0.5038	0.0184	0.6563
0.0044	0.1714	0.0091	0.3445	0.0138	0.5072	0.0185	0.6595
0.0045	0.1752	0.0092	0.3481	0.0139	0.5105	0.0186	0.6626
0.0046	0.1790	0.0093	0.3517	0.0140	0.5139	0.0187	0.6657
0.0047	0.1828	0.0094	0.3552	0.0141	0.5172	0.0188	0.6688
0.0048	0.1866	0.0095	0.3588	0.0142	0.5206	0.0189	0.6720
0.0049	0.1904	0.0096	0.3623	0.0143	0.5239	0.0190	0.6751
0.0050	0.1941	0.0097	0.3659	0.0144	0.5272	0.0191	0.6782
0.0051	0.1979	0.0098	0.3694	0.0145	0.5305	0.0192	0.6813
0.0052	0.2016	0.0099	0.3729	0.0146	0.5338	0.0193	0.6844
0.0053	0.2054	0.0100	0.3765	0.0147	0.5372	0.0194	0.6875
0.0054	0.2091	0.0101	0.3800	0.0148	0.5405	0.0195	0.6905
0.0055	0.2129	0.0102	0.3835	0.0149	0.5438	0.0196	0.6936
0.0056	0.2166	0.0103	0.3870	0.0150	0.5471	0.0197	0.6967

TABLE A-9 (CONT.)   Coefficient of Resistance ($\bar{k}$) versus Reinforcement Ratio (ρ) ($f'_c = 4000$ psi; $f_y = 40,000$ psi; Units of $\bar{k}$ Are ksi)

ρ	$\bar{k}$	ρ	$\bar{k}$	ρ	$\bar{k}$
0.0198	0.6998	0.0236	0.8130	0.0302	0.9934
0.0199	0.7028	0.0237	0.8158	0.0304	0.9986
0.0200	0.7059	0.0238	0.8187	0.0306	1.0037
0.0201	0.7089	0.0239	0.8216	0.0308	1.0088
0.0202	0.7120	0.0240	0.8245	0.0310	1.0139
0.0203	0.7150	0.0241	0.8273	0.0312	1.0190
0.0204	0.7181	0.0242	0.8302	0.0314	1.0240
0.0205	0.7211	0.0243	0.8331	0.0316	1.0291
0.0206	0.7242	0.0244	0.8359	0.0318	1.0341
0.0207	0.7272	0.0245	0.8388	0.0320	1.0391
0.0208	0.7302	0.0246	0.8416	0.0322	1.0441
0.0209	0.7332	0.0248	0.8473	0.0324	1.0490
0.0210	0.7362	0.0250	0.8530	0.0326	1.0540
0.0211	0.7393	0.0252	0.8586	0.0328	1.0589
0.0212	0.7423	0.0254	0.8642	0.0330	1.0638
0.0213	0.7453	0.0256	0.8698	0.0332	1.0687
0.0214	0.7483	0.0258	0.8754	0.0334	1.0735
0.0215	0.7512	0.0260	0.8810	0.0336	1.0784
0.0216	0.7542	0.0262	0.8865	0.0338	1.0832
0.0217	0.7572	0.0264	0.8920	0.0340	1.0880
0.0218	0.7602	0.0266	0.8975	0.0342	1.0928
0.0219	0.7632	0.0268	0.9030	0.0344	1.0976
0.0220	0.7661	0.0270	0.9085	0.0346	1.1023
0.0221	0.7691	0.0272	0.9139	0.0348	1.1071
0.0222	0.7720	0.0274	0.9194	0.0350	1.1118
0.0223	0.7750	0.0276	0.9248	0.0352	1.1165
0.0224	0.7779	0.0278	0.9302	0.0354	1.1212
0.0225	0.7809	0.0280	0.9355	0.0356	1.1258
0.0226	0.7838	0.0282	0.9409	0.0358	1.1305
0.0227	0.7868	0.0284	0.9462	0.0360	1.1351
0.0228	0.7897	0.0286	0.9516	0.0362	1.1397
0.0229	0.7926	0.0288	0.9568	0.0364	1.1443
0.0230	0.7955	0.0290	0.9621	0.0366	1.1488
0.0231	0.7985	0.0292	0.9674	0.0368	1.1534
0.0232	0.8014	0.0294	0.9726	0.0370	1.1579
0.0233	0.8043	0.0296	0.9779	0.0372	1.1624
0.0234	0.8072	0.0298	0.9831		
0.0235	0.8101	0.0300	0.9882		

■■■■■ **TABLE A-10**   **Coefficient of Resistance ($\bar{k}$) versus Reinforcement Ratio (ρ)**
(f'_c = 4000 psi; f_y = 60,000 psi; Units of $\bar{k}$ Are ksi)

ρ	$\bar{k}$	ρ	$\bar{k}$	ρ	$\bar{k}$	ρ	$\bar{k}$
0.0010	0.0595	0.0036	0.2091	0.0062	0.3516	0.0088	0.4870
0.0011	0.0654	0.0037	0.2148	0.0063	0.3570	0.0089	0.4921
0.0012	0.0712	0.0038	0.2204	0.0064	0.3623	0.0090	0.4971
0.0013	0.0771	0.0039	0.2259	0.0065	0.3676	0.0091	0.5022
0.0014	0.0830	0.0040	0.2315	0.0066	0.3729	0.0092	0.5072
0.0015	0.0889	0.0041	0.2371	0.0067	0.3782	0.0093	0.5122
0.0016	0.0946	0.0042	0.2427	0.0068	0.3835	0.0094	0.5172
0.0017	0.1005	0.0043	0.2482	0.0069	0.3888	0.0095	0.5222
0.0018	0.1063	0.0044	0.2538	0.0070	0.3941	0.0096	0.5272
0.0019	0.1121	0.0045	0.2593	0.0071	0.3993	0.0097	0.5322
0.0020	0.1179	0.0046	0.2648	0.0072	0.4046	0.0098	0.5372
0.0021	0.1237	0.0047	0.2703	0.0073	0.4098	0.0099	0.5421
0.0022	0.1294	0.0048	0.2758	0.0074	0.4150	0.0100	0.5471
0.0023	0.1352	0.0049	0.2813	0.0075	0.4202	0.0101	0.5520
0.0024	0.1410	0.0050	0.2868	0.0076	0.4254	0.0102	0.5569
0.0025	0.1467	0.0051	0.2922	0.0077	0.4306	0.0103	0.5618
0.0026	0.1524	0.0052	0.2977	0.0078	0.4358	0.0104	0.5667
0.0027	0.1581	0.0053	0.3031	0.0079	0.4410	0.0105	0.5716
0.0028	0.1638	0.0054	0.3086	0.0080	0.4461	0.0106	0.5765
0.0029	0.1695	0.0055	0.3140	0.0081	0.4513	0.0107	0.5814
0.0030	0.1752	0.0056	0.3194	0.0082	0.4564	0.0108	0.5862
0.0031	0.1809	0.0057	0.3248	0.0083	0.4615	0.0109	0.5911
0.0032	0.1866	0.0058	0.3302	0.0084	0.4666	0.0110	0.5959
0.0033	0.1922	0.0059	0.3356	0.0085	0.4718	0.0111	0.6008
0.0034	0.1979	0.0060	0.3409	0.0086	0.4768	0.0112	0.6056
0.0035	0.2035	0.0061	0.3463	0.0087	0.4819	0.0113	0.6104

TABLE A-10 (CONT.) Coefficient of Resistance ($\bar{k}$) versus Reinforcement Ratio (ρ)
(f'_c = 4000 psi; f_y = 60,000 psi; Units of $\bar{k}$ Are ksi)

ρ	$\bar{k}$	ρ	$\bar{k}$	ρ	$\bar{k}$	ρ	$\bar{k}$
0.0114	0.6152	0.0140	0.7362	0.0165	0.8459	0.0190	0.9489
0.0115	0.6200	0.0141	0.7407	0.0166	0.8501	0.0191	0.9529
0.0116	0.6248	0.0142	0.7452	0.0167	0.8544	0.0192	0.9568
0.0117	0.6295	0.0143	0.7497	0.0168	0.8586	0.0193	0.9608
0.0118	0.6343	0.0144	0.7542	0.0169	0.8628	0.0194	0.9648
0.0119	0.6390	0.0145	0.7587	0.0170	0.8670	0.0195	0.9687
0.0120	0.6438	0.0146	0.7632	0.0171	0.8712	0.0196	0.9726
0.0121	0.6485	0.0147	0.7675	0.0172	0.8754	0.0197	0.9765
0.0122	0.6532	0.0148	0.7720	0.0173	0.8796	0.0198	0.9804
0.0123	0.6579	0.0149	0.7765	0.0174	0.8837	0.0199	0.9843
0.0124	0.6626	0.0150	0.7809	0.0175	0.8879	0.0200	0.9882
0.0125	0.6673	0.0151	0.7853	0.0176	0.8920	0.0201	0.9921
0.0126	0.6720	0.0152	0.7897	0.0177	0.8961	0.0202	0.9960
0.0127	0.6766	0.0153	0.7941	0.0178	0.9003	0.0203	0.9998
0.0128	0.6813	0.0154	0.7984	0.0179	0.9044	0.0204	1.0037
0.0129	0.6859	0.0155	0.8028	0.0180	0.9085	0.0205	1.0075
0.0130	0.6905	0.0156	0.8072	0.0181	0.9116	0.0206	1.0113
0.0131	0.6951	0.0157	0.8115	0.0182	0.9166	0.0207	1.0152
0.0132	0.6998	0.0158	0.8158	0.0183	0.9207	0.0208	1.0190
0.0133	0.7044	0.0159	0.8202	0.0184	0.9248	0.0209	1.0227
0.0134	0.7089	0.0160	0.8245	0.0185	0.9288	0.0210	1.0265
0.0135	0.7135	0.0161	0.8288	0.0186	0.9328	0.0211	1.0303
0.0136	0.7181	0.0162	0.8331	0.0187	0.9369	0.0212	1.0341
0.0137	0.7226	0.0163	0.8373	0.0188	0.9409	0.0213	1.0378
0.0138	0.7272	0.0164	0.8416	0.0189	0.9449	0.0214	1.0416
0.0139	0.7317						

TABLE A-11   Coefficient of Resistance ($\bar{k}$) versus Reinforcement Ratio (ρ)
(f'_c = 5000 psi; f_y = 60,000 psi; Units of $\bar{k}$ Are ksi)

ρ	$\bar{k}$	ρ	$\bar{k}$	ρ	$\bar{k}$	ρ	$\bar{k}$
0.0010	0.0596	0.0055	0.3172	0.0100	0.5576	0.0145	0.7810
0.0011	0.0655	0.0056	0.3227	0.0101	0.5628	0.0146	0.7857
0.0012	0.0714	0.0057	0.3282	0.0102	0.5679	0.0147	0.7905
0.0013	0.0773	0.0058	0.3338	0.0103	0.5731	0.0148	0.7952
0.0014	0.0832	0.0059	0.3393	0.0104	0.5782	0.0149	0.8000
0.0015	0.0890	0.0060	0.3448	0.0105	0.5833	0.0150	0.8047
0.0016	0.0949	0.0061	0.3502	0.0106	0.5884	0.0151	0.8094
0.0017	0.1008	0.0062	0.3557	0.0107	0.5935	0.0152	0.8142
0.0018	0.1066	0.0063	0.3612	0.0108	0.5986	0.0153	0.8189
0.0019	0.1125	0.0064	0.3667	0.0109	0.6037	0.0154	0.8236
0.0020	0.1183	0.0065	0.3721	0.0110	0.6088	0.0155	0.8283
0.0021	0.1241	0.0066	0.3776	0.0111	0.6138	0.0156	0.8329
0.0022	0.1300	0.0067	0.3830	0.0112	0.6189	0.0157	0.8376
0.0023	0.1358	0.0068	0.3884	0.0113	0.6239	0.0158	0.8423
0.0024	0.1416	0.0069	0.3938	0.0114	0.6290	0.0159	0.8469
0.0025	0.1474	0.0070	0.3992	0.0115	0.6340	0.0160	0.8516
0.0026	0.1531	0.0071	0.4047	0.0116	0.6390	0.0161	0.8562
0.0027	0.1589	0.0072	0.4100	0.0117	0.6440	0.0162	0.8609
0.0028	0.1647	0.0073	0.4154	0.0118	0.6490	0.0163	0.8655
0.0029	0.1704	0.0074	0.4208	0.0119	0.6540	0.0164	0.8701
0.0030	0.1762	0.0075	0.4262	0.0120	0.6590	0.0165	0.8747
0.0031	0.1819	0.0076	0.4315	0.0121	0.6640	0.0166	0.8793
0.0032	0.1877	0.0077	0.4369	0.0122	0.6690	0.0167	0.8839
0.0033	0.1934	0.0078	0.4422	0.0123	0.6739	0.0168	0.8885
0.0034	0.1991	0.0079	0.4476	0.0124	0.6789	0.0169	0.8930
0.0035	0.2048	0.0080	0.4529	0.0125	0.6838	0.0170	0.8976
0.0036	0.2105	0.0081	0.4582	0.0126	0.6888	0.0171	0.9022
0.0037	0.2162	0.0082	0.4635	0.0127	0.6937	0.0172	0.9067
0.0038	0.2219	0.0083	0.4688	0.0128	0.6986	0.0173	0.9112
0.0039	0.2276	0.0084	0.4741	0.0129	0.7035	0.0174	0.9158
0.0040	0.2332	0.0085	0.4794	0.0130	0.7084	0.0175	0.9203
0.0041	0.2389	0.0086	0.4847	0.0131	0.7133	0.0176	0.9248
0.0042	0.2445	0.0087	0.4899	0.0132	0.7182	0.0177	0.9293
0.0043	0.2502	0.0088	0.4952	0.0133	0.7231	0.0178	0.9338
0.0044	0.2558	0.0089	0.5005	0.0134	0.7280	0.0179	0.9383
0.0045	0.2614	0.0090	0.5057	0.0135	0.7328	0.0180	0.9428
0.0046	0.2670	0.0091	0.5109	0.0136	0.7377	0.0181	0.9473
0.0047	0.2726	0.0092	0.5162	0.0137	0.7425	0.0182	0.9517
0.0048	0.2782	0.0093	0.5214	0.0138	0.7473	0.0183	0.9562
0.0049	0.2838	0.0094	0.5266	0.0139	0.7522	0.0184	0.9606
0.0050	0.2894	0.0095	0.5318	0.0140	0.7570	0.0185	0.9651
0.0051	0.2950	0.0096	0.5370	0.0141	0.7618	0.0186	0.9695
0.0052	0.3005	0.0097	0.5422	0.0142	0.7666	0.0187	0.9739
0.0053	0.3061	0.0098	0.5473	0.0143	0.7714	0.0188	0.9783
0.0054	0.3117	0.0099	0.5525	0.0144	0.7762	0.0189	0.9827

████████ TABLE A-11 (CONT.)   Coefficient of Resistance ($\overline{k}$) versus Reinforcement Ratio (ρ)
($f'_c = 5000$ psi; $f_y = 60,000$ psi; Units of $\overline{k}$ Are ksi)

ρ	$\overline{k}$	ρ	$\overline{k}$	ρ	$\overline{k}$	ρ	$\overline{k}$
0.0190	0.9871	0.0206	1.0563	0.0222	1.1233	0.0238	1.1881
0.0191	0.9915	0.0207	1.0605	0.0223	1.1274	0.0239	1.1921
0.0192	0.9959	0.0208	1.0648	0.0224	1.1315	0.0240	1.1961
0.0193	1.0002	0.0209	1.0690	0.0225	1.1356	0.0241	1.2000
0.0194	1.0046	0.0210	1.0732	0.0226	1.1397	0.0242	1.2040
0.0195	1.0090	0.0211	1.0775	0.0227	1.1438	0.0243	1.2079
0.0196	1.0133	0.0212	1.0817	0.0228	1.1478	0.0244	1.2119
0.0197	1.0176	0.0213	1.0859	0.0229	1.1519	0.0245	1.2158
0.0198	1.0220	0.0214	1.0901	0.0230	1.1560	0.0246	1.2197
0.0199	1.0263	0.0215	1.0942	0.0231	1.1600	0.0247	1.2236
0.0200	1.0306	0.0216	1.0984	0.0232	1.1641	0.0248	1.2275
0.0201	1.0349	0.0217	1.1026	0.0233	1.1681	0.0249	1.2314
0.0202	1.0392	0.0218	1.1067	0.0234	1.1721	0.0250	1.2353
0.0203	1.0435	0.0219	1.1109	0.0235	1.1761	0.0251	1.2392
0.0204	1.0478	0.0220	1.1150	0.0236	1.1801	0.0252	1.2431
0.0205	1.0520	0.0221	1.1192	0.0237	1.1841		

████████ TABLE A-12   Basic Development Length
(ℓ_{db}) for Compression Bars
(in.) for Grade 60 Bars

Bar size	f'_c (normal-weight concrete), psi			
	3000	4000	5000	6000
3	8.2	7.1	6.8	6.8
4	11.0	9.5	9.0	9.0
5	13.7	11.9	11.3	11.3
6	16.4	14.2	13.5	13.5
7	19.2	16.6	15.8	15.8
8	21.9	19.0	18.0	18.0
9	24.7	21.4	20.3	20.3
10	27.8	24.1	22.9	22.9
11	30.9	26.8	25.4	25.4
14	37.1	32.1	30.5	30.5
18	49.4	42.8	40.6	40.6

Note: See Chapter 5 for calculation of development
length for compression bars.

■ **TABLE A-13   Basic Development Length (ℓ_{hb}) for Hooked Bars with $f_y = 60{,}000$ psi (in.)**

Bar number	f_c' (psi)			
	3000	4000	5000	6000
3	8.2	7.1	6.4	5.8
4	11.0	9.5	8.5	7.7
5	13.7	11.9	10.6	9.7
6	16.4	14.2	12.7	11.6
7	19.2	16.6	14.8	13.6
8	21.9	19.0	17.0	15.5
9	24.7	21.4	19.1	17.5
10	27.8	24.1	21.6	19.7
11	30.9	26.8	23.9	21.8

Note: $\ell_{dh} = \ell_{hb} \times$ modification factors ≥ 6 in. or $8d_b$. For ℓ_{hb} expressions, see the ACI Code, Section 12.5.

Recommended spiral or tie bar number	Core size (in.) = column size − 2 × cover	Circular area (in.²)	Bar number							Square area (in.²)	Bar number						
			#5	#6	#7	#8	#9	#10	#11		#5	#6	#7	#8	#9	#10	#11
3[a]	9	63.6	8	7	7	6	—	—	—	81	8	8	8	8	4	4	4
	10	78.5	10	9	8	7	6	—	—	100	12	8	8	8	8	4	4
	11	95.0	11	10	9	8	7	6	—	121	12	12	8	8	8	8	4
	12	113.1	12	11	10	9	8	7	6	144	12	12	12	8	8	8	8
	13	132.7	13	12	11	10	8	7	6	169	16	12	12	12	8	8	8
	14	153.9	14	13	12	11	9	8	7	196	16	16	12	12	12	8	8
	15	176.7	15	14	13	12	10	9	8	225	16	16	16	12	12	12	8
4	16	201.1	16	15	14	12	11	9	8	256	20	16	16	16	12	12	8
	17	227.0	18	16	15	13	12	10	9	289	20	20	16	16	12	12	8
	18	254.5	19	17	15	14	12	11	10	324	20	20	16	16	16	12	12
	19	283.5	20	18	16	15	13	11	10	361	24	20	20	16	16	12	12
	20	314.2	21	19	17	16	14	12	11	400	24	24	20	20	16	12	12
	21	346.4	22	20	18	17	15	13	11	441	28	24	20	20	16	16	12
	22	380.1	23	21	19	18	15	14	12	484	28	24	24	20	20	16	12
5	23	415.5	24	22	21	19	16	14	13	529	28	28	24	24	20	16	16
	24	452.4	25	23	21	20	17	15	13	576	32	28	24	24	20	16	16
	25	490.9	26	24	22	20	18	16	14	625	32	28	28	24	20	20	16
	26	530.9	28	25	23	21	19	16	14	676	32	32	28	24	24	20	16
	27	572.6	29	26	24	22	19	17	15	729	36	32	28	28	24	20	16

[a]No. 4 tie for No. 11 or larger longitudinal reinforcement.

CHART A-15   Eccentrically Loaded Columns

CHART A-16   Eccentrically Loaded Columns

[a]Charts A-15 to A-26 are reprinted by permission of the American Concrete Institute from ACI Publication SP-17A(90): *Design Handbook,* Volume 2, Columns.

CHART A-17   Eccentrically Loaded Columns

CHART A-18   Eccentrically Loaded Columns

CHART A-19   Eccentrically Loaded Columns

CHART A-20   Eccentrically Loaded Columns

CHART A-21   Eccentrically Loaded Columns

CHART A-22   Eccentrically Loaded Columns

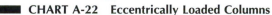

CHART A-23   Eccentrically Loaded Columns

CHART A-24   Eccentrically Loaded Columns

CHART A-25   Eccentrically Loaded Columns

CHART A-26   Eccentrically Loaded Columns

APPENDIX B

Supplementary Aids and Guidelines

B-1 ACCURACY FOR COMPUTATIONS FOR REINFORCED CONCRETE

B-2 $A_{s,max}$ FOR DOUBLY REINFORCED BEAMS

B-3 FLOW DIAGRAMS

B-1

ACCURACY FOR COMPUTATIONS FOR REINFORCED CONCRETE

The widespread availability and use of electronic calculators for even the simplest of calculations has led to the use of numbers that represent a very high order of accuracy. For instance, a calculator having an eight-digit display will yield the following:

$$\frac{8}{0.7} = 11.428571$$

486

It should be recognized that the numerator and denominator, each of one-figure accuracy, resulted in a number that *indicates* eight-figure accuracy. Since the quotient cannot be expected to be more accurate than the numbers that produced it, the result as represented above is a fallacy and may lead one into a false sense of security associated with numbers of very high accuracy. For instance, it is illogical to calculate a required steel area to four-figure accuracy when the loads were to two-figure accuracy and the bars to be chosen have areas tabulated to two- (sometimes three-) figure accuracy. Likewise, the involved mathematical expressions developed in this book and those presented by the ACI Code should be thought of in a similar light. They deal with a material, concrete, that:

1. Is made on site or plant-made, is subject to varying amounts of quality control, and will vary from the design strength
2. Is placed in forms that may or may not produce the design dimensions
3. Contains reinforcing steel of a specified minimum strength but that may vary above that strength

In addition, the reinforced concrete member has reinforcing steel that may or may not be placed at the design location, and the design itself is generally based on loads that may be only "best estimates."

With the foregoing in mind, the following has been suggested by the Concrete Reinforcing Steel Institute as a rough guide for numerical accuracy in reinforced concrete calculations:

1. Loads to the nearest 1 psf; 10 lb/ft; 100 lb concentration
2. Span lengths to about 0.1 ft
3. Total loads and reactions to 0.1 kip or three-figure accuracy
4. Moments to the nearest 0.1 ft-kip or three-figure accuracy
5. Individual bar areas to 0.01 in.^{2}
6. Concrete sizes to the ½ in.
7. Effective beam depth of 0.1 in.
8. Column loads to nearest 1.0 kip

In general (admittedly, not always), the reader will find that in this text we have represented numbers used in calculations to an accuracy of three significant digits. If the number begins with 1, then four significant digits are shown. We round *intermediate and final* numerical solutions in accordance with this rule of thumb. When working on a calculator, however, one will normally maintain all digits and round *only* the final answer. For this reason, the reader may frequently obtain numerical results that are slightly different from those printed in the text. This should not cause undue concern.

B-2

$A_{s,\text{max}}$ FOR DOUBLY REINFORCED BEAMS

A check on ductility of a doubly reinforced concrete beam can be made by determining $A_{s,\text{max}}$ as the steel area that is 75% of the steel area required to produce the balanced condition.

Find the steel area required to produce the balanced condition A_{sb}. From Figure B-1,

$$\frac{c}{0.003} = \frac{d}{0.003 + \epsilon_y}$$

$$c = \frac{0.003d}{0.003 + f_y/E_s} = \frac{0.003dE_s}{0.003E_s + f_y}$$

Substituting $E_s = 29,000,000$ psi and noting that basic units are pounds and inches, at the balanced condition,

$$c = \frac{87,000d}{87,000 + f_y}$$

By equating the resultant forces at the balanced condition,

$$N_{Tb} = N_{Cb}$$

$$A_{sb}f_y = (0.85f_c')\beta_1 cb + A_s'f_s'$$

$$A_{s,\text{max}} = 0.75A_{sb}$$

from which, by substitution,

$$A_{s,\text{max}} = 0.75\frac{(0.85f_c')\beta_1 cb}{f_y} + \frac{0.75A_s'f_s'}{f_y}$$

FIGURE B-1   Balanced condition, doubly reinforced beam.

The ACI Code, Section 10.3.3, states that the 0.75 factor need not be applied to that portion of the tension steel that is equalized by compression steel, however. Adjusting for the preceding and substituting for c,

$$A_{s,max} = \frac{0.75(0.85f_c')\beta_1(87,000)db}{f_y(87,000 + f_y)} + \frac{A_s'f_s'}{f_y}$$

but, from Section 2-8, for singly reinforced beam,

$$\rho_{max} = 0.75\rho_b = \frac{0.75(0.85)f_c'\beta_1}{f_y}\left[\frac{87,000}{f_y + 87,000}\right]$$

Therefore,

$$A_{s,max} = \rho_{max}db + \frac{A_s'f_s'}{f_y} \qquad \text{(B-1)}$$

If $f_s' = f_y$ at the balanced condition, this reduces to

$$A_{s,max} = \rho_{max}db + A_s' \qquad \text{(B-2)}$$

Note that ρ_{max} (or 0.75 ρ_b) for a singly reinforced beam may be found in Table A-5.
   Calculate f_s' *at the balanced condition:*

$$f_s' = \epsilon_s'E_s = \frac{c - d'}{c}(0.003)E_s = \left(1 - \frac{d'}{c}\right)(87,000)$$

Substitute for c:

$$f_s' = \left[1 - \frac{d'(87,000 + f_y)}{87,000d}\right](87,000)$$

$$f_s' = \left[1 - \frac{d'}{d}\left(\frac{87,000 + f_y}{87,000}\right)\right](87,000) \leq f_y \qquad \text{(B-3)}$$

For various values of f_y, the value of (d'/d) may be found for which $f_s' = f_y$. If the actual (d'/d) is less than this value, then $f_s' = f_y$. The values of (d'/d) for which $f_s' = f_y$ are

$$0.37 \text{ for } f_y = 40,000 \text{ psi}$$

$$0.184 \text{ for } f_y = 60,000 \text{ psi}$$

Procedure

1. Calculate the actual (d'/d).
2. For $(d'/d) \leq 0.37$ or 0.184 (as appropriate), use Equation (B-2) for $A_{s,max}$.
3. For $(d'/d) > 0.37$ or 0.184 (as appropriate), use Equation (B-3) for f_s' and Equation (B-1) for $A_{s,max}$.

B-3

FLOW DIAGRAMS

The step-by-step procedures for the analysis and design of reinforced concrete members may be presented in the form of flow diagrams (see Figures B-2 to B-5). To aid the reader in grasping the overall calculation approach, which may sometimes include cycling steps, flow diagrams for the analysis and design of rectangular beams and T-beams are presented here. These flow diagrams represent, on an elementary level, the type of organization required to develop computer programs to aid in analysis and design calculations.

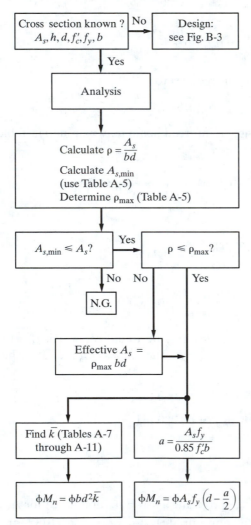

FIGURE B-2   Rectangular beam analysis for moment (tension steel only).

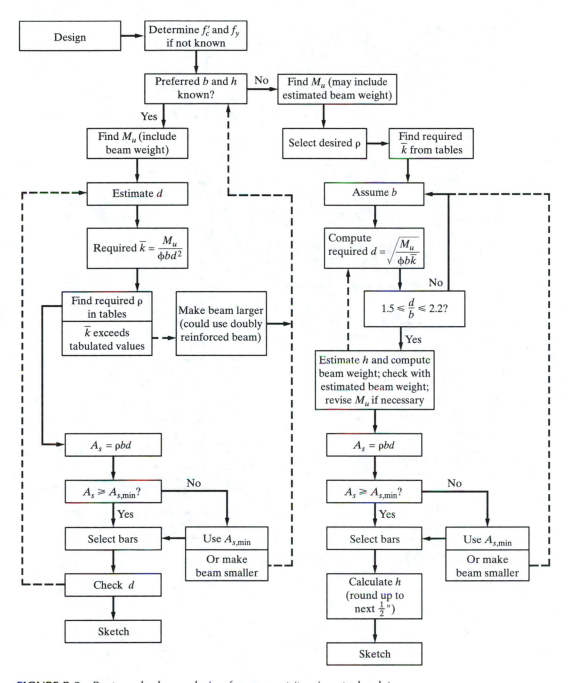

FIGURE B-3   Rectangular beam design for moment (tension steel only).

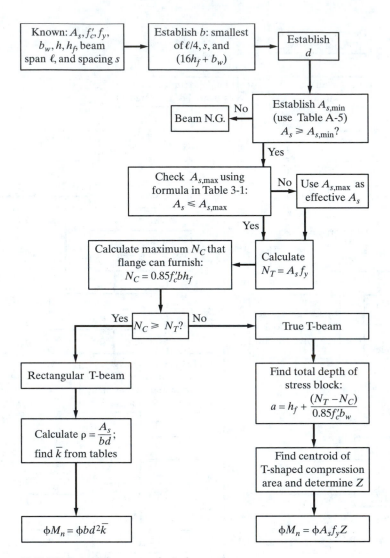

FIGURE B-4 T-beam analysis for moment.

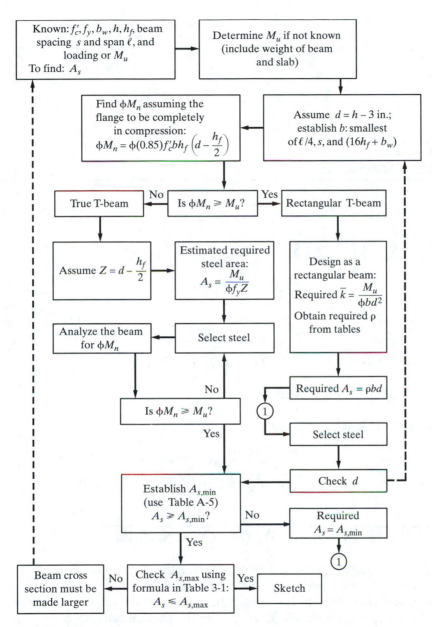

FIGURE B-5   T-beam design for moment.

APPENDIX C

Metrication

C-1 THE INTERNATIONAL SYSTEM OF UNITS (SI)

C-2 SI STYLE AND USAGE

C-3 CONVERSION FACTORS

C-1

THE INTERNATIONAL SYSTEM OF UNITS (SI)

The United States Customary System of weights and measures has been used as the primary unit system in this book. This system actually developed from the English system (British), which had been introduced in the original 13 colonies when they were under British rule. Even though the English system was spread to many parts of the world during the past three centuries, it was widely recognized that there was a need for a single international coordinated measurement system. As a result, a second system of weights and measures, known as the metric system, was developed by a commission of French scientists and was adopted by France as the legal system of weights and measures in 1799.

Although the metric system was not accepted with enthusiasm at first, adoption by other nations occurred steadily after France made its use compulsory in 1840. In the United States, an Act of Congress in 1866 made it lawful throughout the land to employ the weights and measures of the metric system in all contracts, dealings, or court proceedings.

By 1900 a total of 35 nations, including the major nations of continental Europe and most of South America, had officially accepted the metric system. In 1971 the secretary of commerce, in transmitting to Congress the results of a 3-year study authorized by the Metric Study Act of 1968, recommended that the United States change to predominant use of the metric system through a coordinated national program. The Congress responded by enacting the Metric Conversion Act of 1975 that established a U.S. Metric Board to carry out the planning, coordination, and public education that would facilitate a voluntary conversion to a modern metric system. Today, with the exception of a few small countries, the entire world is using the metric system or is changing to its use. Because of the many versions of the metric system that developed, an International General Conference on Weights and Measures in 1960 adopted an extensive revision and simplification of the system. The name *Le Système International d'Unités* (International System of Units), with the international abbreviation SI, was adopted for this modernized metric system.

The American Society of Civil Engineers (ASCE) resolved in 1970 to actively support conversion to SI and to adopt the revised edition of the American Society for Testing and Materials (ASTM) *Metric Practice* guide. In 1988 Congress passed the Omnibus Trade and Competitiveness Act that, among other things, mandated that by the end of fiscal 1992, the federal government would require metric specifications on all the goods it purchased. In 1991, President George Bush signed Executive Order 12770, *Metric Usage in Federal Government Programs,* which required federal agencies to develop specific timetables and milestones for the transition to metric. At this writing, many federal construction programs are fully converted and most of the others will be converted in the near term. Federal construction constitutes a large portion of the nation's construction industry. The authors continue to believe that in the near future, virtually the entire construction industry will go metric.

Metric conversion involves two distinct aspects. On one hand, design calculations and detailing practices will be affected by the new units. Many publications such as specifications, building codes, and design handbooks (and their associated software) are in various stages of production based on the SI. This is essentially a paper (and electronic) change. On the other hand, the physical sizes of some products will be affected. The most significant changes are the sizes and properties of the reinforcing steel. Currently, standardization of the bar sizes and properties using the SI system is based on cross-sectional areas in increments of 100 mm^2. There are eight metric bar sizes as opposed to 11 inch-pound (U.S. Customary) bar sizes, resulting in changes of the nominal diameters of the bars, cross-sectional areas, weight (mass), and deformation requirements. This type of change is called a "hard" conversion. The reinforcing steel industry is pursuing a change in this current metric standardization. It is their proposal to replace the hard metric sizes with a "soft" conversion of the existing inch-pound bar sizes. Most steel companies

■ TABLE C-1   ASTM Standard Deformed Reinforcing Bars (Hard Metric Conversion)

Designation number	Nominal diameter (mm)	Nominal area (mm²)	Nominal mass (kg/m)
10	11.3	100	0.785
15	16.0	200	1.570
20	19.5	300	2.356
25	25.2	500	3.925
30	29.9	700	5.495
35	35.7	1000	7.850
45	43.7	1500	11.775
55	56.4	2500	19.625

support this position. The physical features of the "soft" metric bar sizes would be exactly the same as those of the inch-pound bars. Designations would change: for example, a No. 6 bar (0.75 inch diameter) would become a 19 mm bar.

At this writing, there is not available design information, data, and specifications conforming to the soft metric conversion of ASTM A615, the current inch-pound specification for steel reinforcing bar. Therefore, for purposes of this text, only the "hard" metric conversion values, as shown in Table C-1, are used, in agreement with accepted practice where the SI is being used.

As a means of introducing the SI into reinforced concrete design, this appendix furnishes various design aids, conversion tables, and example using SI units. The examples are solved in accordance with the *Building Code Requirements for Reinforced Concrete* (ACI 318M-89). This code is the metric companion to ACI 318-89. It should be noted that even though ACI 318-95 is the basis for this text, the metric companion ACI 318M-95 is not available at the time of this writing.

Table C-1 presents ASTM standard deformed reinforcing bars for the SI system.

C-2

SI STYLE AND USAGE

The SI consists of a limited number of *base* units that establish fundamental quantities and a large number of *derived* units, which come from the base units, to describe other quantities.

The SI base units pertinent to reinforced concrete design are listed in Table C-2, and the SI-derived units pertinent to reinforced concrete design are listed in Table C-3.

■■■■ **TABLE C-2   SI Units and Symbols**

Quantity	Unit	SI symbol
Length	meter	m
Mass	kilogram	kg
Time	second	s
Angle[a]	radian	rad

[a]It is also permissible to use the arc degree *and its decimal submultiples* when the radian is not convenient.

Since the orders of magnitude of many quantities cover wide ranges of numerical values, SI *prefixes* have been established to deal with decimal-point placement. Si prefixes representing steps of 1000 are recommended to indicate orders of magnitude. Those recommended for use in reinforced concrete design are listed in Table C-4.

From Table C-4, it is clear that there is a choice of ways to represent numbers. It is preferable to use numbers between 1 and 1000, whenever possible, by selecting the appropriate prefix. For example, 18 m is preferred to 0.018 km or 18 000 mm.

■■■■ **TABLE C-3   SI-Derived Units**

Quantity	Unit	SI symbol	Formula
Acceleration	meter per second squared	—	m/s^2
Area	square meter	—	m^2
Density (mass per unit volume)	kilogram per cubic meter	—	kg/m^3
Force	newton	N	$kg{\cdot}m/s^2$
Pressure or stress	pascal	Pa	N/m^2
Volume	cubic meter	—	m^3
Section modulus	meter to third power	—	m^3
Moment of inertia	meter to fourth power	—	m^4
Moment of force, torque	newton meter	—	$N{\cdot}m$
Force per unit length	newton per meter	—	N/m
Mass per unit length	kilogram per meter	—	kg/m
Mass per unit area	kilogram per square meter	—	kg/m^2

■■■■ **TABLE C-4 SI Prefixes**

Prefix	SI symbol	Factor
mega	M	$1\ 000\ 000 = 10^{6}$
kilo	k	$1000 = 10^{3}$
milli	m	$0.001 = 10^{-3}$
micro	μ	$0.000\ 001 = 10^{-6}$

A brief note must be made at this point concerning the presentation of numbers with many digits. It is common practice in the United States to separate digits into groups of three by means of commas. To avoid confusion with the widespread European practice of using a comma on the line as the decimal marker, the method of setting off groups of three digits with a gap, as shown in Table C-4, is recommended international practice. Note that this method is used on both the left and right sides of the decimal marker for any string of five or more digits. A group of four digits on either side of the decimal marker need not be separated.

A significant difference between SI and other measurement systems is the use of explicit and distinctly separate units for mass and force. The SI base unit kilogram (kg) denotes the base unit of mass, which is the quantity of matter of an object. This is a constant quantity that is independent of gravitational attraction. The derived SI unit newton (N) denotes the absolute derived unit of force (mass times acceleration: $kg \cdot m/s^{2}$). The term *weight* should be avoided since it is confused with mass and because it describes a particular force that is related solely to gravitational acceleration, which varies on the surface of the earth. For the conversion of mass to force, the recommended value for the acceleration of gravity in the United States may be taken as $g = 9.81$ m/s^{2}.

As an example, we will consider the "weight" of reinforced concrete, which, in the design of bending members, must be considered as a load or force per unit length of span. In the U.S. Customary System, reinforced concrete weighs 150 lb/ft^{3}. This is equivalent in the SI to

$$150\ \frac{\text{lb}}{\text{ft}^{3}} \times \left(\frac{3.2808\ \text{ft}}{1\ \text{m}}\right)^{3} \times \frac{1\ \text{kg}}{2.2046\ \text{lb}} \approx 2400\ \frac{\text{kg}}{\text{m}^{3}}$$

This represents a mass per unit volume (density) where the unit volume is 1 cubic meter, m^{3}. To use the density of the concrete to obtain a force per cubic meter, Newton's law must be applied:

$$F = \text{mass times acceleration of gravity}$$

$$= mg$$

$$= 2400(9.81)$$

$$= 23\ 500\ \frac{\text{kg} \cdot \text{m}}{\text{s}^2 \text{m}^3}$$

$$= 23\ 500\ \text{N/m}^3$$

$$= 23.5\ \text{kN/m}^3$$

The dead load per unit length of a beam of dimensions $b = 500$ mm and $h = 1000$ mm can then be determined:

$$\left(\frac{500}{1000}\right)\left(\frac{1,000}{1000}\right)(23.5) = 11.75\ \text{kN/m}$$

Thus the load or force per unit length (1 meter) equals 11.75 kN.

C-3

CONVERSION FACTORS

Table C-5 contains conversion factors for the conversion of the U.S. Customary System units to SI units for quantities frequently used in reinforced concrete design.

Although specified in the SI, the pascal is not universally accepted as the unit of stress. Because section dimensions and properties are generally in millimeters, it is more convenient to express stress in newtons per square millimeter (1 N/mm^2 = 1 MPa).

This is the practice followed in recent international structural design standards, including the International Standards Organization (ISO) Draft International Standard for Steel Design.

Reference is made to the ACI Code (318M-89), which furnishes the metric equivalents for equations and data necessary for use in the SI. Other reference sources that contain treatment of the many aspects of metrication in the design and construction field are listed at the end of this appendix.

Example C-1

Find ϕM_n for the beam of cross section shown in Figure C-1. The steel is grade 300, and $f'_c = 20$ N/mm^2.

Solution:

1.
$$f_y = 300\ \text{N/mm}^2$$

$$f'_c = 20\ \text{N/mm}^2$$

■■■■■ **TABLE C-5   Conversion Factors: U.S. Customary to SI Units**

	Multiply		By		To obtain
Length	inches	×	25.4	=	millimeters
	feet	×	0.3048	=	meters
	yards	×	0.9144	=	meters
	miles (statute)	×	1.609	=	kilometers
Area	square inches	×	645.2	=	square millimeters
	square feet	×	0.0929	=	square meters
	square yards	×	0.8361	=	square meters
Volume	cubic inches	×	16 387.	=	cubic millimeters
	cubic feet	×	0.028 32	=	cubic meters
	cubic yards	×	0.7646	=	cubic meters
	gallons (U.S. liquid)	×	0.003 785	=	cubic meters
Force	pounds	×	4.448	=	newtons
	kips	×	4448.	=	newtons
Force per unit length	pounds per foot	×	14.594	=	newtons per meter
	kips per foot	×	14 594.	=	newtons per meter
Load per unit volume	pounds per cubic foot	×	0.157 14	=	kilonewtons per cubic meter
Bending moment or torque	inch-pounds	×	0.1130	=	newton meters
	foot-pounds	×	1.356	=	newton meters
	inch-kips	×	113.0	=	newton meters
	foot-kips	×	1356.	=	newton meters
	inch-kips	×	0.1130	=	kilonewton meters
	foot-kips	×	1.356	=	kilonewton meters
Stress, pressure, loading (force per unit area)	pounds per square inch	×	6895.	=	pascals
	pounds per square inch		6.895	=	kilopascals
	pounds per square inch	×	0.006 895	=	megapascals
	kips per square inch	×	6.895	=	megapascals
	pounds per square foot	×	47.88	=	pascals
	pounds per square foot	×	0.047 88	=	kilopascals
	kips per square foot	×	47.88	=	kilopascals
	kips per square foot	×	0.047 88	=	megapascals
Mass	pounds	×	0.454	=	kilograms
Mass per unit volume (density)	pounds per cubic foot	×	16.02	=	kilograms per cubic meter
	pounds per cubic yard	×	0.5933	=	kilograms per cubic meter
Moment of inertia	inches^4	×	416 231.	=	millimeters^4
Mass per unit length	pounds per foot	×	1.488	=	kilograms per meter
Mass per unit area	pounds per square foot	×	4.882	=	kilograms per square meter

FIGURE C-1   Cross section for Example C-1.

$$b = 250 \text{ mm}, \qquad d = 500 \text{ mm}$$

$$h = 570 \text{ mm}, \qquad A_s = 1500 \text{ mm}^2$$

2.   To be found: ϕM_n.

3.
$$\rho = \frac{A_s}{bd} = \frac{1500}{250(500)} = 0.0120$$

4.
$$0.75\rho_b = 0.0278 = \rho_{\max}$$

$$0.0120 < 0.0278 \qquad\qquad \text{(O.K.)}$$

Check $A_{s,\min}$ based on ACI 318-95 converted to the SI with f_y and f'_c in units of N/mm^2:

$$A_{s,\min} = \frac{0.25\sqrt{f'_c}}{f_y} b_w d \geqslant \frac{1.4}{f_y} b_w d$$

$$\frac{0.25\ \sqrt{f'_c}}{f_y} = \frac{0.25\sqrt{20}}{300} = 0.0037$$

$$\frac{1.4}{f_y} = \frac{1.4}{300} = 0.0047$$

Therefore, use 0.0047. Then

$$A_{s,\min} = 0.0047(250 \text{ mm})(500 \text{ mm}) = 588 \text{ mm}^2$$

$$1500 \text{ mm}^2 > 588 \text{ mm}^2 \qquad\qquad \text{O.K.}$$

5.
$$a = \frac{A_s f_y}{0.85 f'_c b} = \frac{1500(300)}{0.85(20.0)(250)} = 105.9 \text{ mm}$$

6.
$$Z = d - \frac{a}{2} = 500 - \frac{105.9}{2} = 447 \text{ mm}$$

7.
$$M_n = A_s f_y Z$$

8. $\phi M_n = 0.9(A_s f_y Z)$. All the quantities needed for the ϕM_n calculation
have been determined, but some conversion is required to make pre-
fixes compatible. Rather than set up prefix conversion for each lengthy
calculation, it is suggested for situations such as this that quantities be
substituted in units of meters and newtons. The results will be in the
same units. This method also lends itself to the use of numerical values
expressed in powers-of-10 notation. For the ϕM_n calculation,

$$A_s = 1.500 \times 10^{-3} \text{ m}^2, \qquad f_y = 300 \times 10^6 \text{ N/m}^2, \qquad Z = 0.447 \text{ m}$$

from which

$$\phi M_n = 0.9(1.500 \times 10^{-3})(300 \times 10^6)(0.447)$$

$$= 181 \times 10^3 \text{ N·m}$$

$$= 181 \text{ kN·m}$$

Note that the final ϕM_n is simply changed to kN·m. The kilo prefix is the
most appropriate prefix for the majority of flexural problems that are
presented in this book using the U.S. Customary System of units (see
"Bending moment or torque" in Table C-5 for comparison with ft-kips).

Example C-2

Design a rectangular reinforced concrete beam for a simple span of 10 m to
carry service loads of 14.6 kN/m dead load (does not include the dead load of
the beam) and 29.2 kN/m live load. The maximum width of beam desired is
400 mm. Use $f_c' = 20.0 \text{ N/mm}^2$ and $f_y = 400 \text{ N/mm}^2$. Assume a No. 10 stirrup
and sketch the design. (See Chapter 2 for design procedure.)

Solution:

1. $$w_u = 1.4\,w_{DL} + 1.7w_{LL}$$

$$= 1.4(14.6) + 1.7(29.2)$$

$$= 70.1 \text{ kN/m}$$

$$M_u = \frac{w_u \ell^2}{8} = \frac{70.1(10)^2}{8} = 876 \text{ kN·m}$$

2.   Assume that $\rho = 0.0090$ (Table A-5). Note that the given f_c' and f_y correspond approximately to 3000 psi and 60,000 psi, respectively.

3.   From Table A-8,

$$\text{required } \overline{k} = 0.4828 \text{ ksi}$$

Converting to the SI (see Table C-5),

$$\overline{k} = 0.4828(6.895) = 3.329 \text{ N/mm}^2$$

4.   Assume that $b = 400$ mm:

$$\text{required } d = \sqrt{\frac{M_u}{\phi b \overline{k}}}$$

Substituting quantities in terms of meters and newtons yields

$$\text{required } d = \sqrt{\frac{876 \times 10^3}{0.9(0.400)(3.329 \times 10^6)}} = 0.855 \text{ m}$$

$$= 855 \text{ mm}$$

$$\frac{d}{b} \text{ ratio} = \frac{855}{400} = 2.14 \qquad\qquad\qquad\qquad \text{(O.K.)}$$

5.   Estimate the total beam depth for purposes of determining the beam dead load. Assume a No. 35 main bar, a No. 10 stirrup, and a minimum cover of 40 mm. Then

$$h = 855 + 35.7/2 + 11.3 + 40 = 924 \text{ mm}$$

Use a beam depth of 950 mm. From Section C-2, the dead load due to reinforced concrete is 23.5 kN/m³. Therefore, the dead load of the beam per meter length is

$$0.400(0.950)(23.5) = 8.93 \text{ kN/m}$$

6.   The additional M_u due to the beam dead load is

$$M_u = \frac{1.4 w_{DL} \ell^2}{8} = \frac{1.4(8.93)(10)^2}{8}$$

$$= 156.3 \text{ kN·m}$$

$$\text{total } M_u = 876 + 156.3 = 1032 \text{ kN·m}$$

7.   Using ρ, $\overline{k}$, and b as before, the effective depth required is

$$\text{required } d = \sqrt{\frac{1.032 \times 10^6}{0.9(0.400)(3.329 \times 10^6)}} = 0.928 \text{ m} = 928 \text{ mm}$$

$$\frac{d}{b} \text{ ratio} = \frac{928}{400} = 2.32 \qquad\qquad\qquad\qquad \text{(O.K.)}$$

8. $$\text{required } A_s = \rho b d$$

$$= 0.0090(400)(928)$$

$$= 3340 \text{ mm}^2$$

Check $A_{s,\min}$ (use Table A-5 since the given values of f_c' and f_y correspond approximately to 3000 psi and 60,000 psi):

$$A_{s,\min} = 0.0033 b_w d$$

$$= 0.0033(400 \text{ mm})(928 \text{ mm})$$

$$= 1225 \text{ mm}^2$$

$$3340 \text{ mm}^2 > 1225 \text{ mm}^2 \qquad\qquad (\text{O.K.})$$

9. Use four No. 35 bars:

$$A_s = 1000(4) = 4000 \text{ mm}^2$$

The minimum beam width for four No. 35 bars may be determined (closely) from Table A-3, noting that a No. 35 bar is approximately equivalent to a No. 11 bar. Thus

$$\text{minimum } b = 14(25.4) = 356 \text{ mm} < 400 \text{ mm} \qquad (\text{O.K.})$$

10. The total beam depth h may be taken as the effective depth required, plus minimum concrete cover, plus stirrup diameter, plus one-half the main steel diameter:

$$\text{required } h = 928 + 40 + 11.3 + 35.7/2 = 997 \text{ mm}$$

Use $h = 1000$ mm.

11. The design sketch is shown in Figure C-2.

FIGURE C-2   Design sketch for Example C-2.

Example C-3 _____

A simply supported, rectangular, reinforced concrete beam 300 mm wide and having an effective depth of 500 mm carries a total factored load w_u of 70 kN/m on a 9.0 m clear span. (The given load includes the dead load of the beam.) Design the web reinforcement (stirrups). The steel is grade 300, and $f_c' = 20 \text{ N/mm}^2$. Use the ACI Code (318M-89).

Solution:

1. Draw the shear force V_u diagram (see Figure C-3):

$$V_u = \frac{w_u \ell}{2} = \frac{70(9)}{2} = 315 \text{ kN}$$

At the critical section

$$V_u^* = 315 - \frac{500}{1000}(70) = 280 \text{ kN}$$

FIGURE C-3 V_u diagram.

2. Determine if stirrups are required:

$$V_c = \left(\frac{\sqrt{f_c'}}{6}\right) b_w d \qquad\qquad \text{ACI Eq. (11-3)}$$

$$= \frac{\sqrt{20.0}(300)(500)}{6}$$

$$= 111.8 \times 10^3 \text{ N}$$

$$= 111.8 \text{ kN}$$

Stirrups must be provided if $V_u > \frac{1}{2}\phi V_c$:

$$\frac{1}{2}\phi V_c = \frac{0.85(111.8)}{2} = 47.5 \text{ kN}$$

Stirrups *are* required since 280 > 47.5.

3. Find the length of span over which stirrups are required, referencing from the face of the support:

$$\frac{315 - 47.5}{70} = 3.82 \text{ m}$$

Note this location on the V_u diagram as well as the location where $V_u = \phi V_c = 95.0$ kN. This location is obtained from

$$\frac{315 - 95.0}{70} = 3.14 \text{ m}$$

4. Designate "Req'd ϕV_s" on the V_u diagram:

$$\text{required } \phi V_s = \text{max. } V_u - \phi V_c - mx$$
$$= 315 - 95 - 70x$$
$$= 220 - 70x$$

This applies in the range

$$500 \text{ mm} \leqslant x \leqslant 3140 \text{ mm}$$

5. Assume a No. 10 stirrup ($A_v = 200 \text{ mm}^2$) and compute the spacing requirement at the critical section based on the required ϕV_s^*. At this location the stirrups will be most closely spaced. From ACI Equation (11-15),

$$\text{required } s^* = \frac{A_v f_y d}{V_s^*} = \frac{\phi A_v f_y d}{\text{required } \phi V_s^*}$$

where the denominator is determined with reference to Figure C-3:

$$\text{required } \phi V_s^* = V_u^* - \phi V_c$$

Using basic units of meters and newtons,

$$\text{required } s^* = \frac{0.85(200 \times 10^{-6})(300 \times 10^6)(0.500)}{(280 - 95) \times 10^3}$$

$$= 0.138 \text{ m} = 138 \text{ mm}$$

If the required spacing were less than 100 mm, a larger diameter bar would be chosen. We will use a 120 mm spacing as the maximum spacing between the face-of-support and the critical section.

6. Establish the ACI Code maximum spacing requirements. From the ACI Code (318M-89), Section 11.5.4, if V_s at the critical section is less than $(\sqrt{f_c'}/3)b_w d$, the maximum spacing is $d/2$ or 600 mm, whichever is smaller. Therefore, compare V_s^* with this value:

$$\frac{\sqrt{f_c'}b_w d}{3} = \frac{\sqrt{20.0}(300)(500)}{3}$$

$$= 224 \times 10^3 \text{ N}$$

$$= 224 \text{ kN}$$

At the critical section,

$$V_s^* = \frac{\phi V_s}{\phi}$$

$$= \frac{V_u^* - \phi V_c}{\phi}$$

$$= \frac{280 - 95}{0.85} = 218 \text{ kN}$$

Since 218 kN < 224 kN, the maximum spacing will be $d/2$ or 600 mm, whichever is smaller:

$$d/2 = 500/2 = 250 \text{ mm}$$

Wherever $V_s^* > (\sqrt{f_c'}/3)b_w d$, the maximum spacing should be $d/4$ or 300 mm, whichever is smaller.

A second criterion for maximum spacing is based on the code minimum area requirement (ACI Code, Section 11.5.5.3). Code equation (11-14) may be rewritten in the form

$$s_{\max} = \frac{3A_v f_y}{b_w} = \frac{3(200)(300)}{300} = 600 \text{ mm}$$

Of the foregoing two maximum spacing criteria, the smaller value will control. Therefore, the 250 mm maximum spacing controls throughout the beam wherever stirrups are required.

7. Next, determine the spacing requirements based on shear strength. At the critical section the required spacing is 138 mm. The maximum spacing is 250 mm. At other points along the span (x meters from the face of the support), the required spacing may be determined as follows:

$$\text{required } s = \frac{A_v f_y d}{\text{required } V_s} = \frac{\phi A_v f_y d}{\text{required } \phi V_s}$$

where the denominator can be determined from the expression given in step 4, where

$$\text{required } \phi V_s = 220 - 70x$$

Using basic units of meters and newtons, the calculation for required spacing results in

$$\text{required } s = \frac{0.85(200 \times 10^{-6})(300 \times 10^{6})(0.500)}{220 \times 10^{3} - (70 \times 10^{3})(x)}$$

$$= \frac{25.5 \times 10^{3}}{220 \times 10^{3} - (70 \times 10^{3})(x)}$$

$$= \frac{25.5}{220 - 70x}$$

where the resulting spacing is in meters.

The results for several arbitrary values of x are shown tabulated and plotted in Figure C-4. As an example, compute the required stirrup spacing at a distance of 1 m from the face-of-support ($x = 1$ m):

$$\text{required } s = \frac{25.5}{220 - 70(1)} = 0.170 \text{ m} = 170 \text{ mm}$$

Similarly, the required spacing may be found at other points along the beam (see Figure C-4).

FIGURE C-4   Stirrup spacing requirements for Example C-3.

FIGURE C-5   Stirrup spacing Example C-3.

8.   Using Figure C-4, the stirrup pattern shown in Figure C-5 may be developed. Stirrups have been placed the full length of the span, which is a common, conservative practice.

REFERENCES

[1]   *Metric in Construction.* Bimonthly newsletter of the Construction Metrication Council of the National Institute of Building Sciences, 1201 L Street, N.W., Suite 400, Washington, D.C. 20005.

[2]   ANSI/IEEE 268. *American National Standard Metric Practice, 1992.* American National Standards Institute, Inc., 11 W. 42nd Street, New York, N.Y. 10036, 1992.

[3]   ISO 1000. *SI Units and Recommendations for the Use of Their Multiples and Certain Other Units.* American National Standards Institute, Inc., 11 W. 42nd Street, New York, N.Y. 10036.

[4]   ASTM E621. *Standard Practice for the Use of Metric (SI) Units in Building Design and Construction.* American Society for Testing and Materials, 1916 Race Street, Philadelphia, PA 19103, 1984.

[5]   "Building Code Requirements for Reinforced Concrete" (ACI 318M-89). American Concrete Institute, P.O. Box 9094, Farmington Hills, MI 48333.

[6]   "Interim Recommendations for Specifying Soft Metric Reinforcing Bars," Engineering Data Report No. 41. Concrete Reinforcing Steel Institute, 933 N. Plum Grove Road, Schaumburg, IL 60173-4758, 1995.

ANSWERS TO SELECTED PROBLEMS

CHAPTER 1

1-1. (a) w = 467 lb/ft   (b) w = 488 lb/ft
1-3. f_r = 0.356 ksi, ACI f_r = 0.411 ksi
1-5. f_{top} = 0.396 ksi
1-7. M_{cr} = 538 in.-kips
1-9. (a) M_{cr} = 172.7 in.-kips
    (b) P = 3.70 kips

CHAPTER 2

2-1. (a) M_n = 103 ft-kips
    (b) M_n = 158 ft-kips
    (c) M_n = 213 ft-kips
2-3. (a) M_n = 285 ft-kips
    (b) M_n = 294 ft-kips
    (c) M_n = 299 ft-kips
2-5. ϕM_n = 956 ft-kips
2-7. ϕM_n = 169 ft-kips < M_u = 178.6 ft-kips (N.G.)
2-9. 27.2 ft
2-11. ϕM_n = 27.1 ft-kips, service LL = 803 psf
2-13. 3 No. 7 bars
2-15. M_u = 400 ft-kips,
    ϕM_n = 392 ft-kips (N.G.)
2-17. Use h = 26 in., 4 No. 8 bars,
    ϕM_n = 300 ft-kips
2-19. b = 24 in., h = 30 in., 6 No. 9
2-21. b = 24 in., h = 34 in., 7 No. 9
2-23. b = 13 in., h = 27 in., 3 No. 11
2-25. (+ Moment): b = 12 in.,
    h = 23½ in., and 3 No. 8
    (− Moment): same b and h, and 2 No. 7
2-27. (a) 6 in. slab, No. 5 @ 14 in. o.c.
    main steel, No. 4 @ 18 in. o.c.
    shrinkage and temperature steel
    (b) 4 in. slab, No. 5 @ 8 in. o.c.
    main steel, No. 3 @ 14 in. o.c.
    shrinkage and temperature steel

CHAPTER 3

3-1. ϕM_n = 303 ft-kips
3-3. ϕM_n = 439 ft-kips
3-5. (a) ϕM_n = 1527 ft-kips
    (b) A_s = 12.43 in.^{2}
3-7. (a) ϕM_n = 616 ft-kips
    (b) 357 psf (service LL)
3-9. (a) ϕM_n = 392 ft-kips
    (b) ϕM_n = 1620 ft-kips
3-11. 3 No. 9 bars
3-13. (a) 4 No. 9 bars (two layers)
    (b) 4 No. 9 bars (one layer)
3-15. (a) w_{LL} = w_{DL} = 1.79 kips/ft
    (b) ϕM_n = 584 ft-kips (with compression steel), ϕM_n = 388 ft-kips (with tension steel only)
3-17. (a) ϕM_n = 633 ft-kips
    (b) with 4 No. 8 compression bars,
    ϕM_n = 696 ft-kips
3-19. 2 No. 10 bars (comp. steel), 8 No. 9
    bars (two layers, tension steel)
3-21. 2 No. 9 bars (comp. steel), 4 No. 9
    bars (two layers, tension steel)
3-23. 2 No. 10 bars (comp. steel), 5 No. 9
    bars (tension steel, in one layer)

CHAPTER 4

4-1. 8100 lb < 9000 lb (N.G. in shear)
4-3. Max. V_u = 40,300 lb
4-5. s = 10 in. spacing
4-7. No. 3 stirrups (from F.O.S.): 2 in.,
    9 sp @ 4 in., 8 sp @ 5 in., 10 sp @ 10 in.
4-9. No. 3 stirrups (from F.O.S.): 2 in.,
    11 sp @ 5 in., 7 sp @ 10 in.
4-11. No. 3 stirrups (from F.O.S.): in the
    overhang: 3 in., 7 sp @ 12 in.; in the
    center span: 6 in., 10 sp @ 12 in.
4-13. No. 3 stirrups. (a) Single loop
    (from F.O.S.): 2 in., 8 sp @ 7 in., 14
    sp @ 12 in. (b) Double loop
    (from F.O.S.): 2 in., 15 sp @ 4 in.

CHAPTER 5

5-1. 57.9 in.
5-3. 38.4 in.
5-5. 23.8 in.
5-7. Required length of splice = 53.2 in.
5-9. Required length of splice = 26.3 in.
5-11. 2.1′ from F.O.S.
5-13. **(a)** Rectangular beam, b = 16 in., h = 35½ in., 2 No. 10 bars (top), 5 No. 10 bars (bottom)   **(b)** Cut off three interior No. 10 bars at center of support.   **(c)** No. 3 stirrups. In overhang (from F.O.S.): 4 in., 5 sp @ 16 in. In center span (from F.O.S.): 2 in., 11 sp @ 5 in., 7 sp @ 7 in., 3 sp @ 16 in.

CHAPTER 6

6-1. M_u = −3.28 ft-kips, +5.62 ft-kips, −7.87 ft-kips, +4.92 ft-kips, −7.15 ft-kips; V_u = 3.57 kips, 4.11 kips
6-3. b = 12 in., h = 24 in.; end span: 2 No. 6 bars for −M @ end support (with 180° hook), 2 No. 8 bars for +M; interior span: 3 No. 8 bars for −M @ interior support, 2 No. 8 bars for +M

CHAPTER 7

7-1. **(a)** $\bar{y}$ = 11.61 in., I_{cr} = 20,350 in.^{4}
   (b) $\bar{y}$ = 1.68 in., I_{cr} = 72.7 in.^{4}
   (c) $\bar{y}$ = 7.63 in., I_{cr} = 6159 in.^{4}
7-3. **(a)** Δ = 0.36 in.   **(b)** Δ = 0.43 in.
7-5. Δ = 0.34 in. < 0.40 in. (O.K.)
7-7. **(a)** Z = 117.2 < 145   **(b)** Z = 98.4 < 145 (O.K.)
   Both are O.K. for either interior or exterior exposure.

CHAPTER 8

8-1. **(a)** Total H = 7.01 kips/ft   **(b)** Total H = 6.9 kips/ft   **(c)** Total H = 8.0 kips/ft   **(d)** Total H = 12.5 kips/ft

8-3. Overturning F.S. = 3.29, sliding F.S. = 1.35, p_{max} = 0.80 ksf, p_{min} = 0.55 ksf
8-5. No. 7 @ 7½ in. o.c., use a 90° standard hook
8-7. 8 in. thick wall, one layer of steel: vertical No. 4 @ 18 in. o.c., horizontal No. 4 @ 12 in. o.c.

CHAPTER 9

9-1. **(a)** $\phi P_{n(max)}$ = 571 kips, required ties are No. 4 @ 14 in. o.c. **(b)** $\phi P_{n(max)}$ = 1245 kips, required ties are No. 3 @ 18 in. o.c. (three per set)   **(c)** $\phi P_{n(max)}$ = 817 kips, required ties are No. 3 @ 16 in. o.c. (two per set)
9-3. $\phi P_{n(max)}$ = 685 kips, required ties = No. 4 @ 16 in. o.c., $P_{DL} = P_{LL}$ = 221 kips
9-5. $\phi P_{n(max)}$ = 844 kips, required spiral = ⅜ in. diam. @ 2 in. o.c.
9-7. Use 12 No. 9 bars (four per face), required ties are No. 3 @ 18 in. o.c. (three per set)
9-9. Use a column 14 in. × 14 in., 6 No. 9 bars, No. 3 ties @ 14 in. o.c.
9-11. ϕP_n = 302 kips
9-13. Use a column 18 in. × 18 in., 12 No. 9 bars (four per face), No. 3 ties @ 18 in. o.c. (three per set)
9-15. ϕP_n = 232 kips

CHAPTER 10

10-1. Width = 24 in., depth = 12 in., longitudinal steel: 3 No. 4 bars
10-3. Width = 6′-0″, depth = 1′-3″, transverse steel: No. 6 @ 11 in. o.c.; longitudinal steel: 7 No. 5 bars
10-5. 9′-0″ square, depth = 2′-0″, 12 No. 7 bars each way
10-7. Rectangular footing, 7′-0″ × 11′-6″, depth = 2′-0″, 10 No. 8 bars (long direction), 15 No. 6 bars (short direction)

10-9.   Rectangular footing, 19'-6" × 23'-9"

10-11. Footing for column A: 7'-6" square; footing for column B: 8'-2" square

CHAPTER 11

11-1. $f = \pm 0.209$ ksi

11-3. $w = 1.34$ kips/ft

11-5.   Midspan (transfer): $f_{top} = 0.929$ ksi (tens), $f_{bott} = 2.66$ ksi (comp); midspan (full load): $f_{top} = 0.477$ ksi (comp), $f_{bott} = 1.259$ ksi (comp); at end supports (only prestressing stresses exist): $f_{top} = 1.085$ ksi (tension), $f_{bott} = 2.82$ ksi (comp)

11-7. $f_{top} = 2.20$ ksi (comp), $f_{bott} = 0.132$ ksi (comp)

11-9. $\phi M_n = 889$ ft-kips, $M_u = 826$ ft-kips (O.K.)

CHAPTER 12

12-3.   Max. stringer spacing = 72.8 in.

12-5.   Use two 2 × 12 (S4S)

12-7.   Max. shore spacing = 37.0 in.

12-9.   Max. shore spacing = 35.4 in.

12-11. Joists @ 16 in. o.c., stringers @ 7'-0" o.c., 4 × 4 (S4S) shores @ 3'-6" o.c., guy wire bracing @ 12 ft (max.) o.c. on all sides

12-13. Studs @ 12 in. o.c., wales @ 18 in. o.c., max. tie spacing = 36 in. o.c., guy wire bracing @ 25 ft (max.) o.c. on each side of the wall

Index

513